Facing Racism in Education

■ ■ ■

SECOND EDITION

Edited by

Tamara Beauboeuf-Lafontant

and

D. Smith Augustine

Reprint Series No. 28
Harvard Educational Review

Library of Congress Catalog Card Number 95-80692
ISBN 0-916690-30-X

Harvard Educational Review
Gutman Library Suite 349
6 Appian Way
Cambridge, MA 02138

Typesetting: Sheila Walsh
Editorial Production: Dody Riggs

CONTENTS

6/23/96

INTRODUCTION

—■—■—■—

Our present silence on the subject of racism is evidence that we are now living through a downswing of national conscience. . . .

Four recent Supreme Court decisions have dealt severe blows to programs that traditionally have protected the rights of Asian Americans, Blacks, Latinos, and Native Americans. . . .

Our hope is that this collection will renew reflective conversation and generate collective educational response to the problem of racism in an increasingly hostile and indifferent national climate.

—Nitza M. Hidalgo, Ceasar L. McDowell, and Emilie V. Siddle
Facing Racism in Education

The above quote was written in 1990 by the editors of the first edition of *Facing Racism in Education.* Their words remain meaningful as we write in 1995; in fact, they seem even prescient, given the current intensely conservative political and social climate. In the last five years, the nation has moved from a "silence" on the reality of racism to the outright denial of its existence as a privileged few claim that racism is a problem of the past that has been conquered. It is apparent to many of us in education, however, that the "downswing of national conscience" is approaching a moral nadir. In an effort to balance the national budget, the present Congress is attempting to cut programs drastically at all levels of education — from school lunches for low-income children to loans for college students. In addition, as in 1990, recent Supreme Court decisions have dealt not simply severe but possibly fatal blows to affirmative action and other programs designed to encourage the participation of minorities in mainstream institutions. Perhaps most ominous in the present climate is the recent decision by the University of California Board of Regents to eliminate affirmative action in school admissions and in hiring.

Talking about racism is never easy. The speaker, usually a minority member, is often accused of claiming victim status or complaining about an issue that has long been settled. Thus, the speaker is faced with a conundrum —

how to convey the hurt of racism, the "wounding of the spirit,"[1] the killing of dreams without being labeled overly sensitive or paranoid. How does one speak a truth that must be spoken for the good of all? As the editors of this second edition of *Facing Racism in Education,* we feel that these truths must be spoken, must be repeated again and again until all of us can hear the message and decide, finally, that what is spoken is worthy of our attention.

Considering the contemporary climate of our nation and our readers' continuing interest in the subject of racism in education, we decided to assemble this second edition of *Facing Racism in Education.* Response to the first edition was overwhelming: In three years, the book went through five printings. We have retained some the articles from the first edition because we feel that the messages they contain are worthy of repetition, and have added articles published since 1990 that complement and extend these messages. We hope that this second edition will provide our readers with new approaches, insights, and possibilities for change, and also help to continue a much needed dialogue about racism in education.

One of the challenges of editing a book such as this is being able to represent all groups. Perhaps most evident in this book is the lack of articles addressing the educational and racial experiences of Asian Americans. Therefore, their "cultural gifts" remain a mystery to many in the educational community, and we would hope that the editors of future editons will not face the constraint of a lack of articles about any group. At the same time, however, there is the real danger of misrepresenting groups — minority or majority — by treating them as if they were homogeneous. In other words, we advocate the use of caution in attempts to capture salient aspects of the educational experiences of racial groups, as such efforts can in fact reinscribe or reproduce stereotypes and categories and deny the diversity that exists within any group.

As we close this second edition, we hope that our continuation of the dialogue begun by the editors of *Facing Racism in Education* five years ago helps move educators and students, majority and minority members, institutions and communities toward genuine attempts to listen to each other and envision a society enriched by our cultural "gifts."

TAMARA BEAUBOEUF-LAFONTANT
D. SMITH AUGUSTINE
Harvard Graduate School of Education

---

[1] See Carol Locust, "Wounding the Spirit: Discrimination and Traditional American Indian Belief Systems," in this volume.

PART ONE

■ ■ ■

The Experience of Racism

Even if the Negroes do successfully imitate the whites, nothing new
has thereby been accomplished. You simply have a larger number
of persons doing what others have been doing. The unusual gifts
of the race have not thereby been developed, and an unwilling
world, therefore, continues to wonder what the Negro is good for.

— Carter G. Woodson, *The Mis-Education of the Negro*

Though African American historian Carter G. Woodson was referring
specifically to the schooling of Blacks in the United States, his statement
is equally applicable to other groups that have been similarly silenced
in U.S. schools and society. One implication of his quote is that formal
education in the United States has, for the most part, demanded the assimilation of marginalized groups to a European American cultural definition of
academic success. Such assimilation, Woodson argues, results in mis-education and the devaluation of a group's "gifts" — that is, their value systems,
unique histories, and social and educational goals. As a result, schools mis-
interpret or purposely ignore the abilities, behaviors, needs, aspirations, and
gifts of their minority students. Conversely, as the authors of this first section
demonstrate, when minority teachers and students speak for themselves,
what emerges is an examination of their schooling experiences deeply con-
textualized by the histories, power dynamics, and systemic injustices that
affect these people both outside the classroom and within its walls. Thus,
efforts to silence these voices are also attempts to disavow vital aspects of our
society.

A historical problem, racism cannot be understood without our taking a
historical perspective. Yet, in many discussions of racism, this is precisely
what is left out. Spanning the last century, the first two articles of this section
describe the evolution and current state of schooling for Native Americans.
In "Wounding the Spirit: Discrimination and Traditional American Indian
Belief Systems," Carol Locust contends that racism derived from Eurocentric

1

attitudes devalues the significance and meaning of traditional Indian religions. Central to these religions is the belief that one's essence is contained in the spirit, which is in relationship with one's body and mind. Discrimination and racist practices in the classroom that disregard religious beliefs therefore "wound the spirit" of Native American students and violate them at the most intimate level of their being. By elucidating ten basic beliefs shared by most Native American tribes, Locust highlights situations in which U.S. educational practices conflict with and denigrate these beliefs in ways that obstruct the educational success and spiritual harmony of Native American students.

Many of the beliefs and concerns discussed in Locust's article are reflected in Donna Deyhle's richly detailed ethnography of her decade-long experience as a participant-observer among Navajo families in a border reservation community. "Navaho Youth and Anglo Racism: Cultural Integrity and Resistance" portrays the cultural values of the Navajo people and demonstrates how valiantly Navajo students fight to retain their cultural integrity amidst the attempts of their schools to force their assimilation into Anglo culture and values. In addition to showing the impact of racism on the schooling of Navajo youth, Deyhle chronicles the legacy of that schooling and the wider racism in which it is embedded that is evident in the limited and low-paying employment opportunities for these youth once they leave school.

The next two articles of this section discuss the parallel struggles for cultural integrity in which minority graduate students and faculty are engaged. In "Reflections of a Black Social Scientist: Some Struggles, Some Doubts, Some Hopes," Jacquelyn Mitchell highlights the persistent influence of social science deficit theories of minority culture in educational and social institutions. From her experiences as a teacher, graduate student, and researcher, Mitchell offers a rich analysis of the biculturalism and critical consciousness minorities need to have in order to succeed in schools, the academy, and the workplace. She raises the provocative questions, "Does membership in the White academic community preclude membership in a Black one? Do we have to trade one identity for another? If so, at what price? And more important, why?"

María de la Luz Reyes and John Halcón take on this exact question of "why" and examine the forms of overt and covert racism that limit the presence of Chicano professors in the academy. As they illuminate in "Racism in Academia: The Old Wolf Revisited," the racism most prevalent in institutions of higher education manifests itself in covert practices such as tokenism; the "brown-on-brown" research taboo that claims that minorities cannot "objectively" study their own communities; and the "one-minority-per-pot" syndrome that keeps ethnic participation in "mainstream" departments to a minimum except in specifically designated academic areas such as "ethnic studies." Though the authors explore a variety of coping strategies used by some Chicano academics, they advocate that Chicanos join forces with other people of color in order to combat the institutional racism of the academy.

Another frame for discussions of cultural integrity is the notion of "voice" as it is explored in the concluding articles of this section. Beverly McElroy-Johnson's "Giving Voice to the Voiceless" is a compelling discussion of her experiences as an African American teacher who refuses to silence her voice or those of her students.[1] By analyzing her own experiences as a student and later as a teacher, she reveals the depths to which racism deprives students of color of their voices — that is, their identities, places in the world, and relationships to others. For example, McElroy-Johnson notes that though the Holocaust and the bombing of Hiroshima are rightly acknowledged as horrific human experiences, U.S. schools and society are disturbingly silent about the moral injustice and continuing impact of slavery. One result of such "mis-education" is the lack of self-confidence her students feel about themselves as members of a stigmatized group. Essentially, McElroy-Johnson strives to help her students develop a critical consciousness that will allow them to recognize and overcome the destructive consequences of voicelessness induced by systemic injustice.

Lisa Delpit continues McElroy-Johnson's discussion of voice in "The Silenced Dialogue: Power and Pedagogy in Educating Other People's Children," which has become a classic in this field. Telling excerpts from the "silenced" perspectives of minority students and teachers frame her discussion of power differentials and assumptions that guide classroom practices and relationships. Delpit makes it very clear that one method of silencing is the simple refusal of majority educators to hear the voices of minority people. According to Delpit, our goal as educators should be to "come to a viable synthesis of perspectives. . . . To do so takes a very special kind of listening, listening that requires not only open eyes and ears, but open hearts and minds."

[1] Beverly McElroy-Johnson has legally changed her name to Folásadé Oládélé. We have published her article with the name under which she wrote it.

Wounding the Spirit:
Discrimination and Traditional
American Indian Belief Systems

—■ ■ ■—

CAROL LOCUST

Discrimination against persons because of their beliefs is the most insidious kind of injustice. Ridicule of one's spiritual beliefs or cultural teachings wounds the spirit, leaving anger and hurt that may be masked by a proud silence. American Indians* experience this discrimination in abundance for the sake of their traditional beliefs, especially when such beliefs conflict with those of the dominant culture's educational systems.

When Europeans first came to North America their hearts were hungry for one thing — freedom from being discriminated against because of their belief systems. The United States of America was founded on the principle of religious freedom, yet the indigenous peoples whose land was used to establish this country were denied this freedom. Incredibly, American Indians were not granted religious freedom until 1978, when Congress passed the American Indian Religious Freedom Act (Public Law 95-341). The passage of a law, however, cannot bring change quickly after decades of discrimination; racist attitudes toward traditional Indian religions still exist.

---

* As defined in Public Law 93-638, the Indian Self-Determination and Education Assistance Act (1978), an "Indian" means a person who is a member of an Indian tribe, band, nation, or other organized group or community, including any Alaska Native village, regional, or village corporation as defined or established pursuant to the Alaska Native Claims Settlement Act (85 Stat. 688) which is recognized as eligible for the special programs and services provided by the United States to Indians because of their status as Indians. Tribal organization means the recognized governing body of any Indian tribe; any legally established organization of Indians which is controlled, sanctioned, or charactered by such governing body or which is democratically elected by the adult members of the Indian community; to be served by such organization and which includes the maximum participation of Indians in all phases of its activities.

Harvard Educational Review Vol. 58 No. 3 August 1988, 315–330

These attitudes manifest themselves in the U.S. educational system, which was not designed to honor diverse racial and cultural groups. In earlier years, Indian children did not have easy access to public schools, so they were placed in a military-like education system of boarding schools established by the Bureau of Indian Affairs in 1819 (Roessel, 1963). Neither the public schools nor the military system were designed to accommodate either cultural differences, including tribal religions and ceremonies, or language differences. Change is very slow in coming to educational systems in the United States; therefore, even today, very few public or Bureau schools respect Indian traditions and beliefs.

To change this situation in the schools, teachers and administrators must begin to understand that belief systems among Indian people are sacred and holy; moreover, they do not separate the sacred from the secular aspects of life. For example, when a medicine person works with an individual to bring about healing of an illness, it is not just an act of obtaining medical help such as going to see a physician for a cold remedy. Healing and worship cannot be separated, as there is little difference between religious and traditional healing practices of American Indians (Aberle, 1966). Jerrold Levy (1963) described the social behavior of the Indian as inseparable from the culture, sacred narratives, and religion. Clyde Kluckhohn and Dorothy Leighton (1962) noted that there is no distinct term in the Navajo language for "religion" in the Western sense. While doing a study of Tohono O'odham ceremonies, Marvin Kahn and colleagues (1975) observed that no distinction was made between healing and worship. Carol Locust (1985) stated that there is little or no difference between religion and medicine, between a church and a hospital, in the Indian belief system. Carl Hammerschlag, a former psychiatrist at the Phoenix Indian Medical Center and a friend to Indian people, points out that for them the concept of health is not only a physical state, but a spiritual one as well (1985, p. 2). As these studies show, American Indian beliefs about health may be identified as the core beliefs of the cultures themselves. Educators need to learn more about these concepts, since they are fundamental to both the traditional ways of Indian life and the health and spirituality of tribal members. Without this understanding, there can only be discrimination — discrimination that wounds the spirit of Indian people.

There is a long history of misunderstanding of Indian beliefs on the part of the dominant culture. Early, widely referenced scholars (for example, Morgan, 1892, and Reagan, 1930) seem to have assumed that American Indians were pagans (had no religion) or that they worshiped idols, animals, or devils. Such misunderstandings may have occurred because these scholars did not know the language or the customs of the people, and therefore interpreted Indian ceremonies from the perspectives of their own religious backgrounds. For example, eyewitness accounts of Apache culture and religion written by Thomas Morgan (1892) and Albert Reagan (1930) have serious flaws. Thomas Mails (1974) documented his misgivings about the account of the Apaches written by Reagan: Reagan's comments are based on what he saw in only nine months on the western Apache reservations. He was a captain in the Third Cavalry who was among the Apaches from July 1901 until May of 1902. His interpretations of the real meanings and purposes of some acts he saw performed by the medicine men and the Ghan (Mountain Spirit) dancers should not be taken as gospel. More probably, excepting those instances where acts were explained to him, he was not informed or sympathetic enough to make a reliable and profound statement. The fact is that tribal belief systems contain highly structured theological organization, protocol, and ritual, just as other religions do around the world. In most Indian traditions every element of existence and every second of time is perceived as being holy, thereby implying that worship is a constant daily function. The fact that there were no familiar religious objects (no altars, crosses, books) for early observers to see contributed to their conclusion that Indians were "pagan."

One of the reasons many non-Indian people do not understand much about Indian belief systems is that they vary from tribe to tribe and from clan to clan. For example, Apaches believe that supernatural spirits seek out an individual to become a medicine person. The Tohono O'odham, on the other hand, believe that one must be born into a lineage of medicine persons or must be a twin in order to become a medicine person. Yet in spite of these differences, most systems are built on a common set of beliefs. In a previous work I have identified ten common beliefs that are basic to most Indian tribes in the United States (Locust, 1985). These beliefs are presented in this paper as general statements and should be taken as indicators or guides for further study, not as universals or absolutes for all tribes or for any specific tribe. While these are not absolute truths for any one Indian tribal belief system, an understanding of each will help non-Indians begin to comprehend how educational systems suppress and discriminate against the belief systems of Indians.

Several factors may influence the beliefs of an American Indian: subtribe or clan affiliation, tribal sodality (society) membership, formal education, influence of an outside religion, marriage, and length of time and/or experience off the reservation. A tribal member may or may not know many traditional beliefs, and may or may not identify with those that are known. However, the following statements are applicable to the majority of tribal members:

1. American Indians believe in a Supreme Creator. In this belief system there are lesser beings also.

2. Humans are threefold beings made up of a spirit, mind, and body.

3. Plants and animals, like humans, are part of the spirit world. The spirit world exists side by side with, and intermingles with, the physical world.

4. The spirit existed before it came into a physical body and will exist after the body dies.

7

5. Illness affects the mind and spirit as well as the body.

6. Wellness is harmony in spirit, mind, and body.

7. Unwellness is disharmony in spirit, mind, and body.

8. Natural unwellness is caused by the violation of a sacred or tribal taboo.

9. Unnatural unwellness is caused by witchcraft.

10. Each of us is responsible for his or her own wellness.

Educators need to understand the meaning of these beliefs, because Indian sociocultural behaviors rooted in these traditional beliefs strongly affect their formal educational experiences. But an understanding of Indian beliefs is not enough for educators; they must also be able to identify how such beliefs manifest themselves in Indian attitudes and behaviors toward formal educational systems. Below I discuss each of these ten common beliefs and outline ways in which U.S. educational practices come into conflict with these beliefs.

1. American Indians believe in a Supreme Creator. In this belief system there are lesser beings also.

Most tribes identify a Supreme Creator by a name and a personage and usually identify a place of residence for that entity. Although often identified as male, the Supreme Creator is considered both male and female. The name of the Supreme Creator is seldom spoken, for it is sacred. Prayer is usually offered to the Supreme Creator, who is addressed by a term of reverence and endearment, such as "Grandfather." The Creator is usually perceived as omnipotent, in command of all the elements of existence, and as anthropomorphic, but spiritual rather than physical (Lukert, 1977).

Many tribal groups believe in other spirit beings — such as partners, co-creators, mates, or offspring — that are associated with the Supreme Creator. These lesser beings may or may not be impersonated in ceremony. More frequently they are considered exemplary models after which humans are to pattern their own lives. Most Indian tribes also recognize an assemblage of spirit helpers that assist humans. These beings are not gods, nor do they belong to the hierarchy of sacredness; therefore they are not worshipped or prayed to, but they command respect and gratitude. Some of these beneficent spirit helpers may be identified as *Kachinas* (Hopi), *Ghan* (Apache), or *Yei* (Navajo) (Locust, 1985).

2. Humans are threefold beings made up of a spirit, mind, and body.

"Come into this house that has been prepared for you" is a phrase from a Hopi song welcoming an infant into the world. The "house" is the physical body the parents have prepared for the spirit to inhabit. The "I AM" of each person is the spirit that dwells within the physical body. Of the three elements — spirit, mind, and body — the spirit is the most important, for it is the essence of the being. The instrument by which the spirit may express

8

itself is the body. It can learn spiritual lessons and may progress toward the ultimate goal of being united with the Supreme Creator. The mind is the link between the spirit and the body and functions as an interpreter between the two. For example, a person hears a truth by means of the ears of the physical body, and recognizes the truth on a spiritual level. The mind, being aware of the disparity between human desires and spiritual truths, then makes adjustments in the cognitive and response systems within the consciousness to incorporate this new truth.

The element of existence that gives vitality to all creation is often called "energy" or "power." The Supreme Creator is all-powerful; all things he has created have power. This power (energy) is spiritual, so someone referred to as a "powerful" medicine person is identified as a person who has extremely strong personal energy. A stone (such as a crystal) or a plant (tobacco) may be powerful as well. Eagles have very powerful energy, for they fly closest to the sky, which is the abode of the Supreme Creator. Animals are sensitive to human energy; they can sense whether someone is friendly or not. Humans can sense energies also, but most people are not aware of it. For example, a person may meet a stranger that he or she likes immediately and another stranger he or she dislikes immediately. Personal energy is spiritual, and if the personal energy of a newborn infant is extremely strong, medicine people will know that the baby is a medicine person. It is difficult to deceive people who can "see," because energies betray what an individual really is.

Unlike Indian medicine, Western medicine does not incorporate the concept of spiritual illness, and this can create problems for Indian children in non-Indian schools. Suppose, for example, an Indian child is absent from school because of a spiritual sickness. What happens if the school requires a doctor's note to the effect that he or she was seen by a physician, and no note is forthcoming? Non-Indian doctors cannot treat illnesses they do not recognize and were not trained to treat. A spiritual unwellness is frequently more devastating than a physical illness, yet this phenomenon is not recognized by many school nurses. Moreover, Indians believe that an individual's spiritual illness can affect the group (family and friends), and thus group efforts are required to return all members of the group to wellness. As a result, students who are not ill may be absent from school in order to assist a sick relative in returning to wellness. Although this group effort is of vital importance to tribal, clan, and family members, it often becomes a point of antagonism between group membership and school officials, resulting in discriminating actions by school authorities.

Furthermore, many tribal customs revolve around the belief that the body and spirit need not be in the same place at all times. What non-Indians may perceive as inattention, "spacing out," or perhaps a petit mal seizure may be a matter of "spirit traveling" for the Indians. The term "spacing out" implies the act of thinking or seeing things in one's mind, either in recall or in imagination, but confined to creation within the mind. "Spirit traveling" refers to the spirit traveling to another location, assessing the activities and/or situation there (such as in reconnoitering during warfare) and the traveler being able to give an account of the information gathered during the travel. The ability to project the consciousness from the body appears to be common among tribal members, as many people have spoken about it to this researcher. However, it can create conflict in the classroom for students who have not yet learned adequate control of it.

Some tribal groups seem to possess the unique ability to "travel in their spirit bodies," or to manifest themselves in bodily form in another location, as part of the projected consciousness. This ability of bilocation may create frustration for teachers, whose Indian students may leave the physical body sitting at a desk in the classroom while their consciousness and spirit bodies go elsewhere (Locust, 1987).

3. Plants and animals, like humans, are part of the spirit world. The spirit world exists side by side with, and intermingles with, the physical world.

Most American Indians believe that all creation has a spiritual component because all things were made by the Supreme Creator. The earth is our mother, the sky our father, and the animals our brothers and sisters. Water is our friend, and every living thing a relative. Traditionally, thanks and a small gift were given to any animal or plant from which life was taken. No life was taken for sport or fun; hunting, fishing, and harvesting were done to obtain food. Most Indian tribes consider the mutilation of an animal's body to be a direct violation of a brother or sister and believe that what is done to others will be done to them in return. This traditional belief comes into conflict with educational practice, for example, in high school biology classes that require students to dissect animals. When faced with the choice of failing the class or bringing terrible consequences into their own lives or the lives of family members by mutilating an animal's body, most Indian students will choose to fail the class (Locust, 1986a).

The idea that spirit forms inhabit the same living space as humans is not uncommon among Indian people. "My (deceased) father came to see me today" is a common statement, although each tribe may attach a different set of meanings to the visitation. Animals, birds, and fish may also manifest themselves in spirit form without a physical body. When an Indian seeks the meaning of his or her life (this is often called a vision quest), an animal from the spirit world may make itself visible to him or her, thus becoming the symbol for his or her life. Traditionally, American Indian people have been visionaries and have had the ability to see into the spirit world. Tribal members with an extraordinary ability in this area become medicine people.

Indian students are frequently reluctant to express their views about spirit beings to non-Indian school people, because they fear ridicule. Many non-Indians think of spirit beings as terrifying specters; others scoff at anything that smacks of the supernatural. Indian people who acknowledge the spirit world as a normal part of existence have difficulty with both non-Indian views; further, they may refuse to debate the issue because of traditional respect for spirit beings.

4. The spirit existed before it came into a physical body and will exist after the body dies.

American Indians conceive of immortality as circular in nature, having no beginning and no end. In Indian belief systems, when one physical body is worn out, it is shed like an old garment, and the spirit is free to inhabit another body. When that one is worn out, the cycle is repeated until the spirit reaches perfection and returns to the Supreme Creator. This "returning" is basic to the belief of most tribes.

Traditional Indian belief systems do not incorporate an ultimate place of punishment for individuals who have transgressed in this life. But a state of torment is identified for departed spirits who have transgressed and who need chastisement to remind them not to repeat the same errors when they return in another body. Conversely, a peaceful land of rest and plenty occupies a place in Indian religion as a place where existence is carried on. This belief affects burial practices: Indian people provide their deceased with the necessities of life in the next world.

5. Illness affects the mind and spirit as well as the body.

The concept of spirit, body, and mind interacting in humans is basic to most Indian beliefs and traditional healing methods. When Indians become ill, they often ask themselves why they are ill, since the cause of a sickness is as important as the illness itself. If the spiritual energy around a person is strong, he or she will not become ill, and negative things cannot happen to him or her. If an Indian does become ill or experiences difficulties (family problems, for example), he or she must find out why his or her personal energy is low and take steps to correct the situation; otherwise he or she will continue to have problems. And if the source of a student's spiritual weakness is the school, that student may not attend classes until his or her spiritual energy is strong again.

Modern medicine tends to treat the body for illness without treating the spirit. In the Western approach, bodies are cut open, repaired, put back together, cleaned, medicated, and bandaged; but most Western doctors give no thought to the spirit. If the situation indicates emotional or mental problems, the doctor may refer the patient to another doctor who specializes in such illnesses. The physical — and perhaps mental — side of an illness may be taken care of; the spirit, however, is not treated by Western medicine. For this reason many Indians prefer to see a medicine person at the same time that they are being treated by a physician. For example, an Indian may go to the Indian Health Center to have a broken leg cared for. The physician takes care of the physical injury, but to the Indian the spirit must also be cared for properly. Treating the spirit is the process of finding out why the broken leg occurred, understanding the events in a spiritual rather than a

11

physical sense, and then beginning the process of changing whatever it was in the body, mind, or spirit that was out of harmony enough to warrant a broken leg.

In the schools, misunderstandings frequently arise because of the difference between the school systems' definition of "sickness" and the Indian concept of unwellness. Schools may have a list of physical symptoms for which students are automatically sent home: for instance, fever, upset stomach, headache, vomiting, and other obvious symptoms of distress. These physical symptoms are not cause for alarm, however, in most Indian families, whose members have learned to live with minor discomforts and realize that such suffering is usually transient. As a result, Indian parents may be labeled by the school authorities as uncaring, irresponsible, ignorant, or lazy when they send their children to school with a runny nose or a cough, when in fact those symptoms are so common in their culture that they are not considered evidence of illness. In contrast, a child may be kept home several days for traditional treatments for "ghost sickness," a malady of lethargy, apathy, and general nonspecific unwellness caused by the spirits of dead relatives calling for the child to join them. The child may face punishment for his or her absence upon returning to school, since the school's list of excusable illnesses does not include "ghost sickness," and a note from a traditional medicine person — if it could be obtained — would not be considered adequate. Furthermore, a healing ceremony may call for burning powerful, often pungent herbs and enveloping the ill person in the smoke. This treatment usually includes an admonition not to bathe the afflicted person for several days, a practice that precludes the student's returning to school.

6. Wellness is harmony in spirit, mind, and body.

Harmony is the peaceful, tranquil state of knowing all is well with one's spirit, mind, and body. To be in harmony is to be at "oneness" with life, eternity, the Supreme Creator, and oneself. Many Indians who are visionaries describe the energy (aura) around an individual who has harmony as a light or radiance of being, to which all life forms react with joy. But harmony is not found within the environment, nor does it come from others; it comes from within and from the Supreme Creator. It is toward this harmony that American Indians strive, despite the poverty and deprivation in their lives and the discrimination they experience because of their belief in harmony itself.

Harmony is wellness, but it is not utopia, as an older Cherokee man explained. When asked about harmony, an elderly Hopi responded that each person has his proper set of relationships for being in harmony and that no two people are alike. John Coulehan (1980) found a similar perspective among the Navajo. A person can be in harmony, Indians believe, despite the condition of his body, mind, or environment. One person's harmony may include dealing with arthritis. Another person's harmony may include compensating for failing vision. It is not the events that happen to a person, but his or her responses to those events that create harmony. Every human chooses his responses, and thus chooses harmony or disharmony.

7. *Unwellness is disharmony in spirit, mind, and body.*

In contrast to wellness, or harmony, unwellness is characterized by disharmony. One cannot be in a state of disharmony caused by suppressed anger, frustration, heartache, or fear without sooner or later developing unwellness in the physical body from that disharmony. Disharmony may be a vague feeling of things "not being right" in one's life, and a time of meditation may be needed in which to discover what is not right. One can be affected by terminal cancer, but if the spirit, mind, and body are in harmony, the cancer becomes part of the harmony and the person is at peace.

Indian tribes tend to allow each person his or her harmony without forcing absolute conformity to all cultural standards. This custom allows the individuals who are less capable mentally to find a meaningful place in their society in simple physical tasks, such as wood-gathering. A beautiful Hopi man once wept when he recounted the story of his friend "Bear," a big, loving, mentally retarded boy who was the village water carrier. The Bureau of Indian Affairs social worker insisted that Bear go to a school in the city. Bear went, but he was terribly homesick and became violent. He spent the next twenty years in the state hospital for the criminally insane and then returned to his village to die. What a tragic waste of human life! Bear was in harmony in his village carrying water. His retardation was part of his harmony; the state hospital was not.

Avoiding disharmony is desirable in Indian cultures: disharmony is negative and pervasive and can result in unwellness. For instance, Indian parents frequently refuse to go to school when called, because they have learned that being called means their child is in trouble. The negative situation that is certain to develop among school officials, the child, and the parents brings disharmony for all concerned and can result in illness if spiritual energy becomes low. Therefore the parents may choose not to be involved with the disharmony at the school and instead to counsel the child at home in a positive manner. Non-Indians, whose culture dictates swift punishment for students who transgress school rules, may view the Indian response as too lenient or as pampering the child, and may become angry because Indian parents do not respond in the manner the school thinks appropriate. The disparity between the cultural expectations of parental responsibilities and control of children may create dissension and hostility between school officials and tribal members. Students who are faced with a disharmonious situation at school may choose to remove themselves from it in an effort to avoid the possibility of disharmony in their own lives. Physically removing themselves — through leaving school or hiding — is the first defense against disharmony. However, if a student is called before a school official and forced to listen to a tirade full of loud, angry reprimands and accusations, and is therefore endangered by being in proximity to such negativity, the student may choose to protect his or her spirit by removing it through spirit travel if he or she cannot escape physically. At the first available opportunity, the student may also choose to transport his or her body with him or her in the spirit travel and leave an empty chair and a furious school official behind. But to Indians, escaping disharmony does not mean escaping the consequences of an action. Indian children are taught early in life that every thought and every action creates a ripple in their being and that the consequences of those actions are inescapable.

8. *Natural unwellness is caused by the violation of a sacred or tribal taboo.*

Most American Indian tribal beliefs include a distinction between those illnesses that are the result of natural causes and those that result from unnatural causes. Natural unwellness is a consequence of violating a taboo, whether it was done intentionally or unintentionally, and can affect the offender or the offender's family. Although the word *taboo* is not a perfect translation of the concept, it is closer than any other word in English to the meaning of the concept. However, *taboo,* in the Indian sense, carries cultural and religious implications, and to violate a taboo brings spiritual as well as physical consequences.

Each tribe has its own taboos, with specific consequences. In some tribes there is a definite relationship between breaking a certain taboo and experiencing identical consequences. Mutilating an animal's paw or leg, for example, always results in injury to the mutilator's foot or leg. In other tribes, a particular reptile may be seen as a carrier of negative energy, and getting near the reptile may cause a variety of illnesses secondary to "reptile illness."

Most tribes recognize cultural and moral taboos that relate to personal conduct, such as never laughing at a disabled person or at an animal (Gifford, 1940). Religious taboos may concern proper observance of rituals. Some of the prevalent tribal taboos concern death, incest, the female menstrual cycle, witchcraft, certain animals, some types of phenomena such as lightning or an eclipse, particular foods, dead bodies, marrying into one's own clan, and strict observance of religious and ceremonial protocol.

One particular taboo, based on the belief that bodies are sacred to their owners, often creates conflict in schools. For Indians, exposing one's bodily sacredness to the indiscriminate view of others violates the holiness of the being. Thus, violation of the sacredness of the body occurs when students are required to change clothes or shower as a part of their physical education classes, since many of the schools do not provide private showers or changing rooms. Rather than commit the sacrilegious act of exposing their bodies, many Indian students opt to fail physical education, since changing clothes and showering are required to pass the course. Non-Indian educational systems have been extremely slow to respond to the Indians' need for privacy in regard to this issue.

9. Unnatural unwellness is caused by witchcraft.

For almost all tribes, evil is a real and powerful adversary, and one must be continually on guard against it. Evil is seen as a power, and it is also identified as an entity, either human or animal. As part of an attempt to develop a clear definition of evil in Indian belief systems, this writer asked several Indians to explain how they perceived evil. The terms they most often used to identify evil were *bad power, bad energy, negative energy, negative power,* or *dark side.* Some tribes see the bear as a personification of evil, and others see evil as being an owl or a reptile. Most tribes associate a legendary cultural figure with evil. These traditional cultural figures usually only represent evil, and are not seen as the creators of evil. Evil may manifest itself in a multitude of shapes and forms, and can be manipulated by witchcraft.

According to some Indian belief systems, an individual may choose not to walk in the spirit of harmony, and instead choose to walk in the power of malevolent spirits and to do harm to other humans. Indians refer to these individuals as "witches" and to their activities as "witchcraft." Hopi Indians refer to these individuals as *buaka.* In the Yaqui language it is *yesisivome.* These terms are not synonymous with Western concepts of witches and witchcraft — actually, there are no English terms for the Indian concept. The Hopi word *buaka* might be translated as "those who go around at night" or "those from the dark side," as compared with non-witches, who are "beings of light." The Yaqui word *yesisivome* means "one who is on the bad side" of using supernatural power. The Indian term for *witch* refers to both males and females. Tribal groups differ on what the terms "witches" and "witchcraft" mean in their language, but most Indian people understand the use of negative energy against one another. Yet one need not be a witch to cast a spell or to "witch" another person, for most Indians know how to manipulate energy (power), especially mental energy. In intense, destructive cases of witchcraft, however, the witch involved is a skillful professional user of negative power.

Witching usually follows one of two patterns: it may affect the environment around the victim, which in turn affects the person; or it may affect the person directly. If the intended victim's personal power is so strong that the witchcraft cannot affect him or her, a member of the family who is weak will fall victim. Incidences of witchcraft related by Indian people of various tribes indicate that sudden physical illness, sharp pains, accidents, depression, irrational thinking, and unusual behavior are often suspected has having been caused by witchcraft. Protective objects such as medicine bags, certain stones, bits of organic material, and symbolic items of a religious or spiritual nature are frequently worn on the body; their removal (which is often required by school officials) can often create a dangerous vulnerability for the individual.

Keeping one's personal energy strong is the best defense against negative energy. Parents are responsible for the personal protection of their children and of any older, weak family members in their household. When the house is filled with love, caring, and kindness, evil cannot find a weakness by which to enter. If it does enter, therefore, one knows that there is a weakness somewhere and that it must be corrected before more harm is done. Staying away from situations that cause an Indian's personal energy to become weak is a survival behavior that may be frustrating to non-Indians. In the first place, such behavior is not part of their culture, and second, the identification of a harmful situation is culturally determined. Thus, such behavior frequently causes conflict in school settings, and consequently discrimination.

Medicine people are on the "good side" of the use of energy, and are frequently prevailed upon to counteract the negative energy of witchcraft. If the spell is not strong, the victim, with the help of his or her family, may be able to dissolve it. If the negative energy is strong, however, or if the individual does not know where the weakness lies, a medicine person may assist the victim in these areas. (Medicine people never claim to "heal" anyone or to "take off" a spell; properly speaking, they assist other people in healing themselves or in dissolving the negative energy around them.) Medicine people are also healers of the physical body; one may specialize in "bones" and another in childbirth. The visionaries also work with positive energy to counteract negativity, for they have the ability to perceive spiritual matters. In some tribes, healers dedicate themselves to "light" and therefore can never intentionally harm anyone; in others a medicine person may heal someone today and harm someone else tomorrow, depending on the situation. Traditionally, however, medicine people are warriors for "light" and witches are perpetrators of "darkness."

10. Each of us is responsible for his or her own wellness.

Many American Indians believe they are responsible for their own wellness. They can make themselves well and they can make themselves unwell. If an individual allows him- or herself to become upset by something, he or she has allowed disharmony to enter his or her life. This disharmony may create physical symptoms such as a headache or indigestion. Thus, that individual has caused the headache or indigestion by becoming upset. If an individual's spiritual energy is so low that he or she can be affected by witchcraft, then the individual has allowed the witchcraft to affect him or her. Therefore, keeping one's energy strong and keeping oneself in harmony precludes unwellness.

When an Indian is in harmony, his or her spirit, mind, and body are so attuned to the self, the environment, and the universe that transgressions against moral, religious, or cultural taboos do not occur; further, negative energy from witchcraft cannot find a weakness by which to exert its influence. The idea of this powerful protective shield of harmony is articulated in song by the Navajo: "Beauty is above me, beauty is before me, beauty is all around me."

Most tribes believe that a spirit chooses the body it will inhabit. In the case of a handicapped body, the spirit chooses the body knowing its limitations but choosing to use it for some purpose determined by that spirit and the Supreme Creator. Furthermore, tribal members envision the spirit inside a handicapped body as being whole and perfect and capable of understanding everything that goes on in the environment, even when it appears that the physical body cannot comprehend anything. One might express sympathy for the physical condition of the body in which a spirit chose to express itself, to learn lessons, and to teach lessons. One might express respect and honor for the spirit that is strong and wise enough to inhabit such a body, and assist it in accomplishing whatever it came to the earth to do. Indians distinguish between a spirit in a handicapped body and the body itself: the causes of a body's being handicapped may lie with the parents (as in the case of fetal alcohol syndrome), and consequently the blame for (prenatal) mutilation of a body falls on the parents; the choice of being in the body, however, remains with the spirit in the body, not the parents.

Consider, though, that the concept of handicaps is culturally determined; what may be a handicap to a non-Indian may not be considered a handicap to an Indian. Many Navajo, for instance, are born with a congenital hip deformity, but the condition does not disable them and therefore they are not handicapped. When surgery is performed, however, they become unable to sit on a horse comfortably and so become disabled, for riding is still an important mode of transportation in many areas (Rabin & Barnett et al., 1969).

In school systems, children may be classified as mentally retarded, while within their own community they are not retarded but function as contributing members of their society. (Consider the case of Bear described earlier.) Most traditional Indian languages do not have words for retarded, disabled, or handicapped. Dee Brown's book *Bury My Heart at Wounded Knee* (1970) contains many names of individuals that are descriptive of disabilities — No-Eyes, Big-Head, One-Who-Walks-with-a-Limp, Hump, One-Arm — but categories such as "cripples" do not appear in the literature. The Hopi people identify some individuals with the white or snow kachina (albinos), and legends tell them that one deity who was incarnated as a human, the kachina Kokopeli, was humpbacked. Neither of these two conditions constitutes a handicap to the Hopi people (Locust, 1986b). A beautiful term for describing a disabled person comes from the Yaquis: "not completed yet" (Locust, 1987).

Obtaining an education has been a necessity for all Indian children. Traditionally, teaching children who learned at a slower pace than others was as normal as teaching children who learned faster than others, and little difference was shown in the way they were treated. Only when formal education came to the Indian Nations were labels applied to the differences between children. Public Law 94-142, the Education for All Handicapped Children Act (1975), was a two-edged sword for Indian people. On the one

17

hand, it provided educational opportunities for severely disabled children who were once institutionalized off the reservation by the Bureau of Indian Affairs, but on the other hand, it caused multitudes of children to be labeled mentally retarded or learning disabled who up until that time were not considered handicapped in their cultures (Miller, Miller, & Miller, 1987). This is because American Indian cultures reinforce nonverbal communication, visual/spatial memory, visual/motor skills, and sequential visual memory over verbal skills. Psychological evaluations include verbal skills as a large portion of the tests Indian children are given. Tests are conducted in English, a second language to many Indian children. Small wonder, then, that non-Indian tests identify disproportionate numbers of Indian children who score very low in verbal skills.

The formal education process, as well as standardized achievement and intelligence tests, are designed to assist and measure mental functions desirable in the dominant culture. Their use for other cultures is discriminatory; nevertheless, little change has occurred to adjust either the educational or the testing process to accommodate the language or cognition styles of other cultures.

Discussion

Belief systems are integrated into the total being of the American Indian, and discrimination against these beliefs occurs in ways that non-Indians do not easily understand. Indians view immortality and existence as circular rather than linear, and appear to learn best when information is presented to them in a circular manner (Emerson, 1987). Traditional ceremonies are based on the concept of circular completion, just as the spirit continues on the medicine wheel until it reaches completion. Formal education, in contrast, is composed of linear lessons, each of which occupies a linear spot on the year's time chart. Completion is from the top to the bottom of the chart, year after year, until the final year has been reached. Traditional education of Indian youth is not linear and frequently not verbal. Indian children learn by watching their elders, by having the grandparents identify for them the whole of the task, the complete circle, the perfection of completion. The whole is then marked into meaningful parts, just as the wheel of life is divided into the four sacred points of the earth, or the four sacred points of life itself. From these reference points on the circle the elder begins to teach, always relating the parts to the whole, not treating them in isolation — for a part must remain in the whole or the circle is broken — but in reference to the whole, so there is comprehension of the entire task, not just completion of the work. The process may be longer, but at completion the students know why a task is done a certain way, not just how to do it, for they have seen the completion of the circle.

One of the most blatant issues of discrimination against American Indian belief systems involves traditional ceremonial times. School calendars include holidays based on Christian tradition and on national historical events. In most school systems, American Indian children do not enjoy religious freedom, but are penalized for being absent from classes while participating in traditional tribal ceremonies. Consider the case of the Pascua Yaqui Indians near Tucson, Arizona, who attend classes in the Tucson Unified School District. Hundreds of years ago, traditional Yaqui religion was combined with Catholicism, producing a unique belief system with strict religious procedures, ceremonies, and observances in the weeks before the Running of the Gloria (corresponding with Easter Sunday). Each year, scores of Yaqui children are absent from school twice a week for several weeks preceding the Lenten season in the spring, and each year the children suffer the humiliation of having to justify their absences. Each year it was the same; excusable absences did not include participation in traditional tribal functions. However, in 1986 the culturally sensitive school board amended its attendance policy so that the observance of traditional Indian ceremonies and feast days became excusable absences. Unfortunately this bold step toward religious equality in the educational system is an exception, not the norm, for school boards.

The dominant culture's lack of understanding of the tribal concept that the unity of a group is binding also leads to discrimination against Indian people. In years past, it was the unity of the tribe, clan, or even family that enabled its members to survive. This survival instinct is still present in Indian communities, and it dictates behaviors that are frequently misunderstood by non-Indians. For example, the group's survival depends on everyone's working together and sharing. All members work together and contribute to the group, supporting each other in times of stress, for they know that they will find the same network of support for themselves should they require it. Children are expected to contribute to their group, as soon as they are mature enough to do so, so that a four-year-old may have the responsibility of looking after a toddler, and a six-year-old Navajo may act as a shepherd. With this kind of early responsibility comes an early breaking of the maternal bond; children as young as nine and ten "break the apron strings" and are respected as adults, since they participate as adults in the group effort. Responsibility, loyalty, and proper codes of behavior are taught to the children by grandparents, who are the traditional teachers in Indian communities. The U.S. educational system has dealt a severe blow to this group bonding behavior by separating children from the home to send them to school, thus removing from the grandparents the opportunity to teach them properly. Frequently, children are still accorded respect as adults at an early age, but too often they have not had the advantage of traditional teachings. This creates freedom without knowledge of how to accept responsibility, and consequently Indian children are called "delinquent," "wild," and "uncontrolled" by a social system that created this situation for them.

Another aspect of the group membership concept often conflicts with educational systems: that of justifying membership in the group through one's contribution and loyalty. Junior high school girls will stay home to babysit younger siblings while their parents work, enabling the family to have two incomes without the cost of child care. Young boys, pressed to go to work to help buy food and unable to find employment because of their age, may turn to stealing in order to contribute to the group. So strong is the membership bonding that students go hungry rather than ask their parents for lunch money, for in asking they would be putting their needs in front of the group's needs. For the same reason, Indian students may not participate in group sports that require uniforms or equipment that they must purchase, for money spent on those things means that someone else must go without. In an era when unemployment among American Indians is 62 percent on and near reservations (Bureau of Indian Affairs, 1987), and the average annual income of all Indian families in the United States consistently runs $6,000 to $7,000 below that of the general population, money is a great concern (Northern Arizona University and the University of Arizona, 1987, p. 6).

Belief systems are the framework upon which cultures and societies function. It is the bond that holds civilizations together, and it is the small voice inside each of us that urges us to be true to what we have been taught. As Native people, we cannot separate our spiritual teachings from our learning, nor can we separate our beliefs about who and what we are from our values and our behaviors. As Indian people, we ask that educational systems recognize our right to religious freedom and our right, as Sovereign Nations, to live in harmony as we were taught. However, non-Indians must be educated to the traditional beliefs that Indian people may have before they can understand what changes may be needed.

Tribal beliefs vary, as does the extent to which a tribe embraces its traditional cultural beliefs. Each tribal group has distinct and unique beliefs that are basic to that tribe's culture. Most tribes cling to the Old Teachings because they know that, once gone, it means the death of their culture. The majority of American Indians wish to maintain their identity as Sovereign Nations under the Constitution of the United States, and wish to maintain their tribal and cultural belief systems and lifestyles. We remain positive that, once understanding has been established between tribal cultures and educational systems, discrimination will cease.

References

Aberle, D. (1966). *The Peyote religion among the Navajo*. Chicago: University of Chicago Press.
Brown, D. (1970). *Bury my heart at Wounded Knee*. New York: Holt, Rinehart & Winston.
Bureau of Indian Affairs, Department of the Interior. (1987). *Indian service population and labor force estimates*. Washington, DC.
Coulehan, J. (1980). Navajo Indian medicine: Implications for healing. *Journal of Family Practice, 10,* 55–61.
Emerson, L. (1987). *Self-determination through culture and thought processes*. Paper presented at the Indigenous People's World Conference, University of British Columbia, Canada.

Gifford, E. W. (1940). Cultural elements distributions: XII, Apache-Pueblo. *Anthropological Records, 4*(1).

Hammerschlag, C. (1985). *The spirit of healing in groups.* Monograph from a modified text of the Presidential address delivered to the Arizona Group Psychotherapy Society, Oracle, Arizona, April, 1985. Printed by the Phoenix Indian Medical Center.

Kahn, M., Williams, C., Calvez, E., Lujero, L., Conrad, R., & Goldstein, G. (1975). The Papago psychological service: A community mental health program on an American Indian reservation. *American Journal of Community Psychology, 3,* 81–96.

Kluckhohn, C., & Leighton, D. (1962). *The Navajo* (rev. ed.). New York: Anchor Books.

Levy, J. (1963). *Navajo health concepts and behaviors: The role of the Anglo medical man in the Navajo healing process.* A Report to the United States Public Health Service, Indian Health Systems, Bethesda, MD.

Levy, J., & Kunitz, S. (1974). *Indian drinking.* New York: John Wiley & Sons.

Locust, C. (1985). *American Indian beliefs concerning health and unwellness* (Monograph). Tucson: University of Arizona, College of Medicine, Native American Research and Training Center.

Locust, C. (1986a). *Apache beliefs about unwellness and handicaps* (Monograph). Tucson: University of Arizona, College of Medicine, Native American Research and Training Center.

Locust, C. (1986b). *Hopi Indian beliefs about unwellness and handicaps* (Monograph). Tucson: University of Arizona, College of Medicine, Native American Research and Training Center.

Locust, C. (1987). *Yaqui Indian beliefs about unwellness and handicaps* (Monograph). Tucson: University of Arizona, College of Medicine, Native American Research and Training Center.

Lukert, K. (1977). *Navajo Mountain and Rainbow Bridge religion.* Published by the Museum of Northern Arizona, series on American Tribal Religions.

Mails, T. E. (1974). *The people called Apache.* Englewood Cliffs, NJ: Prentice-Hall.

Miller, J., Miller, J., & Miller, D. (1987). American Indian cultural perspectives on disability. Monograph, Native American Research and Training Center, College of Medicine, University of Arizona, Tucson.

Morgan, T. J. (1892). *Report of Indian commissioners.* Washington, DC: National Archives

Northern Arizona University & University of Arizona. (1987). *A study of the special problems and needs of American Indians with handicaps both on and off the reservation* (Vol. 2). Prepared for the U.S. Department of Education, Office of Special Education and Rehabilitative Services, Rehabilitation Services Administration, Washington, DC.

Rabin, D. L., & Barnett, C., et al. (1969, February). Untreated hip disease. *American Public Health Association Supplement Edition, 55* (2), 1–44.

Reagan, A. (1930). *Notes on the Indians of the Fort Apache region.* New York: Anthropological Publications of the American Museum of Natural History, No. 31.

Roessel, R. A., Jr. (1963). *San Carlos Apache Indian education* (Monograph). Tempe: Arizona State University, Indian Education Center.

Navajo Youth and Anglo Racism: Cultural Integrity and Resistance

■ ■ ■

DONNA DEYHLE

Graduation day was near at Navajo High School.[1] Young Navajo men wearing blue jeans, T-shirts, and Nikes stood in the hall talking to the shop teacher. "You learned lots of skills in my class. Try the job services office in town. They can help you find jobs," he told them. One student disagreed. "I haven't really seen any Navajo people working, like in convenience stores or grocery stores. So, the job outlook is pretty slim. Unless you figure out something else to do. Like shoveling snow or something. But the job outlook isn't really great. For Indians, you know."

Several of the students nodded in agreement. The teacher continued, "There are lots of jobs out there. You just have to look for them." As I passed them, I remembered a Navajo parent's comment: "It's the way it has always been. The Anglos keep the jobs for themselves, they don't hire real Navajo. That's the way it is."[2]

I continued down the hall to the library to interview one of the graduating seniors. She was in the top 10 percent of her class and had turned down two college scholarships to stay home with her family on the reservation. "I've always wanted to do things but it's like I couldn't because of school. That's what has held me back. I feel that." Going to college away from the reservation would cause her to miss opportunities to participate in, for example, traditional Navajo ceremonies. She explained her decision: "If I go to college, I will get a job in the city and then I won't come back very often. When am I going to have time to spend with my grandmother learning about my culture? I feel that kind of resentment towards school. I feel cheated out of my own culture."

This article is about the lives, in and out of school, of young Navajo men and women in a border reservation community.[3] Here, school success and failure are best understood as one part of the larger process of racial conflict,

Harvard Educational Review Vol. 65 No. 3 Fall 1995, 403–444

which I have seen fought out in the workplace and in schools in this polarized community. This article will illustrate how Anglos maneuver to acquire the best jobs (some of which are teaching jobs) and how they systematically prepare Navajos for the lowest level jobs. These Navajo people are subject to racial discrimination in the workplace and at school. Young Navajos may respond to the vocational, assimilationist curriculum in their schools by withdrawing or resisting "education." For Navajo students, one of the most life-affirming strategies is to embrace reservation life and traditional Navajo culture. Indeed, the students in my study who were able to maintain Navajo/reservation connections gained a solid place in Navajo society and were also more successful in the Anglo world of school and workplace.

As an anthropologist interested in issues related to American Indian education, I discovered an absence of ethnographic research on American Indian adolescents' lives in and out of school since Murray Wax, Rosalie Wax, and Robert Dumont published *Formal Education in an American Indian Community* in 1964.[4] No such studies existed on the Navajo. In the early 1980s, a doctoral student, who at the time was an elementary school principal in the local school district, invited me to conduct a similar study in his community. District administrators and Navajo parents were concerned with the high dropout rate of Navajo youth, and requested a study that would examine the reasons for the school success and failure of these students. In the fall of 1984, I moved to the community as an ethnographer to start this study. Over the next ten years, I listened to Navajo youth talk about their lives and watched them grow up and have families of their own. I attended their high schools, joining them in over three hundred classes, watching their struggles, successes, and failures. With field notes of observations and casual conversations, audiotapes of meetings and interviews, and ethnohistorical archival data, I documented their lives over the past decade.

Border High School (BHS) is located in a small town of 3,500 people about twenty miles from the Navajo reservation. Almost half of the student population is Navajo. Navajo High School (NHS) is located on the Navajo reservation, and almost 99 percent of the student population is Navajo. Both high schools, as part of one large public school district in one county, are administered from a central district office. They use both state and local standardized curricula.

For this study, I developed a main database that tracked by name all Navajo students who attended BHS and NHS during the school years from 1980–1981 to 1988–1989. This master list contained attendance data, grade point averages, standardized test scores, dropout and graduation rates, community locations, current employment situations, post–high school training, and General Education Diploma (GED) or regular high school graduation diploma received for 1,489 youth. Formal interviews took place with 168 youth who had left school and another one hundred who were either still in school or had successfully graduated. Teachers, administrators, political leaders, parents, and community members also answered my endless questions within the context of formal and casual conversations over the past ten years. During this time, I became involved in extracurricular school activities, including athletic games, plays, dances, and carnivals, and "hanging out" on Main Street and at local fast food restaurants. I attended school and community meetings with Navajo parents. After several years, I was invited to participate in discussions with Navajo parents and to help develop strategies to intervene in school district decisions, such as disciplinary codes, attendance regulations, busing schedules, equal band equipment, and bilingual education. I watched and participated as parents fought for local political control over their children's education and struggled through racist treatment by the Anglo community. These parents were clearly aware of racist practices that occurred, and which I observed, on a daily basis.

I lived for two summers with a Navajo family on the reservation, herding sheep and cooking with children and adolescents. Over the years, as I continually returned to their community, they decided it was worth their time and energy to "educate" me about their cultural norms and values. The oldest daughter, Jan, was a student I had come to know from my initial observations at BHS. She explained her family's decision: "That first year, my Dad said you wouldn't come back. Most people come and study Navajos and leave. He was surprised you came back the next year. And every year you came back. So he said we could trust you." This family introduced me to others, who in turn introduced me to still other families. My hosts graciously explained their perceptions of life, school, and education. I was invited to attend traditional ceremonies as "part of the family." From the ceremony I describe in this article, I have chosen to reveal only dialogue that is relevant to education in order to avoid disclosing any confidential religious beliefs. I have shared drafts of this article over the years with Navajos in the community who have confirmed my observations and who have helped me represent their experiences and concerns more accurately. They have agreed that this article should be published, in order to share with others both the concerns Navajos have for their children's education and the importance of having their children remain faithful to their Navajo traditions.

Anglos living in the community on the border of the reservation also patiently answered my endless questions in over one hundred informal interviews. Approximately 85 percent of the Anglos are members of the Church of Latter Day Saints (LDS), commonly called Mormons. I attended religious meetings at the Indian Ward (a local unit of the LDS Church), seminary classes (religious training) at the two high schools, and interviewed several religion teachers who were bishops in the LDS Church. My research with Navajo youth was a frequent topic of conversations at picnics, dinners, and socials, where Anglos carefully explained their personal understanding, as well as the LDS Church's views, of American Indians. The Anglo voices in this community do not represent a definitive Mormon perspective, but they do illustrate a cultural view that is influenced, in part, by religious beliefs. In the context of this community, Mormon and non-Mormon Anglo voices are consistent in opposition to their Navajo neighbors.[5] As an outsider to both the Navajo and Anglo communities, I was supported, tolerated, and educated by many local people in my efforts to understand the contemporary lives of Navajo people.[6]

Theoretical Framework

Educational anthropologists and sociologists who attempt to explain minority youths' responses to school primarily present either a cultural difference theory or a sociostructural theory.[7] Cultural difference theorists such as Cummins argue that cultural conflicts and other problems develop in minority classrooms because of the differences between students' home and school cultures.[8] Sociostructural theorists such as Ogbu argue that the explanations for minority school failure lie outside of the school itself, specifically in the racial stratification of U.S. society and the economy.[9] Both of these positions provide a useful perspective and have contributed to our understanding of cultural conflict. In particular, I find Ogbu's[10] structural analysis of castelike or involuntary minorities and the job ceiling they face and Cummins's analysis of cultural differences and cultural integrity useful in understanding the situation faced by these Navajo youth.[11]

My research represents a more traditional anthropological approach. I am not attempting to create a general theory of castelike minorities, but rather to represent the specific Navajo experience. In so doing, I take a different position than Ogbu. This ethnographic study speaks to some general claims made by Ogbu, but it does not replace his theory. Specifically, I speak about "racial warfare" to capture two points on which my interpretation and Ogbu's theory diverge: First, Navajos and Anglos conflict economically, politically, and culturally in both the schools and workplace. While Ogbu views the schools as a relatively neutral terrain, I portray the ways in which teachers and students play out this racial conflict. Second, Navajos have substantive ethical disagreements with the Anglo values manifested in the schools and the greater economy. The concept of racial warfare is intended to represent the integrity of Navajo culture and to avoid reducing this culture to a reinterpretation of traditional values in reaction to denial of opportunity in the Anglo-dominated schools and businesses, as I believe Ogbu does.

Young Navajo men and women face a racially polarized landscape, in which historically defined racial conflicts between Navajos and Anglos continue to engulf their lives. As a result, political and economic power remains in the hands of local Anglos who maintain a limited "place" for Navajos. This discrimination is basic to Navajos' attitudes towards schools. As Ogbu has pointed out, any comprehensive understanding of minority students' responses to school must include the power and status relations between minority and majority groups, as well as the variability among different minority groups.

According to Ogbu, the main factor differentiating the more successful from the less successful minorities appears to be the nature of the history of subordination and exploitation of the minorities, and the nature of the minorities' own instrumental and expressive responses to their treatment. In Ogbu's analysis, immigrant groups who came to this country more or less voluntarily arrived with an intact culture developed *before* contact with the dominant group. They viewed schooling as a means for increased opportunity and economic mobility, not as a threat to their cultural identity. In contrast, castelike minorities, which include African Americans, Mexican Americans, and American Indians, have been historically positioned as involuntary subordinates through slavery, conquest, or colonization. Ogbu argues that castelike minorities face schooling with a set of secondary cultural characteristics — a reinterpretation of traditional culture that is developed *after* contact with the dominant White group — to help them cope with the social, economic, political, and psychological history of rejection by the dominant group and its institutions. Schools, as sites of conflict with the dominant group, are seen as a threat to their cultural identity. These castelike minorities have developed oppositional cultural responses to schooling as they reject a system that has rejected them. Ogbu sees this resistance, which takes the form of truancy, lack of serious effort in and negative attitudes toward school, refusal to do classwork or assignments, and delinquency, as an adaptation to their lower social and occupational positions, which do not require high educational qualifications. This, in turn, has been counterproductive to school success. Specifically, pressure from the minority community not to "act White," coupled with feelings that they will not get jobs anyway, further decreases students' school efforts because they struggle with the fear of being estranged from their community if they are successful. The dominant group maintains this "adaptation" by providing inferior education and by channeling the students to inferior jobs after they finish high school.

Although Ogbu's general framework, which combines structural barriers and culturally based reactions, generally "fits" the Navajo situation, there are also striking differences between Navajos and other "castelike" minorities. Navajos have not played the same role in the national economy as other castelike minorities. African Americans, for example, have historically played a central role in the White-dominated economy. Navajos, in contrast, have never been an essential part of the White-dominated economy, except in regard to land procurement. Navajos accurately perceive that they are shut out of the job market, and that their school success is not linked to their economic prosperity.

Whereas Ogbu views the cultures of castelike minorities as a reaction to the dominant White group, I believe that Navajo practices and culture represent a distinct and independent tradition. Navajos do occupy a castelike, subordinate position in the larger social context. However, only a small part of Navajo cultural characteristics can appropriately be called "secondary" or "oppositional." Navajos face and resist the domination of their Anglo neighbors from an intact cultural base that was not developed in reaction to Anglo subordination. An oppositional description of Navajo culture ignores the integrity of Navajo culture and neglects the substantive value disagreements between Navajos and Anglos.

Navajo success is closely tied to family and reservation economic and cultural networks. It is these traditional values that parents seek to pass on to their children. For example, traditional Anglo notions of "success" — school credentials, individual careers, and individual economic prosperity — do not reflect those of the Navajo. The successful Navajo is judged on intact extended familial relations, where individual jobs and educational success are used to enhance the family and the community and aggressive individualism is suppressed for the cooperation of the group. These Navajo values — the communal nature of success and the primacy of the family — exist in well-developed institutional structures on the reservation independent of Anglo culture, and during social and economic crises, help secure the Navajos' identity as a people.

These cultural characteristics in themselves do not necessarily result in school failure, although they contribute to the tension and misunderstanding between Navajos and Anglos. Youth who have little identity as Navajos and who are not accepted by Anglos because they are not White face the greatest risk of school failure and unemployment. To understand this position more fully, it is necessary to turn to Cummins, who argues that the strength of one's cultural identity is a vital factor in the expressive responses to the schooling experience. Cummins states that "widespread school failure does not occur in minority groups that are positively oriented towards both their own and the dominant culture, that do not perceive themselves as inferior to the dominant group, and that are not alienated from their own cultural values."[12] This position suggests that Navajo youth who are better integrated into their home culture will be more successful students, regardless of the structural barriers they face. In other words, the more Navajo students resist assimilation while simultaneously maintaining their culture, the more successful they are in school.

In this article, I draw upon three events — a racial fight, a meeting of the Native American Church, and a high school career day — to portray the race struggle between Navajos and Anglos and the way that struggle manifests itself in schools. My position captures, but also moves beyond, central insights from both cultural difference theory and structural theory. Like cultural difference theorists, I believe that differences in culture play a role in the divisions between Anglo teachers and Navajo students. Anglos do not understand Navajo values, and thus manufacture deficit explanations to account for behavior they assume is unguided by specific beliefs. When Navajo students act on their beliefs, they act in contrast to existing institutional values.

Furthermore, like Ogbu, I believe that these cultural differences become barriers because of the power relations involved. However, Ogbu implies that castelike minority students withdraw from academic effort not only because of the power relations in schools, but also because of the job ceiling and their own communities' social realities or folk theories that undermine the importance of school success. As a result, he takes the accommodationist position that castelike minorities would do better to adopt the strategies of immigrant groups, accept the school's regime, and succeed by its standards. Ogbu does not see culture as a terrain of conflict, nor does he perceive the significance of race as contributing to racial warfare, as I do; rather, he believes it is possible for the culture of the student to be left "safely" at home so that his or her cultural identity can be disconnected from what occurs in school.

This is not possible for Navajo youth. My data supports Navajo students' perception that Anglos discriminate against them and that they have no reason to believe that their cooperation with the educational regime would bring advantages in either schools or in the workplace. The issue for Navajo students is not that doing well in school is to "act White," but that playing by the rules of the classroom represents a "stacked deck." Educational compliance, or succeeding in the *kind* of schooling available to them, does not result in economic and social equality in the Anglo-dominated community. I argue, in this article, that the Navajos' experiences of racial and cultural warfare must be placed at the center of an explanatory model of their education and work experiences.

The Fight: Racial Conflict

Racial polarization is a fact of life in this border community. In 1989, a fight broke out between a Navajo and an Anglo student at BHS. Claiming his younger cousin had been verbally and physically assaulted, a Navajo junior struck an Anglo student across the face in the school hallway during lunch. Navajo and Anglo students quickly gathered at the scene as the principal and the football coach pulled the boys apart. Police were called to the school; the Anglo student was released to his parents, while the Navajo student was taken to jail. The Navajo community demanded a meeting with school officials to discuss the incident, which more than seventy-five Navajo parents attended. The superintendent, the two high school principals, and several teachers also attended, along with the school district lawyer, the DNA lawyer, the local sheriff, and myself.[13] The tension felt in the meeting was a reflection of the larger battles lived out between Navajos and Anglos in the community each day.

The president of the parent association, who served as the meeting translator, spoke first in Navajo and then in English. His son-in-law was the Navajo youth involved in the incident:

> It kinda hurts to hear this information. The parents hurt over this. The parents have come to me with the problem. It hurts the parents and the students. We have to get over this problem. When kids come home and say they have been thrown around, they can't concentrate on their work. It hurts. Word gets around that the Indians are having an uprising. No. It is not true. We want our kids to go to school and do well. They are far behind. We want them to do well in academics. I hope we can talk about this. It gets worse every time we talk. I hear the police came into school and took him away. This is not fair, to knock around youth. If this is happening in school, I want to know about it.

As he sat down, the principal from the high school where the fight occurred stood up. He glanced at notes on a yellow pad, cleared his throat, and spoke:

> Let me express very strongly that there are a lot of things that cannot occur in a school for students to succeed. One thing is that they must feel safe. One of our goals is that it be a safe place. A week ago, following a school dance, a group of Anglos and Navajos got into a fight. They have a history of not getting along. The following week there was a fight in school, only one blow. I didn't talk to the Anglo boy because the police did.

The Navajo student accused of starting the fight interrupted the principal. "You have a problem. The Anglo started it. He was picking on a little kid and I told him to stop. Then he fought me."

The vice principal shook his head in disagreement. Several Navajo students shouted that Anglo students were always picking on and making fun of Navajos.

The principal, still standing, responded, "This is the first time I have heard this. I didn't know the Indian students were being picked on."

Sharon, a Navajo senior who witnessed the fight, stood and faced the principal. "We are never asked. I was not asked. I never get anything from Anglos." Her mother asked, "Why is it so hard for the kids to go to you with their problems?" Sharon persisted in questioning the principal. "I don't like the way Whites treat Indians. Why do you believe what the Anglo students say only? It's one side in this case. Can you guarantee that they won't continue?" The Navajo crowd clapped.

The principal responded, "We can talk about it. No, I can't guarantee. That's what you have to do as an individual. You have to take it." Murmurs of discontent echoed throughout the room. The principal continued, "Rumors of a fight were all around the school on Thursday, so I called in the police. There was no fight that day. Because of the tension we invited the police in to investigate. On Friday morning there was a fight. Both the students were taken in and charged."

The DNA lawyer stood and asked the principal, "Is it true that the Anglo student was not charged and the Navajo student was?" The principal uttered softly, "Yes." Again the crowd muttered their disapproval.

"That cop tried to get me to fight him," shouted the Navajo youth involved in the fight. "He said, 'Come and fight me.' They told me not to step a foot in the school. Not to ever come back."

After a pause for a translation into Navajo, the principal urged parents to come to him with their problems. "If you feel your kids have been made fun of, you should come up to the school. You must come up to the school. We will do everything we can to help. If I can't help, you can go to the superintendent and say, 'That crazy principal can't help us.' That is the avenue we have in the district. We will do everything to help." At this point the superintendent stood and moved to the front of the room to stand by the principal:

> I want to say two things. We expect a lot of our principals, but not to be policemen. We don't expect them to do that. We have a good relationship with the police, so we turn problems over to the police. And then the school gives up jurisdiction. The world is a great place. I hope that the students we turn out have great opportunities. Our schools are good schools, but not perfect.

An elderly Navajo woman brought the discussion back to the issue of discrimination. "Why is it so hard for us to understand that we have this problem? It has been this way for years. I think the problem is that we have the police treating people differently. So you see, the policeman is the problem." A mother added, "I used to go to that high school. I bear the tragedy with the students now. The higher I went, the greater pressure I got. So I left and went to another high school to graduate." An elderly medicine man spoke last:

> We are just telling stories about each other now. Who was in the incident should be up front talking. When my kids were in school it was the same. And we are still trying to solve this problem. These kids who were talking tonight were in elementary school when my kids had this problem in high school. And I think the kids who are in elementary school now will also have this problem. We need to talk about it. Each time we talk about it the problem continues.

The meeting ended shortly before midnight. The school officials quickly left the building. Many of the Navajo parents and children continued to talk in small groups. Although charges against the youth had been dropped, he was not allowed to return to school. "They told me I was eighteen so I could not go to high school any more. I was told to go to adult education to finish."

As I sat with his family, his mother-in-law bitterly complained she should have said the following to the vice-principal, with whom she had gone to school twenty years before: "You know what it is like for the high school kids. You used to do the same things the kids are doing now against Indians. You remember when you put the pins in my seat? All the things that you used to do to Indians, it is still going on here and now. You did it, and now your kids are doing it."

I left with Sharon, the senior who spoke during the meeting, and her mother. We went to my house and continued talking about the incident. Sharon spoke of her own experiences in the racially mixed school. "They always give us trouble. Like there is this one group of guys. I told one, 'Shut up you pale face, or you red neck!' When they are rude to me I call them everything I know. They think Indians stink. I tell them, if you don't like Indians, why did you move here!"

Important public officials, like those who attended the meeting, are Anglos, and their ability to ignore Navajo concerns speaks to the security of their power base. All public institutions in the county are controlled by Anglos and by members of the Mormon Church.[14] The school superintendent, all four high school principals, four out of five elementary school principals, and the administration of the local community college are all LDS members. Over half of the county's population is Navajo, but Navajos account for only 15 percent of the teaching staff, and more than half of those have converted to Mormonism. The few Navajos in power have been sponsored for upward mobility since they joined the LDS church.[15] Locally, these converted Navajos are described by Anglos as "responsible," "good," and the "right kind" of Navajo. Anglo-controlled political and economic networks open slightly for these few individuals. Even for Navajos who hold middle-class jobs, racial stratification limits their place in the community. Navajos and Anglos do not socialize, and they pass each other without acknowledgment in stores, banks, and restaurants. As the meeting revealed, even when Navajos speak they are seldom heard, contributing to a strong sense of disempowerment.

Over the last one hundred years, the Anglo population has expanded and prospered.[16] The Navajo population has also expanded, now comprising 54 percent of the county's population, but they have not prospered. Their life conditions speak loudly of discrimination. A colonized form of government exists in the county where the Anglo population benefits disproportionately from Navajo resources: 60 percent of the county's economic resources comes from the reservation, but only 40 percent is returned in goods and services. Almost 50 percent of the Navajo in the county live without running water or utilities. Their per capita income is $3,572, compared to $11,029 for Anglos. Almost 60 percent of Navajo families have incomes below the poverty level, compared to less than 10 percent of Anglo families. Nearly 90 percent of those in the county on public assistance are American Indian — Navajos or Utes. The unemployment rate of Indians is over 40 percent, four times the unemployment rate for Anglos. Navajo youth and their families are well aware of this economic marginalization. Shoveling snow, envisioned as a job possibility by a young Navajo student at the beginning of this article, speaks powerfully of the job ceiling in this arid, high desert community.

Racial Conflict in the Schools

Racism and cultural beliefs, particularly the issues of assimilation and resistance, are at the heart of the interactions between Navajos and Anglos. The Anglo perspective is informed by a century-old model of assimilation that views Navajo culture and language as a problem to be eradicated. During this period, the Navajo have resisted assimilation and successfully struggled to maintain a Navajo way of life. Faced with continued colonization and discrimination, few Navajos remain silent.

The antagonisms apparent at the meeting also produce tensions in schools. Discrimination takes different forms between teachers and students in classes and in the hallways. Some racism is overt: Anglo students and teachers speak openly about disliking Navajos. Other interactions are more subtle, disguising racism in ostensibly well-intentioned actions, such as teachers lowering their academic expectations to "accommodate" the culture of their Navajo students. Some paternalistic racism exists, such as when teachers assume Navajos are "childlike" and that educators know what is best for "their Navajos." Still other racism is based on superficial stereotypes of Navajo culture, which assume that because Navajo families do not share middle-class Anglo values they hinder their children's success in schools. This section depicts the cultural and racial warfare that comes as a result of dismissing Navajos as being culturally inferior.

Daily encounters with Anglo peers and teachers demonstrate the power of the racial and cultural struggle occurring in schools. Shortly after the meeting, Sharon spoke of her embarrassment and the anger she had towards the science teacher:

> He is prejudiced. He talks about Navajos and welfare. "You all listen, you aren't going to be on welfare like all the other Navajos." He shouldn't talk like that! And then the White students say things like that to us. Like all Navajo are on welfare. I'm not like that. We work for what we have. He shouldn't say things like that. It makes us feel bad.

Some youth use subtle counterattacks when put down by their non-Indian peers. One day in class, two Anglo students teased a young Navajo studying to be a medicine man about his hair bun, lice, and the length of his hair: "Hey, how long did it take you to grow that?" The Navajo boy replied with a soft smile, "Ten minutes." Other confrontations are not so subtle. One young woman, whose last name was Cantsee, explained why she was no longer in math class: "When I came into class late, that teacher said, 'Oh, here is another Indian who can't see how to get to class.' I told him to go to hell and left class."

Teachers' lack of experience in the Navajo community and stereotyping of Navajos results in both the distortion and the dismissal of Navajo culture. During an English class I attended, a teacher was discussing the romantic and realist periods in literature:

> Have you ever dreamed about something that you can't get? That is romanticism, when you dreamed that everything would work out. But then there is the realism period. Some people during this time in your literature text, they lived together six to a room with fleas and lice and everything. They had dreams but they weren't coming true. I hope all of you have bigger dreams than that.

A Navajo student whispered to a friend, "It sounds like he is describing a *hogan* [the traditional Navajo one-room round home]!" In a reading class I observed, the teacher said, "We are studying tall tales. This is something that cannot be true. Like Pecos Bill. They said he lived with the coyotes. You see, it can't be true." Two Navajo students looked at each other and in unison said, "But us Navajo, we live on the reservation with the coyotes." The teacher replied, "Well, I don't know anything about that. Let's talk about parables now."

Although some teachers' actions may be seen as "innocent" or "ignorant," others clearly reveal a hostile edge. Some teachers do know that coyotes are a fact of life on the reservation and still dismiss and mock students' lives. For example, during Sharon's senior year, her career education teacher lectured the class on the importance of filling out job applications. "You must put your address. When you are born, you are born into a community. You are not isolated. You are part of a community at birth. So you have an address." To which a student replied, "But I was born waaaaaaay out on the reservation! Not in a community." "I don't care if you were born out there with the coyotes. You have an address," argued the teacher. Students hooted, groaned, and laughed as several shouted, "Yessss, lady!" to which the teacher shouted back, "You sound like you are all on peyote. Let's go to the occupations quiz in your books."

Just as all Navajo youth are not dropouts, all Anglo teachers are not racist. Some teachers care deeply about their Navajo students. However, continued resistance to their educational efforts frustrates even the best teachers. I shared the frustration of Sharon's English teacher, who urged her Navajo students to perform in class: "You guys all speak two languages. Research shows that bilinguals are twice as smart. Language is not your problem. It's your attitude. You have given up because Whites intimidate you. Don't you want to be a top student?" "No!" the class responded loudly, "we don't care." This teacher, who had expressed a great deal of concern and empathy for her Navajo students three years earlier, recently told me, "You are not going to like what I say about Indians now. I am a racist! I'm not kidding. Working with these Indian kids makes you a racist. They just sit here and do nothing."

Throughout the district, at both elementary and high school levels, administrators and teachers believe Navajo students have difficulties in school because of their language and culture.

Equally damaging to Navajo students' school experiences are teachers who refuse to acknowledge the racial discrimination in the community. By reducing racial conflict to "others' problems" or a thing of the past, the local power struggle is kept out of the classroom. During the last week of studying *To Kill a Mockingbird* in a twelfth-grade English class, the teacher focused on racial conflict between Whites and Blacks, and summarized the discussion of the book by saying:

> It used to be that Whites treated Blacks badly. Remember, this is racial discrimination, when one group treats another badly just because of the color of their skin, and it is against the law. It was a sad part of history and I'm glad it doesn't happen any more.

A Navajo student turned to me and said, "But it happens to us! Why didn't he say that? What about what happens to us?"

Navajo students' attempts to make racial discrimination visible within the school have been silenced by the Anglo students and school administrators. Shortly after the fight and community meeting, Sharon's journalism class called a "press conference" to discuss Navajo education and racial prejudice for an article in the school paper. The journalism teacher, who was also the faculty advisor for the school paper, suggested the conflict between Navajo and Anglo students was an important topic to be covered by the newspaper. The students, fourteen Anglos and two Navajos, voted to invite Navajo parents, the high school principal, the Indian advisor, and myself to be interviewed. We had all attended the community meeting following the fight. At the press conference, an Anglo student who was new to the district spoke first:

> When I came I didn't know about Indians. The kids here tried to scare me, told me about Indian witches and evil spirits. It made me afraid of Indians, that they were weird or gross and they were out to scalp Whites!

The principal suggested that when students hear discriminatory comments they should correct them. Another Anglo student replied, "What do we do when teachers say bad things about Indians? Like the AP [advanced placement] history teacher. We don't have any Indians in there, and he says really awful things about Indians." The principal shook his head, "I'm sure most teachers don't do that. If they do you kids can tell us." He continued, "All students, Anglo and Navajo, are just the same. I don't see the difference. Kids are just kids. The fight between the Anglo and Navajo boy was an isolated incident. We have taken care of the problem." A Navajo parent, who had been silent, then stood and said:

I hear that there was this Anglo kid who was caught stealing a little radio. But then the teacher found out the boy was from an important family here, so the teacher did nothing to the boy. So, you see, we still have this problem.

The bell rang. The press conference was concluded. The students, concerned that discussions of racial prejudice would both demoralize Navajo students and embarrass Anglo students, decided not to print the story.

Racial attitudes are also evident in teachers' and administrators' expectations of Navajo students. These attitudes include assumptions about the "academic place" for Navajos. The sixth-graders from an elementary school feeding into Border High School all scored above the national norm in mathematics on the Stanford Achievement Test. Yet upon entering high school, Navajo children were systematically placed in the lowest level mathematics class. When asked about the placement the principal explained, "I didn't look at the scores, and elementary grades are always inflated. Our Navajo students always do better in the basic classes." These attitudes about race and culture place a ceiling on learners; in a school-administered survey, 85 percent of the teachers in one school indicated that Navajo students had learned "almost all they can learn." Standardized test scores showed an average seventh percentile for the school, the lowest in the state, which the principal explained, saying, "Our district level scores are low and dropout rate high because we have Navajo students."

Racism surfaces not only in ill-intentioned treatment of Navajo students, but also when well-intentioned educators make demeaning assumptions about them, representing a cultural mismatch. Anglos frequently distort Navajo values and view them as inadequate compared to their own cultural values. For example, Navajos are viewed as present oriented and practical minded. "I've never met a Navajo that planned far in the future, to like go to college. It's more [about] what to do tomorrow and the day after," said an Anglo school counselor. Another explained, "The Navajo are very practical minded. They think, 'What value is it to me in my everyday life?' A lot of abstract ideas in education just don't mean anything." Anglo stereotypes of Navajos also include the perception that they work well with their hands. A career education teacher said, "Well, I mean, they are good in spatial things. Working hands-on. They don't learn theoretically. You can talk until you are blue in the face. It's much better if there is practical hands-on application." Anglos intertwine such "descriptions" of Navajo culture with the belief that the Navajo family does not teach children school-appropriate values. A counselor explained:

We [Anglos] were brought up every day with the question, "What are you going to be when you grow up?" And that is something that the Navajo parents never ask. And then I bring them in the counseling office and I ask, "What are you going to be when you finish high school?" That is the first time they have even heard the question. It's just not done at home. And it's my values. The importance of an education and a job. They don't think to the future.

Embedded in this cultural distortion of Navajo values is the assumption that the closeness of Navajo family ties (i.e., "cultural pressure") is problematic for "progress" and that it "causes" school failure. One of the teachers explained it graphically with a story about lobsters:

> You know what they say about lobsters? You can put them in water this high [indicating a depth of a few inches] and they won't get out. As soon as one tries to climb out the others pull him back in. [Laughter] That's what it is like with the Indians. As soon as one of their kind tries to better himself, the others pull him back in.

The owner of a local pottery factory, who employs work-study students from the high school, also saw the problem not as a lack of individual skills, but as one of the demands of family responsibilities:

> Many of them have been through all sorts of training programs. Take Tom. He is a graduate from technical school. A welder. But he came back here and is working here painting pottery. . . . They come back here to live with their families. There is a good and a bad side to that. Over there on the reservation they are getting strangled. It really strangles them over there with families. They can't make it on their own and their families strangle them with responsibilities.

It is within this racially divided community that Navajo youth must navigate the school system. Over the past ten years, in a district with 48 percent Navajos, one out of every three Navajo students left school before graduation; almost 80 percent of the district's dropouts are Navajos.[17] During a district-wide meeting, administrators identified the following as the causes of these youths' school failure: lack of self-esteem; inadequate homes; inadequate preparation for school; lack of parenting skills; poor communication between home and school; poor student attendance; limited vocabulary and language development; limited cultural enrichment opportunities; too academic a curriculum; poor attitude and motivation; and fetal alcohol syndrome. All of these place the blame on deficits of the students and their families. In contrast, only three causes listed found fault with the schools: questionable teacher support, lack of counseling, and non-relevant curriculum.

Navajo students paint a different picture. Acknowledging racism (i.e., citing it as one of the central reasons they leave school), over half of the 168 students I interviewed who had left school said simply, "I was not wanted in school." Over 40 percent of those who left school saw the curriculum as having little relevance for their lives. Although they acknowledge home difficulties, over half of the Navajo youth who left school complained of problems with administrators and uncaring teachers who would not help them with their work.

Assimilation: "Navajoness" as the Problem

Navajos became wards of the federal government in 1868. In accordance with treaty provisions signed at that time, the federal government was to provide schooling for all Navajos. Ever since, schooling has been used by policymakers and educators at the district and federal levels as a vehicle for cultural assimilation. Because public officials considered Navajo culture and language problematic and superfluous, education became a way to eliminate the "Indian problem."

In 1976, the district lost a suit filed by Navajo parents. As a result of the court's decision, the district was required to build two high schools on the reservation and to develop a bilingual and bicultural program for all grades. Construction of the high schools took eight years. The bilingual and bicultural program sat unused, gathering dust in the district's materials center for fifteen years. In 1991, after an investigation by the Office for Civil Rights in the Department of Education, the district was again found out of compliance with federal requirements concerning English as a Second Language (ESL).[18]

The district then created a new bilingual plan, which the newly appointed director of bilingual education presented at a parent meeting at the beginning of the 1993 school year. The district's latest plan calls for a total immersion of Navajo students in the English language to eradicate the Navajo language "problem." It requires that all Navajo students be tested for English-language proficiency, after which, the proposal states, "All Limited English Proficient (LEP) (ESL) [the two terms are used interchangeably] students are placed in the regular classroom with fluent English proficient students to insure optimal modeling of language." This plan will operate even in schools with a 99 percent Navajo population. No special ESL classes will be provided for students who are Navajo-language dominant.

Navajo parents expressed disbelief that the new program would be implemented, and questioned whether Navajo would actually be used for instruction in their children's classrooms. The parents had reason to be concerned. The district had agreed to such a program seventeen years earlier and it still did not exist. The bilingual project director responded, "Trust us. We are now sincere."

The Office for Civil Rights rejected the most recent plan, issuing a citation of non-compliance to the district and turning the investigation over to the Education Litigation Division of the Justice Department. During the summer of 1994, U.S. Attorney General Janet Reno authorized the Justice Department to intervene in this case as "party-plaintiff." Based on a preliminary investigation, the Justice Department believes the school district has discriminated against American Indian students, violating federal law and the

Fourteenth Amendment, by failing to adopt and implement an alternative language program for Limited English Proficient students. The district is accused of denying American Indian students the same educational opportunities and services, such as equal access to certain academic programs, provided to Anglo students, and of denying qualified American Indians employment opportunities equal to those provided to Anglos.

Throughout the district (at both Navajo and Border High Schools), administrators and teachers believe Navajo students have difficulties in school because of their language and culture. This explains, in part, why the district refuses to implement a bilingual program that uses Navajo as a language of instruction. "These kids we get are learning disabled with their reading. Because they speak Navajo, you know," the ESL teacher explained. "The Indian students need to learn English and basic skills to survive in the Anglo world. That bilingual and bicultural stuff is not important for them. The jobs are off the reservation, so they need to learn how to work in the Anglo world." Another teacher, in a letter to the editor of the local newspaper, argued, "Bilingual education will become the greatest obstacle a Navajo student has to overcome and an impediment to the education of all other students."

English language difficulties are acknowledged by Navajo parents; over a two-year period, the topic was brought up at eighteen parent meetings. "Our kids speak Navajo, they need more of those ESL classes to help them learn." But at the same time, they speak of the importance of Navajo culture. "Our kids learn White history. When are you going to have Navajo language and culture, too?" At each meeting, school administrators and teachers assured the parents that their children were getting the help they need to learn English, and that Navajo language and culture were part of the school's curriculum. Over the past ten years of my fieldwork, only four semester-long classes were offered in Navajo language, history, or culture. All ESL classes have been eliminated in the high schools and replaced with general reading classes, even though few teachers in the district are certified in reading education.

This model of assimilation, which views native culture and language as a barrier to be overcome, has always framed educational policy in schools for American Indians.[19] Various programs have attempted to eliminate native cultures, measuring success in part by how many students do not return to their homes and families on the reservation. In the late 1890s, the superintendent of the Carlisle Indian School, the first boarding school for American Indian students, informed a congressional committee that between 25 percent and 30 percent of their students found a job and earned a livelihood away from their home; the remainder returned to the reservation. Even a year or two at school, he said, gave the youth a new life, and only a small percentage go "back to the blanket" and "do nothing."[20]

While the structure has changed somewhat, this educational practice has changed very little in the past one hundred years. In 1990, Sharon's counselor explained, "Most of the kids want to stay right here. On the reservation. It's kinda like, we say, they have 'gone back to the blanket.' They will sit in their *hogan* and do nothing." Counselors cannot comprehend that a youth does not want to leave the reservation. Their typical comments include: "He said he wanted to be a medicine man![21] He can't really mean it. His card [counselor's student aspiration list] says the military," and "It's real progress when they want to get off the reservation. There is nothing for them to do out there." Today, as throughout history, American Indians who resist assimilation by maintaining their culture and remaining on the reservation are described as failures. Such was the case with Sharon. Upon her return to the reservation after college in 1992, I was told by her counselor, "It's too bad. She didn't make it away from here. And I had so much hope for her succeeding." The college graduate is viewed positively, but those who "come home" are labeled "failures" by the Anglo community.

Racial beliefs about Navajos, embedded in a model of assimilation, guide Anglos' "understandings" of how to teach or interact with Navajos. For Anglos, these assimilationist beliefs are generally used to frame either the need to "change" Navajos to fit into the outside world or to adjust educational and economic opportunities downward to be "appropriate" for Navajo culture. Either way, Navajo culture is seen as undesirable. Teachers and administrators believe students fail because of their impoverished homes, culture, and language. Counselors assume Navajo students are not bound for college, and that they therefore should receive practical, vocation-oriented instruction; additionally, they should be encouraged to leave their families for jobs off the reservation. The educational assimilation policies described in this section are part of the larger race war in the community. Within this context, the school curriculum is not "neutral." Navajo youth who resist school are in fact resisting the district's educational goal of taking the "Navajoness" out of their Navajo students.

As Cummins points out, virtually all the evidence indicates that, at the very least, incorporating minority students' culture and language into the school curriculum does not impede academic progress. He argues that Anglos' resistance to recognize and incorporate the minority group's language and culture into school programs represents a resistance to confer status and power (with jobs, for example) on the minority group.[22]

From this angle, Navajo culture is considered *the* reason for academic failure. To accept Navajo culture and language would be to confer equal status, which is unacceptable to the Anglo community. Navajo culture and students' lives are effectively silenced by the surrounding Anglo community. Navajo language and traditions are absent from the school curriculum. Teachers' ignorance of Navajo student's lives results in the dismissal of the credibility of Navajo life. Racial conflict is silenced, either on the premise that it does not exist or that to acknowledge racism is to "cause problems." This "silencing" is a clear denial of the value of the Navajo people's way of life.

Navajoness and School Success

The Anglo community views assimilation as a necessary path to school success. In this view, the less "Indian" one is, the more academically "successful" one will become. Anglos perceive living in town, off the reservation, to be a socially progressive, economically advantageous move for Navajos. In fact, the opposite is true. The more academically successful Navajo students are more likely to be those who are firmly rooted in their Navajo community. This is consistent with Cummins's position that school failure is *less* likely for minority youth who are not alienated from their own cultural values and who do not perceive themselves as inferior to the dominant group. Failure rates are *more* likely for youth who feel disenfranchised from their culture and at the same time experience racial conflict. Rather than viewing the Navajo culture as a barrier, as does an assimilation model, "culturally intact" youth are, in fact, more successful students.

Located on the Navajo reservation, Navajo High School (NHS) is more "successful" than Border High School in retaining and graduating Navajo students. The dropout rate from this school, 28 percent, is slightly less than the national average.[23] These students come from some of the most traditional parts of the reservation. Navajo is the dominant language in most of the homes, and 90 percent of them qualify for subsidized school meals. NHS has four certified Navajo teachers, a group of Anglo teachers with an average of five years' experience, and a school curriculum that is identical to other schools in the district. The differences in Navajo students' performance between BHS and NHS indicate the importance not only of the student's cultural identity, but also of the sympathetic connection between the community and its school. Where there are fewer Anglo students and more Navajo teachers, racial conflict is minimal and youth move through their school careers in a more secure and supportive community context. Nevertheless, even NHS students experience "well-intentioned" racism from some teachers and a vocationalized curriculum.

This pattern — reservation youth succeeding academically more than Navajo town youth — is also repeated *within* the Navajo student population at Border High School (BHS). Almost half the Navajos who attended BHS are bused to school from the reservation. Among Navajos living in town, only 55 percent graduate from BHS, whereas almost 70 percent of the Navajo students living on the reservation graduate from Border High School.[24] In other words, Navajo students who live in town and attend BHS are less successful than those who live on the reservation and attend NHS. Also, within the BHS Navajo population, the Navajos that are bused from the reservation do better than those who live in town. The most successful students, like Sharon, are from one of the most traditional areas of the reservation. In contrast, those who are not academically successful are both estranged from the reservation community and bitterly resent the racially polarized school context they face daily.

Many of the Navajo BHS students who live in town take a confrontational stance toward school: many of their teachers express fear and discomfort with them in their classrooms. Over three-fourths of the school's disciplinary actions involve these Navajo youth. These students' resistance is clear: the schools don't want them and they don't want the schools. The racial conflict in this school is highly charged, with each side blaming the other for the problem.

Faced with a school and community that refuse to acknowledge their "Navajoness" positively, and coming from homes that transmit little of "traditional" Navajo life, these youth clearly are living on a sociocultural border, with little hope of succeeding in either cultural context. Only 15 percent are employed, and fewer than 10 percent of those who leave school attempt educational training later on.

Navajo youth respond in a variety of ways to the racial treatment they experience. Many leave school, while others simply fade into the background of their classrooms. Most report suffering racial discrimination. Sharon's experiences mirror those of many high school graduates. Although Sharon felt unwanted in school, she persisted, and graduated in 1991. Of her six elementary school girlfriends, Sharon was the only one to finish school. Her persistence was framed by her experience growing up on the reservation. Sharon's ability to speak at the meeting and her school success reflect her own sense of confidence — a confidence supported by traditional influences. Her early years were spent with her grandparents in a *hogan* on the reservation. As she explains:

> After I was born my mom was working. My grandma and grandpa, they were the ones that raised me until I started going to school. He was a traditional, a medicine man, so he was strict with us. And he made us go to school all the time. I am thankful to him. His influence is all around me now. . . . I'm modern. I guess I'm kind of old-fashioned, too. I keep all those traditions. I really respect them. I really respect those old people. Like they tell me not to do something. I listen to them. I go to all kinds of ceremonies. I'm proud to be a Navajo.

Sharon places her traditional beliefs alongside those of the dominant culture and honors both. Her grandfather's advice supports her decision. "He told me that it was okay for me to go to both. He said, 'take what was good from both and just make it your life.' So that's what I did. If some old medicine man or somebody told me I needed some kind of ceremony, I'd do it. I'd do it both ways. I'd go for the blessing, too."

Sharon was an academically successful high school and college student. She completed her freshman year at the state university with a 2.8 grade point average, and then decided to return home. This choice securely embedded Sharon within her family and the Navajo community. She reflects on her decision:

I used to think those people that go to college never come back. They always promise to come back to the reservation, but they never do. And now I understand why, because all the jobs are up there [in the city] and I mean, if I major in physical therapy, there is nothing I can do with that down here at home. I thought I could do it without Indians. I thought I could do it by myself, but it does make a difference. It makes me feel more at home. It is good to see some Indian people once in awhile. It really motivates me.

Sharon now lives with her mother on the reservation. She took community college classes for one year to certify as a Licensed Practical Nurse, but left after deciding the classes were boring. "You see, they make the classes easy because most of the students were Navajo. It was too easy and I got tired of it." She occasionally works as a medic on the county's ambulance. With a characteristically broad smile, she said:

Maybe I'll go back [to the university] someday. I sometimes feel sucked in here. Like I'm stuck here. It's so hard to get out. But it feels good to be at my home with Navajo people, even though those Whites sometimes give us trouble. [Reflecting back on the racial fight and community meeting, she said little had changed.] . . . My brother, he is still at that school. And he is fighting back. You just have to keep doing it. Otherwise they just treat you like a dumb Indian. I will always fight. And someday my children will also go to school and fight and get jobs and be Indian.

Despite their treatment by a racist Anglo community that continues to dismiss the values and viability of Navajo life, the Navajo remain a culturally distinct and unified group of people. The continuity of Navajo culture provides a supportive framework or network of family and community for young Navajos, which increases their chances of academic success. This insistence on cultural integrity is visible in life on and near the reservation — where 70 percent of the Navajo youth will choose to live their lives.

The Native American Church: Cultural Integrity

The Native American Church (NAC) and traditional Navajo ceremonies have a central place in the lives of almost of all these Navajo youth. Embedded in Navajo ceremonies are beliefs about the communal nature of success and the primacy of the family. Jobs and educational success are means to enhance the group, not just the individual. Jobs are seen as a means of earning necessary money, not as "good" in and of themselves. This contrasts sharply with Anglo values of hard work for individual mobility, agency, and economic success. To understand the Navajo perspective, it is necessary to experience Navajo life on the reservation, to see the goals and vitality of the Navajo community.

One ceremony I was invited to attend reveals a glimpse into this life. I had been invited by Joe, the father of the family with whom I had lived on the reservation:

> We are going to have a Peyote meeting for the girls.[25] For Jan's birthday, too. To help pray for them to finish school. Jan is trying to graduate this year. If you could come it would help to have an educated person like yourself, a professor.

I was asked to "go in," joining the family and friends for the all-night ceremony in a *tipi* [a traditional Plains Indian structure used for most Native American Church meetings]. Of the twenty-eight participants, I was the only *bilagaana* [Navajo for White person]. We sat around a central fire and a half-moon shaped altar that represented the path of life — from birth to death. The fire and altar were attended to by the Fire Chief. Songs and prayers started with the passing of prayer sticks and a drum, and continued over the next four hours until holy water was brought into the *tipi* at midnight. I spoke and offered prayers during the meeting when I was invited to do so by the Fire Chief, who spoke to Jan and her sister first in Navajo, and then for my benefit in English:

> You are young still. You do not know what will happen to you in ten years. It is important that you take this path, and finish school. Your parents love you very much. You must get your education. I pray for you, it is so important.

He spoke passionately for twenty minutes. Tears were rolling down his face as he pleaded with his kin to succeed in school. As the singing resumed, more participants spoke of their own problems and offered prayers for the hosts' daughters. An uncle spoke:

> I want you to have the good in life. It is hard. It is like a job. You are in school and you must work hard, like a job. We want you to get a good education, and then someday you might have a job like a secretary or something like that, in an office. I can see that. Your parents try hard, but it is up to you to get an education. We know it is hard, but it is important.

The meeting ended at dawn, with a second pail of holy water and ceremonial food. Afterwards, the men remained in the *tipi*, stretched out comfortably as they smoked and told stories. They allowed me to remain and took the opportunity to educate me. The Fire Chief spoke seriously about the general concerns Navajo parents had for their children:

> The things our grandparents knew, we do not know now, and our children will never know. There is a new life, forward, to live in this here dominant culture. This is what I think. Our children need to go out and get the best they can. Go to school and college and get everything they want, and then

44

come back here, to their homes, here between the four sacred mountains. In the past Navajo parents told their children to go out and get an education. Go to college. And they did and they stayed in Albuquerque, in the towns, and then the parents were sad because they said they never saw their children again. But Navajo parents now have to tell their children to go out and get their education. To college. And graduate school. And then to come back home, where they belong. Here on this land. This is where they belong. They need to bring their education back here to the reservation, their home. Then we can be a whole people. This is what I think.

The Native American Church meeting captures the solidarity of the Navajo community and the cultural vitality of its people. Although often invisible to their Anglo neighbors, who view Navajo youths' lives as a "cultural vacuum," ceremonies and family gatherings cloak and support these Navajo youth.[26] The Enemy Way, a five-day ceremony for the purpose of curing illness caused by a ghost, an alien, or an enemy, occurs frequently during the summer months. Additional ceremonial dances occur in the area at least monthly, and a strong Native American Church is active weekly on the reservation. All but one of the young women in the study had their *Kinaalda,* a Navajo puberty ceremony that marks the beginning of Navajo womanhood.[27] Ceremonies are frequently used to bless and support youths' life paths, including their progress in schools and at jobs. In all ceremonies and events, the group serves to support and bond the individual to the Navajo community. Individual economic success becomes a part of the Navajo community's larger economic network.

As was expressed in the NAC meeting, Navajo parents want their children to succeed in both the Anglo and Navajo worlds. However, it is clear that the family and community are of paramount importance, and that educational success brings community and family responsibility. There is a dual side to this message. Navajos are not trying to "get away" from Anglo culture, just from assimilation. Thus, they do want certain material goods and school success, but not at the expense of their cultural identity. As Jan said shortly after her NAC ceremony, "They [parents] tell us to do good in school, but that we will always be Navajo."

Cultural Integrity and Resistance

Traditional Navajo cultural values still frame, shape, and guide appropriate behavior in the Navajo community. Navajo youths' choice to remain a part of the community assures them economic support through local kinship networks unavailable off the reservation. This choice also puts these youth in opposition to the goals set for them by school officials. Specifically, the choice to remain on the reservation and the insistence on maintaining culturally different values are central to the power struggle in the larger community, because these choices are defined as impoverished by Anglos. However, if one understands the viability of the Navajo community, resistance to assimilation is seen as a rational and appropriate choice.

The Navajos are a conquered and colonized people who have successfully resisted assimilation. They have survived over four hundred years of Anglo subjugation and exploitation with a culture that, although changed, has remained distinct in its values, beliefs, and practices. These Navajos have remained on their ancestral land; Anglos are the immigrants. The Navajo Nation, the largest American Indian reservation in the United States, comprises 26,897 square miles, an area approximately the size of West Virginia. Treaty rights recognize sovereignty status, a separate "nation within the nation," for the 210,000-strong Navajo Nation. John David reports that the total personal income in 1991, including wages and salaries, transfer payments, livestock, and crops, was $900,032,754, with a per capita income of $4,106.[28] Accurate portraits of reservation poverty, however, leave non-reservation residents unprepared to understand that there are viable economic and social institutions on the reservation. The Navajo Nation's budget supports an infrastructure of education, law enforcement, and health and human social services with revenues from oil, gas, mining, timber, taxes, and federal and state funds.

Unique to this governmental structure is the infusion of Navajo culture. Traditional home sites that are determined by sheep and cattle grazing rights are maintained by a Land Permit Office; a tribal court system relies on a Navajo legal code, as well as a federal legal code; the Navajo Medicine Men's Association is housed in the complex of the tribal headquarters, with an office at the local hospital; all significant tribal meetings are prefaced with a traditional prayer from a Medicine Man; and the Navajo Nation publishes its own newspaper to provide a Navajo perspective on local and national matters. In 1986, 286 retail businesses, ninety-four of them Navajo owned, operated on the reservation. The Navajo Communication Company provides cable television and telephones to homes with electricity, and the Native American Public Broadcasting Consortium provides local news to radio listeners. The Navajo Community College, a multi-campus institution with seven branches, serves over two thousand students.[29] In 1992, a total of three thousand students were awarded tribal scholarships totaling $3,320,377. This insistence on tribal autonomy and resistance to "blending in" has assured their youth their continuity as Navajos. Specifically, Navajo choices cannot be compared, as in Ogbu's theories, to other minorities, because Navajos only stand to lose by integration into the larger society. The U.S. Commission on Civil Rights explains this unique position:

> Politically, other minorities started with nothing and attempted to obtain a voice in the existing economic and political structure. Indians started with everything and have gradually lost much of what they had to an advancing alien civilization. . . . Indian tribes have always been separate political entities interested in maintaining their own institutions and be-

liefs. . . . So while other minorities have sought integration into the larger society, much of Indian society is motivated to retain its political and cultural separateness.[30]

It is important to realize that Navajo individuals do not monolithically represent "the" Navajo culture. There are hundreds of different ways of "being" Navajo. However, within this cultural constellation, specific values are maintained. These Navajo beliefs and values surround the young as they learn how and what it means to be Navajo. Although the autonomy of the individual regarding possessions and actions is strongly maintained, consensus and cooperation for the good of the group is emphasized over aggressive individualism.[31]

The insistence on recognizing Navajo cultural allegiance begins at an early age and continues throughout life. Children learn to support and be supported by families. "Like there are all these things we do differently," explained Jan, "but I don't know them all. You learn them when you do something wrong. Then they show you what to do right." These lessons are learned and challenged against a backdrop of an Anglo world. Sometimes these worlds successfully co-exist. Matt, Jan's youngest brother, explained how a Navajo ceremony made things "right." Lightning, which is a powerfully negative force in Navajo beliefs, hit the transformer at the trading post. He continued, "We were afraid we could never drink a coke or get candy from there again! But then they had a medicine man do something and it was okay to eat there again."

Other situations provide challenges to the adherence of Navajo values. Navajos feel it is arrogant to try to control nature by planning every detail in the future. After a counseling session during her senior year, Jan explained, "It's dangerous. You can't change things that happen. That's the way it is. But my counselor said I could change everything by planning on a career. I don't think that would work." Navajos have a more humble view of "individual choice," which acknowledges both the dependence of the individual on the group and the importance of the extended family. When receiving sharply negative comments from an Anglo friend about the crowded living conditions at her home, Jan "turned the lens" and expressed disapproval of the Anglo nuclear family: "The way Whites live seems to be lonely. To live alone is kind of like poverty."

The Navajo depend upon extended family networks of economic and social support, critical factors in their lifestyle. On the reservation, the extended family relies on multiple (often minimum wage) incomes to provide support for the group. Joe's 1990 tax forms claimed twelve dependents supported on a $26,000 salary from a uranium plant. Their new pink, double-wide, three-bedroom trailer houses four daughters, two sons, five grandchildren, and the husbands of two of their daughters. Over the past several years, family members supplemented Joe's income with work in the uranium plant and on road construction crews, and as clerks, waitresses, cooks, motel maids, pottery painters, and temporary tribal employees. Sons and daughters move off the reservation in search of employment, and return when temporary employment ends. The family makes "kneel-down bread" with corn from the garden and sells it at fairs and in town.[32] All who can, work at jobs or at home. Pooled resources buy food, clothing, and necessities, and pay for car and insurance bills.

Along with the economic stability the extended family supplies, there is pressure to place the family ahead of individual prosperity and careers. As an elderly Navajo man said, "You can't get rich if you look after your relatives right. You can't get rich without cheating some people."[33] And as Jan said, "In the traditional way and now, the family is the most important thing you can do. Life is too short to worry about jobs. The family is needed for all those ceremonies." Jobs are seen as a way of earning necessary money, not as a way of life in and of itself.

Navajo families struggle with racial and economic discrimination imposed by their Anglo neighbors at the same time they speak with pride of their "freedom" on the reservation. As Jan's father explained, "We don't have electricity, and we don't have electric bills. We haul water, and we don't have water bills. And out here we don't have to pay for a [trailer] space." Nightly television watching, lights, and the vacuum cleaner only require an adapter and a car battery. Jan's aunt added,

> A medicine man warned us about what happens when you leave. He said, "They educate us to be pawns. We are educated to do a thing, and then we become pawns. Must work for money to pay for the water bills, the electricity. We become pawns." So you see, we have our water, even though we haul it from sixteen miles away, we have our warm house, and our meat, and food from the land. In town we have to pay for these things, and then we become dependent.

A move to the city does not necessarily mean an increase in standard of living or "success." For example, in 1992, Jan and her husband moved to a large city to stay with his relatives and seek employment. After three months with only sporadic employment, they returned to her family. "It was lonely in the city," Jan said. "My mother needed us, her daughters, so we moved back. The family is real important. That is the main thing. You depend on the family to teach each other, and to be brought up right. If it is not the whole family being involved in it, then it is like lack of communication." Jan reminded me of a Navajo insult: "She acts as if she doesn't have any relatives." The individual without family is an isolated and unsatisfied person. This echoes the Fire Chief's plea at the Native American Church meeting: ". . . and then come back home. Then we can be a whole people." Jan has successfully followed this life path. She has settled into rearing her own children in the home of her mother on the Navajo reservation.

Submerged in an Anglo-controlled social landscape that restricts employment opportunities for Navajos, over half of the youth who remain on the reservation try, like Jan, to continue their schooling to enhance their chances for employment. After graduating from high school, almost all of them attend the local community college, their last chance to learn job skills to qualify for local employment. This path, starting with the traditional "Career Day" experienced by most U.S. high school seniors, appears egalitarian in that a multitude of opportunities and choices are "open" to youth after high school. For these Navajo youth, however, the Anglo belief of "equal educational opportunity for all" leading to "equal employment opportunities" is racially restricted. Anglos construct educational "choices" or paths for Navajo youth that lead through a vocationalized curriculum in both high school and college. This path dead ends, however, in the secondary labor market.

Post–high school options offered Navajo youth include a combination of local job ceilings, impersonal universities, and the local community college. Navajo students face a world segmented by unattractive choices with which schools and career counselors never come to grips. Although Navajo youth enter high school with high aspirations about their future opportunities, their future aspirations are thwarted by the racism they experience in school. After high school, Navajo youth face a choice between a university-city route that works against their cultural beliefs, and a local job and school market that is totally subject to the racial struggle in the community.

High School Career Day: Racially Defined Choices

On one of my days of observation, I pulled into the small paved parking lot in front of Navajo High School five minutes before school began. The green athletic field stood in sharp contrast to the red dirt and sandstone bluffs. Sheep grazed on the lush lawn, rubbing against the chain-link fence that separated the school from the surrounding Navajo reservation. As I entered the windowless, one-story, red brick school for another day of fieldwork, I was joined by Vangie, a Navajo friend. "It's career day, so you can come with me, Professor, while I learn about schools!" she exclaimed. The juniors and seniors were excused from classes to attend presentations from seven regional colleges and universities, two vocational or technical schools, and the Job Corps. The Navajo Nation's Education Office had a representative to explain tribal scholarships. Students were to attend four information sessions located throughout the school.

Vangie and I attended two regional college presentations. "Some classes are outside and are so much fun. Then there is the choir. You should take that your first year, it is really fun. And you meet all sorts of nice people," a recruiter said. A professionally developed video accompanied the presentation. The second recruiter also showed a polished, upbeat video with smiling faces, a brief glimpse of a professor lecturing in a large amphitheater, shots of athletic events, tennis courts, and leisurely images of students reading books on rolling campus greens. The recruiter said:

If you want to be a policeman don't come here. But if you want to go into the computer field, or nursing, or in-flight training, come here. It is beautiful and the campus is lots of fun. You can do all sorts of things while you are in school.

Students talked excitedly about which college would be more fun.

The representative from a local vocational training school slowly went through a slide presentation as he explained the school's program:

And that girl there, she is working at a real good job in a TV station. And that one, she is underemployed. She could get a real good job if she would leave here! See, in all these pictures we have the old and the totally up-to-date equipment. You never know when you will be working in a small place that has old equipment. So we teach with the old and the new.

Looking at a student audience of only seven Navajo females, he backed up to a previous slide:

See that computer on that slide. If you are going to work in a big office, you have to learn about computers. And then we have a heavy equipment program. We could use more girls. Because of the Equal Opportunity Program, we could place forty girls a year if they completed the program.

The students were quiet and attentive.

We stopped in the library to look at the literature brought by the local community college. District school staff were discussing with the dean of the college their success in sending many of the Navajo youth away to school after graduation. One of the counselors said, "Over 60 percent of the graduating class got accepted to college. Some went to the Job Corps. One year later they are all back. Every one of them!" The Dean of the local community college explained:

We don't recruit our students. They come to us. Many of the Indian students go to large universities and they fail. Then they come to us. After they have been with us, they all — 100 percent who go to larger colleges — will succeed. If we recruited them to start with us, they might think they have missed something. They can get what they need here.

The booth was full of pictures of Navajo students sitting at computers, building houses, working in hospitals, and sitting in lectures. The recruiter was the only Navajo on the professional staff at the college. Raised by a Mormon family, he had recently returned to work at the college.[34] He spoke softly to several Navajo students. "You can get a good education here. And your Pell Grant will pay for everything. It's close to home so your parents can watch you girls!" They laughed and moved on to examine the pamphlets in the Job Corps booth.

The last presentation was by the state's largest university, my employer. Two student recruiters stood in front of the small group and emphasized the importance of filling out the applications correctly and getting financial aid forms into the university on time. "It is very important that you do things on time and correctly. It is a huge university. But we also have support for minority students and we want you to seriously consider coming to the university." The presentation continued with a list of the academic fields offered by the university and the statement, "The classes may be hard, but they are real interesting. And you can get a good education at our university." The presentation was dry, the "fun" of college life was presented as "getting an education," and the recruiters did not smile.

After these presentations, students moved into the auditorium for two films by the College Board on financial aid. Students filled the room, talking about the sessions they had attended, graduation plans, their personal relationships, and after-school activities. The first film pictured an African American man, one of several individuals interviewed who had "made it." He urged others to attend college. "Anyone can go to college. It is worth it. A small sacrifice now to have the money to go to college. But it is worth it. I am glad I went." The second film, a cartoon on how to correctly fill out financial aid forms, covered topics from estimating summer earnings to who in the household was the legal "provider." Students were bored and restless with the films and cheered when the lights came on, and then left for lunch. A counselor spoke to me as we were leaving the auditorium:

> We are the ones that fill out the forms. The students don't do it. About half will go on to some kind of school and almost all of them will be on financial aid grants. And the other half will sit out on the reservation and do nothing.

We left school early. As I was driving Vangie, her brother Sam, and several of their friends home, the conversation turned to what they were going to do after graduation. "I'm thinking about going to Dartmouth. They have a special Indian program. But I don't know if I want to be so far away from home. I might go into the Army. They will pay for my college." Another said, "I'll probably end up with a baby and be stuck here." She laughed, "I really want a baby of my own. I would be really happy, then, at home with my baby. That's what us Navajo do." Vangie jumped into the conversation. "There are a lot of girls that get pregnant. I'm just not going to do it. It will ruin your life if you have a baby. I want to go to college and get away from here so I can get a good job!" One said, "My parents tell me to do what I feel I want to do. I want to go to college. I hear college is a lot of fun. I want to have a business or something and come back to the reservation to live and help my people. I go crazy about thinking about taking care of my parents in the future." Another, who had been silent, softly spoke, "I want to be a race car driver. But my mom thinks it's too dangerous. So I guess I can be a secretary or nurse. She wants me to have a good job like a secretary or something and live at home." Vangie and Sam's home was the last stop. As they climbed out of my car, Sam teased his sister, "I'm not going to have a baby either! At least till I get married and have a job."

Educational and Economic Marginalization

The images shown during Career Day of youth lounging on green fields, smiling faces in a choir, a class, using computers, and laboratories, filled the picture window of opportunities facing youth beyond high school. Few Navajo youth will realize the life depicted in these tableaux. Their dreams of a wide range of occupational choices and jobs in distant big cities dim with the reality of their limited academic skills, which relegate them to semi-skilled jobs. High school career days present hollow images for Sam and most of his peers, who do not face "unlimited" opportunities dependent only on individual achievement, but rather a set of political, economic, and social constraints that intertwine in schools and communities to limit their possibilities. Economic disparity is maintained by the continued role of vocational education in local schools and colleges as one aspect of an ongoing racist strategy to limit the opportunities of Navajo and secure opportunities for Anglos. Navajo youth are trained to remain below the job ceiling.

Sam's experiences, which follow in this section, mirror that of many Navajo youth. Sam and Vangie have ten brothers and sisters. They live on the reservation ten miles from the bus stop in a complex that includes eighteen relatives, a new government home, an older stone home, traditional *hogans,* and a satellite dish. They haul their water from a well six miles away, but have electricity from a nearby oil rig. Shortly before graduation in 1989, while flying kites near their home, Sam talked about what he wanted to do with his life: "I want to go into business or finance. Or maybe electronic engineering. Or maybe the military. I would like to go to Berkeley, in California, but I will need a tribal scholarship. I am working on getting my grades up." He had a 2.1 grade point average. Navajo tribal scholarships require a 3.5, a goal he did not reach. The rhythmic whishing of the oil pump was the only sound on the mesa. Sam proudly pointed out the canyon where their livestock grazed and to the far mountains where his father was born. "I have relatives up there that I don't even know. I would like to come back here to live on the reservation. It would be all right. But they say that it is better to get off the reservation to get jobs." His brother was an example. "My brother, he travels all over the world with his job. He works with computers." But there remains the pull of home. "There are not many jobs here. But I like it here. It is home for us Navajo."

Students' experiences in and out of school modify their expectations about future job possibilities. For the Anglo students, future possibilities increase as students approach graduation. Navajo youths' aspirations, on the other hand, are greater than the future envisioned for them by the schools. After four years in high school, their aspirations often match the vocational orientation constructed by their schools. Even though Sam intended to go to college, with the help of a counselor, he filled his senior year schedule with basic and vocational level classes. The counselor explained:

> We are not supposed to track kids, it is against the law. But by the time these kids are in high school they know what they are going to do. So we have most of our Indian students in vocational classes. After all, most won't go to college anyway.

The assumption that Navajo youth knew they wanted a future in vocational jobs early in high school was not supported by my data. During the 1987–1988 school year, 132 Anglo and Navajo students in grades nine through twelve completed the JOBO, a career inventory test that translated student "interest" into job fields. Although 20 percent of the Navajo ninth-graders indicated interest in professional careers requiring college, twice as many Anglo ninth-graders saw their future jobs as being in professional fields. The reverse was true regarding vocational, semiskilled jobs. Almost half, 47 percent, of the Navajo ninth-graders were interested in such jobs, whereas only 30 percent of the Anglo students saw vocational jobs as part of their desired future. This pattern changed by the twelfth grade. The Anglo students desiring vocational jobs dropped by half, from 30 percent to 15 percent, and over 60 percent now desired professional careers. Just the opposite occurred with the Navajo seniors: 62 percent of these students had readjusted their goals downward, towards vocational jobs, and only 15 percent remained determined to achieve professional careers. These figures must be viewed against the backdrop of the dropout rate: by their senior year, close to 40 percent of Navajo youth had already left school — leaving behind the most academically successful Navajo youth.

Navajo culture and local employment opportunities are used by the Anglo educators as a rationale to limit Navajo students' educational opportunities, while, in reality, a vocational curriculum assures the continuity of the local job ceiling for Navajos. The principal at Sam's high school explained the school's vocational orientation:

> I'm interested in equal educational opportunity. I have been here for ten years. We used to be 75 percent academic and 25 percent vocational. Now we have 75 percent vocational and 25 percent academic. We need to recognize the needs of the people in this local area. I'm not saying we should ignore the academic classes. But the vocational training is where the jobs are for the local Navajo people.

His vice principal added:

Academics are very important in this world, but we've got to realize that half the kids or more out of this high school are not going into academic jobs. They are going to go into vocational. In fact, the majority of jobs in the future are still going to be vocational. They're not going to be in the white-collar type job. But how do you tell them that?

In 1990, the district received a $3.5 million grant to construct a vocational career center. In an open letter to the community, an administrator explained the new thrust of the school district into technology and job preparation. Citing a state statistic that 40 percent of youth finish college or university training when only 20 percent of the available jobs require a four-year degree, he told of the shock facing graduates who have to be retrained in vocational and technical areas. "Since only 20 percent of the jobs in Utah will require a college degree, the secondary schools must take a more active role in preparing students for employment." He explained the necessity for the curriculum to be responsive to employers' needs:

This concept does not mean a lowering of academic standards; to the contrary, most technical jobs now require a strong background in math, physics, and language. Nor does this concept infer that all students should know a specific vocational skill prior to leaving high school. The jobs in our society are changing so rapidly that students will be much better served if they develop certain basic skills and attitudes toward work. Most employers now prefer to train their own employees in specific skill areas. What they want from high schools are students with basic understandings of technology, good basic academic skills, and the flexibility to be retrained as often as the job market requires.

This emphasis in high schools sets the stage for focusing the educational careers of Navajo youth onto vocational paths. The district's "state of the art" vocational school is Navajo High School; the predominantly Anglo high school in the northern part of the district remains college preparatory. This assures college-educated Anglo youth a brighter job future in the community.[35] The administrator's state statistic that 40 percent of youth finish college or university reflects the 97 percent Anglo population of the state, not the local Navajo population served by the district. Almost half of the Navajo youth from the local school district attempt some kind of post–high school education. Out of one thousand youth, one-third eventually attend the local community college, 6 percent attend universities, and 7 percent attend vocational institutions. Regardless of these efforts, less than one-half of 1 percent complete a four-year degree, only 2 percent complete two-year degrees, and 5 percent receive a vocational certificate. None of the youth who attend the community college go on to finish a four-year degree. Over 90 percent of the Navajo youth do not receive a degree higher than their high school diploma. Sam and his friends are in this group.

Sam graduated in 1989 from Navajo High School. During his senior year, he fluctuated among wanting to study business or finance, joining the military, or wanting to go to technical school to learn electronics. He decided to go to the city to hunt for a job. Off the reservation, Navajo family networks are utilized for economic support — both for the family left behind and the person moving to the city. Youth who leave for the city do so only if there is a relative who can assist with housing and the location of a job. The housing tends to be low-income and jobs are usually minimum-wage labor in fast food restaurants, motels, and factories. During the two years following high school, Sam worked at an airplane parts factory in Salt Lake City and did construction work in Phoenix. He lived with relatives in both cities. Back on the reservation to visit his family, he stopped by my house:

> It has been two years since I graduated and I haven't gotten it together to go to college. And now my younger brother is already up at the university ahead of me! I would like to come back here to live on the reservation. It would be all right. But they say that it is better to get off the reservation to get jobs. That's what I did. There are not many jobs here. But I like it here. It is my home. And the air is clear.

Sam stayed on the reservation. He enrolled in the community college in a program that promised good local employment. "It's for electronics. Job Services and the college are running it. I will be able to get a good job with the certificate."

The two-year community college Sam attended is where most Navajos finish their time in higher education. The creation of this community college ten years ago has been an economic boom for the local Anglo community, whose members occupy all of the teaching positions and 99 percent of the administrative and support staff. The college is supported, due to its two-thirds Navajo student population, by federal tuition grants targeted for "disadvantaged" youth and from the Navajos' own oil royalties money.[36]

One Navajo high school counselor explained, "The college comes with scholarship money and says they [youth] can come to the college free. Many don't know about other places. And they need the money to go. And the college needs them to survive." Last year the community college established a scholarship fund for all county residents, using $500,000 from Navajo royalty money to establish matching funds from the state.[37] Prior to this, Navajo students could use their scholarships to attend the college of their choice. Now, under the guidelines of the new scholarship fund, all scholarships are limited to attendance at the local college. By putting these stipulations on the funding, the community college has insured middle-class jobs for the Anglos and vocational training for jobs that do not exist for Navajos.

As in high school, Navajo youth at the community college are encouraged to seek terminal degrees in vocational areas. As the academic dean explained, "We have looked into the economic development of the next decade and it is in the service industry. Our students want to stay in this community and these are where the jobs will be." I argued for encouraging more students to go for four-year professional degrees, reminding him that the better jobs in the county required a college degree. He argued, "Most of the jobs here are in the service industry. We are happy if we can keep a Navajo student for a one-year program. That is success." The mission statement of the college supported his emphasis. Only its concluding goal mentioned preparing students to go on to four-year institutions.[38]

The college has a large vocational program. During the 1992 winter quarter, out of almost one hundred courses offered, two-thirds were in vocational or technical areas. Certificates of Completion, requiring one year of study, are offered in accounting, auto mechanics, general clerical, secretarial occupations, office systems, practical nursing (LPN), stenography, and welding. In addition to these specialties available to all its students, the college offers special vocational programs for Navajo students that are cosponsored by the Navajo tribe. Designed to fill immediate job needs, these latter certificates are offered in marina hospitality training, needle trades (sewing), building trades, sales personnel training for supermarket employment, security officers, building maintenance training, pottery trades, modern office occupations, restaurant management, and truck driving. These latter "Navajo only" certificates are designed to prepare students for local employment. An instructor explained, "These programs are designed to prepare the student for good jobs that are out there. They are extensive, lasting for three quarters. One quarter they are prepared with communication skills. And then how to get along with their bosses. It is the general social skills, work skills, and the particular skills for the job."[39] These programs are not without criticism. Another instructor explained:

> We trained forty or fifty people at a time to run cash registers. That's good. But how many stores around here are going to hire all those people? They're training for limited jobs. Why send everybody to carpenter's school? In this small area we have tons of carpenters. Why teach them all welding? You can do it at home, but how many welders are there in this area? Probably every other person is a welder.

During the last decade at this community college, 95 percent of the vocational certificates were earned by Navajo youth and adults. Even this training, however, did not necessarily result in a job. The Dean of the college explained: "Our marina hospitality program was a good one. And it was going to get a lot of Navajo jobs. The tribe had built a new marina and the tourist dollars were going to be good. But then they had the flood. It wiped out the marina. It hasn't been built again. So all those people, almost one hundred, were trained for jobs that never happened." And then there was the needle trades program. "We trained twenty-four women, but there weren't many jobs. The one sewing factory closed down. The other only hired a few." The employment results from the truck driver program were minimal. "We trained over thirty for that program. The uranium tailings over on the reservation were supposed to be hauled away, so we trained truck drivers. It's still in the courts and so no one was hired. We could have gotten them good jobs in other states, like Oklahoma, but they didn't want to leave the reservation." And the largest program, sales personnel, a joint effort of business, the tribe, and the college, placed students in local supermarkets for "on-the-job training" with the understanding that they would receive employment after completing the program. The supermarkets supervised the student trainees for three months while they learned job-required skills, such as boxing, shelf stocking, and check-out packing:

> We had a real good success with this one. A lot of our students were working in the supermarkets in towns. But then there were problems with the supermarkets not hiring them after the training. Cutbacks, you know. But some people thought they were just using the Navajo students for cheap labor. And then they didn't hire them.

Some vocational training programs lead to jobs. Most do not.

After completing the one-year certificate in electronics, Sam found a job — at a factory in the city. Again, he left the reservation. After eighteen months, he was laid off. In 1993, he returned to his home, this time with a wife and child. Sam said, "I'll find something around here, or we will try the city again. Right now I have things to do at home. My parents need help, after my sister died in the car accident, so I need to be here. I have things to do, you know. My younger sister is going to have her *Kinaalda* and the wood has to be gathered. I can get a job around here." After six months without a job, he enrolled at the community college again. He is studying building trades in a community that saw a 9 percent reduction in the construction industry in 1992.

The only successful job networks Navajo youth have are through their parents or relatives, which are for low-level jobs. Mothers grew up working in the local restaurants and school cafeterias, or as maids in the three local motels. Fathers worked at temporary construction jobs, and in the local oil and uranium fields. Sons and daughters have access into the same lines of employment, especially when the training paths available to them in high school and at the community college limit them to these kinds of jobs.[40] If they remain in their home community (as most do), even Navajo youth with a high school diploma face a future of semi-skilled jobs, training programs, and seasonal work, mirroring the lives of their parents.

High school graduates are twice as likely to have jobs as those who do not finish school.[41] On the surface, this seems like an incentive for youth to finish high school. However, there is little difference in the *kinds* of jobs held by graduates and non-graduates. With rare exceptions, both groups of employed youth work at the same kinds of service industry jobs characterized by low pay with few or no benefits, seasonal employment, and a highly transitional work force: cooks, motel maids, school aides, bus drivers, tour guides, making or painting pottery, clerical workers, electrical assistants, janitors, waitresses, seamstresses, the military, uranium and oil workers, and construction. Working at the same job alongside peers who dropped out of school, many Navajo youths question the relevance of their high school and college diplomas. At the very least, Navajo youth see a successful academic effort paying off less for them than for their Anglo peers. On the one hand, leaving school is not the route most youth choose, as it affects their chances for employment, and completing school is a goal encouraged by their families and the community. On the other hand, they are acutely aware that completing school does not guarantee employment at other than menial jobs. The Navajo youths mentioned at the beginning of this article who disagreed with their shop teacher about the limited job opportunities facing them after high school clearly understood this dilemma.

Regardless of school success or failure, after high school, all of these youth face the same structural barriers in the community because they are Navajo. Here, Ogbu's model partly explains this situation. He argues that the existence of a "job ceiling," intertwined with a "rejection" of the Anglo world, mediates against school success for some castelike minorities. Ogbu states:

> Members of a castelike minority group generally have limited access to the social goods of society by virtue of their group membership and not because they lack training and ability or education. In particular, they face a job ceiling — that is highly consistent pressures and obstacles that selectively assign blacks and similar minority groups to jobs at the lowest level of status, power, dignity, and income while allowing members of the dominant white group to compete more easily for more desirable jobs above that ceiling.[42]

Ogbu implies that the job ceiling affects student attitudes towards school and that vocational tracking is the school's adaptation to the job market. A picture of the economic landscape of the community illustrates the racial stratification that frames the employment possibilities of Navajo youth like Sharon, Jan, and Sam. Although American Indians comprise over half of the local population, they are marginalized to either low-paying jobs or no jobs.[43] The unemployment rate for Indians, 41 percent, is over four times the unemployment rate for Anglos. A breakdown of the jobs in the county by occupation illustrates the different opportunity structures faced by Anglo and American Indian workers. Over 90 percent of official and management jobs are held by Anglos. Only 8 percent of these top-level jobs are held by American Indians. In other professional positions, Anglos hold over two-thirds of the jobs. Twenty-five percent of all jobs in the county are classified in these two management and professional categories, but few American Indians make it into these powerful positions. In other areas, Anglos occupy almost 90 percent of the jobs as technicians, 91 percent of the sales workers, 80 percent of office and clerical workers, and 63 percent of the skilled craft workers. American Indians are employed in the service-maintenance and the construction trades, and as laborers and paraprofessionals. All of the assemblers and hand-working jobs, 75 percent of non-precision machine operators, 50 percent of construction, 61 percent of cleaning and building services, 50 percent of laborers, and 47 percent of food preparation and service jobs are held by American Indians. This job ceiling is faced by all Navajo youth — dropouts, graduates, and community college students.

The Navajo in this community experience a racially defined job ceiling, but student attitudes toward the job ceiling do not result in the rejection of schooling or of the Anglo world. Rather, Navajo reject assimilation as a path they must follow in order to be defined as "successful." Navajo students on the reservation, where there are fewer jobs than in town, are more successful in school, even though they are acutely aware of their limited economic opportunities in the community. Historical experiences and the job ceiling, by themselves, do not explain how Navajo youth respond to school: rather, their response to school is mediated by culture, especially the cultural integrity of the group.

Regardless of students' "cultural stance" (degree of acculturation or assimilation), a key factor in the relationship between schools and students seems to be what schools *do* to students — successful students are still limited by the *quality* of their schooling experience. In viewing schools as sites of conflict, vocational tracking is one part of the racial struggle in this community.

Navajo students are counseled into vocational classes in high school, limiting their access to college preparatory classes. By the time these youth leave high school, their "academic fate" is assured. Almost half of them try schools away from the area, but with minimal academic skills and limited economic resources, they drop out and return home. They then move into the "arms" of the community college to complete the education they will "need" to live, training locally for semi-skilled jobs.[44] Ironically, Navajo youths' failure to succeed educationally "outside" actually enhances the local Anglo economic power base by assuring the continuity of the community college.

Navajo youth are encouraged to leave the area for "good" jobs, which in turn also fits with the Anglos' interest in maintaining good local jobs for their group. Many Navajos work in factories in cities for a while, but, separated from their families, they remain detached, isolated, and poor. Most return home and seek whatever paying job they can find. Unlike middle-class youth, who attach their self-image to the kinds of job they strive for, these Navajo youth view a job as a means of making money, which is necessary for survival. The kind of job they work at does not define their "goodness." That is defined by their family relationships. As Paul Willis argues, the concept of "job choice," from semiskilled to professional jobs, is a middle-class construct.[45] Some people get "jobs," others have "careers." Structural and economic determinants restrict individual alternatives, but choices are made among the remaining possible choices. Navajo youth seek whatever jobs are available to them in their community. In doing so, they support their families with an income and secure the continuity of Navajo culture.

Regardless of the dismal job ceiling, Navajos are persistent in their schooling efforts to enhance their employability. Navajo men and women who do hold the credentials necessary for better jobs are increasingly competitive for these positions. Almost without exception, these educational credentials are earned at schools outside of the county. These few hold positions as teachers, social workers, health care providers, and administrators for tribal and county programs. Without these credentials, however, Navajo people are guaranteed to lack qualifications for positions of leadership and power in the community — a community that has always been their "home" and where most of them will live their lives.

Navajo Lives: Cultural Integrity

Navajos are treated differently from Anglos in this community's educational and economic institutions. However, as John Ogbu, Margaret Eisenhart and M. Elizabeth Grauer, and Margaret Gibson have pointed out, there is intra-group variability in responses to schooling within each minority group.[46] The Navajos are no exception. Clearly, Navajo youth are not homogeneous in their responses to schooling. Some, like Sharon, Jan, and Sam, follow paths that Gibson calls "accommodation without assimilation" and that Ogbu calls an "alternative strategy or the immigrant strategy," even though they are from a "castelike" group. They are successful in the educational system, even though this does not necessarily translate into economic stability. At the same time, they insist on maintaining their place as Navajos within the community. By refusing to accept either assimilation or rejection, these youth force us to look at new ways of viewing success. The school success of these Navajo students, with strong traditions intact, is explained, in part, by a model of "cultural integrity." Supported by a solid cultural foundation, they resist by moving through high school as a short "interruption" in their progression to lives as adult Navajo men and women. For them, high school is something one tolerates and sometimes enjoys; school success does not pose a serious threat to their cultural identity. What is clear from the lives of these Navajo youth, however, is that rather than attempting to erase Native culture and language, schools should do everything in their power to use, affirm, and maintain these if they truly want to achieve equity and promote Navajo students' academic success.

Even though Navajo youth develop a variety of responses to their schooling experiences, what is significant is that the school system issues a homogeneous institutional response to the Navajo youth, regardless of their "good" or "bad" student status. Focusing on student behaviors and their values towards school must be coupled with what schools *do* to these students, such as subjecting them to racial humiliation and vocational tracking. As I have illustrated in this article, the school context and curriculum are not neutral. Racism frames the stage and remains a barrier for all Navajo youth, regardless of their academic success or social compliance. Ironically, academic achievement under these conditions is questionable because of the watered-down curriculum and the persistent discrimination in the job market. This suggests that school reform and changes in the job market must be connected in order to talk about educational success in a meaningful way.

In looking at the variability of Navajo youths' responses to education and the homogeneity of Anglo responses, "cultural identity" is used by both to establish cultural boundaries and borders.[47] Cultural boundaries can be thought of as behavioral evidence of different cultural standards of appropriateness. These can be manifested in different speech patterns, child-rearing practices, and learning styles. The presence of these cultural differences, by themselves, is a politically neutral phenomenon. Navajo youth, securely rooted in their culture, move back and forth between their community and the surrounding Anglo community. The cultural framework surrounding Navajo youth, unlike secondary cultural differences, did not initially arise to maintain boundaries and to provide the ability to cope with Anglo subordination. Cultural boundaries, however, are often turned into cultural borders or barriers during intergroup conflict. In this situation, cultural differences become politically charged when rights and obligations are allocated differently. The Anglo community uses Navajo culture as a border, a reason to deny equality by claiming the privilege of one kind of knowledge over another. Navajo families are judged by what they don't have — money, middle-class Anglo values, higher education, and professional jobs — rather than by what they do have — extended families, permanent homes, strong Navajo values and religious beliefs.

Remaining Navajo is a desired goal, not one settled on by default. Life in homes on the reservation, surrounded by family, friends, and similar "others," is a sound choice for youth, with or without school credentials. The choice to remain on the reservation represents failed attempts to find security and happiness in towns and cities amid racial isolation and under- or unemployment. This choice also represents an ethical commitment and valuing of families and Navajo traditions. The Navajo community provides a place of social acceptance and economic survival unavailable in Anglo-dominated communities off the reservation. This choice, however, situates Navajo youth within a local Anglo community structure that dismisses their lives and limits their educational and economic opportunities.

Cultural and racial differences serve both as reasons used by the Anglo community to deny equal educational or economic opportunity to Navajos and as a means Navajos use to resist cultural homogeneity. Jan, Sharon, and Sam chose a "boundary" strategy, resisting assimilation by maintaining pride in their culture and language, which led them successfully through school. They followed the "rules of the game," even though they knew they faced a "stacked deck." This path, fraught with conflict, uncertainty, and pain, was not easy. For some Navajo youth, however, boundaries become borders. A few cross over and leave their families and lives on the reservation. Most, however, choose their families and Navajo traditions over the illusory promises of wealth in the larger society. As Jan said earlier in this article, "They [parents] tell us to do good in school, but that we will always be Navajo." This choice assures the continuity of the Navajo people, and answers the plea expressed in the NAC meeting: "They need to bring their education back here to the reservation, their home. Then we can be a whole people."

Notes

1. In this article, I use pseudonyms for the schools and the individuals who participated in my research.
2. Although somewhat contested as a term that attempts to represent all majority people, I use the term "Anglo" as it is used by the Navajos in this community, as a political category that unifies all White people.
3. "Border" refers to the economic, social, and political marginalization of the Navajo. It also describes the literal "border" of the reservation community, which is divided geographically by a river. Most of the Anglos live in the North and almost all Navajo live in the South.
4. Murray Wax, Rosalie Wax, and Robert Dumont, *Formal Education in an American Indian Community* (Prospect Heights, IL: Waveland Press, 1989). The original study was published in 1964 by another publisher.
5. I shared my research with LDS and non-LDS Anglos. They also helped me correct my understandings of the Mormon Church.
6. For a more detailed analysis of my fieldwork relations, see D. Deyhle, G. A. Hess, and M. LeCompte, "Approaching Ethical Issues for Qualitative Researchers in Education," in *Handbook of Qualitative Research,* ed. M. LeCompte, W. Millroy, and J. Preissle (San Diego: Academic Press, 1992); Donna Deyhle, "The Role of the Applied Educational Anthropologist: Between Schools and the Navajo Nation," in Kathleen Bennett de-Marrais, *Inside Stories: Reflections on Our Methods and Ethics in Qualitative Research* (New York: St. Martin's Press, in press).
7. See Frederick Erickson, "Transformation and School Success: The Politics and Culture of Educational Achievement," *Anthropology & Education Quarterly, 18* (1987), 335–356; John Ogbu, "Variability in Minority School Performance: A Problem in Search of an Explanation," *Anthropology & Education Quarterly, 18* (1987), 312–334; and Henry T. Trueba, "Culturally Based Explanations of Minority Students' Academic Achievement," *Anthropology & Education Quarterly, 19* (1988), 270–287, for debates on these positions.
8. Jim Cummins, "Empowering Minority Students: A Framework for Intervention," *Harvard Educational Review, 56* (1986), 18–36.
9. John Ogbu, *Minority Education and Caste: The American System in Cross-Cultural Perspective* (New York: Academic Press, 1978).
10. Ogbu, *Minority Education and Caste.*
11. Cummins, "Empowering Minority Students," p. 22.
12. Cummins, "Empowering Minority Students," p. 22.

13. DNA is short for *Dinebeiina Nahiilna be Agadithe*, which translates to English as "people who talk fast to help people out." The DNA is a legal service that provides free legal counsel to low-income Navajos.

14. Racial issues in the county are made more complex by the relationship between the dominant religion, The Church of Latter Day Saints (LDS), or Mormons, and non-Mormons. A majority of the Anglos in the county are Mormons. A majority of the Navajos were either traditionalists or members of the Native American Church. The LDS church teaches that American Indians are "Lamanites," descendants of Laman, Lemuel, and others who, having emigrated to the Americas, rejected the gospel. Righteous groups are White, while those who had rejected the covenants they had made with God received a "sore cursing," even "a skin of blackness . . . that their seed might be distinguished from the seed of their brethren" (*Book of Mormon, 2,* Nephi. 5:21; Alma 3:14). Converting back to the gospel results in the "scales of darkness" falling from Lamanites' eyes and a return to a "white and delightsome" being.

15. For an analysis of the relationship between Mormons and American Indians, see Mark P. Leone, *Roots of Modern Mormonism* (Cambridge: Harvard University Press, 1979); Dan Vogel, *Indian Origins and the Book of Mormon* (Signature Books, 1986); and Wallace Stegner, *Mormon Country* (Lincoln: University of Nebraska Press, 1970).

16. The Anglo population in this county arrived in the 1800s as pioneers from the Church of Jesus Christ of Latter Day Saints (Mormons). Sent by Brigham Young, the 236 settlers were to start a colonizing mission among Navajos and to increase the land base and religious influence of the LDS church throughout the region. From the beginning, cloaked within the assimilationist philosophy of the LDS church, the Mormons dismissed Indians' claims to political and cultural sovereignty.

17. I determined the graduation and dropout rates in this community by following "cohorts" of Navajo youth throughout their school careers. A total of 629 students forming six different cohorts from two schools, from the class of 1984 to the class of 1989, are represented with complete four-year high school records. Combining the data from both schools revealed that 59 percent graduated through either traditional or nontraditional means, 34 percent left school, and 7 percent remained "unknown." The graduation rate of 59 percent is lowered to 49 percent when reporting only students who graduated on time in the traditional high school program. Over half, 55 percent, of the youth that dropped out did so during the twelfth grade.

18. This was based on the *Lau v. Nichols* court decision, which mandated that school districts test and provide special English instruction to non-native English speakers. See, for example, Courtney B. Cazden and Ellen L. Leggett, "Culturally Responsive Education: Recommendations for Achieving Lau Remedies II," in *Culture and the Bilingual Classroom,* ed. Henry T. Trueba, Grace Pung Guthrie, and Kathryn Hu-Pei Au (Rowley, MA: Newbury House, 1981), pp. 69–86, for the educational implications of this court decision.

19. See, for example, Margaret C. Szasz, *Education and the American Indian: The Road to Self-Determination Since 1928* (Albuquerque: University of New Mexico Press, 1977); Gloria Emerson, "Navajo Education," in *Handbook of North American Indians, 10,* ed. Alfonso Ortiz (Washington, DC: Smithsonian Institution, 1983), pp. 659–671; and Estelle Fuch and Robert Havighurst, *To Live on This Earth: American Indian Education* (Albuquerque: University of New Mexico Press, 1972).

20. Robert A. Trennert Jr., *The Phoenix Indian School: Forced Assimilation in Arizona, 1891–1935* (Norman: University of Oklahoma Press, 1988).

21. Navajo medicine men and women are regarded as the most powerful people within Navajo culture. One studies to obtain the knowledge and practices throughout a lifetime, as all of Navajo beliefs about their origin, and reasons and ways to live one's life are intertwined with ceremonies to "balance" and guide themselves for a healthy

life. The medicine men and women are the mediators between the beliefs of a tradition and personal health. In addition to conducting large-scale religious ceremonies, such as the Enemy Way, Navajo medicine men and women perform traditional weddings and *Kinaaldas,* as well as being called upon by families for curing illnesses that range from headaches and nightmares to cancer and diabetes. Most Navajo use the services of both traditional medicine men and women and Western trained medical doctors. See, for an example, Clyde Kluckhohn and Dorothea Leighton, *The Navajo* (Cambridge: Harvard University Press, 1974); Gladys Reichard, *Navaho Religion* (Tucson: University of Arizona Press, 1983); and Leland C. Wyman, "Navajo Ceremonial System," in *Handbook of North American Indians, 10,* ed. Alfonso Ortiz (Washington, DC: Smithsonian Institution, 1983), pp. 536–557.

22. Cummins, "Empowering Minority Students," p. 25.

23. U.S. Department of Education, *State Education Statistics* (Washington, DC: U.S. Department of Education, January 1984 and January 1986).

24. The situation has worsened. The dropout rate among Navajo students has increased over the past five years. Although the combined cohort rate at BHS shows only a dropout average of 41 percent, 75 percent of the 1991 class at Border High School did not graduate. In 1991, the district reported that the dropout rate for Navajo students was five times higher than for Anglo students; 80 percent of the dropouts were Navajos.

25. The Native American Church, commonly referred to as the Peyote religion, is a pan-Indian, semi-Christian, nativistic religious movement in the course of whose ritual believers eat the Peyote cactus, a substance containing more than 10 alkaloids, the best known of which is mescaline. It is pan-Indian in the sense that its ideology emphasizes the unity of Indians and their distinctness from Whites. Its origins are traced to the Plains Indian nativistic religious movements at the turn of the century. It was introduced to the Navajo by the Ute, their neighbors to the north of the reservation. See David Aberle, *The Peyote Religion among the Navajo* (Chicago: University of Chicago Press, 1982). Peyote meetings are jointly conducted by a Fire Chief and a Roadman.

26. This ideology asserts that the Indian home and the mind of the Indian child is meager, empty, or lacking in pattern. See Wax, Wax, and Dumont, *Formal Education,* for an excellent examination of this ideology. This study of a Sioux community and its school was conducted over thirty years ago; many of these researchers' results were mirrored in this Navajo community.

27. With a Navajo girl's first menses, she becomes a young woman and has a "coming of age" ceremony to usher her into adult society. The chief aim of the four-day ceremony is to impart the physical, moral, and intellectual strength she will need to carry out the duties of a Navajo woman, following the example set by Changing Woman in the creation story. Details of the ceremony are reported by Shirley M. Begay, *Kinaalda: A Navajo Puberty Ceremony* (Rough Rock, AZ: Rough Rock Demonstration School, Navajo Curriculum Center, 1983), and Charlotte J. Frisbe, *Kinaalda: A Study of the Navaho Girl's Puberty Ceremony* (Middletown, CT: Wesleyan University Press, 1964).

28. David L. John, *Navajo Nation Overall Economic Development Plan 1992–93* (Window Rock, AZ: The Navajo Nation, 1992).

29. Both Anglos and Navajos teach at the College. The President and Board are Navajo — this is a strong, Navajo-controlled organization. Navajo philosophy, language, and culture are part of the curriculum. The school is currently working on developing a Navajo teacher-training program.

30. U.S. Commission on Civil Rights, *Indian Tribes: A Continuing Quest for Survival* (Washington, DC: U.S. Government Printing Office, 1981), pp. 32-33.

31. Louise Lamphere, *To Run after Them: Cultural and Social Bases of Cooperation in a Navajo Community* (Tucson: University of Arizona Press, 1977).

32. "Kneel-down" bread is a traditional food of the Navajo. A fist-sized ball of ground corn is wrapped in fresh corn leaves and buried in an underground pit oven. The name comes from the process of having to "kneel down" when putting the bread into the pit.

33. Kluckhohn and Leighton, *The Navajo*, p. 300.

34. In 1954, the LDS Church officially adopted, as part of their missionary activities, the Indian Student Placement Program, in which American Indian children were "adopted" by a Mormon family. American Indian youth lived with foster families during the year, went to public schools, and were educated into the LDS Church. Home visits occurred for a few weeks or months during the summer. By 1980, approximately 20,000 Indian students from various tribes had been placed in LDS foster homes. The program is no longer expanding, placing only 1,968 in 1980, and in the future will be focusing on high-school-age children. This program had touched almost all of the Navajo families in this area. In every family, close or distant clan members have experienced LDS foster homes. For some, the experience was positive; for others it was disastrous. See the following for a discussion of this program: J. Neil Birch, "Helen John: The Beginnings of Indian Placement," *Dialogue: A Journal of Mormon Thought, 18* (Winter 1985), 119–129; Lacee A. Harris, "To Be Native American — and Mormon," *Dialogue: A Journal of Mormon Thought, 18* (Winter 1985), 143–152; and M. D. Topper, "Mormon Placement: The Effects of Missionary Foster Families on Navajo Adolescents," *Ethos, 7*, No. 2 (1979), 142–160. There were many reasons for parents to put their children in this program, including the chance for better educational opportunities in the cities, more economic security in White families, and, in situations of extreme poverty, better food.

35. A local county report revealed that two-thirds of the jobs in the county were located in the northern portion of the county, where almost 75 percent of the Anglo population lived. The government ranked as the number one employer, the school district the second, and the county the third. These three provided a total of 750 jobs, or 23 percent of the county's employment. A majority of these jobs required either a college degree or some college education. Specifically, 20 percent of jobs in the state of Utah will require a college degree, 40 percent will require six months to four years post–high school training, and 40 percent will require less than six months of training.

36. In 1933, Congress passed a bill that added this area to the Navajo reservation located in Utah. The bill gave the Navajo people in these areas the right to 37.5 percent of any gas or oil royalties, to be used for tuition for Navajo children, for building or maintaining roads on the lands added to the reservation, and for other benefits for these residents. The state of Utah was the trustee of this trust. In 1956, great quantities of oil were discovered in this area. In lawsuits filed in 1961, 1963, 1977, 1984, and 1987, the Court found in favor of Navajos who claimed the Utah Division of Indian Affairs had failed to comply with the terms of the 1933 Act by using the money for the benefit of non-Navajos. In the most recent lawsuit, in 1992, the Navajos accused the state of breach of trust and breach of fiduciary duties, and are suing to recover millions of dollars lost through this mismanagement. Estimates of how much could be awarded in the case run to more than 50 million dollars.

37. After Navajo complaints of mismanagement, the state attorney general's office audited the trust fund. The audit found a questionable use of funds, including $146,000 to finance the administration building, science building, and dormitories; $35,000 for nursing faculty; and $43,500 for a counselor who administered the scholarship program. The audit questioned using Navajo monies to defray the costs of a state institution.

38. ". . . the curriculum includes associate degree programs, vocational-technical programs, developmental programs, adult and community education programs and courses which are transferable towards four year degrees."

39. During the 1992 Winter Quarter, this instructor taught twenty-four one- to six-credit cooperative education classes. Each class covered a different subject area, such as anthropology, auto mechanics, geology, drafting, and secretarial work, with a title that included, "Work Experience."

40. Out of two hundred employed graduates from my database, 25 percent of the males were in the military, the National Guard, or the Marines, and 75 percent were in trade types of occupations, particularly construction, welding, electrical, and oilfield work. Most of the women were in traditional low-paying pink collar jobs, such as LPN, office worker, seamstress, pottery painter, and clerk. One woman had a bachelor's degree and was teaching; one other was a supervisor at K-Mart.

41. All the Navajo youth, from the high school classes of 1982 to 1989 in two different schools, were tracked in my database over the past eight years to determine what happened to them after they had graduated or left school. Two-thirds of these youth were successfully located. The percentages given are based on these youth. Out of 732 youth, both graduates and non-graduates, 32 percent were employed, 39 percent were unemployed, and 29 percent were students. Higher employment, lower unemployment, and more student status were revealed by examining the high school graduates separately. Out of 499 graduates, 39 percent were employed, 26 percent unemployed, and 35 percent were students. The image is bleaker when looking at the youth who left school prior to graduation. Of these 233 youth, only 19 percent were employed, 66 percent were unemployed, and 15 percent were students. There were slight gender differences. More men were employed, 37 percent, compared to 27 percent of the women. Close to half, 47 percent, of the women were unemployed, compared to 34 percent of the men. An equal number of men and women were students. The label "student" is one that needs to be viewed cautiously. Over 80 percent of these were enrolled in the local community college. Many of these youth attended school on a part-time basis, lived at home, and were otherwise unemployed.

42. John Ogbu, "Societal Forces as a Context of Ghetto Children's School Failure," in *The Language of Children Reared in Poverty,* ed. Lynne Feagans and Dale C. Farren (San Diego: Academic Press, 1982), p. 124.

43. In this rural county, existing jobs are limited. The services industry sector (lodging, personal, business, repair, health, and educational services) was the largest contributor of jobs in the county, accounting for 21 percent in 1986. The largest occupational group, representing 36 percent of all jobs in 1986 and 37 percent in 1991, was in production, operations, and maintenance — basically in the blue collar group of occupations. These jobs were concentrated primarily in the goods-producing industries of agriculture, mining, construction, and manufacturing. Second in the number of jobs hierarchy are the professional, paraprofessional, and technical groups, followed by service and clerical occupations. The Utah Department of Employment Security published a projected occupations outlook from 1986 to 1991 specific for this county. The occupations listed as being in demand included: blue collar workers, supervisors, cashiers, combined food preparation and service workers, continuous mining machine operators, conveyor operators and tenders, electricians, underground mining machinery mechanics, maintenance repairers (general utility), roof bolters, secretaries, sewing machine operators, and shuttle car operators. This local profile mirrors that of the state in general. The services and trade industry will account for half of all jobs in Utah by 1991 and will claim 58 percent of all new job growth over the same period. Brad M. McGarry, "Utah's Affirmative Action Information 1987: A Blueprint for Hiring," Utah Department of Employment Security Labor Market Information Services, May 1988; John T. Matthews and Michael B. Sylvester, "Utah Job Outlook: Statewide and Service Delivery Areas 1990-1995," Utah Department of Employment Security Labor Market Information Services, January 1990.

44. For a discussion of how community colleges function to "cool out" students, limiting rather than leading them to professional degrees, see Steven Brint and Jerome Karabel, *The Diverted Dream* (New York: Oxford University Press, 1989); Burton Clark, "The 'Cooling-Out' Function in Higher Education," *American Journal of Sociology, 45* (1960), 569–576; Kevin J. Dougherty, "The Community College at the Crossroads: The Need for Structural Reform," *Harvard Educational Review, 61* (August 1991), 311–336; and W. Norton Grubb, "The Decline of Community College Transfer Rates," *Journal of Higher Education, 62* (March/April 1991), 194–222.

45. Paul Willis, *Learning to Labour* (Westmead, Eng.: Saxon House, 1977).

46. Ogbu, *Minority Education and Caste;* John Ogbu, "Variability in Minority School Performance: A Problem in Search of an Explanation," *Anthropology & Education Quarterly, 18* (1987) 312–334; John Ogbu, "Understanding Cultural Diversity and Learning," *Educational Researcher, 21* (November 1992), 5–14; Margaret A. Eisenhart and M. Elizabeth Grauer, "Constructing Cultural Differences and Educational Achievement in Schools," in *Minority Education: Anthropological Perspectives,* ed. Evelyn Jacob and Cathie Jordan (Norwood, NJ: Ablex, 1993); and Margaret A. Gibson, *Accommodation Without Assimilation: Sikh Immigrants in an American High School* (Ithaca: Cornell University Press, 1988).

47. Erickson, "Transformation and School Success," p. 346.

Although they must remain unnamed, I wish to thank the hundreds of Navajo and Anglo women, men, children, and young adults who have patiently listened to my questions, tirelessly corrected my misconceptions, and honestly tried to teach me about their lives. Without their help this research would not have been possible. I would like to thank Frank Margonis, John Ogbu, Harvey Kanter, Laurence Parker, Beth King, Audrey Thompson, and the members of the Cultural, Critical, and Curriculum Group in the Department of Educational Studies at the University of Utah for their insightful critiques on numerous drafts of this article. I bear sole responsibility, however, for the interpretations presented. I would also like to acknowledge the financial support for this research from the Spencer Foundation and the University of Utah.

Reflections of a Black Social Scientist:
Some Struggles, Some Doubts,
Some Hopes

—■—■—■—

JACQUELYN MITCHELL

I first became aware of the influence of social science theories on social and educational policies affecting minority people when I was a young teacher in a compensatory education program in the 1960s. This was a decade when a great deal of research was devoted to the perceptual, cognitive, and linguistic processes of poor Black children. Cultural and linguistic deprivation, said to result, in part, from maladaptive mother-child interactional styles, had been cited as factors contributing to these children's poor school performance and low scores on IQ and standardized achievement tests. Based on these studies, legislation and federal monies created preschool compensatory education programs designed to improve academic performance. After working in the program and with families in the Black community for a while, I began to question many of the assumptions on which the program was based. My own experience did not fit these deprivation theories, and I began the attempt to understand the contradictions between theory and experience that have since guided much of my work. Now as a social scientist I have come to question the science itself and my role in it.

Social scientists are often uncertain of the influence they wield. It is their research which provides the justification for a great many of the social policies enacted in this country. Minorities, since the 1960s, have become increasingly involved in policymaking, as it has had significant effects on our lives. But we must make larger contributions to research, or policy will never reflect our true concerns. I want to stress that I am not writing as a spokesperson for Black social scientists. Some Black researchers may not identify at all with my experiences. It is my hope, however, that other minority re-

Harvard Educational Review Vol. 52 No. 1 February 1982, 27–44

searchers involved in struggles like mine will realize that the contradictions and ambivalent feelings that they experience are not simply personal problems; they are, rather, an aspect of being a minority in a White-dominated society.

The Sixties: Changing Black Consciousness and the Social Sciences

The 1960s was a decade of political, economic, and racial turmoil in the United States. It was a particularly critical period in my life, the time when my political and ethnic values were formed, a decade that still affects me today. As the civil rights movement gained momentum, Black and other minority groups began actively to erase the social injustices of the past and develop political and economic autonomy. We were frustrated, and that frustration, arising from continuous denial of political, economic, and social assimilation, sparked angry — and sometimes violent — confrontations between Blacks and Whites in many of our communities.

Much legislation designed to reduce social inequality was passed during this period; however, few of us were notably influenced by increased opportunities in employment, housing, and education. What we saw instead was that most Blacks remained below the national income average, continued to live in blighted physical environments, and attended segregated, inferior schools. The resulting frustration produced a more radical and ethnic consciousness within the Black community, a consciousness that spawned an even greater desire for political change, to embrace the growing awareness in all of us of the fundamental cultural origins of Black people. It is from this perspective of a striving for equality and autonomy that I viewed social science research emerging during the same period.

The contrast between these parallel movements is stark and even ironic: the very existence of a distinct Afro-American culture was being questioned or denigrated by many engaged in social science research, while at the same time we were developing ethnic pride and an appreciation for Black culture. In 1963 Glazer and Moynihan had declared that "the Negro is only an American and nothing else. He has no values and culture to guard and protect" (p. 53). Even earlier, Lewis had introduced the notion of a "culture of poverty" to characterize American minorities and provide an explanation for why the poor remain poor (see Lewis, 1966). Lewis asserted that the poor develop a unique configuration of shared understandings in adapting to their common circumstances. They raise their young to deal with the circumstances they are familiar with, thus creating a vicious cycle of poverty. Culture, based on socioeconomic status rather than common history, became the superordinate factor in the explanation of ethnic differences and failure.

It was from this perspective that social scientists began to study the Black family. Moynihan (1965) stigmatized the Black family as the force promoting and perpetuating a "tangle of pathology," which he described as "the principal source of the aberrant, inadequate, or antisocial behavior that . . .

serves to perpetuate the cycle of poverty and deprivation" (p. 76). He urged that a "national effort towards the problem of Negro Americans must be directed towards the question of family structure . . . to enable it to raise and support its members as do other families" (p. 93).

Extrapolating from these environmentalist ideas about the role of experience in the development of intellect, psychologists began to link Black children's low IQ and achievement scores to the lack of intellectual stimulation in their homes (see, for example, Klaus & Gray, 1968). Part of the "tangle of pathology" was said to be a pattern of mother-child interaction that did not promote useful problem-solving skills. Children already assumed deficient in basic information faced the added burden of lacking the tools needed to process unfamiliar material.

Since one essential tool for social interaction is language, both the language of mother-child interactions and the language of Black people in general came under a great deal of scrutiny. Early analyses of the speech of Head Start children emphasized the impoverished nature of the children's language in the classroom and their nonstandard grammar and pronunciation. In their early, extreme form, psychological theories of Black children's speech describe these children as virtually deprived of a distinct language, a consequence of their presumed cultural deprivation (see, for example, Brottman, 1968). Highly structured language tutorials were prescribed and implemented in an effort to teach Black children to speak in ways regarded as appropriate (Bereiter & Englemann, 1966). The ascendancy of language deficit theories was short-lived, however, as a flood of researchers offered the explanation that Black children's language was a dialect variation (Shuy, 1967), and psychologists and linguists began to talk about the socially determined nature of language production (Labov, 1966). (Language deficit theories remain in curricula today, but in modified form and with somewhat more sophisticated rationales. The Distar early reading program is one such example.)

British sociologist Bernstein's (1961) theories, which characterized social interactions between members of the working class by their use of a restricted linguistic code that relied heavily on shared context for meaning, were used to add credence to the "tangle of pathology." By extension, conditions of "cultural deprivation" in the United States could be expected to foster the use of restricted linguistic codes. In fact, such restricted linguistic codes were quickly discovered in parent instructional talk (Hess & Shipman, 1965). It was assumed poor children would be at a distinct disadvantage when they went to school, where elaborated codes were the norm (Bereiter & Englemann, 1966).

Operation Head Start was one of the government programs initiated to redress these cultural "deficits" and economic disadvantages. However, after several years, Head Start came under heavy attack on several fronts. School performance had not changed dramatically (Datta, 1970; Gottfried, 1973; Smith & Bissell, 1970); Blacks had become more militant and were questioning programs conceived by the White majority. In addition, a new theory of social inequality challenged the assumptions of Head Start. Jensen (1969) announced that the Head Start programs had failed because Blacks are not only culturally deprived, but are also genetically inferior. Many academics disputed this theory, but their criticisms failed to stem a growing conviction that something even more basic than cultural deprivation was wrong with Black people. A new kind of early compensatory education was called for, one tailored to limited intellectual capacities and employing rote learning, for which Blacks were said to be better suited.

So, for different reasons, American academics and the federal government implemented additional remedial programs designed to change the way Blacks learn and think (Klaus & Gray, 1968). It was under such circumstances that I began to take a professional interest in the lives of Black people.

The Sixties: Teaching in a Compensatory Preschool Program

The compensatory program in which I taught was in a suburban town approximately fifty miles north of New York City. Most of the Black people lived in an area called "The Flats," a neighborhood of single dwellings, apartment houses, and public housing projects. Visitors to "The Flats" were impressed by the endless flow of traffic and the large congregations of people on the street. Friends and neighbors gathered in apartment yards and on street corners for camaraderie and gossip. Male teenagers stood in front of stores to "rap." There were several ethnic restaurants, bars, and record shops, and an occasional storefront church. Sounds of children's laughter, barking dogs, and horn blasts from impatient drivers pervaded the streets. Colorful graffiti, with slogans such as "Black Power" and crudely drawn clenched fists, decorated apartment doors, walls, and sidewalks.

Before I began to teach in the program, I was "given" a set of beliefs about the backgrounds of the children I would teach and about the kind of classroom I would have to create if these children were to succeed academically. I attended in-service workshops that introduced the social science literature on low-income Black children and offered training on ways to provide effective learning environments. I was also told what to expect in the homes I would visit: Black mothers would be uneducated, strict disciplinarians; absent fathers would be the norm; books would be rare; and the children would be inattentive, hyperactive, and demanding. I was taught that the Black child's environment hindered learning because it lacked intellectual stimulation. But I was also warned that Black children were overwhelmed by other stimuli — too much music, too much noise, too many people. Black children, it seemed, didn't have enough of anything except music, noise, and people — and they had too much of those.

Each of the ten classrooms of fifteen children in the pre-kindergarten/ day-care program was taught by a teacher certified in early childhood education. I was the only Black teacher. Each class was also staffed with a White teaching assistant who had at least fifteen units of college credit. Aides with high school diplomas worked in those classrooms which included the very youngest children and children who attended school a full day. All the aides were Black. Presumably, their presence was to give the school its ethnic flavor — the program's attempt to assimilate the values of the community into the school.

The program was often described as innovative, as one that met the needs of the child. However, I found the characterization of "needs" patronizing when I realized that the children were regarded as linguistically deprived and often treated as if they had no language at all. Once in a planning meeting on our program's goals and objectives I challenged a major objective — "to teach the children to speak *acceptable* English." I was reminded of the life circumstances and the future outlook of the children I was teaching: standards of living are lower and job opportunities are limited for the poor and minorities in this country, especially poor minorities who do not speak standard English. Keeping this reality in mind, I planned my language lessons accordingly. But I felt uneasy with the notions of language competence that seemed to go along with the goal of teaching acceptable English; my colleagues seemed to be confusing "acceptable" as a social as well as a linguistic category.

Before the start of each school year, all teachers visited the homes of the new children. Home visits were mandatory and afforded us the opportunity to see firsthand the restrictive mother-child interactions, to acquaint us with the culture of poverty, to broaden our understanding of the detrimental effects of cultural deprivation — to dramatize the literature, so to speak. However, I saw the visits as a chance to get acquainted with the parents and the children in a nonthreatening environment.

Often during these first home visits I became annoyed by the attitudes of White staff members, and, at times, angry. My anger was not clearly directed, but resulted from the implicit denigration of the milieu of Black culture. I was angry at the sham. Teacher involvement in a program created primarily for poor Blacks should imply an underlying respect for Black culture as an idea independent of the harsh reality. Many teachers were afraid to walk through Black neighborhoods: they were, for the first time in their lives, strikingly visible as a minority. Some did not know how to respond to the shouts and wisecracks of men on the street. What was the culturally appropriate behavior in an environment in which one did not know the rules?

Although I was Black and less conspicuous than my White colleagues, I also attracted attention, but in a different sense. My professional attire identified me, in this community, as a "middle-class," "siddity," "uppity," "insensitive" school teacher who had made her way out of the ghetto, who had returned to "help and save," and who would leave before dark to return to the suburbs. My speech set me up as a prime candidate for suspicion and distrust. Speaking Standard English added to the badges that my role had already pinned on me. The tags with which I was labeled during my initial

73

encounters with the women were often painful, and in my attempts to shake them off I felt compelled, at every opportunity, to clarify my identity. In retrospect, I can see that I was patronizing at times — a trait I had often associated with Whites — in my attempts to demonstrate the extent of my sincerity and my "Blackness."

The mothers were as curious about me as I was about them. Although I thought the research literature prepared me for what to expect in the children's homes, the mothers had been prepared in a very different way for what to expect from me. The social system in this country formalizes the relationships between the middle class and the poor. Class differences become pronounced when interaction between women in different social classes is minimal and when their contact is channeled only through such institutions as schools and social service agencies. As a result, the middle-class Black woman is often perceived by the poor women in the Black community as an agent of the system, rigid in mannerisms and judgmental in attitude.

During my orientation visit with the parents, I outlined the program's philosophy and described the kinds of activities planned for the children. I used the opportunity to suggest ways their children should dress for school, emphasizing the advantages of wearing old clothing. I warned them that school activities such as finger painting, cooking, and playing in mud would ruin their children's clothing. Yet each year I was struck by the numbers of mothers who disregarded my suggestions and by the intensity of their protests. Invariably the children arrived on the first day of school impeccably attired in brand-new apparel. At the time, the mothers' actions seemed senseless to me, and I questioned the logic of their behavior.

After several visits to the homes, however, my attitudes started to change. I began to develop rapport with the families and to gain some understanding of how members in the community perceived their reality. No longer wary of me, the mothers began to confide and disclose their fears that if their children wore old clothes to school, White teachers would consider them unkempt and neglected and treat them as such; the teachers would doubly judge their children — by outward appearance alone and by their appearance as Black children. White children, they reasoned, were likely to be seen as children who got dirty playing; Black children were likely to be seen as just raggedly dressed kids whom no one cared enough about to keep neat. They recognized the consequences of labeling and negative teacher attitudes and sought to ease their children's entry into the culture of the school even if it meant substantial sacrifice to buy them new clothes.

Other misconceptions regarding members of the Black community came to light during my tenure in the compensatory education program. Prior to teaching in the preschool, I had taught in an elementary school and had noticed that the number of Black parents who attended PTA meetings and parent conferences seemed disproportionately low compared to the number of White parents present. Many, in fact, never had any contact with school personnel. At the time, I believed that the parents' absence at these functions reflected lack of interest in their children's education and school affairs. But when I encouraged the mothers to visit the preschool classroom and attend school meetings, they were reluctant, citing White teacher attitudes as reasons for their hesitation, attitudes which became particularly visible when one did not speak "standard English." The few who did attend school functions remained silent rather than risk embarrassment. Although teachers and school officials might have perceived this silence as hostile, the mothers regarded it as a defense.

The preschool children demonstrated similar behavior. The language they had learned at home was criticized in school. What the teacher called *incorrect* in school was *correct* in their community. I believe that this constant criticism and correction led many children to conclude that it was safest to remain silent. Consequently, in school those children came to be labeled nonverbal.

Sentiment regarding art and art instruction was a minor value conflict, but it too contributed to the school/community polarization. The other teachers and I felt that children would learn best by experimenting with different kinds of art materials. The Black paraprofessional aides argued for teacher-made patterns, claiming that both they and the parents preferred the traditional approach to art instruction over the free-style methods. With patterns, the finished product would always be identifiable and well made. I advocated the *process* of creating the art object; they advocated the finished *product*. The parents' and paraprofessionals' beliefs and values were shaped largely from past experiences in which they were often judged from a dominant-culture perspective and had to learn adaptive behaviors to survive daily doses of prejudice. It is no wonder that the school failed to recognize the significance of the art product to the parents, and the preparation that it represented for their children to survive, cope, and succeed. As the aides predicted, the patterned, adult-designed art work was indeed displayed more frequently in homes than were the child-designed collages and finger paintings.

All of the parents wanted their children to have a better start in life than they had had, and hoped that the program would provide a "headstart." Opportunity brought hope; and hope, they believed, together with hard work and a little luck, made success a possibility. For some, success meant having access to the economic resources which they had heretofore been denied. To others, it represented getting the rights, privileges, and respect that they deserved. Many parents socialized their children for success in this country by teaching them to interact competently both in their own environment and in mainstream society. The mothers sought to prepare their children to be bicultural — simultaneously acculturated and socialized in two separate cultures, yet able to draw from the experience and values of both.

They saw more problems ahead for their children than the school did as it naively tried to prepare the children for a monocultural life in the larger society.

As I worked with the families and in the program and read the current research, several questions haunted me: How can Blacks prepare themselves to move effectively in mainstream society and still maintain their own culture? How can educational institutions be effective settings for the development of Black people? How can research more adequately reflect and account for the reality of Black people's lives? Later, in graduate school and postdoctoral work, I found that the contradictions and questions were very persistent. They are a part of the system.

The Seventies: Experiences in Graduate School

These questions prompted me to return to school to pursue graduate studies. My goal was to investigate the Black experience from a Black perspective. The questions became specifically focused at an in-service workshop that introduced me to the concept of Black English as a legitimate dialect. At the workshop I learned about the research of linguists and anthropologists such as Labov (1970); Labov, Cohen, Robins, and Lewis (1968); Stewart (1969, 1971); and Abrahams (1970). I realized that the language instruction I had been using in my classroom, though modified considerably from the structured Distar program used in other compensatory programs, nevertheless supported the belief that "Black English" and "bad English" were synonymous. Although I had difficulty accepting this position completely, I cannot honestly say that I rejected the premise that Black English was inferior and an improper way to speak standard English.

The workshop leaders claimed that Black English had its own complex set of rules, grammar, vocabulary, and structure. For the first time I felt that I had a sound perspective from which to attack the sixties studies of Black behavior and the scholarship which presumed that Black and White children develop cognitive styles along the same lines, one well, the other poorly. I realized that characteristics indigenous to the Black experience, and the way that this experience is reflected in language, were being treated ethnocentrically.

My experiences teaching, and the questions resulting from those experiences, plus the ideas generated by the workshop leaders, kindled my desire to go to graduate school. I sought alternative explanations for the research findings on the social, cultural, and cognitive modes of Black children and hoped to develop new theories to refute those findings. My focus would be Black language as cause, consequence, and mediator of the Black experience. In retrospect, the central dilemma of my professional training also became clear: I am a Black child — one of the subjects whose behavior needed an alternative explanation. By enrolling in graduate school, I was embedding myself in an environment that denied the complexity of my experience. I sought to reeducate myself. I expected to develop new methods through activity that was based on the premises and methods of the very system I questioned. If I were successful, I might have to regard myself as a failure.

Although Blacks and other minority people are trained to be bicultural in their homes and communities, graduate school — yet another "culture" — poses special problems. Students learn fairly early that there is a pre-scribed way to talk in a graduate community and that the name of that language is "academese." Professional jargon serves both to obscure meaning and to define group membership. White social science students must learn to negotiate in the two spheres of their everyday and academic lives, whereas Blacks and other already bicultural minority students have to develop a third set of interactional styles and become, in effect, tricultural. Those who can-not master this requirement are destined to fail.

Since a significant portion of graduate minority students cannot rely on their family members for financial support during their studies, many are forced to work to meet daily living and educational expenses. This was not always the case. During the 1960s, universities actively recruited minority students by offering them scholarships and stipends. However, this period of support was short-lived. In the quiet of the seventies, few scholarships or stipends were given. Minority status no longer qualified one for special con-siderations. Ironically, many Whites continue to associate ethnicity with scholarship money and assume that Blacks receive financial support from universities and philanthropic organizations, monies for which the White students are often ineligible. These assumptions of "reverse discrimination" perpetuate and aggravate the divisive climate that exists between Black and White students.

Financial constraints cause many poor Black graduate students to com-plete their academic requirements more promptly than do affluent students. As a result, they forfeit many of the advantages and pleasures associated with a leisurely pursuit of an academic degree. More significantly, many minority students are not able to devote adequate time to explore the issues, methods, and theories relevant to their research. Those who, in addition, are unpre-pared to deal with the institution's academic demands are doubly vulner-able.[1] Still, they are forced to contend with the rigorous demands thrust upon all graduate students. They soon encounter a third jeopardy: their success, their failure, their smallest actions are seen not merely as their per-sonal attainments, but as representative of *all* minority people.

I often discussed the problem of representativeness and visibility with Black and other students of color. Most agreed that we monitor our behavior according to our perception of White attitudes, and hide, at times, behind

[1] The issue of whether Blacks are usually less prepared than Whites for graduate work needs consideration beyond the scope of this article. But I will says that virtually *nothing* is being done to help those who are less prepared to catch up. They are left to flounder and struggle on their own.

a face. Hiding, or maintaining face, is an emotionally exhausting and draining experience, depleting energy that could be more advantageously directed toward school work.

We were reminded of our minority status in a number of ways. Because it was the school's policy to support affirmative action enrollment we were the visible evidence of our university's reparations for society's past injustices. At the same time, we heard comments about how our minority admissions — Puerto Ricans, Native Americans, Chicanos, never Blacks to a Black — were lowering the academic standards of the university. Professors said the intellectual caliber of students was declining; White students were afraid that their degrees would be devalued, just like those homes in suburbia when neighborhoods become integrated and homeowners fear declining property values. We had to deal with the reality that often the institutional forces promoting reparations were the same as those worrying about declining quality. Not only did the institutions transmit mixed messages to us, but individual statements could be seen as double-edged: "You're okay, but some of the others . . ." or "Well, you're an exception."

We were representatives, different from some of the others and the "unexceptional" mass of minority status people, but representing them just the same. We were at the same time the failures depressing academic standards and the successes who, by our very success, ceased to be members of the group whom we were supposed to represent. My minority student colleagues and I tried to support each other as we dealt with the terrible bind: if I fail, the minority students fail; if I succeed, I only highlight a general minority student failure by being an exception and thus jeopardize my membership in minority culture. We had to be tricultural, make up for lack of preparation, be both representative and exceptional, and find some way to neither succeed nor fail. These jeopardies are not totally new; they are simply exaggerated in graduate school.

The folk wisdom of the mothers who lived in "The Flats" came to mind again and again during graduate school: you can't wear old clothes to school because the teacher will judge you accordingly; art is better if it resembles something real; it is better to remain silent, because you know you will be evaluated far more for how you say something than for what you say. I saw parallels between the attitudes of the mothers and those of the students at the university. I noticed, for example, both in the undergraduate and graduate departments, that Black students seemed to dress more stylishly than White students, though for the most part they were financially less able to do so.

I also noticed that many minority students neither shared their work nor asked their professors or peers for help. We did not want to confirm White students' beliefs that we were, in fact, unprepared and lowering university standards. At the same time, we were apprehensive about the reaction of minority peers. In our private joking routines, we often bantered that the computer had somehow erred and the university was unaware of its faux pas regarding our admittance. It was far easier to hide our intellectual uncertainty from each other with a joke than to admit openly that a great deal of our insecurity had been internalized and was very real to us. Although we could reject such fears intellectually, the repetitive messages transmitted in the university environment had their impact.

To some extent, this situation parallels the attitudes favoring a standardized art product which were frequently expressed in the compensatory program: the products of the art instruction should be "finished" and able to be evaluated on clear standards, and the children should be taught to "finish" and do so "correctly." For graduate students, avoiding contact with professors until there is a finished product means that there is only one occasion for evaluation, and we found that evaluation is routinely made with the minority status of the student in mind. If it is judged as good, as satisfactorily matching the standard product, then that minority student is seen as exceptional; if it is judged as poor, then the student is seen as a typical minority student.

Many faculty members have difficulty separating a student's work from his or her ethnicity; they either expect poor work because of it or are surprised if it is good. These expectations seem reasonable to them in light of the public knowledge of the difference between White and minority scores on Graduate Record Examinations and Miller's Analogy Tests discussed during admissions debates. Realizing that we are thought to lower academic standards, and having the finished product the only product made public does not solve the problem for Black students; but knowing the biases by which we may be judged makes it manageable.

Black students were often reluctant to speak in class or in public, to ask for clarification, or to offer an opinion. Avoidance was partly due to our recognition that our questions and opinions were seldom heard without awareness of the color of the speaker. Whenever a minority student took a stand on an issue related to ethnicity, it was assumed that the silent minority students shared that same opinion. As a result, an awesome burden was placed upon the vocal Black student who felt commissioned to serve as an unofficial spokesperson for all Blacks. Many of us resented this yoke, but at the same time recognized our social responsibility to pursue and explain ethnic issues. Strangely enough, we often demanded from ourselves what Whites expected from us, while realizing the futility of accomplishing this goal to anyone's satisfaction.

There are no easy solutions. One might speculate that the problems Black students encounter in graduate school might be lessened if they were shared with Black faculty members. The Black student/Black faculty ratio obviously works against such a solution. Black professors are particularly overburdened by the sheer number of Black students who seek their help and advice. Furthermore, some are in comparable situations, experiencing similar difficulties, and cannot afford to overextend themselves or become too involved in nonacademic problems. They are forced to engage in university politics and play the tenure game for their own survival, and this, unfortunately, often takes precedence over active involvement with and support of Black students.

Frequently, students turn to organizations like the Black Student Union for support. These organizations offer a supportive and comfortable environment in which students can discuss issues, feelings, frustrations unique to their experience. Although involvement in these organizations can be worthwhile, it takes time away from study. In addition, there are other problems associated with dependence on student ethnic organizations for moral support. When these groups are one's primary support group, for example, everyone involved represents everybody else. If students openly admit their confusion, they can both discourage their colleagues and risk negative sanctions by providing evidence that outside of the group they may be acting as representatives of weakness or incompetence, not strength and ability. It is ironic that in the Black Student Union, we could publicly admit our need to wear masks when we dealt with the White power structure, but rarely shared our need to maintain face among ourselves. A negative sanction from one's own ethnic group was far more devastating than one received from Whites. So in essence, some of us wore masks behind our masks. While Black faculty members and student organizations provide support for the student, neither is sufficient to solve all the problems.

I was fortunate in having several mentors who, as friends, eased the stresses I encountered in graduate school and, as professionals, encouraged me to explore nontraditional approaches to research on Black children. By challenging my ideas, they forced me to clarify my intuitive, but unsubstantiated criticisms of ethnically related research issues. Under their tutelage, I concentrated on course work emphasizing qualitative research methods. I sought courses which would provide a different research lens with which to reexamine the "cultural-deficient" theories postulated in the sixties and which still, in more subtle forms, exist today. Many Black students who did not find the support they needed experienced "non-paranoid paranoia," a state which the sociologist Davidson (1973) claims is non-paranoid because "it is based in reality; but 'paranoid' nevertheless, because it is excessive and sometimes demoralizing" (p. 37). Davidson refers specifically to Black students' fear of being co-opted, a fear that evolves from hearsay or from personally having had a term paper written on the Black experience "used for purposes of 'intelligence' or 'surveillance' aimed at Black people" (p. 38).

Black students who were aware of the phenomenon of academic exploitation feared being used and often became suspicious or distrustful of projects offering research experience if the project was investigating aspects of the Black experience. The students felt that rather than gaining research training in these circumstances, they were being taken advantage of and used as pawns for easy access into the Black community for data collection. Davidson (1973) claims that these fears were not totally ungrounded but in many cases were real situations. Student research assistants volunteering for or employed by such exploitative research projects are usually "under the illusion that [they are] somehow [making] a contribution to the needs of [Black] people" (p. 33). He further suggests that many Black graduate students and research assistants who have been co-opted come to recognize eventually how "totally their careers are determined by White academic standards and to develop a sense of abject powerlessness . . ." (p. 42). Rather forebodingly, Davidson prophesies that Black students will never resolve their inner turmoil.

I had not anticipated these problems before entering graduate school. The clear-cut solutions that I had sought simply were not there. I also did not suspect that even after completing a doctorate, and being allowed to enter the esoteric world of social science, the turmoils would persist. These turmoils follow me and other minority students beyond graduate school, into our places of employment, to research organizations, businesses, postdoctoral training programs, to all academic environments.

The Eighties: Renewed Hopes or Faded Dreams

Rather than diminishing, my problems have increased and intensified. New ones have appeared. Most significantly, a role and identity conflict has crystallized: I am expected somehow to be an objective social scientist yet have a Black perspective. This role is a contradiction, and I have begun to experience feelings of anxiety and futility, emotions that paralyze and inhibit my creativity and productivity. As a Black scholar I am both within and outside White academia: my visibility and minority status are inseparable, ever-present, always apparent to me and to my colleagues. Becker (1966) addresses this dilemma in *Outsiders*. He maintains that "whether one is a physician [a social scientist in our case] or middle-class or female will not protect [us] from being a Negro first and any other of these things second" (p. 33).[2] This was the case at the day-care center and in graduate school, and also is the case in the academic community where my behavior is often assessed in terms of race and ethnicity, regardless of my personal traits. The rules, though tacit, are quite clear: if I fail to conform to the behavior that is socially defined and sanctioned by the academic community, I will be held accountable and labeled. The tricultural interactional skills that I mastered in graduate school have taken on even greater significance in academia, and I am learning the fine art of "switching hats" depending on the race or status of my colleagues, and on the context.

In fulfilling our academic roles, we interact increasingly more with the White power structure and significantly less with members of our ethnic community. This is not without risk or consequence; some minority scholars feel in jeopardy of losing their distinctive qualities. Behavior which is sanc-

[2] Whereas the problems encountered in White male-dominated academic settings by Black professionals per se are the focus here, the additional (and some have argued more complex and emotionally loaded) problems of the female Black researcher seem to encompass these frustrations and more.

tioned in the university environment may be devalued in our ethnic community and actually create conflict. Coping with conflicts between different belief systems is not a new experience for minority scholars. Black undergraduate students experienced this same phenomenon in the sixties and "feared that total immersion in White college life styles socialized them into a carbon copy of a White person, made them a 'print-out-sheet' representing something Whites programmed, designed, and fed into a giant computer, somehow transforming Blacks into something Whites like, or at least [could] tolerate" (Noble, 1978, p. 114). Little has changed. Two decades later, Black academics continue to wrestle with these same forces and fears.

We enrolled in graduate school with naive visions of acquiring the methodological skills with which to challenge social science theories pertaining to minorities. We were not prepared, however, for the personal transformations we would undergo. In pursuit of our goals, it was easy to overlook how extended interactions with White colleagues and exposure to different ways of thinking could alter our world view and change the way we think. Some of us become the prodigal sons and daughters in our communities, returning to our grassroots only to discover painfully that we have changed and are now strangers — marginal members within our ethnic group and communities. "What usually happens is that Blacks become detached from their own . . . ethnic world, and alienated from the Black masses" (Noble, 1978, p. 149).

What ensues is a state of double marginality, a condition far more emotionally draining than one would experience under most demoralizing circumstances. It is of little consequence that we may be recognized and respected for our contributions and scholarship; our ever-present visibility never allows us to experience complete membership in White academia. At the same time, these marginal feelings begin to affect our ethnicity as well. We thus experience double marginality, belonging to and feeling a part of two worlds, yet never at home in either.[3] It is as though the split we experience is a zero-sum game. Does membership in the White academic community preclude membership in a Black one? Do we have to trade one identity for another? If so, at what price? And more important, why?

Multiple demands accompany the two identities. As Erikson (1978) wrote, "If he is careful to observe one set of demands imposed upon him, he runs the immediate risk of violating some other and thus may find himself caught in a deviant stance no matter how earnestly he tries to avoid it" (p. 25). Problems and stresses already inherent in being a minority and an academic

---

[3] The notion of "double consciousness" was described by W. E. B. Du Bois (1961) as "a peculiar sensation, this double consciousness, this sense of always looking at one's self through the eye of others, of measuring one's soul by the tape of a world that looks on in amused contempt and pity. One ever feels his two-ness — an American, a Negro; two souls, two thoughts, the unreconciled strivings; two warring ideals in one dark body whose dogged strength alone keeps it from being torn asunder" (pp. 16–17).

become compounded when the ideologies of the two reference groups contradict and conflict. In the attempt to sustain a feasible balance between our cultural and social identities, we undergo feelings of strain, anomie, and alienation. We are in a no-win situation; if we "sell out" and totally embrace the White system, we might enjoy some of its rewards, yet negate valued parts of ourselves. Selling out connotes a permanence, a closure, and a denial of culture that, for me, is the ultimate compromise that a Black researcher can make. Yet complete rejection of White academia may not be any better for a concerned, minority researcher. If we reject the system, we forfeit our opportunity to influence it in ways which will create a more receptive and responsive atmosphere for our input. So we "buy in."

Buying into the system might be considered as a viable alternative for those minorities who are uncomfortable with the closure implicit in selling out. Buying in might be seen as a more temporary adaptation than selling out and become a strategy to gain power within the system and thus ultimately to influence social and educational policy. It is availing ourselves of the resources and personnel at hand and having the opportunity to expose White scholars to alternative theories and interpretations of research data and findings. Perhaps our ethnic integrity will be less compromised by buying into the system and negotiating for power within it. In essence, what is required is a summation and integration of our personal and professional experiences into a meaningful synthesis for both self and the profession.

If ethnic researchers decide to buy in, they need continually to assess their perceptions of this concept in order to determine how close it comes to selling out. The difference between one position and another is sometimes indiscernible, and, unless they are keenly astute, researchers can easily compromise themselves. Minority researchers who feel that they have compromised their ethnic integrity within the system — that they have sold out — can become guilt-ridden. However, it is that very feeling of guilt, that fear of having gone a step too far, that I believe distinguishes the concerned social scientist from the "sell out." As social scientists we are continually at risk, vulnerable to charges from either side of having sold out or of being written off as nothing more than an agitator rather than a serious academic.

As social scientists, we "deal intimately with the White power structure and cultural apparatus, and the inner realities of the Black world at one and the same time" (Cruse, 1967, p. 451). Although our role as spokesperson is self-imposed, it is nevertheless exhausting and stressful, and takes a mental toll on minority researchers who strive to be effective. Furthermore, we are burdened with the responsibility of *not misrepresenting* our people's realities. We realize that our statements can be potentially harmful to people of color if they result in distorted conclusions. As a result, like other minority researchers I am often overly cautious before I speak and write, hoping that the statements I make and opinions I give reflect fairly accurately the Black experience in general, not merely myself in particular. Thus I forego a bit of my own autonomy, knowing that this is inherent in such a responsibility.

These problems also occur when we decide which research projects to pursue. Since many of us purposely chose careers in research as a vehicle for effecting social change, we ought to consider beforehand the possible consequences that our work might have for social and educational legislation. Our position is precarious: both the research we conduct and our ethnicity can be exploited. Either can be used to effectively validate denigrating theories. By declaring that research projects have minority scholarship or input, White social scientists can use our endorsements to disclaim any racist implications which might be embedded in their work.

Low-income Blacks have been subjected to countless research investigations, possibly more than any other group in this country, but now the Black community is beginning to react: speaking out, expressing distrust, and questioning the kinds and the quality of studies that are being conducted in Black communities. As a result of the negative consequences of some past research, many Blacks are not receptive to the notion that it can have positive outcomes. They are suspicious and hostile toward research groups seeking entry into their communities. This mistrust includes Black researchers as well. In fact, Black scholars who conduct research in Black communities experience double hostility: we are seen as perpetrators of racist research and are viewed as amoral "sell outs" who would use our positions and ethnicity to the detriment of our own people.

We find ourselves in still another quandary: we want to continue research with subjects from our own ethnic group, but are forced to do it by using dominant-group theories and methodologies. As a result, Black and other minority researchers must explain why minority groups do so "poorly" in light of prevalent theories, or we must continually challenge the theories. Both situations are double-edged. In the first case, the researcher has implicitly come to accept these theories and applies them to study minority groups, thereby perpetuating the problem. The second alternative — challenging the validity of existing theories — is more difficult. The minority researcher must not only criticize, but pose viable theoretical alternatives or be perceived as another ideologue who is all rhetoric and no results.

Objectivity is a critical issue for the minority researcher. Being members of the ethnic group that we are studying can have both advantages and disadvantages. We can bring a two-pronged analysis to our data by attempting to apply an "objective" interpretation as well as a sociocultural perspective unavailable to the White researcher. It becomes particularly difficult, however, to remain objective about research issues when they affect you, even indirectly.[4] How does one objectively study a population that is consid-

---

[4] I am aware that research cannot be value-free, nor can we as researchers maintain true objectivity. Many minority researchers, however, feel compelled to strive for this goal. Paradoxically, and this is where minorities are really in a bind, we must follow all of the research standards of our profession or risk our careers as researchers. As minority group members, we can see how the values, beliefs, and priorities of minority people are violated by existing research methods, yet we must not violate the standards of those methods if we are to be considered respectable researchers.

ered "deviant" when the researchers themselves, although considered exceptions, are members of that deviant population? Although our empathy for the population under study might guide the nature of our research, it might also hamper it. "While a certain amount of empathy is necessary if one wishes to understand fully the persons he studies, empathy, sympathy, sentimentality, or whatever label one prefers, sometimes presents itself as a stumbling block to [Black] researchers" (Sawyer, 1973, pp. 368–369).

We are forced to proceed slowly and with caution. We are tempted at times to withhold our research results because we are aware that our findings can be used to affect in a negative way the lives of Black people. Many of us seriously consider the possible consequences of making public our "shared secrets" — those aspects of ethnic life that we as a minority group want to keep private so that the "deviant" labels that have been attributed to us will not be reinforced (Sawyer, 1973). Shared secrets revealed outside the context of the Black experience can be incorrectly analyzed by Whites. For us the question really becomes which role takes priority: being a Black or being an objective researcher. I feel that this dilemma will never be resolved and will always present problems for me.

Black researchers must also consider the issue of audience; with what readership do we wish to create a dialogue? As a social scientist I am naturally concerned with the academic community's reception and evaluation of my work, but as a Black I am equally concerned with the reactions of my Black colleagues. They evaluate my work from an ethnic as well as a scientific perspective. Receiving a positive response from both audiences is rare. For minority scholars undergoing tenure review who have intentionally selected ethnic journals as forums for their work, further problems arise: ethnic journals are not, as a whole, valued or respected by the academic community. In terms of career advancement, it is advantageous to publish in prestigious journals, regardless of their readership. Many minority scholars are therefore compelled to publish in prestigious as well as ethnic journals to satisfy both professional and personal needs.

Another major problem associated with publishing in professional journals is the limited audience that is reached. Seldom are our findings relayed or filtered to advocates of social change, to people directly involved with our sample population. On many occasions, I have questioned colleagues who have collected data in ethnic communities and schools. The people who volunteer for their studies are rarely given feedback or results when the researchers leave the field, nor are local social service agencies and policy makers who are directly involved with our subjects. Perhaps I am naive to have supposed that educational theories formulated within the context of academic scholarship are ultimately translated into social policies that will substantially improve the quality of life for people in this country who are poor, oppressed, and ethnically different.

I am currently reassessing my reasons for having chosen a career in social science. The past has shown that research has not been particularly instrumental in changing social and economic conditions for minority people. We seem to have come full circle; Black grievances that erupted in the sixties in violence and riots are reappearing in our Black ghettos today. The economic and social situations of Blacks have not improved markedly. An article in *Newsweek* attests to this fact:

> The middle-class fourth of the Black population often written about as "burgeoning," has in fact not grown in a decade, and the fourth living in poverty has not shrunk. But the rate of Black unemployment has doubled since 1969, to 13.5 percent . . . and the number of unemployed Blacks has nearly tripled, to 1.4 million. The rates run devastatingly high among Black teenagers; a new generation is coming of riot age with short work, few skills, stunted hopes — and no memory whatever of the victories so painfully won by their parents. (Goldman, Borger, Shannon, Foote, & Kirsh, 1980)

As the quote from *Newsweek* indicates, the need for researchers who can analyze the Black experience and aid in Black attainment of full economic and political rights is as great now in the early 1980s as it was in the 1960s. Yet the education of Black researchers is being obstructed by cultural and structural problems which beset Black education in predominantly White institutions. The problems and coping strategies I observed in the Black graduate students with whom I studied were the same as those I observed among poor mothers of children in the ghetto school in which I taught. To a large degree, the primary school system remained ignorant of the Black mothers' perspectives on education, and misinterpreted their behavior. At the graduate level, educational theory, research, and practice ignored and continues to ignore Blacks' perceptions of bias in being distinguished and assessed, and in their strategies for prevailing in spite of these biases. Educational institutions cannot solve the political and economic problems of Black Americans alone. Their contributions toward this end, however, can be significant if researchers allow Black perceptions of social reality to become a central focus in all fields of educational theory, research, and practice concerning Blacks.

The Eighties: Where I Am Now

Skeptical, frustrated, yet somewhat optimistic, I sought answers, and looked for different questions, in a postdoctoral research training program. The program applied a cross-cultural, interdisciplinary perspective to the study of children's problem-solving skills in everyday contexts. Inductive methods of ethnographic research are used to describe behaviors in natural situations (including schools) and to investigate behavior in terms of experiences and practices that are culturally relevant to the children. The ethnographic data enable us to understand how contexts affect and guide particular behavior. We then apply a cognitive-psychological framework to the ethnographic observations to design instructional environments which are based on what people do in their everyday problem solving from the perspective of their own culture. "These new programs are still in their infancy and seem to be an absolute requirement for developing a theory of culture and behavior and a valuable approach to overcoming the shortcomings and paradoxes posed by current procedures for the study of children's lives" (Laboratory of Comparative Human Cognition, 1979, pp. 831–832). If this is not *the* answer, at least it is one beginning.

The contradictions that I have experienced still comprise an organizing force in my life, and the goals which began to form in the 1960s preschool compensatory program still hold: to contribute to research that adequately reflects and accounts for the reality of Black people's lives and to change educational institutions so that they become effective settings for the development of Black children. Currently, I am at a major university training minority undergraduate students to evaluate critically current research, to challenge it, and to develop new methods. I hope that my experience can help to ease the dilemmas of this new generation of potential researchers and to deal with those contradictions of the sixties by which many Blacks are still ensnared today. From these students can come real solutions to minority problems; we former students, now teachers, can advance them and hasten solutions.

I have not attempted to answer questions in these reflections, merely to raise them. Perhaps the answers that I am seeking lie in the interdisciplinary approach to understanding the relationship between culture and cognition that I am now exploring — and then again perhaps they do not. Nevertheless, I begin the eighties with renewed hope, remembering the dreams of the day-care mothers and of people's struggles in the 1960s for political, social, and economic autonomy.

References

Abrahams, R. D. (1970). *Deep down in the jungle.* Chicago: Aldine.

Becker, H. (1966). *Outsiders: Studies in the sociology of deviance.* New York: Free Press.

Bereiter, C., & Englemann, S. (1966). *Teaching disadvantaged children in the preschool.* Englewood Cliffs, NJ: Prentice-Hall.

Bernstein, B. (1961). Social class and linguistic development: A theory of social learning. In A. H. Halsey, J. Floud, & A. Anderson (Eds.), *Education, economy and society.* New York: Free Press.

Brottman, M. A. (1968). Language remediation for the disadvantaged preschool child. *Monographs of the Society for Research in Child Development,* 168, *33* (8, Serial No. 124).

Cruse, H. (1967). *The crisis of the Negro intellectual from its origins to the present.* New York: Morrow.

Datta, L. E. (1970). *A report on evaluation studies of Project Head Start.* Washington, DC: Office of Child Development, U.S. Department of Health, Education and Welfare.

Davidson, D. (1973). The furious passage of the Black graduate student. In J. Ladner (Ed.), *The death of white sociology.* New York: Vintage.

Du Bois, W. E. B. (1961). *The souls of Black folk: Essays and sketches.* Greenwich, CT: Fawcett.

Erikson, K. T. (1978). Notes on the sociology of deviance. In E. Rubington & M. Weinberg (Eds.), *Deviance: The interactional perspective.* New York: Macmillan.

Glazer, N., & Moynihan, D. P. (1963). *Beyond the melting pot: The Negros, Puerto Ricans, Jews, Italians, and Irish in New York City.* Cambridge, MA: MIT Press.

Goldman, P., Borger, G., Shannon, E., Foote, D. M., & Kirsh, J. (1980, June 2). The mood of ghetto America. *Newsweek*, pp. 32–34.

Gottfried, N. W. (1973). The effect of early intervention programs. In K. S. Miller & R. M. Dregen (Eds.), *Comparative studies of Black and White in the United States.* New York: Seminar Press.

Hess, R. D., & Shipman, V. (1965). Early experience and socialization of cognitive modes in children. *Child Development, 36,* 869–886.

Jensen, A. (1969). How much can we boost I.Q. and scholastic achievement? *Harvard Educational Review, 39,* 1–123.

Klaus, R., & Gray, S. (1968). The early training project for disadvantaged children: A report after five years. *Monographs of the Society for Research in Child Development, 33*(4), (Serial No. 120).

Laboratory of Comparative Human Cognition. (1979). Cross-cultural psychology's challenges to our ideas of children and development. *American Psychologist, 34,* 827–833.

Labov, W. (1966). *The social stratification of English in New York City.* Washington, DC: Center for Applied Linguistics.

Labov, W. (1970). The logic of non-standard English. In F. Williams (Ed.), *Language and poverty.* Chicago: Markham Press.

Labov, W., Cohen, P., Robins, C., & Lewis, J. (1968). A study of the nonstandard English of Negro and Puerto Rican speakers in New York City. *Phonological and grammatical analysis* (Vol. 1); *The use of language in the speech community* (Vol. 2). Final Report, Cooperative Research Project No. 3288. Washington, DC: Office of Education.

Lewis, O. (1966). *Anthropological essays.* New York: Random House.

Moynihan, D. P. (1965). *The Negro family: A case for national action.* Washington, DC: U.S. Government Printing Office.

Noble, J. (1978). *Beautiful also are the souls of my Black sisters: A history of the Black women in America.* Englewood Cliffs, NJ: Prentice-Hall.

Sawyer, E. (1973). Methodological problems in studying so-called "deviant" communities. In J. Ladner (Ed.), *The death of White sociology.* New York: Vintage Books.

Shuy, R. W. (1967). *Discovering American dialects.* Champaign, IL: National Council of Teachers of English.

Smith, M. S., & Bissell, J. S. (1970). Report analysis: The impact of Head Start. *Harvard Educational Review, 40,* 47–49.

Stewart, W. A. (1969). Historical and structural bases for the recognition of Negro dialect. In J. E. Alatis (Ed.), *Monograph Series on Languages and Linguistics,* (No. 22).

Stewart, W. A. (1971). Observation (1966) on the problems of defining Negro dialect. *Florida F.L. Reporter, 9*(1/2), 47–49.

The preparation of the manuscript was supported by grant awards from the Ford Foundation 780-0639, 780-0639A; the Carnegie Corporation DC15 Dept. 06184; and NIMH ADAMNAHM 15972-01 and 02.

The author acknowledges the following colleagues at the Laboratory of Comparative Human Cognition, University of California, San Diego, for their helpful comments and suggestions during the writing of this manuscript: Alonzo Anderson, Denise Borders-Simmons, Sondra Buffett, Esteban Diaz, Elette Estrada, Hugh Mehan, J. Lee Meihls, Luis Moll, Warren Simmons, and especially Michael Cole and Peg Griffin.

Racism in Academia:
The Old Wolf Revisited

■ ■ ■

MARIA de la LUZ REYES
JOHN J. HALCON

A Chicano candidate was being interviewed for a tenure-track faculty position. The small conference room, with a seating capacity of twelve, was filled beyond its limits. Extra chairs were brought in as faculty from various departments sat elbow to elbow. Just a week before, it had been impossible to round up four warm bodies to interview a White male candidate applying for another faculty position in the School of Education.

At the head of the table, in a dark pin-striped suit, sat the invited candidate. He smiled as he waited for another question. At the center of the table, an older Anglo professor leaned forward, brushed back his thinning white hair, adjusted his glasses, and peered at the waiting candidate.

"Dr. Fuentes,[1] I see here in your vita that you have a bachelor's degree in Chicano Studies, a specialization in bilingual education, your publications deal mostly with minority issues, and you have been keynote speaker at two Chicano commencements."

"Yes, that's correct," replied Dr. Fuentes.

"Well, Dr. Fuentes, I have a problem with these things."

"What's the problem?" queried Dr. Fuentes.

"Frankly, I am concerned that if we hire you, you will be teaching separatism to our impressionable young administrators. . . ."

The blood rushed to the candidate's face, and the anger in his eyes was difficult to conceal. The audience grew silent.

* * *

[1] In the tradition of ethnographic field work and because of politically sensitive settings for other minorities, pseudonyms for actual persons and institutions are used throughout the essay to protect their identities and to maintain confidentiality. Accounts are based on actual interviews (May 1986). The incidents reported in this article were either experienced by us personally or were reported to us by others.

Harvard Educational Review Vol. 58 No. 3 August 1988, 299–314

As minorities, we know from personal experience that racism in education is vigorous and pointed. We realize that, in spite of bona fide college degrees, our credentials are challenged by pervasive racist attitudes, and our efforts toward full incorporation into academic positions in institutions of higher education (IHE's) are hampered by layers of academic stratification. We find that, even with earned Ph.D.'s, the academic road is the beginning of another Sisyphean climb. If current patterns of minority hiring persist, the best we can expect is to occupy positions outside the mainstream ranks, those most peripheral to the hub of governance and power.

Not long ago, as graduate students, we believed that successful completion of our graduate programs would be our license to "play in the big leagues." In our naiveté, we assumed that attainment of our advanced degrees would mark the end to our "language problems," our experiences with educational tracking, low expectations, negative stereotyping, use of tests to denote our ranking and placement in the system, and a myriad of other institutional obstacles. In a sense, we assumed — or maybe hoped — that the frequent encounters with racism which we experienced in schools were confined to the lower echelons of the educational ladder. We believed that our Ph.D.'s paved the way to an egalitarian status with mutual respect among professional colleagues, where the new rules of competition would be truly based on merit. We were wrong. Instead, we find that even in academia, we face the same racism under different conditions — the old wolf in new clothing.

The racism experienced by Chicanos in academia is not new. Chicano scholars have characterized it as "academic colonialism" (Arce, 1978; Ornelas, Ramirez, & Padilla, 1975). Many Chicano writers blamed this form of racism for their inability to penetrate the elitist, White, male-dominated system which excluded them from full and significant participation (Arvizu, 1978; Candelaria, 1978; Casso & Roman, 1975; Valverde, 1975). But to those of us new to academe, the manifestations of racism at the professorial level appear new. This sense of newness may be attributed to the fact that the majority of racial incidents are generally associated with the experiences of minorities at elementary, secondary, and baccalaureate levels. The very idea that racism could exist among the *educated* elite is disconcerting to new academicians of color, and might come as a surprise to aspiring novices looking in from the outside.

In the early 1970s, some believed that there were only about one hundred Chicano Ph.D.'s in the United States (C. de Baca, 1975). The most recent data indicate that full-time Hispanic faculty (including Cubans, Chicanos, Puerto Ricans, and South Americans) in higher education institutions as of fall 1983 numbered 7,356 (*Digest of Education Statistics 1985–86* and *1987*). There is no specific breakdown for Chicanos provided in these data, but the fact is clear that today we have more Hispanic academics than ever before.

From personal observations and from what we have learned through our interactions with other Hispanics in academe, we believe that for the first time there exists a noticeable number of over-qualified, under-employed

Hispanic Ph.D.'s unable to gain access to faculty positions in IHE's. Ten to fifteen years ago we might not have been able to name ten Chicano Ph.D.'s; today many of us can easily name six to ten Hispanic Ph.D.'s unable to obtain academic positions. This observation is at once ironic and paradoxical: we are considered the elite and best-educated members of a minority community that is still struggling desperately to graduate its members from high school, and yet, rather than finding a payoff at the end of the educational tunnel, we find a dark path draped in full academic regalia — for aspiring Chicano academics, this is indeed a sobering and humbling reality.

As Chicano academics, we have personally met or have come to know about a large number of Chicano Ph.D.'s, through a loose, informal network across the country. This network provides information about the experiences of other Chicano academicians from which we have collected examples of racism in IHE's. This essay is an attempt on the part of two Chicanos to describe incidents of racism in IHE's that we, and other Chicano colleagues, have experienced.

Definition of Racism

Dube's (1985) definition of racism provides a useful framework for our discussion of racism in academia. He describes three types of racism: overt, covert, and reactive. This article will focus on the overt and covert forms found in academia. According to Dube, overt racism is based on the notion that some races are inherently superior to others. It is the most easily identified form, "open and up-front" (p. 88), and publicly displayed like that of the Ku Klux Klan, for example. In contrast, covert racism stems from a more subtle philosophy, "at times taking the form of superior virtue . . . believed to be common only to virtuous 'races'" (p. 88). Although not easy to identify, it has negative consequences for minorities.

In our experiences within educational systems, we find that examples of these two types of racism occur regularly. In some cases, long and well-established patterns of behavior are so entrenched that they function as standard operating procedures. In the following pages we will discuss manifestations of these types of racism primarily as they affect Chicano academics.

Overt Racism

Overt racism at IHE's usually occurs in isolated events such as the interview described at the beginning of this article. Although "open and up-front," overt racism is usually not exhibited publicly beyond the campus. It is most common in situations where minorities are being considered for positions occupied primarily by Whites, as in the case of minorities vying for tenure-track faculty positions at predominantly White colleges and universities.

A recent series of incidents comes to mind. Five Chicano Ph.D.'s applied for various faculty positions at a southwestern college located in a community with a 40 percent Chicano constituency. Over the course of a year and a half, they each surfaced as finalists and were interviewed for tenure-track positions. The strong pool of Chicano candidates resulted from active recruitment efforts by Chicano faculty who wanted to improve academic opportunities for other Chicanos.

Some faculty and school deans were surprised to learn that five Chicano applicants had been invited to interview, especially since the dean of arts and sciences had reported that previous faculty recruitment efforts had yielded "no qualified minorities." Although the number of candidates seemed significant compared to previous searches, it was small when compared to the twenty-five to thirty-five White candidates interviewed during the same period. Chicano candidates drew a large number of faculty spectators to their interviews, while non-minority applicants went virtually unnoticed — even in the departments to which they had applied. On at least two occasions, one department chair in education reported at a faculty meeting that only two faculty members had attended the interviews for the math and science education candidates (two White males). Given the predominance of White faculty across the campus, the seemingly frequent and obvious presence of Chicanos within a relatively short span of time prompted one school dean to remark, "What do they think this is, Taco University?" That racial slur resurfaced each time another Chicano was to be interviewed.

Optimistically, one might believe that the faculty came to meet and listen to the candidate, but that was not the case. Instead, many appeared to attend the interviews chiefly to find fault with the candidate or to offer their reasons for not hiring the candidate. In one case some faculty members came with copies of previously circulated petitions, attempting to halt the search on the grounds that they did not agree with the job description used in the national search. No formal objection to the job description had been made before the search committee let it be known that a Chicano had emerged as the top candidate.

The tragedy was that those overt racist tactics were successful — none of the five Chicanos was hired. According to personal accounts from the candidates in subsequent communications, they were told they were rejected on the basis of "inexperience," "lack of sufficient qualifications," or "incompatibility" with the faculty in the departments in which they had applied. Four of the five positions were left vacant, and in the fifth, a White male who had served as an adjunct instructor was hired on a temporary basis. A year later, one of the Chicano applicants was hired, but only after a series of confrontations between minority faculty and the administration as well as pressure from Chicano and Black students and from members of the Hispanic community.

Covert Racism

Covert racism is the most pervasive form of racism in higher education. Because of its elusive nature, however, covert racism is ignored by those who have never experienced it, and denied by those who contribute to it. As

92

discussed previously, our interactions with other Chicanos in academe have allowed us to compile typical examples of covert racism in higher education. We have organized those examples under the following categories: tokenism, the typecasting syndrome, the one-minority-per-pot syndrome, the brown-on-brown research taboo, and the hairsplitting concept. Below we discuss each category, examining closely the implications for Chicano academics.

Tokenism. The civil rights movement of the 1960s ushered the way for Executive Order 11246, the federal blueprint for affirmative action (Holmes, 1975). This Department of Labor regulation required that all federal contractors and subcontractors take affirmative action in all employment activity, assuring equal opportunity to job applicants and barring discrimination on the basis of "race, color, religion, sex, or national origin." For Hispanics, this order opened up new opportunities. They found themselves appointed to important positions in both private and public agencies. During the same period, fellowships to pursue graduate degrees at universities across the country, especially in education, became available primarily through the Ford Foundation and Title VII of the Elementary and Secondary Education Act. Those funding sources and others like them allowed a larger number of Hispanics, who might not otherwise have afforded it, to pursue higher education.

In the mid-1970s, when minority quota systems were being implemented in many nonacademic agencies, the general public was left with the impression that Chicano or minority presence in professional or academic positions was due to affirmative action, rather than to individual qualifications or merit. But that impression was inaccurate. Generally, IHE's responded to the affirmative action guidelines with token positions for only a handful of minority scholars in nonacademic and/or "soft" money programs. For example, many Blacks and Hispanics were hired as directors for programs such as Upward Bound, Talent Search, and Equal Opportunity Programs (EOP) (Valverde, 1975). Other minority faculty were hired for bilingual programs and ethnic studies programs, but affirmative action hires did not commonly extend to tenure-track faculty positions. The new presence of minorities on college campuses, however, which occurred during the period when attention to affirmative action regulations was at its peak, left all minority professionals and academics with a legacy of tokenism — a stigma that has been difficult to dispel.

Actual gains in academic faculty positions due to affirmative action regulations could not have been anything but minuscule. As early as 1975, Peter Holmes, then Director of the Civil Rights Commission, reported at the National Institute on Access to Higher Education for the Mexican American that the spirit of the affirmative action regulations was based on the notion of an "availability pool." This concept was interpreted such that the regulations applied *only* in situations where it could be proven that there were significant numbers of available minorities in the respective employment areas. Since the number of Hispanics with Ph.D.'s constituted less than one percent of available persons in many academic fields at that time (*Minorities in Higher Education,* 1984), Holmes believed it was impossible for higher education institutions to comply with the regulations (see also "Discrimination in Higher Education," 1975). The University of California at Berkeley, for example, negotiated an affirmative action plan with the former Department of Health, Education and Welfare, and mutually identified *only three* departments where projected goals for minority hiring were required under affirmative action regulations (Holmes, 1975).

Despite the minimal gains for minorities in tenure-track positions, we continue to be plagued with the assumption that we are mere tokens and have been hired without the appropriate credentials, experience, or qualifications. The legacy of tokenism and its negative implications has led to a current situation, in which unspoken pressure is put on minority academics to continually prove that they are as good as White academics. Tokenism has also had the effect of reducing minority-occupied positions to a subordinate status, providing an easy excuse to ignore or minimize our presence and our efforts.

The Typecasting Syndrome. A by-product of tokenism is the typecasting syndrome. This is an underlying attitude or belief that Hispanics can only, or should only, occupy minority-related positions, such as those in Bilingual Education, Chicano Studies, foreign languages (Spanish), or student support services such as EOP.

An actual case of this typecasting syndrome occurred recently to a Chicana colleague during the negotiation of her contract with a state university on the West Coast. Two tenure-track positions were announced at the university where she applied for a faculty position. One position was in the teacher education program with a rank of associate professor, and the other position was in the bilingual education program at the assistant professor level. Although her qualifications and experience were equally strong in both areas, she applied for the teacher education position, because she had recently been promoted to associate level and because she recognized the need for integrating minority scholars into the mainstream programs. Much to her surprise, she received an invitation to interview for the teacher education and the bilingual position, without having applied for the latter.

When the interviews were completed, she was informed that she was the top candidate for both positions and that the university would make her an offer. A couple of weeks later, the dean called to offer her the bilingual position because "they believed that it was her main area of expertise" and that it was "where she would be most happy." She was quite aware that the position in teacher education meant breaking through an all-White faculty, while the position in bilingual education would have confined all Hispanics to the same unit. As a result, she refused the offer for the bilingual position, reminding the dean that she had not applied for it, and that since she was the top candidate in both positions, she should be allowed to select the position she preferred.

The negotiations slowed as she was informed of a "new policy" requiring candidates to "update" all college transcripts, provide proof of earned doctorate degree, and proof of good teaching evaluations from previously taught classes. She learned from the other Chicanos at the university that the "new" requirements were familiar tactics intended to discourage her from accepting the position. It took the threat of legal action to convince the Dean to offer her the associate level position in teacher education.

Arce (1978) and Olivas (1986) argue that this practice of specialized minority hiring for minority slots "is a more formal co-optation of Hispanic concerns . . . which relieves the institution of the need to integrate throughout their ranks" (Olivas, 1986, p. 14). The worst part for the few Chicanos in academia is that the typecasting syndrome segregates them in ethnically related professions. Arciniega and Morey (1985), for example, reported that in 1983 only 3.5 percent of the California State University faculty were Hispanic, and that the majority of those were in ethnic studies departments.

Another negative consequence of the typecasting syndrome is that often the only avenues for Hispanic promotion are in ethnically related fields. A report entitled, "The Status of Chicanos/Latinos at the University of California" (Gordon, 1988) bears this out. A coalition of Hispanic faculty members from the U.C. system complained in the report that there were only three Chicanos/Latinos in high-level academic administrative positions, and they reported that "there are no, repeat no, Chicano or Latino academic deans or department heads outside of ethnic or Chicano Studies" (Fields, 1988, p. A17). If this is the case at the University of California system, in a state with 6.6 million Hispanics (Fields, 1988), it is not likely that Hispanic academics are faring much better in other states where their numbers are smaller.

Typecasting is indeed pervasive, and is simply another form of stereotyping that prevents Chicanos from becoming fully integrated into all areas of academia. The larger social consequences of confining minorities to the outer fringes of academia include severely limiting White students' access to ethnically diverse points of view — resulting in a shallow education from a monocular perspective (Fishman, 1975). In an increasingly pluralistic society, this practice has the added effect of depriving White students of social skills necessary for mutual respect and co-existence with other cultural groups. The alarming increase in racial incidences involving White college students against minorities (Farrell, 1988a, 1988b, 1988c, 1988d; McCurdy, 1988; Williams, 1987) is ample evidence of this deprivation.

The "One-Minority-per-Pot" Syndrome. Many colleges and universities operate under an unwritten quota system that manifests itself as reluctance to hire more than one minority faculty member per department. We refer to this practice as the "one-minority-per-pot" syndrome. Two or three minority faculty may be hired for ethnic studies, bilingual education, or foreign languages, but departments of education, sociology, history, English, or psychology, for example, seldom hire more than one minority per department.

We believe that implicit in this practice is a deep-seated belief that minorities are not as qualified as non-minorities. This conviction stems from an unspoken fear that the presence of more than one minority faculty member in a mainstream, traditional department might reduce the department's academic reputation. We have participated in faculty meetings in which the subject of additional faculty has been discussed. In these meetings, the suggestion that minority candidates be considered has generally evoked pat responses along these lines: "We don't want to hire anyone because of their ethnicity, we want *fully qualified* candidates" (see Blum, 1988a; Heller, 1988), or "This isn't a position for bilingual education," or "We hired a minority last year." Typically, consideration of minority candidates occurs only when there is pressure applied to diversify the faculty.

Scott Heller (1988) offers evidence of the deeply ingrained belief among faculty that hiring minorities reduces the caliber of the faculty already on board. In one college president's attempt to discover the reasons for the institution's inability to hire Black faculty, several faculty members revealed their reservations in private interviews when they "questioned whether affirmative action hiring wasn't tantamount to lowering academic standards" (p. A16). In a seeming contradiction, these same faculty members welcomed a pool of candidates that included minorities. Apparently, an applicant pool that includes minorities is considered by White faculty as evidence of a "good faith effort" in hiring and integrating minorities — even if minorities are not ultimately hired.

The "one-minority-per-pot" concept applies to administrators as well as faculty. Recently, a Chicano colleague of ours applied for an associate deanship at his institution. Prior to completing his application, he was forewarned by the academic vice president that he was not likely to be considered for the position. According to our colleague, the vice president told him that "there were already three other Chicano administrators at the college." Recognizing the futility of his effort, the candidate withdrew his name from consideration.

Another familiar theme closely associated with the "one-minority-per-pot" syndrome is the practice of requiring additional documentation from minorities above and beyond the standard curriculum vitae, transcripts, and letters of recommendation. For example, it is not uncommon for minorities to be required to submit copies of their dissertations, evaluations of their teaching, bibliographies from their published papers, and copies of funded proposals. Since it is usually minorities who are singled out to provide additional documentation and the requests are usually made *after* they have become top candidates, there is adequate ground for suspecting that covert racism is at work. The intent of this tactic is to discourage minority candidates from accepting faculty positions. Both points were illustrated previously in the case of our Chicana colleague who was offered a position for which she had not applied. For minority academics, this particular practice has the simultaneous effect of publicly demeaning their professional reputations while chipping away at their self-esteem.

Additionally, the limitation on minority hiring that is part of the "one-minority-per-pot" syndrome has the effect of restricting the career goals and aspirations of Hispanics and other minority faculty. We believe that the lack of minority faculty in academic departments today (Blum, 1988a, 1988b; Fields, 1988; Higher Education Research Institute, 1982; Harvey, 1987; *Minorities and Strategic Planning at the University of Colorado*, 1987) is more likely the result of this unwritten quota system than it is of the lack of available candidates in some hypothetical pool.

The "Brown-on-Brown" Research Taboo. As Hispanic academics, our research interests often stem from a recognition that we have endured racial discrimination and from a compelling need to lend a dimension of authenticity to the prevailing theories about our communities. Said another way, we want to provide our own perspectives regarding prevailing negative assumptions about our values, culture, and language. This explains our interest in such topics as dropouts, bilingual education, second-language literacy, Chicano literature, and the education of minority students. Our interest in these areas is also motivated by a concern for assisting our community in improving its second-rate status in the educational, economic, and political arenas. Tired of reading about ourselves in the social science literature written by non-minorities, we want to speak for ourselves, to define, label, describe, and interpret our own condition from the "inside out." We feel strongly about providing a balance to the existing literature and research on Chicanos.

Our efforts, like those of other minority scholars, often meet with covert disapproval by our White colleagues, who judge the quality and validity of our scholarly work, our research, and our publications (Blum, 1988a, 1988b). Quite often, our research interests are dismissed as minor or self-serving. The general perception is that minority-related topics do not constitute academic scholarship — as was the case in the incident described in the introduction — and that they are inappropriate and narrow in scope. The assumption is that minority researchers cannot be objective in their analyses of those problems which are so close to their life experiences. In this regard we have to agree with Kushner and Norris (1980–1981) who suggest that the devaluing of minority research interests deprives minorities of the "dignity of contributing to theorizing about their worlds" (quoted in Lather, 1986, p. 264).

The perception that "brown-on-brown" research is somehow not valuable pervades academic circles. This paternal attitude from a White, male-dominated profession is a double standard that lends full credibility to Whites' conducting research on White populations, but discredits minority academics' research on minority issues. White-on-White research is accorded legitimacy, but "brown-on-brown" research is questioned and challenged at the same time that many White social scientists are establishing their professional careers as experts on minority issues. What appears to be at the heart of the objection to "brown-on-brown" research is not the credibility of our research, but an unspoken objection to a potential undermining of White expertise on minority issues.

Many minorities believe that another objection to "brown-on-brown" research is that the traditional Eurocentric perspective used to evaluate their scholarship puts nontraditional research at a disadvantage because predominantly White male academics lack the appropriate cultural perspectives from which to judge its real merit (O'Neale in Blum, 1988a; Wilson in Blum, 1988b). The problem of judging minority scholarship may also be exacerbated by the high concentration of minority academics in education, the arts, and the humanities, "where the evaluation of research is more subjective than in such fields as engineering or the natural sciences" (Wilson in Blum, 1988b, p. A17).

Referring to women in academia who share experiences similar to those of ethnic minorities, especially regarding the devaluing of their research, Simeone (1987) states:

> While the system employs the rhetoric of merit, its determination is far from objective. Even if there were agreement on the most important criteria, for example, agreement on means of assessment and actual performance would be difficult to reach. The process which is constructed to sort out the mediocre and the merely good at each level may be sorting factors other than merit, as well. Some of these may include political or social affiliations, intellectual perspective, or perceived congeniality. (p. 28)

The devaluing of minority research in promotion and tenure decisions is difficult to prove. Yet many Hispanics, Blacks, and Native Americans cite cases from their own experiences, or that of their colleagues, as examples of unfair evaluation of their research during promotion and tenure reviews (see Blum, 1988b, and Fields, 1988). A recent example is that of a Black woman in the English Department at Emory University, who lost a three-year battle to overturn her denial of tenure (Blum, 1988a). She was the only Black woman in the department, and her expertise was in Black literature. The scholar in question and her supporters claim that the decision to deny her tenure was based on institutional racism that devalues scholarship by minorities on ethnically related subjects. On the other hand, both the committee on tenure who reviewed her case and university administrators claim that the decision was based on "her weakness as a scholar" (p. A15). Several students and faculty who were interviewed did not discount racism as a factor. A member of the committee stated, ". . . it's a kind of covert or unconscious racism deflected into the belief that a certain specialty or a certain journal that is outside of established fields is not good enough" (Baker in Blum, 1988a, p. A17).

The devaluing of "brown-on-brown" research stems from the values undergirding institutions of higher education, which reflect culturally monolithic systems. These systems judge the quality of scholarship from the normative perspective of their own cultural group. As a result, the work of those individuals who depart from those standards is deemed inferior (Ramirez, 1988). The obvious consequence, then, of the tenure and promotion processes based on White males' definition of research and scholarship is that few minorities make the grade.

The Hairsplitting Concept. This last type of covert racism is rather elusive, but it is no less real. We describe the hairsplitting concept as a potpourri of trivial technicalities, or subjective judgment calls, which prevent minorities from being hired or promoted. When minorities have met all the academic criteria, jumped the hurdles, and skipped through all the specified hoops, the final decision is based on highly subjective and arbitrary points. At times, these decisions border on paternalism, with White males defining and deciding what is best for us, as in the case cited earlier of the Chicana professor being told in which department she would be most happy. At times minority candidates are second-guessed and eliminated, not on the basis of their qualifications, but on the personal opinions of the decisionmakers (Heller, 1988). A minority candidate, for example, might not get a position because the committee might assume that she or he would not be happy in a predominantly White community (Wilson in Blum, 1988; Fields, 1988; Heller, 1988). Decisions that are publicly acclaimed as objective are, in fact, highly subjective. Politics, personality, and even intellectual orientation almost always color decisions and serve to exclude those who are different (Candelaria, 1978; Ramirez, 1988; Simeone, 1987).

Hairsplitting practices are dangerous because the exclusion of Chicanos is justified by minor, arbitrary, and inconsequential factors that prevent them from reaping the benefits of their education. What appears to be consistent in the application of hairsplitting practices is that often when White-dominated selection committees feel threatened by a minority candidate, they base their selection decision on an arbitrary, hairline difference favoring the White candidate. When IHE's use arbitrary hairsplitting practices as grounds for their final decisions, the unspoken rule seems to be that it is better to support the candidate who best reflects the status quo.

Each of the above forms of covert racism has contributed to the current status of Chicanos in academia and, in part, explains the dearth of minority academicians. We have discovered a painful truth: It is difficult to escape the tentacles of racism, which touched our earlier educational experiences. The sad reality is that the "old wolf" is still around, now dressed in token assumptions, the typecasting syndrome, the one-minority-per-pot syndrome, the brown-on-brown research taboo, and the hairsplitting tactics.

Some Responses to Racism

Chicanos, like other minority academics, find ways to cope with racism. In talking with other Chicanos, we have identified four prevalent responses to racism: give in, give up, move on, or fight back.

Chicanos in the "give in" group play the academic game at all costs. They yield easily to the demands to assimilate. In some cases, they attempt to divest themselves of all obvious cultural traits. At the same time, they work diligently at mainstreaming their research interests, and steer clear of minority-related issues. Individuals in this group might even deny racism, explaining the dearth of minority academics simply from a "pick-yourself-up-by-your-bootstraps" philosophy. They behave as if they were convinced that the key to success in academia is simply a matter of hard work and that politics, personal preferences, and subjectivity have little to do with merit. A few in this group succeed in infiltrating the system and blending well in their academic settings. Others give in completely, but despite their full conversion, they encounter rejection by those in the system who continue to perceive them as outsiders, or "tokens." Chicanos who deal with racism in this manner may feel alienated and out of touch with the Hispanic community at large. Indeed, their own Chicano community may have little respect for them and may perceive them as sell-outs.

Chicanos in the "give up" group are usually found in institutions and departments where displays of racism are overt. These Chicanos tend to struggle against academic racism at all costs. Most of their energies are used to combat injustices instead of pursuing scholarship. These individuals tend to become so demoralized that racism destroys both their spirit and their self-esteem. The lack of a support network to assist them to survive and succeed in such an academic environment makes it almost impossible to tolerate any direct or subtle attack.

These individuals soon experience "burnout" as they see the futility of their efforts to change the system. At times, the direct or underlying hostility and alienation that these individuals experience have a disabling effect that gradually leads to a self-fulfilling prophecy regarding their academic potential. Repeated invalidation of their work serves to convince them that their efforts are substandard and their work inferior. Instead of hanging on, they give up — becoming disillusioned or convinced that they "don't have what it takes" to be an academic; that academia is not suited to their ultimate priorities, or that they "don't need the hassles." These Chicanos may leave academia altogether, and they may not return.

Chicano academics who cope with institutionalized racism by moving on to greener pastures compose the "move on" group. Individuals in this group maintain a strong affiliation with their community and feel a strong sense of responsibility to improve the status of other Chicanos in the larger community. They neither assimilate easily, nor readily ascribe to mainstream perspectives. As a result of their strong cultural awareness and assertiveness, they may often be perceived by their White peers as "arrogant." These individuals recognize manifestations of racism in the academy and fully understand that as minority academics they are in "tenuous-track" positions. They are realists. And, although they clearly fight against racism, they learn how to "pick their fights," realizing that taking on every minority issue can render them totally ineffective. They carefully evaluate their situations, looking at such factors as the key players, their support networks, and the odds of succeeding in their institutions. When they recognize that the price of the struggle is not worth their efforts *in that particular environment,* they move on. They do so instead of seriously jeopardizing their careers, damaging their self-esteem, and exhausting all their energies in futile struggles. Although few find the ideal university, many of these Chicanos eventually find the "best fit" for them.

Finally, Chicano academics in the "fight back" group respond in two ways, one of which is similar to the response of the "move on" group. That is, they fight back but recognize their limitations and the importance of succeeding in the system. They do so — not because institutions of higher education are perfect systems — but because they recognize that if institutional racism is to be eradicated, they must participate in the decisionmaking arenas controlled by tenured faculty, and where the key decisions for admission and full incorporation are made. They understand that this must be done from the inside out. So they persevere. They learn to play the game, without compromising either their integrity or their ethnicity. They comply with the rules only insofar as issues related to scholarship will earn them tenure. They may temporarily limit their involvement with the Chicano community in order to attain tenure. Once they are tenured, however, many redirect their attention to minority concerns and minority-related research that will help improve the condition of their community. A characteristic of Chicanos in this group is an unwavering tenacity and resilience that enables them to continue their efforts even when they encounter stiff opposition. Chicanos in this group often join together to plan effective strategies for combatting racism and demanding equity. Their fight against racism motivates them to surpass the limited expectations the dominant community has for them as minorities.

Another response of Chicanos in the "fight back" group is to exert every effort to prove the oppressor wrong, regardless of the consequences. These Chicanos often sacrifice their academic careers to effect a significant change that will pave the way for other Chicano academics. They are generally politically astute and know how to mobilize the minority community behind certain issues. They are often perceived as the martyrs and prophets of the community, who appear to be filled with a kind of reckless zeal to right injustices. As a result, they may pay the price of being excluded from academia altogether.

The different responses to racism that we have observed are often variations of the above four themes. For example, an individual may respond to racism in any of these four ways, depending on the specific circumstances. The most critical dividing line in these responses lies between the coping strategies that ultimately separate Chicano academics from their community and those that allow Chicanos to maintain close ties with their community.

Conclusions

Discriminatory policies and the manifestations of racism in educational institutions have changed very little over the years. In spite of the changing demographics that indicate a dramatic rise in the Hispanic population, and in spite of the new focus on recruitment and retention of minorities by educational institutions, Chicano academics today are generally experiencing many of the same kinds of racial prejudices experienced by those who preceded them into the academy a generation ago. Forms of tokenism, typecasting, limitations on minority hiring, devaluing of Chicano research, and hairsplitting practices are prevalent manifestations of racism in academia. Each of these factors contributes to maintaining the small number of Chicano academics currently in IHE's, and to the inability of a growing number of Chicano Ph.D.'s to break into the system. The latter are experiencing the disillusionment of being over-qualified, under-employed, or unemployed. They are in a Catch-22 situation: unable to get an academic job because they lack university teaching and publishing experience, and unable to acquire that experience because they cannot get an academic position. To our knowledge, no surveys have been conducted to determine the actual count, but we know that a good number of unemployed potential Chicano academics exist because the network is small, and we know many of them. This is a disturbing reality for members of a minority community who work hard to convince their youth that education is the great social equalizer that generally brings with it a guaranteed economic return.

How can we eliminate or reduce racism in academia? Eradicating institutional racism in academia will not be an easy task. Hispanic Ph.D.'s (which include Cubans, Chicanos, Puerto Ricans, and Central and South Americans) compose a mere 2.1 percent of all doctorate degrees (*Minorities in Higher Education*, 1987). Of those, Chicano academics in universities across the country represent an even smaller number. Further, we know from experience that unless the dominant majority recognizes the value of a culturally diverse professoriate, we cannot expect them to take the lead in eliminating precisely the kind of racism they tacitly condone.

On the other hand, we cannot change the system alone. Chicano academics will have to form coalitions and join forces with other Hispanic, Black, Native American, and Asian academics who share similar experiences. Together we must work at dispelling the myth of tokenism that surrounds minority hiring. We must press for an end to the typecasting syndrome, to the limit on minority hiring by certain departments, and to hairsplitting practices. We must promote instead the idea that departments should be rewarded when they can demonstrate diversity among their faculty, and at the same time, we must lobby and press for a reexamination of the criteria for review, promotion, and tenure, for a redefinition of scholarship, and for inclusion of so-called "minority journals" among those classified as premier journals.

Minority academics will have to work at convincing their institutions that minority faculty are the *key* to recruitment, retention, and promotion of other minorities, both students and faculty. They will have to press for *full incorporation* and *integration* into the various branches of the institution, not just in minority slots. Anything less than that will render them powerless to assist other minorities to move successfully through the academic hurdles. Without minority role models at all levels of the educational structure, but especially in the centers of power — the ranks of tenured professors — it will be difficult to convince young Hispanic, Black, and Native American students that they can benefit from higher levels of education.

As minority academics, we realize that we need an exceptional amount of ability, drive, dedication, and discipline to meet the requirements for academic advancement and the added demands of serving as role models for minority students. One way to compensate and to make allowances for this extra work is to exert pressure to have universities assign some weighted value to minority contributions of this type. We believe Valverde (1975) had a good idea in arguing that universities should give Chicanos (and other minorities) their "full measure by ascribing proportional value to such characteristics as language, ethnic perspective, cultural knowledge, diversity of ethnic mix in the network of people, and the power to attract other minority students into higher education" (p. 110).

To accomplish these goals, we will have to be each other's biggest fans; that is, we must seize and even create opportunities for publicly recognizing the qualifications and the contributions made by members of our own ethnic group and other minorities. We must go out of our way to promote minority scholars, to highlight their expertise, to disseminate minority publications among our non-minority colleagues, to suggest ways in which they can integrate minority perspectives into their classes and use books written by, or which include articles written by, minority scholars. We must push for diversification of the curriculum.

We recognize that it will take courageous leadership among minority academics to effect changes in the current situation and that the burden of initiating those changes lies squarely on our shoulders. No one else has the vested interest that we have. No one else can do it for us. We must tackle it ourselves because it is obvious that non-minority academic leaders are ambivalent about the role of minorities in higher education. On one hand, they pay lip service to the diversification of faculty on their campuses, but on the other hand, they do nothing to bring that about. Once we fully understand this and once we understand how institutions have excluded us from full participation, we can join forces with other people of color, set priorities, and harness our energies to combat racism in academia. If we fail to do this, we will find ourselves a generation from now still facing the same "old wolf" . . . in yet another fleecy robe.

References

Arce, C. (1978). Chicano participation in academe: A case of academic colonialism. *Grito del Sol: A Chicano Quarterly, 3,* 75–104.

Arciniega, T., & Morey, A. I. (1985). *Hispanics and higher education: A CSU imperative.* Long Beach, CA: Office of the Chancellor.

Arvizu, S. F. (1978). Critical reflections and consciousness. *Grito del Sol: A Chicano Quarterly, 3,* 119–123.

Bayer, A. E. (1973). *Teaching faculty in academe: 1972–73.* American Council on Education, Research Report 8(2). Washington, DC: American Council on Education.

Blum, D. E. (1988a, June 22). Black woman scholar at Emory U. loses 3-year battle to overturn tenure denial, but vows to fight on. *Chronicle of Higher Education,* pp. A15–A17.

Blum, D. E. (1988b, June 22). To get ahead in research, some minority scholars choose to "play the game." *Chronicle of Higher Education,* p. A17.

C. de Baca, F. (1975). White House perspective. In H. J. Casso & G. D. Roman (Eds.), *Chicanos in higher education.* Albuquerque: University of New Mexico Press.

Candelaria, C. (1978). Women in the academy. *Rendezvous: Journal of Arts and Letters, 13*(1), 9–18.

Casso, H. J., & Roman, G. D. (Eds.). (1975). *Chicanos in higher education.* Albuquerque: University of New Mexico Press.

Digest of education statistics, 1985–86, and *1987.* Washington, DC: U.S. Department of Education, Office of Education Research and Improvement.

Discrimination in higher education. (1975, Spring). *Civil Rights Digest, 7*(3), 3–21.

Dube, E. (1985). The relationship between racism and education in South Africa. *Harvard Educational Review, 55,* 86–100.

Farrell, C. S. (1988a, January 27). Black students seen facing "New Racism" on many campuses. *Chronicle of Higher Education,* pp. A1, A37–A38.

Farrell, C. S. (1988b, January 27). Stung by racial incidents and charges of indifference, Berkeley to become model integrated university. *Chronicle of Higher Education,* pp. A37–A38.

Farrell, C. S. (1988c, February 17). Rising concerns over campus racial bias marked at Northern Illinois University. *Chronicle of Higher Education,* pp. A37–A38.

Farrell, C. S. (1988d, February 24). Students protesting racial bias at U. of Massachusetts end occupation of campus building after 5 days. *Chronicle of Higher Education,* p. A41.

Fields, C. M. (1988, May 11). Hispanics, state's fastest-growing minority, shut out of top positions at U. of California, leaders say. *Chronicle of Higher Education,* pp. A9–A10.

Fishman, J. (1975). *An international sociological perspective of bilingual education.* Keynote Address. National Association for Bilingual Education Conference, San Antonio, Texas.

Gordon, L. (1988, June 14). Second report criticizes UC on its policy towards hiring Latinos. *Los Angeles Times,* p. 3.

Harvey, W. B. (1987, May/June). An ebony view of the ivory tower. *Change, 19*(3), 46–49.

Heller, S. (1988, February 10). Some colleges find aggressive affirmative action efforts are starting to pay off, despite scarcity of candidates. *Chronicle of Higher Education,* p. A12.

Higher Education Research Institute. (1982). *Final report of the commission on the higher education of minorities.* Los Angeles: Jossey-Bass.

Holmes, P. (1975). The ineffective mechanism of affirmative action plans in an academic setting. In H. J. Casso & G. Roman (Eds.), *Chicanos in Higher Education* (pp. 76–83). Albuquerque: University of New Mexico Press.

Kushner, S., & Norris, N. (1980–81). Interpretation, negotiation and validity in naturalistic research. *Interchange, 11*(4), 26–36.

Lather, P. (1986). Research as praxis. *Harvard Educational Review, 56,* 257–277.

McCurdy, J. (1988, June 8). Nullification of Latino students' election sparks melee at UCLA. *Chronicle of Higher Education,* p. A23.

Minorities and strategic planning at the University of Colorado. (1987). Boulder: Office of the Associate Vice President for Human Resources.

Minorities in higher education. Third Annual Status Report. (1984). Washington, DC: American Council on Education.

Minorities in higher education. Sixth Annual Status Report. (1987). Washington, DC: American Council on Education.

Olivas, M. A. (1986). Research on Latino college students: A theoretical framework and inquiry. In M. A. Olivas (Ed.), *Latino college students* (pp. 1–25). New York: Teachers College Press.

Ornelas, C., Ramirez, C. B., & Padilla, F. V. (1975). *Decolonizing the interpretation of the Chicano political experience.* Los Angeles: UCLA Chicano Studies Center Publications.

Professional women and minorities: A Manpower data resource service. (1984). Washington, DC: Scientific Manpower Commission.

Ramirez, A. (1988). Racism toward Hispanics: The culturally monolithic society. In P. A. Katz & D. A. Taylor (Eds.), *Eliminating racism profiles in controversy* (pp. 137–157). New York: Plenum Press.

Simeone, A. (1987). *Academic women working towards equality.* South Hadley, MA: Bergin & Garvey.

Valverde, L. (1975). Prohibitive trends in Chicano faculty employment. In H. J. Casso & G. D. Roman (Eds.), *Chicanos in higher education* (pp. 106–114). Albuquerque: University of New Mexico Press.

Williams, A. A. (1987, October 12). Advice/dissent. *Colorado Daily.*

Giving Voice to the Voiceless

—■-■-■—

BEVERLY McELROY-JOHNSON

Every person has a different voice, just as every person has a different genetic inheritance. A person's voice is like a fingerprint, an identifying mark. There are squeaky, low, cheerful, harsh, angry, strident, weak, and sweet voices — all different kinds. In fact, most people have two voices — an outer voice that other people hear when they speak, and an inner voice that other people may not hear at all. There are people who have a particularly difficult time making contact with their inner voice with any confidence, and thus often take the authority of external voices as their own. Some people are so used to hearing their own voices that they hardly hear anything else, while others have been silenced or unheard for so long that they either never learned to speak or have forgotten how.

When I use the term *voice*, I am thinking of a strong sense of identity within an individual, an ability to express a personal point of view, and a sense of personal well-being that allows a student to respond to and become engaged with the material being studied, the other students in the classroom, and the teacher. Voice, in this sense, is having a place within the academic setting, other than just a desk and a book. Voice is the student's participation in and acceptance of the academic and intellectual process. It is the student's desire to express ideas in a clear, coherent way, because that student understands that his or her thoughts are important. It is the solid understanding of why an individual must communicate clearly and effectively, the recognition of self within the student that gives that student the ability to express with confidence the answers to important questions within the academic setting. Voice is identity, a sense of self, a sense of relationship to others, and a sense of purpose. Voice is power — power to express ideas and convictions, power to direct and shape an individual life towards a productive and positive fulfillment for self, family, community, nation, and the world.

Harvard Educational Review Vol. 63 No. 1 Spring 1993, 85–104

The students I teach have different voices. They come from thirty-nine different countries and speak twenty-nine different languages. I teach eighth- and ninth-grade English classes (and previously seventh-grade English class as well) at Westlake Junior High School, which is located in the central section of Oakland, California, close to the downtown business district. The school's student population consists of three major groups: 44 percent African American; 42 percent Asian (including Chinese, Vietnamese, Laotian, Thai, and other Pacific groups, mostly immigrant); and 12 percent Hispanic (mostly Mexican). The remaining 2 percent are made up of other diverse groups from around the world. The school is divided into two sections, one devoted primarily to English-as-a-Second-Language (ESL) students, which is called the International Department. The other section, which has no official name, is for native English speakers, primarily African Americans. Our faculty is predominantly European American; the support staff is predominantly African American.

Since arriving at Westlake Junior High School, I've had only one Caucasian student. Most of my students are Asian, African American, and Hispanic. Because their inner and outer voices have often been historically muted and stifled, they have little sense of security when they speak during class discussions.

In this article, I will focus on the educational status of African American students and my connection to them culturally and ethnically. My concerns stem from my own personal observations and experience, which is supported by statistical information collected within my district. These statistics, compiled by the District Curriculum and Instruction Department, show that African American students are unable to: 1) complete high school disproportionately to other groups; 2) function within certain classrooms (88% of suspensions at my school are of African American students, mostly males); 3) read and write at a level that enables them to be socially and economically successful within the school environment and in the larger work world; 4) have a sense of personal power and worth.

The fact that I am an African American teacher and a woman is obviously a strength for me in teaching African American students, because of our shared historical connections and collective experience in this country. I was brought up to believe in the significance of the ancestral African role of woman, her significance as mother and teacher in the beginning years of a young person's life. Some may ask, "Can you teach other children as well?" This question is misguided at best and racist at worst, and reveals an underlying negative assumption. My response is simple: Does anyone ever ask the many White teachers all over the world who teach non-White children, including African American children, if they (Whites) can teach them as well as Blacks, or if their whiteness somehow limits their work with "other" people's children?

As a teacher, my dedication to teach all students as they are is essential to my instructional practices. However, recognition of my own background as a woman and as an African American contributes to my strong sense of self, my personal/cultural history, and my identity. It is this personal sense of strength that makes me a credible person and teacher.

Like all human beings, I am affected by my cultural/ethnic condition and gender. By acknowledging and accepting my own identity, I am able to accept others and assist my students, whoever they are, in building their own identities as readers, writers, and human beings. I am also able to study what I do not know about others, to do research, to ask for assistance from more knowledgeable sources, and, thereby, to encourage student progress in learning.

To me, successful students are those who are able to master the necessary tools, whatever they may be, to ensure their completion of high school, college, vocational school, and/or apprenticeships in order to make positive lives for themselves. Success especially involves the ability to read and write, so that students have the power of communication and the necessary proficiencies for seeking employment. Success also means students being able to navigate, in a disciplined way, within a diverse society that is sometimes hostile to them, without falling apart and/or being self-destructive.

However, as an observer of student successes, I am disturbed that the failures of the educational system seem to be reflected disproportionately in the African American culture, and, more specifically, among African American males. Why is this? Perhaps part of the answer lies in the status of African Americans as a minority group and in their history. While Asians, for example — who are often referred to by the dominant culture as the "model minority" — voluntarily immigrated to the United States to seek a better life, African Americans were forcibly brought in chains. In his article "Minority Status and Literacy," John Ogbu (1990) points out that Asian immigrants

> have chosen to move to the United States or to some other society, in the belief that this change will lead to an improvement in their economic well-being or to greater political freedom. These expectations influence the way they perceive and respond to white Americans and to institutions controlled by whites. . . . Castelike or involuntary minorities are people initially brought into the United States through slavery, conquest or colonization. Resenting the loss of their former freedom and perceiving the social, political, and economic barriers against them as part of an undeserved oppression, American Indians, black Americans, Mexican Americans and native Hawaiians are characteristic American examples of these involuntary minorities. (p. 145)

The failure of the current urban educational system is that, in general, it does not address the needs of all those it serves. Educators who force a Eurocentric curriculum upon students from non-European backgrounds assume that these students: 1) want to be like European Americans; 2) understand this Eurocentric framework; and 3) bring with them the necessary knowledge and empowerment to navigate in such foreign waters.

The failure of the educational system extends further, in my opinion, into the political and psychological nature of the teaching body, primarily consisting of European American females who, for whatever reasons, are too often unaware of the non-European learners' needs, who ignore the need to translate curriculum and instruction into language readily accessible to these learners, and/or who rigidly oppose acknowledging diversity and instead work for the "oneness of all" in "their image" of what that is. This destroys the self-concept and individual power of non-European students, forcing them either into personal conduct that is destructive in nature or into a "white-washed" imitation of the European American ideal, an uneasy identity that is in opposition to their own natural cultural, ethnic, and racial identities.

Another way of addressing the reason for the failures of African American students within the U.S. educational system is to study in depth the collective history of African Americans, and the psychological implications of their history on this group of people. It has never ceased to amaze me that, when the subject of African American history is raised and the impact of slavery on this group is addressed, the response is often negative and resistant. If the subject were the dropping of the atomic bomb on innocent people at Hiroshima, one would select words carefully in raising any objection to the voicing of the terror of that deed and the effect it has had on the Japanese people and the world. If it were the Holocaust, one would be ill-advised to raise an objection to the constant reminders of these horrors in print, on television, and in film. We are encouraged to feel empathy and concern for the Southeast Asian people, who have fled oppression, or the Central American people, who are suffering from the ravages of war. Yet, when the subject of the psychological, moral, emotional, spiritual, and physical effects of slavery upon African American men, women, and children comes up, the responses are often very different, even hostile.

Since my sophomore year in high school, I have heard these negative attitudes and responses expressed, at times overtly and at other times more subtly. I attended Male High School in Louisville, Kentucky, and graduated with honors in 1965. The name of the school itself explains some of its limitations; previous to my enrollment, the school's student body had been all White and all male. I received no college counseling while there, even though I graduated second in a class of 500 students that was roughly 15 percent African American, second only to the valedictorian, a White male, who did receive such counseling.

However, my experience of this attitude extends into every aspect of my adult life, notably my professional and volunteer environments. When I was hired to be assistant manager of press relations at Kaiser Steel, I was told by the head of our department that I filled two quotas — "You're Black and a woman, and we need the federal subsidies that go with that." My personal accomplishments and abilities were not discussed. Whenever I expressed concerns about the racist/sexist overtones at work, including the hostile jokes or slanders, I was not taken seriously and was even told that I had "an axe to grind." Sometimes this attitude took the form of asking me questions like, "Don't you like being a woman?" or, "Do you have a problem being Black?"

After leaving that profession, I experienced similar attitudes in the volunteer work I did. European Americans would express prejudices that were often explicit and sometimes implicit, such as, "You're very intelligent. You're really different from most Black people. How did you turn out so well?" (shock) or, "My, you're so articulate" (surprise). Others would dwell on my physical appearance — "You're so attractive" or "You look nice" (condescending) — in situations where the issues being addressed had nothing to do with physical attributes. My intelligence and ideas were often ignored. When I complained that these comments and attitudes smacked of racism, sexism, or both, and were extremely painful for me to deal with, I was told, "Well, that's the past. Things have changed" or "Here we go again."

As far as I am concerned, those of us who have persisted in insisting that we be heard and that our voices be acknowledged have done so at great personal sacrifice. In the face of ridicule and denial, we still attempt to make contact with our brothers and sisters of different cultures, especially our European American coworkers in education, in this democratic society where individual voice is ostensibly supreme.

The African American experience over the past twenty-five years, including my own, has been a particularly painful one — an experience rooted in a past of great ancestral beauty in Africa and the sorrow of slavery in America. It involves the realization that the few of us who have passed through a window of time and opportunity have often done so at great personal cost and with the neglect of our own inner spirits as human beings. For me, poet Paul Laurence Dunbar (1990) eloquently captures this state of being in "Sympathy":

> I know why the caged bird sings, ah me,
> When his wing is bruised and his bosom sore, —
> When he beats his bars and would be free;
> It is not a carol of joy or glee,
> But a prayer that he sends from his heart's deep core,
> But a plea, that upward to Heaven he flings —
> I know why the caged bird sings!
> (p. 45)

I also identify with the words Dunbar (1990) expresses in "We Wear the Masks":

> We wear the mask that grins and lies,
> It hides our cheeks and shades our eyes, —
> This debt we pay to human guile;
> With torn and bleeding hearts we smile,
> And mouth with myriad subtleties.

111

Why should the world be over-wise,
In counting all our tears and sighs?
Nay, let them only see us, while
We wear the mask.

We smile, but, O great Christ, our cries
To thee from tortured souls arise.
We sing, but oh the clay is vile
Beneath our feet, and long the mile;
But let the world dream otherwise,
We wear the mask.
(p. 251)

For me, the denial has ended. I can no longer tolerate the refusal of most European Americans to see that we African Americans are, independently of them, living, breathing, thinking human beings with a culture, a history, and an origin of our own. Our complaints are as real as those of our Japanese American brothers and sisters who have received recognition and restitution for their grievances. The genocide, the destruction of our will, the enslavement of our ancestors has been, for us, and I dare say for the rest of humanity, as vile as the Holocaust. I think we need to be heard and to be recognized, but not for revenge or restitution — there can be no restitution or revenge to equal the death and destruction of millions of African souls traversing the middle passage to the Americas in slave ships. We have no country but this one, no education but the one offered here, no language but English, no nationality but the one we have here.

Everything of Africa that we had including language was taken away from us. All we had left was our skin. So, I guess my ethnic background is the Black-American ethnic culture which has built itself on half-remembered scraps of things from Africa and been incorporated with the new American experience from the plantations. I am not African and I am not accepted as being American, yet. Have I no ethnicity? I think not. (Gandesbery, 1970, p. 10)

We must have full recognition and participation. We cannot be dismissed. And yet, we are. Many of the images, culture, values, and concerns reflected in every institution of this country, including the media, television, and schools tell us to "sit down, shut up, and accept what you have. It's not that bad. Be glad you have what you have. Things have changed." But what changes is a matter of who has the power. Change — when our children are not graduating from high school? Change — when young African American males are killed in the streets or ending up in prison? Feels like the past to me.

The persistent tendency to think of dark skin as unattractive, kinky hair as "bad" hair, and African features as less appealing than Caucasian features, come from this sense of inferiority. Our lack of respect for African American experts comes from this sense of inferiority. The disastrously high Black-on-Black homicide rate is in many ways indicative of fundamental disrespect for Black life growing out of this same sense of inferiority. It is a simple fact that people who love themselves seek to preserve their lives — not destroy them. (Akbar, 1991, p. 22)

My African American students are often afraid that they are unacceptable, stupid, or not capable of making it in school because of fears of inferiority, which have been reinforced by a racist society. These students are thus afraid to write, because nothing exposes voice more clearly than written pieces. Many of my other students, who are voluntary immigrants, express themselves differently; their fear motivates them to make high marks so that they can succeed in their new country, socially and economically.

Recently, one of my African American students asked me, in a rather defensive tone, how he was doing, and I told him, "Fine." "But I always fail English," he said, sounding depressed. This baffled me, since he is at the appropriate grade level for his age. We talked about it, and I discovered that what he really meant is that he *feels* like a failure. Since that time he has approached me several times with a self-denigrating attitude, and I have given him the affirmation he needs. He is doing well, and his attitude seems to be improving as he experiences that he is capable, and that he may be a better student than he thinks he is or than his past experiences have shown him to be. Students need to feel safe, free from ridicule and disrespect. They don't want to be rejected.

I like to use Maya Angelou's (1969) book, *I Know Why the Caged Bird Sings*, to explore the idea of voice. After extensive work in curriculum development with other ninth-grade teachers in Oakland, we chose this book as a core nonfiction work for ninth graders under the thematic umbrella, "The Individual and Society."[1] For me this is a good choice, because Angelou's life, which was fraught with difficulties — silence, loneliness, oppression, abuse — demonstrates victory over all of these and testifies to the power of courage, hope, love, and spiritual joy. It is a testament to the individual's victory over what could have been overwhelming odds. She represents a model of a person who regarded learning, reading, writing, and understanding as important, someone for whom education was the key to liberation. Students need to see this model.

When Angelou was eight years old, she was raped by her mother's lover. She was devastated — violated, silenced, and without voice in matters affecting her life. She subsequently entered a period of silence, and it wasn't until she met her first great teacher, Mrs. Flowers, that she found a reason to

---

[1] This theme, "The Individual and Society," was chosen by English teachers in our district because it would cover a broad range of literary materials, from Angelou's *I Know Why the Caged Bird Sings* to Shakespeare's *Romeo and Juliet* to Orwell's *Animal Farm*.

speak. She loved Mrs. Flowers, and she loved the poetry that Mrs. Flowers brought into her life.

The image of a teacher whom the student respects and loves so much that the student wants to communicate has had a profound effect upon me and my teaching. I learned to speak, to read, to want to communicate because I loved my teachers, beginning with my mother. It was this love that has led me into deeper understanding. I consider myself very ordinary. In fact, I think I am a slow learner, but the love of others has taught me to think and to love. It is out of deep gratitude to those teachers that I do the best I can with what I have been given. Therefore, *I Know Why the Caged Bird Sings* is a wonderful model of human accomplishment, victory, and identity for me, as well as for my students.

The problems associated with prejudice, difficult parental relationships, divorce, sexual relationships, pregnancy, abuse, and homelessness are also presented in Angelou's book, in a way that demonstrates how they can be overcome by education. This is good for my students, many of whom, regardless of race or culture, are beset by seemingly insurmountable problems in their own environments. Angelou's work shows that even tremendous problems can be conquered, that amazing things are possible, and that one can forgive the hurts of life, can acknowledge what is not good and choose to live life at the highest level, being good and true to oneself.

In the opening chapter of *I Know Why the Caged Bird Sings*, Angelou writes about a Sunday in church when, wearing a faded purple dress made from an old White woman's throwaway, she is ridiculed by the other children. Her fantasy is that these children will one day be sorry when they realize that she is really a little White girl with blonde hair, and they will then have to give her the respect she deserves:

> Wouldn't they be surprised when one day I woke out of my black ugly dream, and my real hair, which was long and blond, would take the place of the kinky mass that Momma wouldn't let me straighten? My light-blue eyes were going to hypnotize them after all the things they said about "my daddy must of been a chinaman" (I thought they meant made out of china, like a cup) because my eyes were so small and squinty. Then they would understand why I had never picked up a Southern accent, or spoke the common slang; and why I had to be forced to eat pigs' tails and snouts. Because I was really white and because a cruel fairy stepmother, who was understandably jealous of my beauty, had turned me into a too-big Negro girl, with nappy black hair, broad feet and a space between her teeth that would hold a number-two pencil. (Angelou, 1969, p. 2)

When I read the first chapter, including this passage, to my students, their reactions are mixed. The entire class begins to brainstorm as to the effects of Angelou's self-view on the eventual outcome of her life. Students participate by offering physical, mental, and emotional characteristics that they feel would be significant to Angelou's development as a person. I write their ideas on butcher paper, and then they group related ideas into categories. They look at how her attitude affects the successes or failures of her life — in other words, they make predictions. Since most of them know nothing about her, and those with any knowledge are unsure of themselves, they have little to go on besides the book's first chapter. In one class, a great deal of giggling was generated around her physical qualities: "She got nappy hair, and she's stanky," yelled out one young man.

This remark reminded me of what it was like growing up in Louisville, Kentucky, where I had "good" hair — not as good as White folks, but not as nappy as Black folks.[2] At least that was the case until Nanny, my father's mother, took a hot comb to it. But this article isn't really about Nanny and my problems. It's not even about hair texture and skin color. Those are merely metaphors for what is really going on in the internal world of many African Americans: the sense of self-contempt and self-hatred that many of us take in stride with a sense of humor, and which are reflected nowhere more clearly than in the classroom. The student who yelled out "she got nappy hair" was voicing the self-view that many African Americans have accepted consciously or, even more unfortunately, unconsciously:

> Even today there is an unnatural equation of Caucasian physical features with beauty, intelligence, authority, and so forth. A disproportionate number of professional, educated so-called "beautiful" African Americans have prominently Caucasian features. . . . "Good hair" and "nice features" are still thought to be those characteristics most like Caucasians. Contrary to popular belief, these attitudes have not changed substantially among African American youth who have grown up since the "Black Power" movement of the 1960's. (Akbar, 1991, p. 32)

For me, this hair consciousness began on my first day of school. The day began as if it were my birthday. My Mom had been preparing me for weeks, telling me how grown up I was, how special I was to begin first grade at five years old. That morning she woke me up saying, "How's my first grader? Come on big girl. Get up. Let's get a bath!" As I rubbed sleep out of my eyes, I was filled with nervousness, excitement, and a sense of my new-found maturity. I was the star of the day!

---

[2] Good hair is European hair or European American hair, the kind featured in most of the television shampoo commercials, and magazine advertisements. In fact, blonde hair might be considered the ultimate. After all, "blondes have more fun."

For most African Americans, this straight hair can only be approximated through the use of chemical relaxers or straighteners. Hair is a metaphor and a reality for the differences between Blacks and Whites. White people have beautiful hair. Black people have ugly hair. Many African American people believe this consciously and/or unconsciously.

No chemical can really make a Black person White. However, because of rape and miscegenation, some Blacks have come closer to European standards of beauty. Historically, for African Americans, hair texture and skin color reflect one's proximity to European Americans and their power. The straighter the hair, the lighter the skin, the better the person. African American literature and experience are full of examples of this problematic sense of values.

After Mama's breakfast of bacon, eggs, toast, orange juice, and milk, I dressed for my new adventure. I was proud to be going to first grade at five, since my birthday wasn't until November, and I had already begun reading by looking at newspapers, cutting out words, identifying them, and learning them with my Mom's help. My head was full of wonderful stories of princesses who turned frogs into princes with a kiss. Flowers fascinated me and brought me great joy. So, wearing a pretty white dress and a yellow rose from my mother's rose bush in my tightly braided shoulder-length hair, I set out for Virginia Avenue Elementary School. I was all the more joyous because it had also been my Mom's school. The principal had been her principal, and the teachers knew her. My excitement knew no limits. Besides going to school for the first time, I had my daddy beside me. I was always in love with him, because he was tall and beautiful. We walked up the street — me bursting with pride — all the way past Leonhardt's Grocery, through the Greenwood Cemetery shortcut, and on to Virginia Avenue and the school.

I don't remember my first-grade teacher. It seems that I should, and if someone told me her name, perhaps I would. My most vivid impression of my first school day — in fact of my first year of school — centers around a girl named Sherylanne. Sherylanne had really short hair in rubber bands and barrettes all over her head, and she was lighter than I in complexion. By now I was painfully aware from my neighborhood friends of being "yellow" or "high yellow" or "yellow belly," or sometimes "macaroni and cheese," a take-off on my last name, McElroy.

We hadn't been in the room half an hour before Sherylanne apparently had decided she couldn't stand me. All I remember is her coming up to me and smacking me, saying, "You think you cute you yellow thing, cause you got long hair." As she ripped the yellow rose out of my hair and stomped on it, all I could do was cry. Why did she attack me? I was mute, shocked, hurt. I didn't understand. Tears streamed down my face until Daddy came. When I asked him "Why?" he could only answer, "She's just jealous," and give me a pat on the head.

I don't remember my first-grade teacher intervening at all with Sherylanne and me. She was either unaware of what was going on, or she didn't care. And it didn't matter what color she was — we both needed her help.[3] Sherylanne needed someone to train her in how to treat other people. I needed someone to teach me how to stand up for myself. We needed help in understanding ourselves, to get in touch with our voices. Sherylanne and I needed to speak up about what was bothering us, needed to be given an inner voice of self-worth. Where was the teacher? A good teacher would have "seized the day," would have talked about "good" hair versus "bad" hair, dark skin versus light skin. My school was full of pictures of African Americans of all hues. A good teacher would have used those pictures and had us draw pictures to

---

[3] I attended segregated schools until high school, and all of my teachers were Black in elementary and junior high.

teach us about our heritage and to instill pride in us for who we were and where we came from — pride in our history. Instead, on that first day of school I waited in a state of distress, fear, and sadness for my Dad to pick me up.

A good teacher creates an environment in which the child grows and develops, replacing the environment of the child's home. A child leaves the safety of the home at five years old and is completely vulnerable, spending from four to six hours a day in a foreign environment. A good teacher tries to address the needs of the student, whatever those needs may be. A bad teacher resists those needs, blaming them on someone else at best, or ignoring them at worst. A good teacher succeeds in assisting students to handle their needs and become successful within the school system. A bad teacher fails to help her students adapt to the school environment, ignores the children, or is too self-involved, ignorant, or self-assertive to look at the individual, cultural, and human needs of the student.

I know now that Sherylanne's behavior was more than just jealousy. It was part of a predicament shared by many African Americans, one reflected in the attitudes of most of my students. I relate the story about Sherylanne not because of its personal significance to me, but to illustrate the need for teachers of children who come from an African American background to be vigilant in helping them understand that these kinds of attitudes reflect self-denial and self-hatred. Students, and young people in general, can be resilient and forgiving — often among my students, in the face of awesome odds. But resiliency does not negate the reality of how deeply African American people are affected by the forces of racism. No matter how strong people are, the power of these forces has an impact on the lives of all of African Americans, and ultimately all people. Through conscious development of personal/cultural and historical self-knowledge, a person can deal effectively with the limitations placed on them by our society.

In my classroom, as I have stated earlier, many students arrive with attitudes about themselves and their appearances that are often negative. I teach directly to these problems. Beginning with the first day of school, I tell my students that it doesn't matter to me what they look like, what color they are, what country they come from, how much money they have, what kind of hairdo they have, what kind of clothes, shoes, and jewelry they own. My only concern is what they have in their heads and in their hearts. I ask them three questions: How much do you know about the English language? How well do you think? Can you communicate your thoughts intelligently in speaking and in writing? These three questions are the basis of our relationships in the classroom.

I divide all of my classes into groups of four students each, which are mixed by race and gender. I tell the students that they must leave all that old racist/sexist baggage outside my door. If they want to, they can pick it up again when they leave the room, but I don't think most of them really want that excess baggage.

The word "educate" comes from the Latin *educare*, which means "to lead forth." By returning students to the source — to themselves and to their inner understandings of identity, culture, responsibility, and self-worth — it is possible to "lead them forth" to an expanded view of self and of others through an English curriculum designed to give them knowledge, skill, and competence to communicate intelligently. As a teacher, it is my job to guide them through the process of learning what they will need to know about themselves and others, through reading, writing, and communication, in order to live in a larger environment, no matter what it is. Knowledge gives them power, a voice in the development of their own lives. This kind of education gives them power to make positive lives for themselves and others.

Education involves taking personal experience, objectifying it, and relating it to universal themes that are important to all people. A teacher, for example, must be aware that all children need to be loved, affirmed, and appreciated, to be given guidance, direction, and instruction. Teachers have a captive audience and a great deal of time each day to impart important basic values to their students. But at the same time that we share universal characteristics, we are also different from one another. We all have our own ancestors, culture, religion, and history, and these differences must be recognized by the teacher. We must begin by leading our students back to the cause of their attitudes in order to move them forward to understand their experience and take charge of their lives.

As an English teacher, I am aware that adolescence is fraught with the drama of life. It is the time when young people make basic decisions about the kind of people they are going to hang out with and the kind of people they are going to be. It is a time of rebellion against parents, a time of first love, and a time for making big decisions and choices about future educational, professional, and employment goals. In today's schools, many of these adolescents have lost their way, have no knowledge of who they really are, and it's our job as teachers to educate them, to help them find their way. Perhaps their parents should have given them an African American consciousness, but many parents don't have it themselves. No one can blame the children or their parents for this failure. For four hundred years, African Americans have had their history, language, culture, and self-worth destroyed by the forces of slavery and segregation. It is no secret that African American people have long been seen as less than human by the forces of White supremacy. A teacher needs to have a consciousness and understanding of these conditions in order to teach African American students successfully. All teachers, not just African American teachers, have a responsibility to help these students discover who they are. I am talking about an African American rather than African consciousness. It is no more possible for people of African descent born in America to have an African consciousness than it is for them to have a Chinese or European consciousness. Most of us have never been to Africa, and while our roots are there, we live in America.

118

In my class examining Maya Angelou's *I Know Why the Caged Bird Sings* —
after the students have made a list of Angelou's characteristics and made
projections on her life — we discuss how they feel about the words they've
put on the board. This is both a pre-writing lesson and an inductive reasoning lesson, the object of which is both academic and cultural. Students use
the lists of words generated by the class to come up with categories of ideas,
such as prejudice, emotions, adult/child relationships, peer relationships,
and self-esteem. Then they make predictions based upon their reasoning,
and eventually they will write a speculative essay on the causes and effects of
prejudice.

The cultural objective of this lesson is to educate students about larger
concerns in the African American community: about the need for African
American people to build a strong sense of self-worth and to build understanding of the causes of the current predicament in order to survive in the
future. It also opens a way for students from various cultures to build their
own sense of identity: by looking at the struggle of others they also can learn
to understand them, and themselves.

But, before letting a class discuss what they've generated, I show the list
to another class and have them make observations about the attitudes of the
students who made the list. The list by one class of ninth-graders, which
included the words "stanky," "ashy," and "nappy hair," drew a great deal of
comment from two other classes. In a seventh-grade class, the students compared this "stanky" list to the list produced by another ninth-grade class.
They did not talk about words like "stanky" and "nappy" specifically, although they noted that those words were derogatory; however, they found
the second class's list to be more respectful and more mature. This prompted
me to take the "stanky" list to the more "mature" ninth-grade class in order
to get their reactions. They were incensed. Not only were they angry with
Angelou for writing about herself that way, but one Black male stated that
"she was very ignorant and ashamed of her color, and the person in your
other class is even more stupider. That what's wrong with Black people."

I shared the responses from the other classes with the ninth-grade class
that had originally generated the "stanky" list. The student who had yelled
out "stanky" was quite subdued, but he insisted it was the truth because of
what she had said about herself, which he said identified her lack of self-esteem. His statement, in defense of his previous remarks, illustrates his understanding of "self-hatred," as well as his acknowledgment of Angelou's
state of being. "I think it's really sad," remarked an Asian girl, a recent
immigrant from Hong Kong. "She is ashamed of who she is. She care what
White people say. It disgraces her. She need to know who she is, take pride
in herself. I think this [is the] result of slavery." Students agreed that a sense
of inferiority still affects Blacks in many ways, and they made a variety of
observations about Maya Angelou. African American students said things
like, "She don't know who she is," "She wanna be White," "She hates herself."
Akbar's words illustrate the underlying theme of these feelings:

So, dark skin became equated with the reason for slavery. The skin color of the slave became associated with other kinds of subhuman traits. On the other hand, the slave master's pale skin became equated with superhuman traits. In fact, God, all the Saints and the entire heavenly hosts, became identified with the pale skin. The logical conclusion of the abused, oppressed slave was that the basis for his condition was his skin color, and the way out of his condition was to change that color. (Akbar, 1991, p. 32)

When we were growing up, everyone was color-struck and caught up in hair-consciousness. We couldn't escape it. Sherylanne is a metaphor for all the beautiful Black girls who have suffered, because they are not White, at the hands of insensitive teachers. I don't think Sherylanne liked school very much. She was a pretty girl, with long eyelashes and beautiful skin. The boys loved her — and she was pregnant at the end of sixth grade. Now that I look back on it, she may have suffered more at the hands of insensitive teachers than I did. Some teachers, then and now, refuse to teach to the circumstances of students. Instead, they teach to a curriculum as if it were set in stone. Many don't know anything about the backgrounds or life circumstances of their students, and maintain a distance that borders on indifference. How does a twelve-year-old get pregnant without anyone observing it? What kind of interest was expressed towards this girl? I am not saying that the teacher was responsible for Sherylanne's pregnancy, but I am saying that the teacher might have contributed to the girl's lack of knowledge about other possibilities for her life.

But, I did have teachers who transcended such insensitivity. Helen King, my fourth-grade teacher, helped all of her students do their best. She cared about all aspects of our beings, our personal values, and our futures. Mrs. King was somebody too, a strong, successful woman, a Creole from New Orleans with brilliant green eyes that shone with love and affection; but, she could snap a person in two if needed. She had sung with the New York City Opera, so our quiet times were full of arias from "Madama Butterfly," "La Traviata," "La Boheme," "I Pagliacci," "Suor Angelica," "Louise," "Meditation de Thais," and so on. Mrs. King never began a day without singing and playing on the piano James Weldon Johnson's "Lift Every Voice and Sing." We had his picture in the classroom. We also had Sojourner Truth, Harriet Tubman, Madame C. J. Walker, Paul Laurence Dunbar, Countee Cullen, Frederick Douglas, W.E.B. DuBois, Carter G. Woodson, Langston Hughes, Mahalia Jackson, and Marian Anderson staring at us daily from their pictures on the wall. Mrs. King helped us have some self-respect. She encouraged my love for music and expanded my horizons. When she asked us to listen, we listened. She loved us.

Another special teacher was Mrs. McQuinney, who had also been my mother's sixth-grade teacher. My mother, like many other African American parents, believed strongly in the rule, "Spare the rod, spoil the child." When she would spank or whip me, she would usually do it with a belt. I know some people look aghast at such punishment, but my people learned these practices as a part of their history. Slaves were beaten with whips and chains, so a belt was nothing. Anyway, Mama would always cry when she whipped me, so there would be the two of us crying together. My skin was fair enough that all marks showed easily, and my legs would welt up. We had to wear dresses to school, and I went to Mrs. McQuinney's class not thinking about the marks. But she called me to her desk one day during play time while the other kids were busy and asked, "Beverly, what on earth happened to your legs?"

"I got a whippin," I answered.

"Well, I'll have to talk to your Mama about that," she replied.

I didn't have any anxiety about her talking to my Mom, because I knew Mama respected her, and I figured I could use the assistance if it would keep me from getting any further such punishment.

That evening, while I was washing dishes and getting ready to do my homework at the kitchen table, the phone rang in the back of the house. I started my homework and was pretty involved in it when my Mom came in with big tears in her eyes. She told me Mrs. McQuinney phoned and gave her a good talking to. Mama said, "You're too old for whipping, and I'm not going to do it again, but don't think you're going to just do any old thing. You're a McElroy and there's certain things you do and certain things you don't do." I was greatly relieved. After that I received different kinds of lessons in cause and effect, but whipping was eliminated. Obviously, Mrs. McQuinney remained one of my favorite teachers.

Home training and school training must work together to create a sense of interrelatedness, a sense of community. Parents do the best they can in most instances. I was the eldest child and my mother was young. She was anxious for me to get an education to improve my life circumstances, and she was very strict. My mother's training of obedience, academic achievement, and self-respect was reinforced by Mrs. McQuinney, but she also helped my mother see that whipping was unnecessary; she was training my Mom as well. In this sense, training is education.

When teachers care about students, they view them within a whole context. They make contact with parents and assist them in helping the child develop a sense of pride and self-respect. By calling my mother, Mrs. McQuinney showed that she cared about both of us. By extending herself personally to my Mom, Mrs. McQuinney helped a young parent deal with the frustrations of raising a strong-willed, highly verbal child, which also helped my Mom assess some of her long-held beliefs about child rearing. These two women were connected in their concern for my well-being and for their own. They were connected, interrelated. School and home were part of one system, sharing a common interest and concern — the students.

My elementary school was a beautiful place to me. The teachers represented all the hues and shades of African Americans and were highly skilled educators. The school walls were covered with pictures of famous African

Americans. My best teachers reinforced the images that I saw on the walls. They taught me my history as a Black person living in North America. They taught me to look at the beauty of my people through reading our poetry and singing our songs. I grew to appreciate the courage, strength of character, and love that African Americans had developed and demonstrated, not only during slavery, but during our constant oppression in this country. They addressed the question of purposes. They showed me that life has meaning and that learning, knowledge, enlightenment can and must be passed on from one generation to the next. They encouraged me to dream about what I could give back to my parents, to my people, to my community. Anything I thought I could do, including singing, writing, even becoming a teacher, they supported with the affirmation that it would be possible if I were willing to put in the effort. I loved them, and I wanted to be like them.

While I don't remember my first-grade teacher, I remember Mrs. King and Mrs. McQuinney vividly. These two teachers, in particular, taught me to have a sense of pride and courage. They also gave me a sense of past reality and future possibility. They helped me answer questions like "Who am I?" "Why am I here?" and "What am I supposed to do?" They gave me a voice.

> Teaching is a complex and demanding profession, more complex than medicine, according to one scholar who has studied both professions. Thus, career-long opportunities for growth, renewal, and access to new information are essential. (Anderson, 1985, p. 102)

My own goal in teaching is not just to create literate, accomplished student writers who make it in the world. Although those are important goals, they are not big enough for the world in which we live today. Our students come to us with a great deal of confusion, from many different backgrounds, cultures, races, and socioeconomic situations. They are confused and frightened, and often can't express their own opinions. Many express opinions that have little personal or practical meaning for them, opinions that have been instilled in them by adults (parents, teachers, television and radio personalities, and writers). They need assistance in defining their own values and identity. They need to understand the role of the individual and of society. They need and want direction. Teachers need to understand the cultural differences of their students, especially minority students. In particular, they need to understand the background of the resistance many African American children display in relation to school and learning, as explained by Ogbu:

> In their folk theory of "making it," involuntary minorities wish they could advance through education and ability as white Americans do, but know they cannot. They come to realize that it requires more education and effort to overcome the barriers set up against them. . . . The public schools for example cannot be relied upon to provide minority children with the "right education." Involuntary minorities find no justification for the preju-

122

dice and discrimination they find in school and society, which appears to be institutionalized and enduring. . . . Involuntary minorities perceive their cultural frames of reference not merely as different from but as opposed to the cultural frames of reference of their white "oppressors". The cultural and language differences emerging under these conditions serve as boundary making mechanisms. Involuntary minorities do not interpret language and cultural differences encountered in school or society as barriers to overcome; they interpret such differences as symbols of their identity. Their culture provides a frame of reference that gives them a sense of collective or social identity, a sense of self-worth. (Ogbu, 1990, pp. 153–154)

As I began this article, I pointed out that I am greatly concerned about the number of African American students who are falling into chasms of failure in our current educational system, while teachers argue over rules of pedagogy. These students need a voice to express themselves in creative, productive ways. They need a sense of history, models of successful human beings from their race and others, and ways of dealing with pent-up emotions resulting from living in a society that has not valued them. Teachers who refuse to deal with this issue are leaving these students voiceless. As opposed to majority White students, who already have these things in place, African American students need structure, clarity, and a disciplined environment. They need challenges, and teachers must maintain high standards and expectations for them. Again, Ogbu explains:

Minority children receive inferior education also through what occurs inside the schools, inside the individual classrooms. Among the mechanisms discovered to affect minority education adversely, none is more important than teachers' low expectations. So, also, too many minority children are treated as having educational "handicaps." A disproportionate number are channeled into "special education," a pseudonym for inferior education. Problems that arise from cultural and language differences are inadequately attended to. The failure of school personnel to understand the cultural behaviors of minority children often results in conflicts that affect the children's capacity to adjust and learn. While minority children have an obligation to understand and relate to the culture and language of the schools, this is a two-way thoroughfare. (Ogbu, 1990, p. 156)

In "The Silenced Dialogue: Power and Pedagogy in Educating Other People's Children," Lisa Delpit states:

The Black child may perceive the middle-class teacher as weak, ineffectual, and incapable of taking on the role of being the teacher; therefore, there is no need to follow her directives. In her dissertation, Michelle Foster (1987) quotes one young Black man describing such a teacher. "She is boring, boring. She could do something creative. Instead she just stands there. She can't control the class. She asked me what she was doing wrong. I told her she could be meditating for all I know. She says that we're supposed to know what to do. I told her I don't know nothin unless she tells me. She just can't control the class. I hope we don't have her next semester." (Michelle Foster quoted in Delpit, 1988, p. 290)

What is obvious to me in this discussion between the teacher and the student is that the teacher thinks that the student has the problem. She thinks the students should "know what to do." My belief is that if they knew what to do, students wouldn't need teachers. By contrast, when a teacher takes charge and addresses the real needs of her or his students, the response from them is very different:

A young Black man is discussing a former teacher with a group of friends: "We had fun in her class, but she is mean. I can remember she used to say, 'Tell me what's in the story, Wayne.' She pushed, she used to get on me and push me to know. She made us learn. We had to get in the books. There was this tall guy and he tried to take her on, but she was in charge of that class and she didn't let anyone rule her. I still have the book we used in her class. It's a bunch of stories in it. I just read one on Coca-Cola again the other day." (Michelle Foster quoted in Delpit, 1988, p. 209)

In order for students to develop their voice, the teacher's voice must be clear, distinct, and above board. Students shouldn't be expected to second-guess a teacher's instruction or motivation; they needn't be clairvoyant. Black students need the security of knowing that someone is in charge. I'd venture to say that many students, including second-language students, need to hear a teacher's strong voice in order to feel secure in developing their own voices.

My experience has shown me that students think a teacher does not care about the students if he or she does not control the class. Many of my students need a teacher who establishes him- or herself as a person who "won't take no mess." They expect the teacher to establish an environment where profanity, name calling, and violence are not allowed. To my students, the classroom environment is as important as the material we study. My students also want me to "know my stuff," to give them the reasons why they must study the material I'm teaching. They want to know how their studies are going to contribute to their lives. They want a teacher who knows something about their different cultures, histories, and backgrounds. They want a teacher who can relate to and is respectful of their parents. They want a relationship with the teacher as real human beings. Whenever I hear students say a teacher "ain't teachin notin," I know that they feel ignored, undisciplined, and unaccepted.

Recently, I ran into a former student at a yogurt shop. The young woman was distraught about her new English class in a suburban school near Berkeley, California. She said that there were only two other African American students in her tenth-grade, Advanced Placement English class of thirty-five students. She went on to tell me:

We're studying MacBeth and I hate it. Whenever I ask that teacher to explain something, she says I should change my class, because it's obviously too hard for me. All she does is throw us into these groups where the White kids basically ignore us, and we're supposed to come up with the answers but we're scared of each other. She never deals with any of the things that go on in those groups. We work in those stupid groups while she works at her desk. When we did Romeo and Juliet with you, it came alive. That's because you related it to our lives, to what's happening around us. Not her. She treats us like we're stupid and don't belong there. She's the one who's dumb.

Needless to say, I spent a good deal of time while eating my frozen yogurt trying to convince my former student to stick in there with the teacher and Macbeth, but I must admit it really troubled me. The teacher is White, and although I am not saying that this alone is the problem (there are also Black teachers who are disconnected from their students), several aspects of what the student told me made me feel that the teacher's race contributed to the problem. She treated the student in a way that made her feel as if she were "stupid and didn't belong in an advanced placement class" without considering how the student must feel being an African American in a predominantly White environment. She asked the student on her first day of class, "Are you sure you're in the right class?" She would not answer the student or give her assistance when she asked for help. The student's perception was that the teacher did not like her and did not want to help her because she is African American.

I don't know what the teacher's perceptions are. I do know from working with European American teachers that they often find African American students more difficult to teach: the teachers don't want to be authoritarian and yet they often believe that "Black kids seem to like that." However, my feeling is that students want an authorita*tive* not authorita*rian* teacher, a sensitive, helpful, and knowledgeable person who provides a disciplined, supportive environment for student learning. I don't think that's too much to ask.

At the end of my classes' study of *I Know Why the Caged Bird Sings*, after difficult writing assignments exploring a variety of ideas brought up in the book, one of my students wrote me this note:

Dear Ms. Johnson,

You are a meaningful teacher to me in Westlake. Although I didn't have your class till the last semester, I really learned a lot from your class. I learned how to develope [sic] my own thoughts in writing and how to write a good essay. Even though I didn't do a good job in your class but at least I tried my best! I will remember and miss you all my life!!! Forget me not.

Love always,

Joann Chou 6-10-91

Joann was a lot harder on herself than I ever was. She earned good marks consistently. What strikes me most about her is not that she feels that she didn't do a good job in my class, but that she knows she did her best. To me this says that Joann has high standards that she may or may not reach. However, the underlying message she carries is one of triumph: "I did my best."

I share this not because I feel good about it (although of course I do!), but to emphasize the important role a teacher has in helping students develop voice. When we help a young person find a little bit of who he or she is, then we are successfully doing our jobs. When we ignore the issues facing our students, we contribute to their failures. There were many reasons for Sherylanne's problems; no teacher could accept responsibility for all of them. But, a teacher must be vigilant in order to help students think more clearly about their situations and not contribute to negative outcomes. I don't know if any teacher tried to help Sherylanne get beyond the fixation on hair and color, or whether she ever developed a sense of pride in herself and her race. I don't know if she was able at some point to give rise to her voice and speak out about her problems. I only know that the experience Sherylanne and I had in the first grade represents the teacher's failure to exert her power in a positive and constructive way — a way that would have helped us, and all her students. While the unfortunate Sherylanne dropped out of school, I graduated second in my class in high school, graduated from college, went on to graduate school, and held several positions before returning to teaching. When I graduated from high school, some said I did well because I was "high yellow" and had "good hair." I like to believe, however, that I succeeded because of my talent and hard work — like Joann Chou, I did my best. But more importantly, I owe my success to the brave, wonderful, creative teachers who gave me a sense of who I am, and a voice with which to say it.

References

Akbar, N. (1991). *Chains and images of psychological slavery.* Jersey City, NJ: New Mind Productions.

Angelou, M. (1969). *I know why the caged bird sings.* New York: Bantam/Random House.

Anderson, R. (1985). *Becoming a nation of readers: The report of the Commission on Reading.* Washington, DC: National Institute of Education.

Delpit, L. (1988). The silenced dialogue. *Harvard Educational Review, 58,* 280–298.

Dunbar, P. L. (1990). "Sympathy" and "We wear the mask." In *African American literature* (an anthology). Austin, TX: Holt, Rinehart & Winston.

Gandesbery, J. (1970). Denying origins. *The Quarterly of the National Writing Project and the Center for the Study of Writing, 13*(2), 10–12, 20.

Ogbu, J. U. (1990). Minority status and literacy in comparative perspective. *Daedalus, 119*(2), 141–167.

The Silenced Dialogue:
Power and Pedagogy in Educating
Other People's Children

■ ■ ■

LISA D. DELPIT

A Black male graduate student who is also a special education teacher in
a predominantly Black community is talking about his experiences in
predominantly White university classes:

> There comes a moment in every class where we have to discuss "The Black
> Issue" and what's appropriate education for Black children. I tell you, I'm
> tired of arguing with those White people, because they won't listen. Well,
> I don't know if they really don't listen or if they just don't believe you. It
> seems like if you can't quote Vygotsky or something, then you don't have
> any validity to speak about your *own* kids. Anyway, I'm not bothering with
> it anymore, now I'm just in it for a grade.

A Black woman teacher in a multicultural urban elementary school is
talking about her experiences in discussions with her predominantly White
fellow teachers about how they should organize reading instructions to best
serve students of color:

> When you're talking to White people they still want it to be their way. You
> can try to talk to them and give them examples, but they're so headstrong,
> they think they know what's best for *everybody*, for *everybody's* children. They
> won't listen, White folks are going to do what they want to do *anyway*.
>   It's really hard. They just don't listen well. No, they listen, but they don't
> *hear* — you know how your mama used to say you listen to the radio, but
> you *hear* your mother? Well they don't *hear* me.
>   So I just try to shut them out so I can hold my temper. You can only
> beat your head against a brick wall for so long before you draw blood. If I
> try to stop arguing with them I can't help myself from getting angry. Then

Harvard Educational Review Vol. 58 No. 3 August 1988, 280–298

I end up walking around praying all day "Please Lord, remove the bile I feel for these people so I can sleep tonight." It's funny, but it can become a cancer, a sore.

So, I shut them out. I go back to my own little cubby, my classroom, and I try to teach the way I know will work, no matter what those folk say. And when I get Black kids, I just try to undo the damage they did.

I'm not going to let any man, woman, or child drive me crazy — White folks will try to do that to you if you let them. You just have to stop talking to them, that's what I do. I just keep smiling, but I won't talk to them.

A soft-spoken Native Alaskan woman in her forties is a student in the Education Department of the University of Alaska. One day she storms into a Black professor's office and very uncharacteristically slams the door. She plops down in a chair and, still fuming, says, "Please tell people, just don't help us anymore! I give up. I won't talk to them again!"

And finally, a Black woman principal who is also a doctoral student at a well-known university on the West Coast is talking about her university experiences, particularly about when a professor lectures on issues concerning educating Black children:

If you try to suggest that that's not quite the way it is, they get defensive, then you get defensive, then they'll start reciting research.

I try to give them my experiences, to explain. They just look and nod. The more I try to explain, they just look and nod, just keep looking and nodding. They don't really hear me.

Then, when it's time for class to be over, the professor tells me to come to his office to talk more. So I go. He asks for more examples of what I'm talking about, and he looks and nods while I give them. Then he says that that's just my experiences. It doesn't really apply to most Black people.

It becomes futile because they think they know everything about everybody. What you have to say about your life, your children, doesn't mean anything. They don't really want to hear what you have to say. They wear blinders and earplugs. They only want to go on research they've read that other White people have written.

It just doesn't make any sense to keep talking to them.

Thus was the first half of the title of this text born — "The Silenced Dialogue." One of the tragedies in the field of education is that scenarios such as these are enacted daily around the country. The saddest element is that the individuals that the Black and Native American educators speak of in these statements are seldom aware that the dialogue *has* been silenced. Most likely the White educators believe that their colleagues of color did, in the end, agree with their logic. After all, they stopped disagreeing, didn't they?

I have collected these statements since completing a recently published article (Delpit, 1986). In this somewhat autobiographical account, entitled

"Skills and Other Dilemmas of a Progressive Black Educator," I discussed my perspective as a product of a skills-oriented approach to writing and as a teacher of process-oriented approaches. I described the estrangement that I and many teachers of color feel from the progressive movement when writing-process advocates dismiss us as too "skills oriented." I ended the article suggesting that it was incumbent upon writing-process advocates — or indeed, advocates of any progressive movement — to enter into dialogue with teachers of color, who may not share their enthusiasm about so-called new, liberal, or progressive ideas.

In response to this article, which presented no research data and did not even cite a reference, I received numerous calls and letters from teachers, professors, and even state school personnel from around the country, both Black and White. All of the White respondents, except one, have wished to talk more about the question of skills versus process approaches — to support or reject what they perceive to be my position. On the other hand, *all* of the non-White respondents have spoken passionately on being left out of the dialogue about how best to educate children of color.

How can such complete communication blocks exist when both parties truly believe they have the same aims? How can the bitterness and resentment expressed by the educators of color be drained so that the sores can heal? What can be done?

I believe the answer to these questions lies in ethnographic analysis, that is, in identifying and giving voice to alternative world views. Thus, I will attempt to address the concerns raised by White and Black respondents to my article "Skills and Other Dilemmas" (Delpit, 1986). My charge here is not to determine the best instructional methodology; I believe that the actual practice of good teachers of all colors typically incorporates a range of pedagogical orientations. Rather, I suggest that the differing perspectives on the debate over "skills" versus "process" approaches can lead to an understanding of the alienation and miscommunication, and thereby to an understanding of the "silenced dialogue."

In thinking through these issues, I have found what I believe to be a connecting and complex theme: what I have come to call "the culture of power." There are five aspects of power I would like to propose as given for this presentation:

1. Issues of power are enacted in classrooms.

2. There are codes or rules for participating in power; that is, there is a "culture of power."

3. The rules of the culture of power are a reflection of the rules of the culture of those who have power.

4. If you are not already a participant in the culture of power, being told explicitly the rules of that culture makes acquiring power easier.

5. Those with power are frequently least aware of — or least willing to acknowledge — its existence. Those with less power are often most aware of its existence.

The first three are by now basic tenets in the literature of the sociology of education, but the last two have seldom been addressed. The following discussion will explicate these aspects of power and their relevance to the schism between liberal educational movements and that of non-White, non-middle-class teachers and communities.[1]

1. Issues of power are enacted in classrooms.

These issues include: the power of the teacher over the students; the power of the publishers of textbooks and of the developers of the curriculum to determine the view of the world presented; the power of the state in enforcing compulsory schooling; and the power of an individual or group to determine another's intelligence or "normalcy." Finally, if schooling prepares people for jobs, and the kind of job a person has determines her or his economic status and, therefore, power, then schooling is intimately related to that power.

2. There are codes or rules for participating in power; that is, there is a "culture of power."

The codes or rules I'm speaking of relate to linguistic forms, communicative strategies, and presentation of self; that is, ways of talking, ways of writing, ways of dressing, and ways of interacting.

3. The rules of the culture of power are a reflection of the rules of the culture of those who have power.

This means that success in institutions — schools, workplaces, and so on — is predicated upon acquisition of the culture of those who are in power. Children from middle-class homes tend to do better in school than those from non-middle-class homes because the culture of the school is based on the culture of the upper and middle classes — of those in power. The upper and middle classes send their children to school with all the accoutrements of the culture of power; children from other kinds of families operate within perfectly wonderful and viable cultures but not cultures that carry the codes or rules of power.

4. If you are not already a participant in the culture of power, being told explicitly the rules of that culture makes acquiring power easier.

In my work within and between diverse cultures, I have come to conclude that members of any culture transmit information implicitly to co-members.

---

[1] Such a discussion, limited as it is by space constraints, must treat the intersection of class and race somewhat simplistically. For the sake of clarity, however, let me define a few terms: "Black" is used herein to refer to those who share some or all aspects of "core black culture"

However, when implicit codes are attempted across cultures, communication frequently breaks down. Each cultural group is left saying, "Why don't those people say what they mean?" as well as, "What's wrong with them, why don't they understand?"

Anyone who has had to enter new cultures, especially to accomplish a specific task, will know of what I speak. When I lived in several Papua New Guinea villages for extended periods to collect data, and when I go to Alaskan villages for work with Alaskan Native communities, I have found it unquestionably easier — psychologically and pragmatically — when some kind soul has directly informed me about such matters as appropriate dress, interactional styles, embedded meanings, and taboo words or actions. I contend that it is much the same for anyone seeking to learn the rules of the culture of power. Unless one has the leisure of a lifetime of "immersion" to learn them, explicit presentation makes learning immeasurably easier.

And now, to the fifth and last premise:

5. Those with power are frequently least aware of — or least willing to acknowledge — its existence. Those with less power are often most aware of its existence.

For many who consider themselves members of liberal or radical camps, acknowledging personal power and admitting participation in the culture of power is distinctly uncomfortable. On the other hand, those who are less powerful in any situation are most likely to recognize the power variable most acutely. My guess is that the White colleagues and instructors of those previously quoted did not perceive themselves to have power over the non-White speakers. However, either by virtue of their position, their numbers, or their access to that particular code of power of calling upon research to validate one's position, the White educators had the authority to establish what was to be considered "truth" regardless of the opinions of the people of color, and the latter were well aware of that fact.

A related phenomenon is that liberals (and here I am using the term "liberal" to refer to those whose beliefs include striving for a society based upon maximum individual freedom and autonomy) seem to act under the assumption that to make any rules or expectations explicit is to act against liberal principles, to limit the freedom and autonomy of those subjected to the explicitness.

I thank Fred Erickson for a comment that led me to look again at a tape by John Gumperz[2] on cultural dissonance in cross-cultural interactions. One

---

(Gwaltney, 1980, p. xxiii), that is, the mainstream of Black America — neither those who have entered the ranks of the bourgeoisie nor those who are participants in the disenfranchised underworld. "Middle-class" is used broadly to refer to the predominantly. White American "mainstream." There are, of course, non-White people who also fit into this category; at issue is their cultural identification, not necessarily the color of their skin. (I must add that there are other non-White people, as well as poor White people, who have indicated to me that their perspectives are similar to those attributed herein to Black people.)

[2] *Multicultural Britain: "Crosstalk,"* National Centre of Industrial Language Training, Commission for Racial Equality, London, England, John Twitchin, Producer.

of the episodes showed an East Indian interviewing for a job with an all-White committee. The interview was a complete failure, even though several of the interviewers appeared to really want to help the applicant. As the interview rolled steadily downhill, these "helpers" became more and more indirect in their questioning, which exacerbated the problems the applicant had in performing appropriately. Operating from a different cultural perspective, he got fewer and fewer clear clues as to what was expected of him, which ultimately resulted in his failure to secure the position.

I contend that as the applicant showed less and less aptitude for handling the interview, the power differential became ever more evident to the interviewers. The "helpful" interviewers, unwilling to acknowledge themselves as having power over the applicant, became more and more uncomfortable. Their indirectness was an attempt to lessen the power differential and their discomfort by lessening the power-revealing explicitness of their questions and comments.

When acknowledging and expressing power, one tends toward explicitness (as in yelling to your ten-year-old, "Turn that radio down!"). When de-emphasizing power, there is a move toward indirect communication. Therefore, in the interview setting, those who sought to help, to express their egalitarianism with the East Indian applicant, became more and more indirect — and less and less helpful — in their questions and comments.

In literacy instruction, explicitness might be equated with direct instruction. Perhaps the ultimate expression of explicitness and direct instruction in the primary classroom is Distar. This reading program is based on a behaviorist model in which reading is taught through the direct instruction of phonics generalizations and blending. The teacher's role is to maintain the full attention of the group by continuous questioning, eye contact, finger snaps, hand claps, and other gestures, and by eliciting choral responses and initiating some sort of award system.

When the program was introduced, it arrived with a flurry of research data that "proved" that all children — even those who were "culturally deprived" — could learn to read using this method. Soon there was a strong response, first from academics and later from many classroom teachers, stating that the program was terrible. What I find particularly interesting, however, is that the primary issue of the conflict over Distar has not been over its instructional efficacy — usually the students did learn to read — but the expression of explicit power in the classroom. The liberal educators opposed the methods — the direct instruction, the explicit control exhibited by the teacher. As a matter of fact, it was not unusual (even now) to hear of the program spoken of as "fascist."

I am not an advocate of Distar, but I will return to some of the issues that the program — and direct instruction in general — raises in understanding the differences between progressive White educators and educators of color.

To explore those differences, I would like to present several statements typical of those made with the best of intentions by middle-class liberal educators. To the surprise of the speakers, it is not unusual for such content to be met by vocal opposition or stony silence from people of color. My attempt here is to examine the underlying assumptions of both camps.

"I want the same thing for everyone else's children as I want for mine."

To provide schooling for everyone's children that reflects liberal, middle-class values and aspirations is to ensure the maintenance of the status quo, to ensure that power, the culture of power, remains in the hands of those who already have it. Some children come to school with more accoutrements of the culture of power already in place — "cultural capital," as some critical theorists refer to it (for example, Apple, 1979) — some with less. Many liberal educators hold that the primary goal for education is for children to become autonomous, to develop fully who they are in the classroom setting without having arbitrary, outside standards forced upon them. This is a very reasonable goal for people whose children are already participants in the culture of power and who have already internalized its codes.

But parents who don't function within that culture often want something else. It's not that they disagree with the former aim, it's just that they want something more. They want to ensure that the school provides their children with discourse patterns, interactional styles, and spoken and written language codes that will allow them success in the larger society.

It was the lack of attention to this concern that created such a negative outcry in the Black community when well-intentioned White liberal educators introduced "dialect readers." These were seen as a plot to prevent the schools from teaching the linguistic aspects of the culture of power, thus dooming Black children to a permanent outsider caste. As one parent demanded, "My kids know how to be Black — you all teach them how to be successful in the White man's world."

Several Black teachers have said to me recently that as much as they'd like to believe otherwise, they cannot help but conclude that many of the "progressive" educational strategies imposed by liberals upon Black and poor children could only be based on a desire to ensure that the liberals' children get sole access to the dwindling pool of American jobs. Some have added that the liberal educators believe themselves to be operating with good intentions, but that these good intentions are only conscious delusions about their unconscious true motives. One of Black anthropologist John Gwaltney's (1980) informants reflects this perspective with her tongue-in-cheek observation that the biggest difference between Black folks and White folks is that Black folks *know* when they're lying!

Let me try to clarify how this might work in literacy instruction. A few years ago I worked on an analysis of two popular reading programs, Distar and a progressive program that focused on higher-level critical thinking skills. In one of the first lessons of the progressive program, the children are introduced to the names of the letter *m* and *e*. In the same lesson they are then taught the sound made by each of the letters, how to write each of the letters, and that when the two are blended together they produce the word *me*.

As an experienced first-grade teacher, I am convinced that a child needs to be familiar with a significant number of these concepts to be able to assimilate so much new knowledge in one sitting. By contrast, Distar presents the same information in about forty lessons.

I would not argue for the pace of the Distar lessons; such a slow pace would only bore most kids — but what happened in the other lesson is that it merely provided an opportunity for those who already knew the content to exhibit that they knew it, or at most perhaps to build one new concept onto what was already known. This meant that the child who did not come to school already primed with what was to be presented would be labeled as needing "remedial" instruction from day one; indeed, this determination would be made before he or she was ever taught. In fact, Distar was "successful" because it actually *taught* new information to children who had not already acquired it at home. Although the more progressive system was ideal for some children, for others it was a disaster.

I do not advocate a simplistic "basic skills" approach for children outside of the culture of power. It would be (and has been) tragic to operate as if these children were incapable of critical and higher-order thinking and reasoning. Rather, I suggest that schools must provide these children the content that other families from a different cultural orientation provide at home. This does not mean separating children according to family background, but instead, ensuring that each classroom incorporate strategies appropriate for all the children in its confines.

And I do not advocate that it is the school's job to attempt to change the homes of poor and non-White children to match the homes of those in the culture of power. That may indeed be a form of cultural genocide. I have frequently heard schools call poor parents "uncaring" when parents respond to the school's urging, that they change their home life in order to facilitate their children's learning, by saying, "But that's the school's job." What the school personnel fail to understand is that if the parents were members of the culture of power and lived by its rules and codes, then they would transmit those codes to their children. In fact, they transmit another culture that children must learn at home in order to survive in their communities.

"Child-centered, whole language, and process approaches are needed in order to allow a democratic state of free, autonomous, empowered adults, and because research has shown that children learn best through these methods."

People of color are, in general, skeptical of research as a determiner of our fates. Academic research has, after all, found us genetically inferior, culturally deprived, and verbally deficient. But beyond that general caveat, and despite my or others' personal preferences, there is little research data supporting the major tenets of process approaches over other forms of literacy

instruction, and virtually no evidence that such approaches are more effica-
cious for children of color (Siddle, 1986).

Although the problem is not necessarily inherent in the method, in some
instances adherents of process approaches to writing create situations in
which students ultimately find themselves held accountable for knowing a
set of rules about which no one has ever directly informed them. Teachers
do students no service to suggest, even implicitly, that "product" is not important. In this country, students will be judged on their product regardless
of the process they utilized to achieve it. And that product, based as it is on
the specific codes of a particular culture, is more readily produced when the
directives of how to produce it are made explicit.

If such explicitness is not provided to students, what it feels like to people
who are old enough to judge is that there are secrets being kept, that time
is being wasted, that the teacher is abdicating his or her duty to teach. A
doctoral student in my acquaintance was assigned to a writing class to hone
his writing skills. The student was placed in the section led by a White professor who utilized a process approach, consisting primarily of having the
students write essays and then assemble into groups to edit each others'
papers. That procedure infuriated this particular student. He had many angry encounters with the teacher about what she was doing. In his words:

> I didn't feel she was teaching us anything. She wanted us to correct each
> others' papers and we were there to learn from her. She didn't teach any-
> thing, absolutely nothing.
>
> Maybe they're trying to learn what Black folks knew all the time. We
> understand how to improvise, how to express ourselves creatively. When
> I'm in a classroom, I'm not looking for that, I'm looking for structure, the
> more formal language.
>
> Now my buddy was in [a] Black teacher's class. And that lady was very
> good. She went through and explained and defined each part of the struc-
> ture. This [White] teacher didn't get along with that Black teacher. She
> said that she didn't agree with her methods. But *I* don't think that White
> teacher *had* any methods.

When I told this gentleman that what the teacher was doing was called a
process method of teaching writing, his response was, "Well, at least now I
know that she *thought* she was doing *something*. I thought she was just a fool
who couldn't teach and didn't want to try."

This sense of being cheated can be so strong that the student may be
completely turned off to the educational system. Amanda Branscombe, an
accomplished White teacher, recently wrote a letter discussing her work with
working-class Black and White students at a community college in Alabama.
She had given these students my "Skills and Other Dilemmas" article (Delpit,
1986) to read and discuss, and wrote that her students really understood and
identified with what I was saying. To quote her letter:

One young man said that he had dropped out of high school because he failed the exit exam. He noted that he had then passed the GED without a problem after three weeks of prep. He said that his high school English teacher claimed to use a process approach, but what she really did was hide behind fancy words to give herself permission to do nothing in the classroom.

The students I have spoken of seem to be saying that the teacher has denied them access to herself as the source of knowledge necessary to learn the forms they need to succeed. Again, I tentatively attribute the problem to teachers' resistance to exhibiting power in the classroom. Somehow, to exhibit one's personal power as expert source is viewed as disempowering one's students.

Two qualifiers are necessary, however. The teacher cannot be the only expert in the classroom. To deny students their own expert knowledge *is* to disempower them. Amanda Branscombe, when she was working with Black high school students classified as "slow learners," had the students analyze RAP songs to discover their underlying patterns. The students became the experts in explaining to the teacher the rules for creating a new RAP song. The teacher then used the patterns the students identified as a base to begin an explanation of the structure of grammar, and then of Shakespeare's plays. Both student and teacher are expert at what they know best.

The second qualifier is that merely adopting direct instruction is not the answer. Actual writing for real audiences and real purposes is a vital element in helping students to understand that they have an important voice in their own learning processes. Siddle (1988) examines the results of various kinds of interventions in a primarily process-oriented writing class for Black students. Based on readers' blind assessments, she found that the intervention that produced the most positive changes in the students' writing was a "mini-lesson" consisting of direct instruction about some standard writing convention. But what produced the *second* highest number of positive changes was a subsequent student-centered conference with the teacher. (Peer conferencing in this group of Black students who were not members of the culture of power produced the least number of changes in students' writing. However, the classroom teacher maintained — and I concur — that such activities are necessary to introduce the elements of "real audience" into the task, along with more teacher-directed strategies.)

"It's really a shame but she (that Black teacher upstairs) seems to be so authoritarian, so focused on skills and so teacher directed. Those poor kids never seem to be allowed to really express their creativity. (And she even yells at them.)"

This statement directly concerns the display of power and authority in the classroom. One way to understand the difference in perspective between Black teachers and their progressive colleagues on this issue is to explore culturally influenced oral interactions.

In *Ways With Words,* Shirley Brice Heath (1983) quotes the verbal directives given by the middle-class "townspeople" teachers (p. 280):

- "Is this where the scissors belong?"
- "You want to do your best work today."

By contrast, many Black teachers are more likely to say:

- "Put those scissors on that shelf."
- "Put your name on the papers and make sure to get the right answer for each question."

Is one oral style more authoritarian than another?

Other researchers have identified differences in middle-class and working-class speech to children. Snow et al. (1976), for example, report that working-class mothers use more directives to their children than do middle- and upper-class parents. Middle-class parents are likely to give the directive to a child to take his bath as, "Isn't it time for your bath?" Even though the utterance is couched as a question, both child and adult understand it as a directive. The child may respond with "Aw Mom, can't I wait until . . . ," but whether or not negotiation is attempted, both conversants understand the intent of the utterance.

By contrast, a Black mother, in whose house I was recently a guest, said to her eight-year-old son, "Boy, get your rusty behind in that bathtub." Now I happen to know that this woman loves her son as much as any mother, but she would never have posed the directive to her son to take a bath in the form of a question. Were she to ask, "Would you like to take your bath now?" she would not have been issuing a directive but offering a true alternative. Consequently, as Heath suggests, upon entering school the child from such a family may not understand the indirect statement of the teacher as a direct command. Both White and Black working-class children in the communities Heath studied "had difficulty interpreting these indirect requests for adherence to an unstated set of rules" (p. 280).

But those veiled commands are commands nonetheless, representing true power, and with true consequences for disobedience. If veiled commands are ignored, the child will be labeled a behavior problem and possibly officially classified as behavior disordered. In other words, the attempt by the teacher to reduce an exhibition of power by expressing herself in indirect terms may remove the very explicitness that the child needs to understand the rules of the new classroom culture.

A Black elementary school principal in Fairbanks, Alaska, reported to me that she has a lot of difficulty with Black children who are placed in some White teachers' classrooms. The teachers often send the children to the office for disobeying teacher directives. Their parents are frequently called in for conferences. The parents' response to the teacher is usually the same:

"They do what I say; if you just *tell* them what to do, they'll do it. I tell them at home that they have to listen to what you say." And so, does not the power still exist? Its veiled nature only makes it more difficult for some children to respond appropriately, but that in no way mitigates its existence.

I don't mean to imply, however, that the only time the Black child disobeys the teacher is when he or she misunderstands the request for certain behavior. There are other factors that may produce such behavior. Black children expect an authority figure to act with authority. When the teacher instead acts as a "chum," the message sent is that this adult has no authority, and the children react accordingly. One reason this is so is that Black people often view issues of power and authority differently than people from mainstream middle-class backgrounds.[3] Many people of color expect authority to be earned by personal efforts and exhibited by personal characteristics. In other words, "the authoritative person gets to be a teacher because she is authoritative." Some members of middle-class cultures, by contrast, expect one to achieve authority by the acquisition of an authoritative role. That is, "the teacher is the authority because she is the teacher."

In the first instance, because authority is earned, the teacher must consistently prove the characteristics that give her authority. These characteristics may vary across cultures, but in the Black community they tend to cluster around several abilities. The authoritative teacher can control the class through exhibition of personal power; establishes meaningful interpersonal relationships that garner student respect; exhibits a strong belief that all students can learn; establishes a standard of achievement and "pushes" the students to achieve that standard; and holds the attention of the students by incorporating interactional features of Black communicative style in his or her teaching.

By contrast, the teacher whose authority is vested in the role has many more options of behavior at her disposal. For instance, she does not need to express any sense of personal power because her authority does not come from anything she herself does or says. Hence, the power she actually holds may be veiled in such questions/commands as "Would you like to sit down now?" If the children in her class understand authority as she does, it is mutually agreed upon that they are to obey her no matter how indirect, soft-spoken, or unassuming she may be. Her indirectness and soft-spokenness may indeed be, as I suggested earlier, an attempt to reduce the implication of overt power in order to establish a more egalitarian and non-authoritarian classroom atmosphere.

If the children operate under another notion of authority, however, then there is trouble. The Black child may perceive the middle-class teacher as weak, ineffectual, and incapable of taking on the role of being the teacher; therefore, there is no need to follow her directives. In her dissertation,

---

[3] I would like to thank Michelle Foster, who is presently planning a more in-depth treatment of the subject, for her astute clarification of the idea.

Michelle Foster (1987) quotes one young Black man describing such a teacher:

> She is boring, bo::ing.* She could do something creative. Instead she just stands there. She can't control the class, doesn't know how to control the class. She asked me what she was doing wrong. I told her she just stands there like she's meditating. I told her she could be meditating for all I know. She says that we're supposed to know what to do. I told her I don't know nothin' unless she tells me. She just can't control the class. I hope we don't have her next semester. (pp. 67–68)

But of course the teacher may not view the problem as residing in herself but in the student, and the child may once again become the behavior-disordered Black boy in special education.

What characteristics do Black students attribute to the good teacher? Again, Foster's dissertation provides a quotation that supports my experience with Black students. A young Black man is discussing a former teacher with a group of friends:

> We had fu::an in her class, but she was mean. I can remember she used to say, "Tell me what's in the story, Wayne." She pushed, she used to get on me and push me to know. She made us learn. We had to get in the books. There was this tall guy and he tried to take her on, but she was in charge of that class and she didn't let anyone run her. I still have this book we used in her class. It's a bunch of stories in it. I just read one on Coca-Cola again the other day (p. 68).

To clarify, this student was *proud* of the teacher's "meanness," an attribute he seemed to describe as the ability to run the class and pushing and expecting students to learn. Now, does the liberal perspective of the negatively authoritarian Black teacher really hold up? I suggest that although all "explicit" Black teachers are not also good teachers, there are different attitudes in different cultural groups about which characteristics make for a good teacher. Thus, it is impossible to create a model for the good teacher without taking issues of culture and community context into account.

And now to the final comment I present for examination:

"Children have the right to their own language, their own culture. We must fight cultural hegemony and fight the system by insisting that children be allowed to express themselves in their own language style. It is not they, the children, who must change, but the schools. To push children to do anything else is repressive and reactionary."

A statement such as this originally inspired me to write the "Skills and Other Dilemmas" article. It was first written as a letter to a colleague in response

* *Editor's note:* The colons [::] refer to elongated vowels.

to a situation that had developed in our department. I was teaching a senior-level teacher education course. Students were asked to prepare a written autobiographical document for the class that would also be shared with their placement school prior to their student teaching.

One student, a talented young Native American woman, submitted a paper in which the ideas were lost because of technical problems — from spelling to sentence structure to paragraph structure. Removing her name, I duplicated the paper for a discussion with some faculty members. I had hoped to initiate a discussion about what we could do to ensure that our students did not reach the senior level without getting assistance in technical writing skills when they needed them.

I was amazed at the response. Some faculty implied that the student should never have been allowed into the teacher education program. Others, some of the more progressive minded, suggested that I was attempting to function as gatekeeper by raising the issue and had internalized repressive and disempowering forces of the power elite to suggest that something was wrong with a Native American student just because she had another style of writing. With few exceptions, I found myself alone in arguing against both camps.

No, this student should not have been denied entry to the program. To deny her entry under the notion of upholding standards is to blame the victim for the crime. We cannot justifiably enlist exclusionary standards when the reason this student lacked the skills demanded was poor teaching at best and institutionalized racism at worst.

However, to bring this student into the program and pass her through without attending to obvious deficits in the codes needed for her to function effectively as a teacher is equally criminal — for though we may assuage our own consciences for not participating in victim blaming, she will surely be accused and convicted as soon as she leaves the university. As Native Alaskans were quick to tell me, and as I understood through my own experience in the Black community, not only would she not be hired as a teacher, but those who did not hire her would make the (false) assumption that the university was putting out only incompetent natives and that they should stop looking seriously at any Native applicants. A White applicant who exhibits problems is an individual with problems. A person of color who exhibits problems immediately becomes a representative of her cultural group.

No, either stance is criminal. The answer is to *accept* students but also to take responsibility to *teach* them. I decided to talk to the student and found out she had recognized that she needed some assistance in the technical aspects of writing soon after she entered the university as a freshman. She had gone to various members of the education faculty and received the same two kinds of responses I met with four years later: faculty members told her either that she should not even attempt to be a teacher, or that it didn't matter and that she shouldn't worry about such trivial issues. In her desperation, she had found a helpful professor in the English Department, but he left the university when she was in her sophomore year.

We sat down together, worked out a plan for attending to specific areas of writing competence, and set up regular meetings. I stressed to her the need to use her own learning process as insight into how best to teach her future students those "skills" that her own schooling had failed to teach her. I gave her some explicit rules to follow in some areas; for others, we devised various kinds of journals that, along with readings about the structure of the language, allowed her to find her own insights into how the language worked. All that happened two years ago, and the young woman is now successfully teaching. What the experience led me to understand is that pretending that gatekeeping points don't exist is to ensure that many students will not pass through them.

Now you may have inferred that I believe that because there is a culture of power, everyone should learn the codes to participate in it, and that is how the world should be. Actually, nothing could be further from the truth. I believe in a diversity of style, and I believe the world will be diminished if cultural diversity is ever obliterated. Further, I believe strongly, as do my liberal colleagues, that each cultural group should have the right to maintain its own language style. When I speak, therefore, of the culture of power, I don't speak of how I wish things to be but of how they are.

I further believe that to act as if power does not exist is to ensure that the power status quo remains the same. To imply to children or adults (but of course the adults won't believe you anyway) that it doesn't matter how you talk or how you write is to ensure their ultimate failure. I prefer to be honest with my students. Tell them that their language and cultural style is unique and wonderful but that there is a political power game that is also being played, and if they want to be in on that game there are certain games that they too must play.

But don't think that I let the onus of change rest entirely with the students. I am also involved in political work both inside and outside of the educational system, and that political work demands that I place myself to influence as many gatekeeping points as possible. And it is there that I agitate for change — pushing gatekeepers to open their doors to a variety of styles and codes. What I'm saying, however, is that I do not believe that political change toward diversity can be effected from the bottom up, as do some of my colleagues. They seem to believe that if we accept and encourage diversity within classrooms of children, then diversity will automatically be accepted at gatekeeping points.

I believe that will never happen. What will happen is that the students who reach the gatekeeping points — like Amanda Branscombe's student who dropped out of high school because he failed his exit exam — will understand that they have been lied to and will react accordingly. No, I am certain that if we are truly to effect societal change, we cannot do so from the bottom up, but we must push and agitate from the top down. And in the meantime, we must take the responsibility to *teach*, to provide for students who do not already possess them, the additional codes of power.[4]

But I also do not believe that we should teach students to passively adopt an alternate code. They must be encouraged to understand the value of the code they already possess as well as to understand the power realities in this country. Otherwise they will be unable to work to change these realities. And how does one do that?

Martha Demientieff, a masterly Native Alaskan teacher of Athabaskan Indian students, tells me that her students, who live in a small, isolated, rural village of less than two hundred people, are not aware that there are different codes of English. She takes their writing and analyzes it for features of what has been referred to by Alaskan linguists as "Village English," and then covers half a bulletin board with words or phrases from the students' writing, which she labels "Our Heritage Language." On the other half of the bulletin board she puts the equivalent statements in "standard English," which she labels "Formal English."

She and the students spend a long time on the "Heritage English" section, savoring the words, discussing the nuances. She tells the students, "That's the way we say things. Doesn't it feel good? Isn't it the absolute best way of getting that idea across?" Then she turns to the other side of the board. She tells the students that there are people, not like those in their village, who judge others by the way they talk or write.

> We listen to the way people talk, not to judge them, but to tell what part of the river they come from. These other people are not like that. They think everybody needs to talk like them. Unlike us, they have a hard time hearing what people say if they don't talk exactly like them. Their way of talking and writing is called "Formal English."
>
> We have to feel a little sorry for them because they have only one way to talk. We're going to learn two ways to say things. Isn't that better? One way will be our Heritage way. The other will be Formal English. Then, when we go to get jobs, we'll be able to talk like those people who only know and can only really listen to one way. Maybe after we get the jobs we can help them to learn how it feels to have another language, like ours, that feels so good. We'll talk like them when we have to, but we'll always know our way is best.

Martha then does all sorts of activities with the notions of Formal and Heritage or informal English. She tells the students,

---

[4] Bernstein (1975) makes a similar point when he proposes that different educational frames cannot be successfully institutionalized in the lower levels of education until there are fundamental changes at the post-secondary levels.

In the village, everyone speaks informally most of the time unless there's a potlatch or something. You don't think about it, you don't worry about following any rules — it's sort of like how you eat food at a picnic — nobody pays attention to whether you use your fingers or a fork, and it feels *so* good. Now, Formal English is more like a formal dinner. There are rules to follow about where the knife and fork belong, about where people sit, about how you eat. That can be really nice, too, because it's nice to dress up sometimes.

The students then prepare a formal dinner in the class, for which they dress up and set a big table with fancy tablecloths, china, and silverware. They speak only Formal English at this meal. Then they prepare a picnic where only informal English is allowed.

She also contrasts the "wordy" academic way of saying things with the metaphoric style of Athabaskan. The students discuss how book language always uses more words, but in Heritage language, the shorter way of saying something is always better. Students then write papers in the academic way, discussing with Martha and with each other whether they believe they've said enough to sound like a book. Next, they take those papers and try to reduce the meaning to a few sentences. Finally, students further reduce the message to a "saying" brief enough to go on the front of a T-shirt, and the sayings are put on little paper T-shirts that the students cut out and hang throughout the room. Sometimes the students reduce other authors' wordy texts to their essential meanings as well.

The following transcript provides another example. It is from a conversation between a Black teacher and a Southern Black high school student named Joey, who is a speaker of Black English. The teacher believes it very important to discuss openly and honestly the issues of language diversity and power. She has begun the discussion by giving the student a children's book written in Black English to read.

Teacher: What do you think about that book?

Joey: I think it's nice.

Teacher: Why?

Joey: I don't know. It just told about a Black family, that's all.

Teacher: Was it difficult to read?

Joey: No.

Teacher: Was the text different from what you have seen in other books?

Joey: Yeah. The writing was.

Teacher: How?

Joey: It use more of a southern-like accent in this book.

Teacher: Uhm-hmm. Do you think that's good or bad?

Joey: Well, uh, I don't think it's good for people down this a way, cause that's the way they grow up talking anyway. They ought to get the right way to talk.

Teacher: Oh. So you think it's wrong to talk like that?

Joey: Well . . . [*Laughs.*]

Teacher: Hard question, huh?

Joey: Uhm-hmm, that's a hard question. But I think they shouldn't make books like that.

Teacher: Why?

Joey: Because they not using the right way to talk and in school they take off for that and li'l chirren grow up talking like that and reading like that so they might think that's right and all the time they getting bad grades in school, talking like that and writing like that.

Teacher: Do you think they should be getting bad grades for talking like that?

Joey: [*Pauses, answers very slowly.*] No . . . No.

Teacher: So you don't think that it matters whether you talk one way or another?

Joey: No, not long as you understood.

Teacher: Uhm-hmm. Well, that's a hard question for me to answer, too. It's ah, that's a question that's come up in a lot of schools now as to whether they should correct children who speak the way we speak all the time. Cause when we're talking to each other we talk like that even though we might not talk like that when we get into other situations, and who's to say whether it's —

Joey: [*Interrupting.*] Right or wrong.

Teacher: Yeah.

Joey: Maybe they ought to come up with another kind of . . . maybe Black English or something. A course in Black English. Maybe Black folks would be good in that cause people talk, I mean Black people talk like that, so . . . but I guess there's a right way and wrong way to talk, you know, not regarding what race. I don't know.

Teacher: But who decided what's right or wrong?

Joey: Well that's true . . . I guess White people did.

[*Laughter. End of tape.*]

Notice how throughout the conversation Joey's consciousness has been raised by thinking about codes of language. This teacher further advocates having students interview various personnel officers in actual workplaces about their attitudes toward divergent styles in oral and written language. Students begin to understand how arbitrary language standards are, but also how politically charged they are. They compare various pieces written in different styles, discuss the impact of different styles on the message by making translations and back translations across styles, and discuss the history, apparent purpose, and contextual appropriateness of each of the technical writing rules presented by their teacher. *And* they practice writing different forms to different audiences based on rules appropriate for each audience. Such a program not only "teaches" standard linguistic forms, but also explores aspects of power as exhibited through linguistic forms.

Tony Burgess, in a study of secondary writing in England by Britton, Burgess, Martin, McLeod, and Rosen (1975/1977), suggests that we should not teach "iron conventions . . . imposed without rationale or grounding in communicative intent, . . . [but] critical and ultimately cultural awareness" (p. 54). Courtney Cazden (1987) calls for a two-pronged approach:

1. Continuous opportunities for writers to participate in some authentic bit of the unending conversation . . . thereby becoming part of a vital community of talkers and writers in a particular domain, and

2. Periodic, temporary focus on conventions of form, taught as cultural conventions expected in a particular community. (p. 20)

Just so that there is no confusion about what Cazden means by a focus on conventions of form, or about what I mean by "skills," let me stress that neither of us is speaking of page after page of "skill sheets" creating compound words or identifying nouns and adverbs, but rather about helping students gain a useful knowledge of the conventions of print while engaging in real and useful communicative activities. Kay Rowe Grubis, a junior high school teacher in a multicultural school, makes lists of certain technical rules for her eighth graders' review and then gives them papers from a third grade to "correct." The students not only have to correct other students' work, but also tell them why they have changed or questioned aspects of the writing.

A village teacher, Howard Cloud, teaches his high school students the conventions of formal letter writing and the formulation of careful questions in the context of issues surrounding the amendment of the Alaska Land Claims Settlement Act. Native Alaskan leaders hold differing views on this issue, critical to the future of local sovereignty and land rights. The students compose letters to leaders who reside in different areas of the state seeking their perspectives, set up audioconference calls for interview/debate sessions, and, finally, develop a videotape to present the differing views.

To summarize, I suggest that students must be *taught* the codes needed to participate fully in the mainstream of American life, not by being forced to attend to hollow, inane, decontextualized subskills, but rather within the context of meaningful communicative endeavors; that they must be allowed the resource of the teacher's expert knowledge, while being helped to acknowledge their own "expertness" as well; and that even while students are assisted in learning the culture of power, they must also be helped to learn about the arbitrariness of those codes and about the power relationships they represent.

I am also suggesting that appropriate education for poor children and children of color can only be devised in consultation with adults who share their culture. Black parents, teachers of color, and members of poor communities must be allowed to participate fully in the discussion of what kind of instruction is in their children's best interest. Good liberal intentions are not enough. In an insightful study entitled "Racism without Racists: Institutional Racism in Urban Schools," Massey, Scott, and Dornbusch (1975) found that under the pressures of teaching, and with all intentions of "being nice," teachers had essentially stopped attempting to teach Black children. In their words: "We have shown that oppression can arise out of warmth, friendliness, and concern. Paternalism and a lack of challenging standards are creating a distorted system of evaluation in the schools" (p. 10). Educators must open themselves to, and allow themselves to be affected by, these alternative voices.

In conclusion, I am proposing a resolution for the skills/process debate. In short, the debate is fallacious; the dichotomy is false. The issue is really an illusion created initially not by teachers but by academics whose world view demands the creation of categorical divisions — not for the purpose of better teaching, but for the goal of easier analysis. As I have been reminded by many teachers since the publication of my article, those who are most skillful at educating Black and poor children do not allow themselves to be placed in "skills" or "process" boxes. They understand the need for both approaches, the need to help students to establish their own voices, but to coach those voices to produce notes that will be heard clearly in the larger society.

The dilemma is not really in the debate over instructional methodology, but rather in communicating across cultures and in addressing the more fundamental issue of power, of whose voice gets to be heard in determining what is best for poor children and children of color. Will Black teachers and parents continue to be silenced by the very forces that claim to "give voice" to our children? Such an outcome would be tragic, for both groups truly have something to say to one another. As a result of careful listening to alternative points of view, I have myself come to a viable synthesis of perspectives. But both sides do need to be able to listen, and I contend that it is those with the most power, those in the majority, who must take the greater responsibility for initiating the process.

To do so takes a very special kind of listening, listening that requires not only open eyes and ears, but open hearts and minds. We do not really see through our eyes or hear through our ears, but through our beliefs. To put our beliefs on hold is to cease to exist as ourselves for a moment — and that is not easy. It is painful as well, because it means turning yourself inside out, giving up your own sense of who you are, and being willing to see yourself in the unflattering light of another's angry gaze. It is not easy, but it is the only way to learn what it might feel like to be someone else and the only way to start the dialogue.

There are several guidelines. We must keep the perspective that people are experts on their own lives. There are certainly aspects of the outside world of which they may not be aware, but they can be the only authentic chroniclers of their own experience. We must not be too quick to deny their interpretations, or accuse them of "false consciousness." We must believe that people are rational beings, and therefore always act rationally. We may not understand their rationales, but that in no way militates against the existence of these rationales or reduces our responsibility to attempt to apprehend them. And finally, we must learn to be vulnerable enough to allow our world to turn upside down in order to allow the realities of others to edge themselves into our consciousness. In other words, we must become ethnographers in the true sense.

Teachers are in an ideal position to play this role, to attempt to get all of the issues on the table in order to initiate true dialogue. This can only be done, however, by seeking out those whose perspectives may differ most, by learning to give their words complete attention, by understanding one's own power, even if that power stems merely from being in the majority, by being unafraid to raise questions about discrimination and voicelessness with people of color, and to listen, no, to *hear* what they say. I suggest that the results of such interactions may be the most powerful and empowering coalescence yet seen in the educational realm — for *all* teachers and for *all* the students they teach.

References

Apple, M. W. (1979). *Ideology and curriculum.* Boston: Routledge & Kegan Paul.

Bernstein, B. (1975). Class and pedagogies: Visible and invisible. In B. Bernstein, *Class, codes, and control* (Vol. 3). Boston: Routledge & Kegan Paul.

Britton, J., Burgess, T., Martin, N., McLeod, A., & Rosen, H. (1975/1977). *The development of writing abilities.* London: Macmillan Education for the Schools Council, and Urbana, IL: National Council of Teachers of English.

Cazden, C. (1987, January). *The myth of autonomous text.* Paper presented at the Third International Conference on Thinking, Hawaii.

Delpit, L. D. (1986). Skills and other dilemmas of a progressive Black educator. *Harvard Educational Review, 56,* (4), 379–385.

Foster, M. (1987). *It's cookin' now: An ethnographic study of the teaching style of a successful Black teacher in an urban community college.* Unpublished doctoral dissertation, Harvard University.

Gwaltney, J. (1980). *Drylongso.* New York: Vintage Books.

Heath, S. B. (1983). *Ways with words.* Cambridge: Cambridge University Press.

Massey, G. C., Scott, M. V., & Dornbusch, S. M. (1975). Racism without racists: Institutional racism in urban schools. *Black Scholar, 7*(3), 2–11.

Siddle, E. V. (1986). *A critical assessment of the natural process approach to teaching writing.* Unpublished qualifying paper, Harvard University.

Siddle, E. V. (1988). *The effect of intervention strategies on the revisions ninth graders make in a narrative essay.* Unpublished doctoral dissertation, Harvard University.

Snow, C. E., Arlman-Rup, A., Hassing, Y., Josbe, J., Joosten, J., & Vorster, J. (1976). Mother's speech in three social classes. *Journal of Psycholinguistic Research, 5,* 1–20.

I take full responsibility for all that appears herein; however, aside from those mentioned by name in this text, I would like to thank all of the educators and students around the country who have been so willing to contribute their perspectives to the formulation of these ideas, especially Susan Jones, Catherine Blunt, Dee Stickman, Sandra Gamble, Willard Taylor, Mickey Monteiro, Denise Burden, Evelyn Higbee, Joseph Delpit Jr., Valerie Montoya, Richard Cohen, and Mary Denise Thompson.

PART TWO

—■-■-■—

The Dimensions of

> The intellectual activity of those without power is always charac-
> terized as nonintellectual. I think this issue should be understood,
> not just as a dimension of pedagogy, but a dimension of politics as
> well. This is difficult to do in a society like that of the United States,
> where the political nature of pedagogy is negated ideologically. It
> is necessary to negate the political nature of pedagogy to give the
> superficial appearance that education serves everyone, thus assur-
> ing that it continues to function in the interest of the dominant
> class.
>
> — Paulo Freire, *Literacy: Reading the Word and the World*

In this section, we present five articles that locate the experience of racism
within the social, economic, and political realities that shape interactions
between racial groups. As Freire clarifies, masking over the political nature of education ensures the maintenance of systemic privileges accorded
exclusively to members of the dominant class or to those subdominant people who reject their cultures for assimilation into dominant norms.

David Wallace Adams analyzes the historical and social contexts of the
schooling experiences of Native Americans in "Fundamental Considerations:
The Deep Meaning of Native American Schooling, 1880–1900." By delineat-
ing the religious, economic, and cultural beliefs of White settlers, Adams
traces the intimate connections that existed between Capitalism, Republicanism, and Protestantism. These connections, in turn, guided the U.S. approach to Native American schooling as a campaign to derascinate students
from their languages and cultures, which were seen as inferior and antitheti-
cal to those of the dominant culture. By fabricating the inferiority of Native
Americans and necessitating their attendance in boarding schools, White
settlers accomplished two goals: the "civilization" of "savages" and the appro-
priation of their lands. Schools, as Adams maintains, became the major "civi-

this campaign to dispossess Native Americans of their land
g them away from their traditions.

Spener similarly examines the ties between educational policy and
omic demands in "Transitional Bilingual Education and the Socializa-
ion of Immigrants." Asserting that the U.S. economic system creates the
need for low-paying, low-status jobs, Spener examines how schools systematically prepare immigrants and minorities to occupy subdominant social and
economic positions. In his analysis, Spener deconstructs xenophobic arguments that assert that "illegal aliens" take jobs away from citizens; that the
United States has always been a melting pot promising upward mobility for
all; and that depriving immigrants of instruction in their native languages
(or at least of validation of their cultures) is the only way to promote their
English proficiency. By addressing these legal, pedagogical, and economic
arguments, Spener asserts that English-only movements are part and parcel
of the disempowerment that the U.S. educational system encourages among
language minority students in order to maintain an expendable, rootless
class of workers to fill low-level jobs.

The last three articles illustrate the effects of economic and political dis-
enfranchisement on the schooling experiences of a particular group — African Americans. In "Racelessness as a Factor in Black Students' School Success: Pragmatic Strategy or Pyrrhic Victory?" Signithia Fordham explores how
some African American students feel compelled to become raceless by denying their cultural ties in their efforts to achieve academic success. Based on
her ethnography of high-achieving Black high school students, Fordham
claims that the European American emphasis on individual success is a powerful contextual factor in the psychosocial experience of schooling for these
students. Though "racelessness" may appear pragmatic to individual students, as Fordham posits, it is destructive to their cultural integrity.

Emilie Siddle Walker and Janie Ward take up the issue of cultural integrity
in two settings: legalized segregation and the present-day economic marginalization of African Americans, respectively. In "Caswell County Training
School, 1933–1969: Relationships between Community and School," Siddle
Walker documents the affirming cultural interactions that existed in a segregated school in North Carolina. From the perspectives of teachers, administrators, parents, and former students, she describes how an oppressed community valued and supported its school, and shared responsibility for the
moral, cultural, and academic development of its children. Her work offers
a definition of parent involvement that emphasizes a two-way, rather than a
one-way, community-school relationship.

In "Cultivating a Morality of Care in African American Adolescents: A
Culture-Based Model of Violence Prevention," Ward similarly describes a
tradition of community and caring among African Americans. Highlighting
the current epidemic of violence and its connection to the economic and

political conservatism of the last fifteen years, she defines violence as a "relational breakdown." Ward therefore suggests that by cultivating healthy racial identities that embody cultural traditions of caring and connection, African American adults can help adolescents counter mainstream values of excessive individualism and disconnection from others that legitimize violence.

Fundamental Considerations:
The Deep Meaning of Native American
Schooling, 1880–1900

—■-■-■—

DAVID WALLACE ADAMS

This they tell, and whether it
happened so or not I do not know;
but if you think about it,
you can see that it is true.
              — John Neihardt, *Black Elk Speaks*

"These are great evils; and it must be added that they appear to me to be
irremediable." Alexis de Tocqueville used these terms to characterize
the ways that the young republic treated its native peoples in his now
classic *Democracy in America*. Tocqueville's judgment was not the result of
casual speculation. In his tour of America he had observed firsthand the
tragic consequences that occurred when Indian societies stood in the path
of "the most grasping nation on the globe."

> At the end of the year 1831, while I was on the left bank of the Mississippi,
> at a place named by Europeans Memphis, there arrived a numerous band
> of Choctaws. . . . These savages had left their country and were endeavoring
> to gain the right bank of the Mississippi, where they hoped to find an
> asylum that had been promised them by the American government. It was
> then the middle of winter, and the cold was unusually severe; the snow had
> frozen hard upon the ground, and the river was drifting huge masses of
> ice. The Indians had their families with them, and they brought in their
> train the wounded and the sick, with children newly born and old men
> upon the verge of death. They possessed neither tents nor wagons, but only
> their arms and some provisions. I saw them embark to pass the mighty river,

Harvard Educational Review Vol. 58 No. 1 February 1988, 1–28

and never will that solemn spectacle fade from my remembrance. No cry, no sob, was heard among the assembled crowd; all were silent. Their calamities were of ancient date, and they knew them to be irremediable. The Indians had all stepped into the bark that was to carry them across, but their dogs remained upon the bank. As soon as these animals perceived that their masters were finally leaving the shore, they set up a dismal howl, and plunging all together into the icy waters of the Mississippi, swam after the boat.[1]

Tocqueville understood all too well that removal was at best only a temporary solution to the "Indian problem." As White settlers pushed ever westward, oblivious and contemptuous of Indian ways and treaty agreements, the same uneven confrontation between the two races would be repeated on succeeding frontiers, and with the same results. Indian removal only postponed the long-term question of what place, if any, the Native American would have in the American empire. The keen-eyed Frenchman was pessimistic: "I believe that the Indian nations of North America are doomed to perish, and that whenever the Europeans shall be established on the shores of the Pacific Ocean, that race of men will have ceased to exist."[2]

Throughout the nineteenth century, two visions of the Indian's future struggled for dominance in the minds of policymakers. One of them predicted, as Tocqueville's did, that the Indian was doomed to extinction. In this vision Indians, like characters in a Cooper novel, would retreat ever deeper into the forest in an attempt to live out their last days as a dying race in accordance with ancestral customs. According to this view, even if the hand of philanthropy were extended by a beneficent government, the "Red Man" would be either unable or unwilling to grasp it. Reinforced by the frontier mentality of Indian hating and the continued call for land concessions, this attitude prevailed all too often in the councils of Washington. But a second and contradictory vision is also evident throughout the course of Indian-White relations. From this perspective, Indians, like most other members of the human family, were creatures of environmental and historical circumstance, fully capable of being transformed and assimilated once exposed to the "superior" influences of White society. This was clearly the view of the Congress in 1819, when it created a "civilization fund" to support missionaries on the frontier. The House Committee on Indian Affairs exhorted the Congress thus: "Put into the hands of their children the primer and the hoe, and they will naturally, in time, take hold of the plow; and as their minds become enlightened and expand, the Bible will be their book, and they will grow up in habits of morality and industry, leave the chase to those of minds less cultured, and become useful members of society."[3]

By mid-century, the Indian's fate was still unresolved, and, by 1880, the time for postponement had run out. The earlier policies of removal had now reached their logical conclusion in the form of the Indian reservation. Now, with the near extinction of the buffalo, with renewed demands by Whites for Indian land, and with the iron rails of the locomotive snaking their way across the vast stretches of prairie, it was clear that the days of the Indian were numbered. Census figures told the story. The Indian population continued to decline with each decade: 1850—400,764; 1860—339,421; 1870—313,712; 1880—306,543; 1890—248,253.[4] It was in this context that policymakers moved aggressively to assimilate the Indian into the mainstream of American life. Their efforts were greatly aided by the rise of several organizations devoted specifically to the reform of Indian policy, notably the Indian Rights Association, the Lake Mohonk Conference, and the Women's National Indian Association. These groups, together with the older Board of Indian Commissioners, led a well-coordinated effort to solve the "Indian problem" along humanitarian lines.[5]

Much of this assimilation campaign focused on education. Annual congressional appropriations for Indian education rose from $75,000 in 1880 to nearly $3 million in 1900.[6] In 1891 Congress declared that school attendance for Indian children should be compulsory. Two years later it added teeth to the measure by authorizing the Indian Bureau to "withhold rations, clothing, and other annuities" from those parents who resisted sending their children to school.[7] While these measures held weight only where schools were in existence, they provided the legal basis for stricter enforcement of school attendance. In fact, between 1880 and 1900 the number of Indian children enrolled in school more than quadrupled from 4,651 to 21,568, the latter figure representing over one-half of all Indian children of school age.[8] By 1900, Congress had created a network of Indian schools composed of 147 reservation day schools, 81 reservation boarding schools, and 25 off-reservation boarding schools.[9]

This dramatic growth in Indian schooling reflects the sublime faith that Americans in general, and reformers in particular, placed in schools as agencies for social cohesion and assimilation. The extent of that faith is captured by Annie Beecher Scoville, a missionary to the Sioux, in her remarks at Lake Mohonk in 1901. Having observed the government's feverish efforts to construct schools among the Sioux, she observed:

> If there is an idol that the American people have, it is the school. What gold is to the miser, the schoolhouse is to the Yankee. If you don't believe it go out to Pine Ridge, where there are seven thousand Sioux on eight million acres of land incapable of supporting these people, and find planted over that stretch of territory thirty-two schoolhouses, standing there as a testimony to our belief in education. There is something whimsical in planting schoolhouses where no man can read, far from the highways, unneighbored by farms, and planted, not at the request of the Sioux, but because we believed it was good for them! It is a remedy for barbarism we think, and so we give the dose. Uncle Sam is like a man setting a charge

of powder. The school is the slow match. He lights it and goes off whistling, sure that in time it will blow up the old life, and of its shattered pieces he will make good citizens.[10]

My purpose in this article is to reveal the fundamental considerations that underlay the late nineteenth-century campaign for the establishment of Indian schools. To characterize this campaign as merely another use of the common school as an instrument for assimilation misses, in my view, the deeper historical significance of the determined crusade to school the Native Americans in the ways of White society. I will examine the subject from three interpretive vantage points, and while I will occasionally discuss life in Indian schools for the purpose of illustration, my primary focus will be on the rhetoric of reform. This article, then, is largely a study of reformers' motives and how those motives were translated into educational policy.

The Protestant Ideology

The first interpretive perspective I will utilize is that of the so-called Protestant ideology.[11] In the work of John Higham, Carl Kaestle, and David Tyack and Elizabeth Hansot, ideology is seen as a set of interconnected and mutually reinforcing beliefs and values that provide members of a given society with a sense of who they are as a collective cultural enterprise and where they fit into the historical scheme of things.

Using this broad definition, historians have undertaken the difficult task of sorting out the various strands of American ideology that gave rise to the common school in the first half of the nineteenth century. The result has been an emerging consensus around the importance of three seminal elements in American thought: Protestantism, capitalism, and republicanism. Briefly stated, the thesis is that the pan-Protestant values of common-school reformers — the importance of Bible reading, individual salvation, and personal morality — were conveniently linked to the secular values inherent in nascent capitalism; namely, the emphasis on personal industry, the sanctity of private property, and the ideal of "success." The fusion of religious and economic values made the dominant ideology powerful enough, but when these ideals were incorporated into a larger vision of national destiny — an aspect of republican thought that went beyond idealizing constitutional democracy as a form of government — the ideology assumed truly mythic proportions. As Higham notes: "America began to be seen as the spiritual center of Christendom. Thus, the Protestant ideology, instead of enshrining a single creed, exalted a sacred place."[12] By providential intention, America had a millennial destiny to impose its system onto those who stood in the path of its march to the Pacific. And if Protestantism, capitalism, and republicanism constituted the core of the ideology, the common school was seen as the natural instrument for transmitting it to rising generations of American youth.[13]

The question before us is the following: Can the Protestant ideology, which played such an important role in defining the goals of the common-school movement in the first half of the nineteenth century, also aid us in understanding the aims of Indian education in the last two decades of that century? At first, one might think not. Higham argues, for instance, that in the late nineteenth century the integrating force of the Protestant ideology gradually began to wane and give way to the more intensified and cohesive force of "technical unity."[14] Tyack and others have clearly established how this development manifested itself in the sphere of education, where a new generation of educational leaders labored to apply the principles of centralization, specialization, standardization, and meritocracy to all aspects of school life.[15] The quest for the "one best system" makes for an important story, yet it would be a misreading of the period to assert that the rise of educational bureaucracies somehow condemned evangelical Protestants to playing bit parts in the new educational drama. Quite the contrary. As demonstrated by Robert T. Handy, Protestantism in post–Civil War America continued to be an "aggressive dynamic form of Christianity that set out confidently to confront American life at every level, to permeate, evangelize, and Christianize it."[16] Most important, Protestants continued to wield immense influence over the course of the nation's schools. William J. Reese argues correctly that "American Evangelical Protestants of the turn of the century could still rejoice that the schools were safely theirs."[17]

Particularly significant to this story is the fact that those involved in reshaping the nation's Indian policy were firmly rooted in the Protestant tradition and, more to the point, were thoroughly imbued with the three cardinal elements of that ideology: Protestantism, capitalism, and republicanism. Indeed, by slightly recasting these three themes into Protestantism, individualization, and Americanization, we are provided with a useful angle for understanding late nineteenth-century Indian schooling. As it turns out, all three themes figured prominently in discussions concerning Indian education.

The importance placed on individualization stemmed from the belief that the greatest barrier to the Indians' assimilation was their attachment to the tribal community over and above their own individual advancement. This attachment reflected two aspects of Indian society that reformers viewed as particularly loathsome: the Indian's longstanding adherence to communal values and their general disdain for the White man's work ethic. The problem was especially acute given the fact that many reservations were almost totally dependent upon government rations for day-to-day subsistence.

With the eradication of the buffalo and the rise of the reservation system, hunting-oriented economies all but collapsed. Young warriors who had once been honored for their hunting skill were now reduced to gathering at the agency for biweekly distributions of flour, sugar, coffee, and, periodically, beef. What was particularly infuriating to reformers was that, in the face of such humiliating dependency, all too many Indians remained contemptuous of what Whites saw as the only path the self-respecting manhood; namely, the endless toil associated with eking out an existence from the soil. The situation was even more complicated by the Indian's lack of desire to accumulate more wealth than his neighbors; and indeed, once he did accumulate it, to squander it in elaborate gift-giving ceremonies.[18] It followed that a major objective of policymakers was to convert the Indian child to the ideal of the self-reliant man. This effort took two forms: industrial training and the inculcation of values.

In boarding schools, which accounted for a majority of Indians enrolled, half of the student's day was devoted to some form of manual or industrial training. This practice followed from the belief, as expressed by one school superintendent, that "the best education for the aborigines of our country is that which inspires them to become producers instead of remaining consumers." He maintained that although acquiring rudimentary academic skills was surely important, it was even more fundamental to teach the Indian child how to work: "A string of textbooks piled up in the storehouses high enough to surround a reservation if laid side by side will never educate a being with centuries of laziness instilled in his race."[19] Because policymakers believed that the Indian's future depended upon the schools' success at transforming hunters into farmers, it followed that boys were taught those skills required for self-sufficient farming: plowing, planting, harvesting, fence building, stock raising, wagon making, harness making, carpentry, and blacksmithing. Likewise, Indian girls were taught skills deemed appropriate for the rural housewife and mother: cooking, cleaning, and sewing.[20]

Individualization also entailed persuading the student to embrace a cluster of related values and beliefs that, taken together, served to portray capitalism as a model social order and the rugged individualist as an ideal personality. For U.S. Senator Henry Dawes, the solution to the Indian problem was to "teach him to stand alone first, then to walk, then to dig, then to plant, then to hoe, then to gather, and then to *Keep*" — the last step being a vital one.[21] Similarly, Merrill Gates reminded those at Lake Mohonk in 1896 that the primary challenge to philanthropy was to awaken "wants" in the Indian. Then, and only then, Gates argued, could the Indian be coaxed "out of the blanket and into trousers and trousers with a *pocket that aches to be filled with dollars!*" [emphasis added][22] Commissioner of Indian Affairs John Oberly believed that the Indian student should be taught the "exalting egotism of American civilization, so that he will say 'I' instead of 'We,' and 'This is mine' instead of 'This is ours.'"[23] Thus did educators seek to create in the Indian student's mind the mental and moral concept of possessive individualism. In textbooks, classrooms, workshops, and sermons, the importance of the key American values of industriousness, thrift, perseverance, and acquisitiveness was continually drummed home. For the students at Phoenix Indian School, the message of individualism came in the form of a poem, "There's Always a Way," printed in the school newspaper:

There's always a way to rise, my boy,
Always a way to advance;
Yet the road that leads to Mount Success
Does not pass by the way of chance
But goes through the stations of Work and Strife,
Through the valley of Persevere.
And the man that succeeds, while others fail,
Must be willing to pay most dear.[24]

The Protestant ideology also required that the Indian child be Christianized and, ideally, Protestantized. Reformers invariably dismissed the Indian's native religion as a hodgepodge of barbaric rites and ceremonies totally devoid of any moral content. Beyond this, native beliefs were condemned for encouraging in Indians a naive and childish tendency to seek spiritual meanings and truth in the natural world, for their failure to acknowledge any association between religious activity and material advancement, and finally, for their acceptance of polygamous marriage and extended kinship relationships as legitimate and desirable social arrangements.[25] What reformers were objecting to was the fact that Native American religions reinforced and reflected the values and cultural patterns of Indian life, something they were committed to erasing.[26]

It followed that the religious aims of Indian schooling fell into two categories. On the one hand, reformers believed that Indian children should be introduced to essential Christian doctrine, and in the process come to feel the "pulsing life-tide of Christ's life." On the other hand, they should be subjected to a rigorous program of moral training. It was in this realm that the religious and acquisitive values of Protestant America were to be given complementary expression. Indian children must be taught to love their neighbor, but they must also be told about "the road that leads to Mount Success."[27]

The Christian message was communicated in a number of ways. In day schools, it came in the form of *McGuffey Readers,* classroom prayers, and hymn singing. In boarding schools, it was expressed in the form of Sunday church services, nightly prayer meetings, and a host of religious clubs. Native American autobiographies from this period clearly show that the Protestant impulse profoundly influenced life in Indian schools. For instance, Jason Betzinez, an Apache, tells us that his introduction to Christianity came at Carlisle Indian School in Pennsylvania, where, as a result of attending church on Sundays and frequent prayer meetings, the "influence became stronger and stronger as I came to understand English better. It changed my whole life."[28] Similarly, Thomas Wildcat Alford, a Shawnee, who on the eve of departure for a distant boarding school was instructed by tribal chiefs not to listen to the White man's preaching, also fell under the spell of the evangelical promise. At first, Alford was able to resist the religious onslaught, "but as time passed," he explains, "and the interest of my teachers became stronger, their pleas more insistent, I could not ignore the subject. I began to consider the religious beliefs and to study the Gospel of Jesus Christ." In time, he wrote, he came to know "deep in my soul that Jesus Christ was my Savior."[29] Don Talayesva, a Hopi boy who attended an off-reservation school in Riverside, California, tells us of being torn between his ancestral Hopi beliefs and the White man's religion. He remembers conjuring up this sermon for the school YMCA meeting:

> Well, my partners, I am asked to speak a few words for Jesus. I am glad that I came to Sherman and learned to read and cipher. Now I discover that Jesus was a good writer. So I am thankful that Uncle Sam taught me to read in order that I may understand the Scriptures and take my steps along God's road. When I get a clear understanding of the Gospel I shall return home and preach it to my people in darkness. I will teach them all I know about Jesus Christ, the Heavenly Father, and the Holy Ghost. So I advise you boys to do your best and pray to God to give us a good understanding. Then we will be ready for Jesus to come and take us up to heaven. I don't want any of my friends to be thrown into the lake of hell fire where there is suffering and sorrow forever. Amen.[30]

These passages should not be taken as representative responses to the Christian message; many students, to the exasperation of school officials, stubbornly adhered to their native beliefs. These passages simply illustrate the extent to which the evangelical spirit permeated the atmosphere of Indian schooling.

When policymakers turned to the third aim of Indian schooling — Americanization — they were primarily addressing the issue of the Indian's future political status. Two issues were involved here: the status of the tribal unit as a collective political entity (that is to say, tribal sovereignty), and the individual Indian's citizenship status. In the minds of reformers the two issues were inextricably linked: the elimination of tribal sovereignty would facilitate the individual Indian's entry into citizenship. The political sovereignty of Indian tribes had, in fact, been eroding steadily throughout the nineteenth century. By 1871, when Congress declared that the government would no longer conduct its relations with Indians by treaty, the process was nearly complete; henceforth, Indians were to be regarded as mere "wards" of the government.[31] Meanwhile, the Indian reservation was an anomaly in the American system. Only when Indians were separated from the larger tribal unit, the government held, would they be truly fit for citizenship. Congress could simply declare them citizens, but was hesitant to do so. Most policymakers agreed with Commissioner of Indian Affairs Ezra Hayt, who contended that Indians needed "as long tutelage before launching them into the world to manage their own affairs."[32] On two questions, then, reformers were in agreement: First, the Indians' connections to their tribal unit and the reservation had to be severed if they were to be absorbed into the larger body politic; and second, the government had a special responsibility to

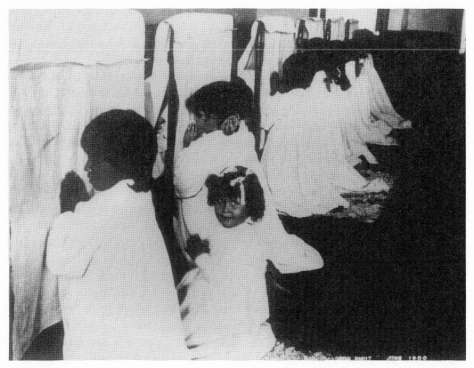

"Good Night," Phoenix Boarding School, 1900.

prepare them for citizenship. In this matter the schools would have a special role to play.

Education for citizenship focused on language instruction and political socialization. The connection between language and citizenship stemmed from the belief that, along with all citizens, the Indian child should be compelled to read, write, and speak the English language. As Commissioner of Indian Affairs J. D. C. Atkins argued in 1887: "If we expect to infuse into the rising generation the leaven of American citizenship, we must remove the stumbling blocks of hereditary customs and manners, and of these language is one of the most important elements." According to Atkins, "no unity or community of feeling can be established among different peoples unless they are brought to speak the same language and thus become imbued with the like ideas of duty."[33] That same year, John Riley, Superintendent of Indian Schools, echoed the sentiments of his superior. Teaching English to the Indian, he argued, would reduce the Indian's prejudice toward the White man's ways, would enhance the Indian's understanding of the "spirit of the laws and institutions under which they are to live," and finally, would lessen their vulnerability to "unprincipled white men."[34] The bottom line was that Indians, as a colonized people, could legitimately be expected to take on the tongue of their conquerors. Again, according to Atkins, citizenship required a certain amount of cultural absorption and "nothing so surely and perfectly stamps upon an individual a national characteristic as language." Besides, Atkins continued, "this language, which is good enough for a white man and a black man, ought to be good enough for the red man."[35]

If the issue of language was largely instrumental, the real focus of citizenship education was the Indian's political socialization. On the one hand, this meant instruction in the rights and duties of citizenship and in the principles of the U.S. Constitution. No less important, however, was the need to awaken a "fervent patriotism" in Indian students. They should, according to Commissioner Morgan, "be taught to look upon America as their home and upon the United States Government as their friend and benefactor."[36] The campaign to win the Indian's political allegiance was in part carried out in the traditional U.S. History course.[37] Beyond textbook instruction, schools were encouraged to teach students patriotic songs, political recitations, and, perhaps most important, involve them in patriotic rituals, including the celebration of national holidays.

Since boarding-school students wore special government uniforms and were subjected to a daily routine of marching and drilling, these patriotic rituals occasionally assumed elaborate proportions. When President William McKinley visited Phoenix Indian School in 1901, for example, the entire student body performed a highly disciplined marching routine before lining up in front of the President, who looked on from the reviewing stand. "There they stood for an instant, 700 pairs of eyes gazing sharply and intently at the 'great father,'" the school newspaper reported, and then at the sound of a bugle, the Indians roared in unison: "I give my head and my heart to my country; one country, one language, and one flag."[38]

In remote outposts, patriotic rituals were more modest, but equally pointed. A Hopi memoir describes an observance at a reservation boarding school in the Southwest: "In May we had a decoration celebration. We stuck little flags in our caps, took bunches of flowers, and marched out to the graves of two soldiers who had come out here to fight the Hopi and had died."[39] In another school, students were asked to participate in a political pageant celebrating the day that Europeans first set foot on the shores of the New World. An Indian student, dressed as Columbus, recited the lines:

> Then boomed the Pinta's signal gun!
> The first that ever broke
> The sleep of the new world — the sound
> Echoing to forest depths profound,
> A continent awoke![40]

A continent awoke? From what? This question suggests another line of investigation, one that explores the idea that reformers, in their discussion of Indian policy in general and Indian schooling in particular, were forced to draw upon images more fundamental than those generated by the Protestant ideology, images at least as old as that fateful day in 1492, when Columbus and his band of voyagers first confronted not only a New World, but, as Tzvetan Todorov has put it, "the question of the other," the people Columbus called *Indios*.[41]

The Civilization–Savagism Paradigm

When Europeans, and later, European Americans, first encountered the Native American's "otherness," they made a distinction between Indians and Whites that by the late eighteenth century had become the central reference point for explaining the cultural chasm that separated the two races. The basic idea was that peoples on the globe were at various stages in their evolution from "savagism" to "civilization." As the theory went, while the Whites were for the most part civilized, Indians were still largely savages. There was room for minor variations where particular groups or societies were involved, but the generalization was said to be true in the main. Because Indians — and here the images came flooding forth — indulged in barbaric religious practices, relied on hunting and gathering for subsistence, were disdainful of private property and wealth, and generally lived out their lives in pagan ignorance of all things civilized, they were culturally worthless. Sometimes noble, sometimes ignoble, they were nevertheless savages.[42]

Central to the civilization–savagism paradigm was the concept of historical process. History was seen as the story of man's progressive movement toward the ideal of civilization. If one wished to see the process unfold, one had only to look at America. Near the end of his life Jefferson wrote to a friend:

> Let a philosophic observer commence a journey from the savages of the Rocky Mountains, eastwardly towards our sea-coast. These he would observe in the earliest stage of association living under no law but that of nature, subsisting and covering themselves with the flesh and skins of wild beasts. He would next find those on our frontiers in the pastoral state, raising domestic animals to supply the defects of hunting. Then succeed our own semi-barbarous citizens, the pioneers of the advance of civilization, and so in his progress he would meet the gradual shades of improving man until he would reach his, as yet, most improved state in our seaport towns. This, in fact, is equivalent to a survey, in time, of the progress of man from the infancy of creation to the present day.[43]

Just as savagery must give way to civilization, Jefferson and his contemporaries reasoned, so Indian ways must give way to White ways. Whether Indians as a people would survive remained an open question. Jefferson seems to have genuinely hoped and believed that they would. In any event, traditional Indian ways were destined to perish. The alternatives before them were clear: civilization or extinction.[44]

Throughout the nineteenth century, the idea of civilization remained a fixed reference point in all discussions of the Indian question. Coincidentally, in 1877, just as the movement to reform Indian policy was getting under way, the idea received impressive scholarly support with the appearance of Lewis Henry Morgan's *Ancient Society*.[45] A cultural evolutionist, Morgan identified seven stages in the path to human progress: lower savagery, middle savagery, upper savagery, lower barbarism, middle barbarism, upper barbarism, and civilization. On Morgan's scale, North American Indians fell somewhere between middle savagery and middle barbarism, depending upon the particular attributes of a given culture. Numerous factors determined where Morgan placed various societies on his categorical scale, but three were deemed to be of particular importance in the passage to civilization: the acceptance of monogamous marriage and the nuclear family as the basic unit in society, the reliance on agriculture as the basis for subsistence, and a firm belief in private property as the proper basis for economic and social organization. Morgan found Indian societies wanting in one or more of these criteria. Nevertheless, he was convinced that Indians, with proper guidance from a benevolent government, were fully capable of acquiring civilized ways and eventually being absorbed into the mainstream of American life.[46]

Late nineteenth-century reformers subscribed not only to the law of civilized progress, but also to its corollary, that the Indians' only hope for survival depended upon their assimilation into mainstream American society. According to Commissioner of Indian Affairs Henry Price: "Savage and civilized life cannot live and prosper on the same ground. One of the two must die."[47] As Secretary of the Interior Carl Schurz pointed out, time was of the essence: "To civilize them, which was once only a benevolent fancy, has now become an absolute necessity, if we mean to save them." Indians were a dying race.[48]

Since Indians were on the brink of extinction, the civilization–savagism paradigm posed a question that was of immense importance to the Indians' destiny: Must the process of social evolution be as painstakingly slow for Indians as it had been for Whites? No, reformers answered; where human progress was involved, historical time was to be measured in relative rather than absolute terms. Moreover, the school could be the instrument for hastening the evolutionary process. As Commissioner Morgan pointed out, a civilizing education was capable of carrying a single generation of Indian youth across "the dreary chasm of a thousand years of tedious evolution."[49] Addressing the Lake Mohonk Conference, U.S. Commissioner of Education William Torrey Harris concurred:

> But shall we say to the tribal people that they shall not come to these higher things unless they pass through all the intermediate stages, or can we teach them directly these higher things, and save them from the slow progress of the ages? In the light of Christian civilization we say there is a method of rapid progress. Education has become of great potency in our hands, and we believe that we can now vicariously save them very much that the white race has had to go through. Look at feudalism. Look at the village community stage. . . . We have had our tribulation with them. But we say

to lower races: we can help you out of these things. We can help you avoid the imperfect stages that follow them on the way to our level. Give us your children and we will educate them in the Kindergarten and in the schools. We will give them letters, and make them acquainted with the printed page. With these comes emancipation from mere personal authority, from the authority of the master, from the authority of the overseer and the oracle. With these comes the great emancipation, and the school will give you that.[50]

Schools, then, could not only civilize; they could civilize quickly.

It should be clear by now that where the education of Indians was concerned, fundamental and unique considerations come into play that are unaccounted for in the Protestant ideology. To be sure, there is nothing in the first interpretation that contradicts the one emerging here. Indeed, one might reasonably argue that nineteenth-century discussions on the fate of the Indian were simply the by-product of the historical forces unleashed by one of the most consequential strands in the Protestant ideology; namely, the belief that it was America's destiny to extend European American institutions and ways of life across the continent. Moreover, the doctrine of progress was certainly as deeply embedded in the tradition of evangelical Protestantism as it was in the Enlightenment tradition of Jefferson. The fact remains, however, that when policymakers turned their attention to the Indian question, they invariably shifted to a frame of reference and a descriptive language tailor-made for the occasion — they shifted to the civilization–savagism model. Needless to say, to define the Indian's "otherness" in terms of savagery was more than a little self-serving. To dismiss the Indian as a savage was surely a convenient means of legitimizing the history of Indian-White relations, a history that, if viewed objectively, might cast a shadow over the righteous pretensions of the American empire.

It should be noted that the Protestant ideology, including its educational prescriptions (Protestantization, individualization, and Americanization), was certainly relevant to the discussion of what it would take to civilize the Indian. When policymakers spoke of christianizing Indians, they always assumed that their conversion would be an important step in civilizing them as well. Thus, Merrill Gates proclaimed at Lake Mohonk that introducing the Indian to Christianity could "do in one generation most of that which evolution takes centuries to do."[51] And although the reformers preferred that Protestantism prevail over Catholicism in the battle for the Indian's heart and soul, most saw the Indian's conversion from paganism to any Christian faith as progress. Even Herbert Welsh, well known for his anti-Catholic sentiment, could appreciate the fact that "the great religious bodies, the Roman communion on the one side, and the Protestant communions on the other, should try to recognize the value of each other's work, at least as an instrument of civilization."[52] Citizenship education was regarded as a civilizing force as well. Instruction in the rights and duties of citizenship would prepare the Indian child for full participation in the political life of one of the most civilized nations on earth. As for language instruction, Commissioner Atkins was convinced that "the first step to be taken toward civilization, toward teaching the Indians the mischief and folly of continuing in their barbarous practices, is to teach them in the English language."[53] Finally, the Indian's individualization would surely advance the cultural elevation process. "There is an utter barbarism in which property has almost no existence," claimed Merrill Gates. "The tribal organization tends to retain men in such barbarism. It is a great step gained when you awaken in an Indian the desire for the acquisition of property of his own, by his own honest labor."[54] In this respect, as in others, the Protestant ideology shaped reformers' thinking as to what they must teach the Indians if they were to civilize them.

The idea of civilization, however, remained a fundamental frame of reference for discussions on Indian education. Its impact on the overall direction of Indian schooling can be illustrated in three ways. First, it set the boundaries for one of the most troublesome questions confronting the Indian Bureau: What type of institution — the day school, the reservation boarding school, or the off-reservation boarding school — was best suited to accomplish the Indian child's transformation? This question forced policy-makers to return to first principles. In time, they would conclude that the civilizing process could be carried out most effectively if it were conducted in an environment isolated from the countervailing influence of savagery, that is, at a distance from the tribal community. By the late 1870s, this resulted in a general preference for the reservation boarding school over the day school. The problem with the day school, officials in the field complained, was that although children were taught the curriculum of civilization during the day, they were instructed in the ways of savagery at night. By removing children from the camp and cloistering them in a boarding school for nine months of the year, the civilizing process could be carried on much more efficiently.[55]

By the early 1880s, however, the enthusiasm for reservation boarding schools had begun to wane. Students, it seemed, still felt the pull of traditional life beyond the school fence, and they frequently ran away. Furthermore, during the annual summer vacation, many students suffered severe cases of "relapse." More than one Indian agent would observe "how soon they seem to forget all they have been taught, after they return to camp."[56] According to another agent:

> Immediately following the close of the school the children laid aside the clothing furnished them and donned the kind the camp Indians wear. A number of them continue to come about the agency, but not a word can one be induced to speak in English. They attend our Sabbath services, but they can not be prevailed upon to sing, while in school the majority of them sing elegantly. These are some of the reasons why the results of the school

are not satisfactory to me. I really believe that one year's schooling away from the influence of the camp Indians would do the child more good than four at the agency.[57]

A good number of policymakers and reformers agreed. The result was the creation of a new institution, the off-reservation boarding school, where students were schooled in the ways of Whites for an uninterrupted period of five years before returning home. As it turned out, both types of boarding schools, reservation and off-reservation, would remain the cornerstone of the Indian school system for years to come. One thing remained certain: in order for savagism to be countermanded, the Indian child had to be educated in an isolated environment. Hence, by 1900 close to 85 percent of Indian children enrolled in school were attending boarding schools.[58]

A second impact of the idea of civilization on Indian schooling can be seen by examining the nature of the educational program itself; namely, the sheer comprehensiveness of it. A close examination of the institutional life of Indian schools reveals that they were waging an all-out assault on the child's "otherness." For the war against savagery to be successful, reformers decided, it must be waged uncompromisingly on every aspect of the child's being. Thus, while their bronze skin would never wash white, the Indian children could otherwise be taught to look, dress, eat, walk, and think like civilized Whites. The alteration process can be seen in the following account of the opening day at Pine Ridge boarding school in South Dakota, about 1880. The description was written by Julia McGillycuddy, wife of the government's agent, Valentine McGillycuddy.

On the opening day, hundreds of curious Indians — bucks, squaws, and children — hung about the building wondering just what was going to happen to the 200 youngsters sequestered within it. McGillycuddy advised pulling down the shades at the windows in the large bathroom on the ground floor to exclude the gaze of the inquisitive.

The first step toward civilizing these primitive children was to purge them of various uncleanliness. The several bathrooms as well as the laundry were the scenes of activity, the hair-cutting to be accomplished first, followed by a bath which would include washing the heads as a labor-saving device.

In each bathroom a teacher armed with shears was prepared to begin operations. Curious peepers stood close to the windows on the ground floor, deeply regretful of the drawn shades which barred their observation of the activities carried on behind them. There the matron seated a small boy and taking a lousy braid in one hand, raised the shears hanging by a chain from her waist. A single clip and the filthy braid could be severed. But unfortunately, at that moment a breeze blew back the shade from the window. The previously baffled effort of a youngster plastered against the casing on the outside of the window was now rewarded by a fleeting glimpse

Bobtail and son, Cheyenne, Carlisle Indian Boarding School, circa 1880.

of his playmate seated in the chair and a tall lean woman with a pair of shears in her hand prepared to divest the boy of his hair — Delilah bringing calamity upon an embryo Samson.

Like a war whoop rang out the cry: "*Pahin kaksa, pahin kaksa!*" The enclosure rang with alarm, it invaded every room in the building and floated out on the prairie. No warning of fire or flood or tornado or hurricane, not even the approach of an enemy could have more effectively emptied the building as well as the grounds of the new school as did the ominous cry. "They are cutting the hair!" Through doors and windows the children flew, down the steps, through the gates and over fences in mad flight toward the Indian villages, followed by the mob of bucks and squaws as though all were pursued by a bad spirit. They had been suspicious of the school from the beginning; now they knew it was intended to bring disgrace upon them.

McGillycuddy's raised hands, his placating shouts, and his stern commands were less effective than they had been on occasions of threatened outbreak. He was impotent to stem the flight. He calmed the excited teachers, assuring them that the schoolhouse would soon again be filled with children. But their faces expressed disappointment as well as chagrin over the apparent failure of his attempt to civilize the Sioux.[59]

All this was necessary, we are expected to understand, because Indians were too savage to know what was good for them. This leads us to a third implication of the civilization ideal — namely, the belief that the student must be made to embrace the essential elements of the civilization–savagism paradigm. The Indian child must come to know what Whites already knew — that Whites were civilized and Indians were savages. The entire boarding school experience, of course, implied this message, but occasionally the point had to be made outright. At Hampton Institute in Hampton, Virginia, for instance, where Indians were educated along with Blacks, it appears to have permeated the entire curriculum.[60] Thus, the following section of a student's examination was published in the school newspaper under the heading "Work and Fun in the Geography Class":

9. To what race do we all belong?
9. The Human race

10. How many classes belong to this race?
10. There are five large classes belonging to the Human race.

11. Which are the first?
11. The white people are the strongest.

12. Which are the next?
12. The Mongolians or yellows.

13. The next?
13. The Ethiopians or blacks.

14. Next?
14. The Americans or reds.

15. Tell me something of the white people.
15. The Caucasian is away ahead of all of the other races — he thought more than any other race, he thought that somebody must made the earth, and if the white people did not find that out, nobody would never know it — it is God who made the world.[61]

An underlying assumption of the civilization–savagism paradigm was that although Indians were at the bottom of the ladder of civilization, the ladder could eventually be climbed. The proper note to be struck, then, was one that simultaneously inspired both humiliation and hope in the student. In 1893, Philip Garrett, an influential member of the Indian Rights Association, attempted to strike just this note when addressing the graduating class of

Carlisle Indian School. Garrett began by reminding his audience that their race had been "thrown by the providence of God in the pathway of a mighty and resistless tide of civilization." Since the only path of survival was to adopt civilized ways, Garrett continued, the Indian would have to make the best of a difficult situation. Indeed, they ought to be thankful for their situation. Left to their own resources and the painstakingly slow process of social evolution, they might have been mired in the backwaters of savagery for several generations. Instead, a benevolent government was offering them a different and brighter prospect: Students had a "unique opportunity to show the marvelous change that can be wrought in a single generation by the aid of good schools, and the lessons of centuries."[62]

As one considers these statements, the question comes to mind: What were the ultimate concerns that drove reformers to make such statements? The answer, in part, no doubt lies in the fact that they truly believed them. As philanthropic spokesmen for Protestant America, they appear to have been utterly convinced that the Indian's only hope for survival lay in embracing White civilization. But there was another, perhaps more fundamental, consideration at work as well. And this leads us to still another perspective on the meaning of Indian schooling.

Taking the Land

This third perspective begins with the rude fact that in the beginning Indians possessed the land and Whites desperately wanted it. On the proposition that Indian land would eventually become White land there was never any serious debate. Both the Protestant ideology and the civilization–savagism paradigm presupposed and demanded it. In the meantime, the question of how the great transfer of real estate might be managed loomed large.[63]

The problem facing policymakers in Jefferson's time was how to dispossess Indians of large tracts of land without doing undue violence to their philanthropic ideals. Their ingenious solution to this dilemma was rooted in the conviction that it required much more land to support a nomadic hunting society than a like-sized population of sedentary farmers. Thus, the willingness of Indians to sell their land would be directly proportionate to their ability to acquire civilized ways. Moreover, in the civilizing process, they would be drawn inevitably into the White economy; they would come to hunger for the goods of Whites just as the White man hungered for Indian land. The pieces of the puzzle began to fall into place. "When [Indians] shall cultivate small spots of earth, and see how useless their extensive forests are," Jefferson wrote, "they will sell from time to time, to help out their personal labor in stocking their farms, and procuring clothes and comforts from our trading houses."[64] On another occasion he remarked: "While they are learning to do better on less land, our increasing numbers will be calling for more land, and thus a coincidence of interests."[65] The so-called "coincidence of interests" between the two races amounted to this: Indians possessed the land and needed civilization; Whites, on the other hand, had civilization but needed land. The philanthropic solution to the Indian question was now clear: a fair exchange whereby Whites would give the Indians civilization in return for land cessions — land the Indians would no longer require once they were civilized. This was the basis for an Indian policy characterized by one historian as "expansion with honor."[66]

As it turned out, there was very little honor to be had. The White hunger for land was far in excess of congressional willingness to fund civilization programs. Moreover, Native Americans proved to be less enthusiastic about committing cultural suicide than the Jeffersonians had surmised. The result was that Indian nations were first simply moved farther West, and in time were concentrated on reservations so that Whites might circumvent them in their rush across the continent. But the march of civilized progress was not to be stopped; eventually, even the reservation itself was looked upon as a new source of land. As Henry Pancoast, cofounder of the Indian Rights Association, noted in 1882: "The rush of Western settlement grows more and more; an enormous army pours forth continually into our Eastern seaports to spread itself over the West. However can we keep these still places in the midst of the current, a bit of stone age in the crush and fever of American enterprise?"[67] The answer, of course, was that it would be impossible; the only solution was civilization, which, once accomplished, would free up more land. As Commissioner Morgan reminded philanthropists in 1892: "A wild Indian requires a thousand acres to roam over, while an intelligent man will find a comfortable support for his family on a very small tract."[68]

Thus, while reformers were earnestly striving to save Indians from extinction by a process of assimilation, the were also mindful of the fact that under the reservation system Indians still possessed more land than they would ever need once they were transformed into farmers. Some reformers were even willing to challenge the idea that the Indians really owned the land to begin with. In the words of Lyman Abbott:

> It is sometimes said that the Indians occupied this country and that we took it away from them; that the country belonged to them. This is not true. The Indians did not occupy this land. A people do not occupy a country simply because they roam over it. They did not occupy the coal mines, nor the gold mines, into which they never struck a pick; nor the rivers which flow to the sea, and on which the music of a mill was never heard. The Indians can scarcely be said to have occupied this country more than the bisons and the buffalo they hunted. Three hundred thousand people have no right to hold a continent and keep at bay a race able to people it and provide the happy homes of civilization. We do owe the Indians sacred rights and obligations, but one of those duties is not the right to let them hold forever the land they did not occupy and which they were not making fruitful for themselves or others.[69]

171

Not all reformers went as far as Abbott, but all were convinced that the reservation system should be abandoned.

I do not mean to create the impression that reformers were primarily motivated by their desire to dispossess Indians of their land. Their opposition to the reservation system was rooted in several factors, not the least of which was the fact that it forestalled the Indian's absorption into national life. As we can see from the discussion above, however, the issues of land and national economic growth clearly figured into their considerations. In any event, the reservation system came under increasing attack in the 1880s from reformers, and, not surprisingly, from Western land interests, who had their own reasons for wanting to abolish the Indian reservation.

The result of this unholy alliance was one of the most important and devastating pieces of Indian legislation of the late nineteenth century — the General Allotment Act of 1887, more commonly called the Dawes Act after its chief sponsor, Senator Henry Dawes of Massachusetts. The Dawes Act authorized the President to select those reservations he deemed suitable for allotment, after which the following provisions came into effect. First, the reservation would be divided into individual allotments, the head of each family receiving 160 acres, with smaller allotments made to unmarried women and orphans. Second, to protect the new landholders from land-hungry Whites, title to the land would be held by the government for a period of twenty-five years, after which it would pass to its lawful owner. Third, holders of allotments would be granted U.S. citizenship. Finally, the surplus, unallotted lands would be sold off to Whites, the funds gained therefrom to be spent for the Indians' benefit, mainly for education.[70] Reformers looked upon the Dawes Act as a major milestone in their crusade to solve the Indian problem. In a single piece of legislation they believed they had found the mechanism to smash tribalism, transform hunters into farmers, and grant the Indians U.S. citizenship. Even the selling of the surplus lands would facilitate the process; as White settlers established productive homesteads on the available lands, they would inevitably prove to be positive role models for their Indian neighbors.[71]

Against this background, the campaign to educate the Indians takes on new meaning. First, allotment enables us to understand why educators placed so much emphasis on individualization and citizenship training — both were essential if the Indians were going to survive in their new citizen-farmer roles. Without such preparatory education, reformers pointed out, allotment would prove to be a cruel hoax. "Put an ignorant and imbruted savage on land of his own, and he remains a pauper, if he does not become a vagrant and a thief," claimed Lyman Abbott.[72] Charles Painter, lobbyist for the Indian Rights Association, agreed: "The reservation walls being down" he said, "and the retraining power of the agent broken, he [the Indian] and his children will become a race of wanderers and beggars, unless they are met . . . with influences wise enough and large enough to teach them the nobility of manhood and the uses of freedom." Painter then added: "There is now scope and hope for the schoolmaster."[73] The Dawes Act, then, helped to remind educators of what they must teach Indians if they were to survive and prosper as citizens.

A second connection between education and allotment stems from the fact that, in theory, the allotment process was to be set into motion on a given reservation only when the President, with the advice of the Indian Bureau, deemed a given Indian population capable of making the transition to a freeholding agricultural economy. Since surplus lands could not be sold until allotment was completed, it followed that educating Indians was a necessary preliminary to divesting them of excess lands. The connection between education and surplus lands would provide Commissioner Morgan with one of his most effective arguments for funding Indian education.

[The] great economical fact is that the lands known as Indian reservations now set apart by the Government for Indian occupancy aggregate nearly 190,000 square miles. This land, for the most part, is uncultivated and unproductive. When the Indians shall have been properly educated they will utilize a sufficient quantity of those lands for their own support and will release the remainder that it may be restored to the public domain to become the foundation for innumerable happy homes; and thus will be added to the national wealth immense tracts of farming land and vast mineral resources which will repay the nation more than one hundred fold for the amount which it is proposed shall be expended in Indian education.[74]

Third, the issue of Indian land loss was inextricably connected to the school's efforts at citizenship education. The point here is that school officials occasionally felt compelled to address the issue that was at the heart of so much Indian-White conflict — the fact that Whites had nearly succeeded in dispossessing the Indians of the entire continent. The objective was to persuade the students to accept the idea that it was inevitable and entirely justified that the Indians lose their ancestral lands to a more progressive people. Some students did in fact come to internalize this point of view, as evidenced by this account of Indian-White relations by a Hampton pupil:

Centuries ago we undoubtedly held full control over this fair land — this vast domain from east to west. Bodily we were free to roam, but our freedom of thought lay dormant as we slumbered heavily by the camp-fires of prosperity. What did the fertile valleys, the rich plain, the mineral treasures concealed in the hillsides mean to us? They simply told us that here was a good hunting ground, and there a good site for temporary habitation. But when the white man came he put everything in a new light. He saw how everything in nature could render him a service. 'Twas not long before we saw his engines making their way across our domains west-ward. Mountains were in his way, but he climbed them. Rivers were there, but he crossed them. When he was killed by our arrows, he, as it were, sprang up from his own ashes. He brought with him civilization and freedom. These constituted the power which made him a most formidable adversary. Our wanderings along his track proved a hindrance to his progress and we were driven away until finally we found ourselves penned on reservations with nothing to do and nothing to expect. . . . Since then we have entered upon a stage of civilization which brings with it problems hard for us to handle. This is our past.[75]

One suspects that such sentiments were relatively rare among Indian students, but this passage illustrates the ultimate political purpose to which the civilization theme might be applied. The civilization–savagism paradigm called for establishing political and cultural hegemony over Indians as a first step to their incorporation into American life. In the instance above, the process may be said to have merely reached its logical conclusion.[76]

School officials also made concerted efforts to win student support for the Dawes Act. Just two years after its enactment, Commissioner Morgan instructed school superintendents to observe annually the anniversary of the law's passage, along with other national holidays. The occasion might be used, explained Morgan, "to impress upon Indian youth the enlarged scope and opportunity given them by this law and the new obligations which it imposes."[77] For the next decade or so, especially at larger off-reservation schools, special efforts were made to celebrate the day with speeches, dramatic sketches, and elaborate pageants. In 1890, the Carlisle celebration of "Franchise Day" required students to listen to a recitation of a poem titled "A Message from Carlisle Students to the Indians." Apparently written by one of the school staff, but read by a student, the purpose of the poem was to dispel Indian fears that the Dawes Act, despite its promise of citizenship, was in reality nothing but a scheme to dispossess the Indian of more real estate. As the poem admits, taking land from the Indian was an old American story.

> You say we are poor, though a splendid dominion
> Of forests and rivers and mountains of gold
> Were ours, e'er the greed of the white man detained it;
> You are sorry and grumble that now it is sold.

The poem continues by pointing out that the government was now offering the Indian redress:

> Redress in this way, that though we as a Nation
> No more may hold sway o'er a boundless domain,
> Though tribes may be scattered like leaves of the maple
> And the pipes of our councils be smoked not again.

> Yet prospects more pleasant than these in the future
> And riches far better, our people may see,
> When learning, shall bring us a wealth more resplendent
> Than title to millions can possibly be.

Education, then, would compensate for the past dispossession of Indian lands, and presumably for those lost as a consequence of the Dawes Act as well.

> But welcome the ruin, if now by our losses,
> We gain thousand fold in a better estate.
> A man may be chief in the empire of reason.
> Education, not land, makes a citizen great.[78]

Celebrations of the Dawes Act were intended to evoke in students a genuine enthusiasm for the provision of the bill that awarded citizenship to allottees. One student responded:

> Now we are citizens
> We give him applause;
> So three cheers, my friends,
> To Senator Dawes![79]

For those students converted to the idea of civilization and the Protestant ideology, the Dawes Act indeed gave them something to celebrate. For others, those still not won over to the White man's way of thinking, the price of citizenship must have appeared too severe: the further loss of the tribal estate.[80]

Conclusion

This essay has been an attempt to peel away the layers of meaning behind the late nineteenth-century effort to school Native Americans in the ways of Whites. My investigations have caused me to conclude that while the Protestant ideology tells us a great deal about the aims of Indian schooling during this period, it leaves a good deal unexplained as well. In particular, it leaves unexplained reformers' preoccupation with the concept of civilization and its counterpart, savagism. It also fails to make any direct connection between the objectives of Indian schooling and the most fundamental fact of Indian-White conflict, the fact that Whites were aggressively dispossessing Native Americans of their land. It might be argued that I have engaged in a bit of hairsplitting: that while the Protestant ideology failed to address the Indian question directly, its glorification of the American empire certainly implied the cultural inferiority of people who stood in its path; and that the Indian's loss of land was always rather blatantly assumed — in short, the handwriting was on the wall. Perhaps so, but this does not explain away the fact that when policymakers went about the business of designing an Indian school system, both the civilization–savagism paradigm and the issue of land possession became the fundamental points of reference for discussion. It is entirely understandable that this should be so. Although Protestant ideology might provide the necessary spiritual and ideational energy to propel the American empire westward, ever deeper into Indian country, it could not address in precise terms what it was about the Indians' "otherness" that justified systematic political and cultural subjugation, including the taking of their land. Still, it was not irrelevant either. The Protestant ideology helped shape policymakers' ideas of what it meant to be civilized, of what Indians must become if they were to be saved from extinction. In the end, I would argue, the Protestant ideology, the civilization–savagism paradigm, and the White hunger for Indian land were all mutually reinforcing and hopelessly intertwined as factors influencing the educational campaign to assimilate the Indian.

A visual depiction of historical forces at work can be seen in George A. Crofutt's chromolithograph "American Progress," published in 1873 after an earlier painting by John Gast, and issued with an accompanying text, in which Crofutt sought to capture the quintessential spirit and meaning of the American experience.[81] At center stage is one of the most powerful icons of nineteenth-century America, Columbia, who, with the "Star of the Empire" on her forehead, drifts majestically westward over the American landscape. In one hand she carries the "talking wires" of the telegraph, a symbol of American progress, and in the other a large volume, which one would expect to be the Bible. Closer inspection, however, reveals the inscription "Schoolbook."

Crofutt's print can be read at several levels. On the one hand, it is an attempt to dramatically show a persistent strain in the Protestant ideology — the idea that America is a sacred place with a millennial destiny. But "American Progress" is about the idea of civilization as well; it is about the triumph of civilization over Indian savagism. Indeed, one can scarcely look at it without calling to mind Jefferson's vision of America as a panoramic representation of "the progress of man from the infancy of creation to the present day." In fact, the accompanying text relates:

> On the right of the picture is a city, steamships, manufactories, schools, and churches, over which beams of light are streaming and filling the air — indicative of civilization. The general tone of the picture on the left declares darkness, waste and confusion. From the city proceed the three great continental lines of railway, passing the frontier settlers' rude cabin, and tending toward the Western Ocean. Next to these are the transportation wagons, overland stage, hunters, gold seekers, pony express, the pioneer emigrant and the war-dance of the "noble red man." Fleeing from "Progress," and towards the blue waters of the Pacific, which shows itself on the left of the picture beyond the snow-capped summits of the Sierra Nevadas, are the Indians, buffaloes, wild horses, bears, and other game, moving Westward — ever Westward the Indians, with their squaws, papooses, and "pony lodges," . . . as they flee from the presence of the wondrous vision. The "Star" is *too much for them*.[82]

And finally, of course, there is the land. As the Indian is pushed off the canvas of American life, the land remains for the taking.

176

"American Progress," chromolithograph, issued by George Crofutt, 1873.

Crofutt's print is a depiction of the national myth of the day. But let us imagine that he had issued the print several years later, let us say 1883. Would the vision have been altered? Probably little would have been changed, except that now Columbia, with an outstretched arm, would be seen offering the "Schoolbook" to the "vanishing American." For the school-book contained within it the Americanizing lessons of Christianity, capital-ism, and republicanism. The schoolbook would save the Indian from extinc-tion. If only Indians would accept the gift of the book, they would come to enjoy the blessings of civilized progress. But even then — and this was always clearly understood — they must continue to give up the land. Such was the deep meaning of Indian education.

Notes

1. Tocqueville, *Democracy in America*, Vol. 1 (1935; rpt., New York: Alfred A. Knopf, 1980), p. 340.
2. Tocqueville, *Democracy*, p. 342.
3. For an overview of nineteenth-century Indian-White relations, see Francis Paul Prucha, *The Great Father: The United States Government and the American Indians* (Lincoln: University of Nebraska Press, 1984), vol. 1; Wilcomb E. Washburn, *The Indian in*

America (New York: Harper & Row, 1975), pp. 146–249; Arrell Morgan Gibson, *The American Indian: Prehistory to the Present* (Lexington, MA: D. C. Heath, 1980), pp. 249–484; Robert M. Utley, *The Indian Frontier of the American West, 1846–1890* (Albuquerque: University of New Mexico Press, 1984); Robert F. Berkhofer, Jr., *The White Man's Indian: Images of the American Indian from Columbus to the Present* (New York: Alfred A. Knopf, 1978); and Brian W. Dippie, *The Vanishing American: White Attitudes and U.S. Indian Policy* (Middletown, CT: Wesleyan University Press, 1982), pp. 3–196. The House Committee on Indian Affairs quotation is taken from Henry Warner Bowden, *American Indians and Christian Missions: Studies in Cultural Conflict* (Chicago: University of Chicago Press, 1981), p. 167.

4. Dippie, *The Vanishing American*, p. 200.
5. The assimilation campaign is examined in Francis Paul Prucha, *American Indian Policy in Crisis: Christian Reformers and the Indian, 1865–1900* (Norman: University of Oklahoma Press, 1976); Loring Benson Priest, *Uncle Sam's Stepchildren: The Reformation of United States Indian Policy, 1865–1887* (New Brunswick, NJ: Rutgers University Press, 1942); Frederick E. Hoxie, *A Final Promise: The Campaign to Assimilate the Indians, 1880–1920* (Lincoln: University of Nebraska Press, 1984); Henry E. Fritz, *The Movement for Indian Assimilation, 1860–1890* (Philadelphia: University of Pennsylvania Press, 1961); and Robert Winston Mardock, *The Reformers and the American Indian* (Columbia: University of Missouri Press, 1971). For the role of reform organizations, see, in addition to the above, William T. Hagan, *The Indian Rights Association: The Herbert Welsh Years, 1882–1904* (Tucson: University of Arizona Press, 1985); Vine Deloria, Jr., "The Indian Rights Association: An Appraisal" in *The Aggressions of Civilization: Federal Indian Policy Since the 1880's,* ed. Sandra L. Cadwalder and Vine Deloria, Jr. (Philadelphia: Temple University Press, 1984), pp. 3–18; Larry E. Burgess, "'We'll Discuss It at Mohonk'," *Quaker History, 60* (Spring 1971): 14–28; Larry E. Burgess, "The Lake Mohonk Conferences on the Indian, 1883–1916," Diss., Claremont Graduate School, 1972; Helen M. Wanken, "'Women's Sphere' and Indian Reform: The Women's National Indian Association, 1879–1901," Diss., Marquette University, 1981. The role of the Board of Indian Commissioners is assessed in Robert H. Keller, Jr., *American Protestantism and United States Indian Policy, 1869–1882* (Lincoln: University of Nebraska Press, 1983), chap. 4; and Henry E. Fritz, "The Board of Indian Commissioners and Ethnocentric Reform, 1878–1893," in *Indian-White Relations,* ed. Jane Smith and Robert Kvasnicka (Washington, DC: Howard University Press, 1976), pp. 57–78.
6. *Annual Report of the Secretary of the Interior,* 1913, Administrative Reports, Vol. II, p. 183.
7. The legislative history on compulsory education for Indians during this period is traced in Theodore Fischbacher, *A Study of the Role of the Federal Government in the Education of the American Indian* (San Francisco: R. and E Research Associates, 1974), pp. 125–131.
8. *Annual Report of the Commissioner of Indian Affairs,* 1900, House Doc. No. 5, 56th Cong., 2nd sess., 1900–1901, serial 4102, p. 643; and Laurence F. Schmeckebier, *Office of Indian Affairs* (Baltimore: Johns Hopkins Press, 1927), p. 209.
9. Schmeckebier, *Office of Indian Affairs,* p. 214.
10. *Proceedings of the Nineteenth Annual Meeting of the Lake Mohonk Conference,* 1901, pp. 17–18.
11. John Higham, "Hanging Together: Divergent Unities in American History," *Journal of American History, 61* (June 1974), 5–28; Carl F. Kaestle, *Pillars of the Republic: Common Schools and American Society, 1780–1860* (New York: Hill & Wang, 1983), chap. 5; Carl F. Kaestle, "Ideology and American Educational History," *History of Education Quarterly, 22* (Summer 1982), 123–138; and David Tyack and Elizabeth Hansot, *Managers of Virtue: Public School Leadership in America, 1820–1980* (New York: Basic Books, 1982), pt. 1.
12. Higham, "Hanging Together," p. 10; Kaestle, *Pillars of the Republic,* p. 76.

13. Kaestle argues that the Protestant ideology was largely composed of ten interlocking propositions:

> "the sacredness and fragility of the Republican polity (including ideas about individualism, liberty, and virtue); the importance of the individual character in fostering social morality; the central role of personal industry in defining rectitude and merit; the delineation of a highly respected but limited domestic role for women; the importance for character building of familial and social environment (within certain racial and ethnic limitations); the sanctity and social virtues of property; the equality and abundance of economic opportunity in the United States; the superiority of American Protestant culture; the grandeur of America's destiny; and the necessity of a determined public effort to unify America's polyglot population, chiefly through education." See Kaestle, "Ideology and American Educational History," pp. 127–128.

14. Higham, "Hanging Together," p. 23.
15. Tyack and Hansot, *Managers of Virtue*, pp. 94–180; Tyack, *The One Best System: A History of American Urban Education* (Cambridge: Harvard University Press, 1974), pts. 2, 4.
16. Handy, "The Protestant Quest for a Christian America, 1830–1930," *Church History, 22* (March 1953), 10. See also Handy, *A Christian America: Protestant Hopes and Historical Realities* (New York: Oxford University Press, 1971), chaps. 3–4; and Winthrop S. Hudson, *American Protestantism* (Chicago: University of Chicago Press, 1961), pp. 109–127.
17. Reese, "The Public Schools and the Great Gates of Hell," *Educational Theory, 32* (Winter 1982), 14. See also David B. Tyack and Thomas James, "Moral Majorities and the School Curriculum: Historical Perspectives on the Legalization of Virtue," *Teachers College Record, 86* (Summer 1985), 513–535.
18. Reformers' assessments of the Indian's economic value system were both exaggerated and misinformed. Still, the sharing and cooperative tradition of most Indian societies is richly documented in ethnographic literature. See, for instance, De Mallie, "Pine Ridge Economy, Cultural and Historical Perspectives" in *American Indian Economic Development*, ed. Sam Stanley (The Hague: Monton Publishers, 1978), p. 250; Royal B. Hassrick, *The Sioux* (Norman: University of Oklahoma Press, 1964), pp. 36–37, 296; Edward P. Dozier, *Hano: A Tewa Indian Community in Arizona* (New York: Holt, Rinehart & Winston, 1966), pp. 88–89; Malcolm McFee, *Modern Blackfeet: Montanans on a Reservation* (New York: Holt, Rinehart & Winston, 1972), p. 46; and E. Adamson Hoebel, *The Cheyennes: Indians of the Great Plains* (New York: Holt, Rinehart & Winston, 1962), p. 94.
19. *Annual Report of the Commissioner of Indian Affairs*, 1886, House Exec. Doc. No. 1, 49th Cong., 2nd sess., 1886–1887, Serial 2467, pp. 221–22.
20. "Rules for Indian Schools," *Annual Report of the Commissioner of Indian Affairs*, 1890, House Exec. Doc. No. 1, 51st Cong., 2nd sess., 1890–1891, Serial 2841, pp. CXLVI, CLLII.
21. *Journal of the Thirteenth Annual Conference with Representatives of Missionary Boards*, in the *Annual Report of the Board of Indian Commissioners*, 1883, House Exec. Doc. No. 1, 48th Cong., 2nd sess., 1883–1884, Serial 2191, pp. 731–732.
22. *Journal of the Fourteenth Annual Meeting of the Lake Mohonk Conference*, 1896, pp. 11–12.
23. *Annual Report of the Commissioner of Indian Affairs*, 1888, House Exec. Doc. No. 1, 50th Cong., 2nd sess., 1888–1889, Serial 2637, p. 89.
24. *Native American*, September 13, 1902, p. 1.
25. The Protestant missionary effort has been examined in Robert F. Berkhofer, Jr., *Salvation and the Savage: An Analysis of Protestant Missions and American Indian Response, 1787–1862* (New York: Atheneum, 1972); Bowden, *American Indians and Christian Missions;* and Keller, *American Protestantism and United States Indian Policy.*
26. Hopelessly ethnocentric, reformers had little appreciation for the richness and diversity of Native American religious life. For an introduction to this aspect of Indian

societies, see Joseph Epes Brown, *The Spiritual Legacy of the American Indian* (Crossroad: New York, 1982); Ake Hultkrantz, *Belief and Worship in Native North America* (Syracuse: Syracuse University Press, 1981); Hultkrantz, *The Religions of the American Indians* (Berkeley: University of California Press, 1979); Hartley Burr Alexander, *The World's Rim: Great Mysteries of the North American Indians* (Lincoln: University of Nebraska Press, 1953); Sam D. Gill, *Native American Religions: An Introduction* (Belmont, CA: Wadsworth Publishing, 1982).

27. See the remarks of Merrill Gates in the *Proceedings of the Eleventh Annual Meeting of the Lake Mohonk Conference*, 1893, pp. 11–12; and Daniel Dorchester, "Moral Training in Indian Schools," *Annual Report of the Commissioner of Indian Affairs*, 1891, House Exec. Doc. No. 1, 52nd Cong., 1st sess., 1891–1892, Serial 2934, p. 542.

28. Jason Betzinez, *I Fought with Geronimo* (Harrisburg, WV: Stackpole, 1959), p. 156.

29. Alford, *Civilization, as Told to Florence Drake* (Norman: University of Oklahoma Press, 1936), pp. 105–106.

30. Leo W. Simmons, ed., *Sun Chief: The Autobiography of a Hopi Indian* (New Haven: Yale University Press, 1942), pp. 116–117.

31. The changing legal status of the American Indian during this period is reviewed in Prucha, *American Indian Policy in Crisis*, chap. 11; Walter L. Williams, "From Independence to Wardship: The Legal Process of Erosion of American Indian Sovereignty, 1810–1903," *American Indian Culture and Research Journal*, 7 (1984), 5–32; and Alvin J. Ziontz, "Indian Litigation," in Cadwalder and Deloria, *Aggressions of Civilization*, chap. 7.

32. *Annual Report of the Commissioner of Indian Affairs*, 1878, House Exec. Doc. No. 1, 45th Cong., 3rd sess., 1878–1879, Serial 1850, p. 444. All Indians were granted citizenship by an Act of Congress in 1924. See Gary C. Stein, "The Indian Citizenship Act of 1924," *New Mexico Historical Review*, 47 (July 1972): 257–274.

33. *Annual Report of the Commissioner of Indian Affairs*, 1887, reprinted in Francis Paul Prucha, *Americanizing the American Indians: Writings by the "Friends of the Indian," 1880–1900* (Cambridge: Harvard University Press, 1973), pp. 201–203.

34. *Annual Report of the Commissioner of Indian Affairs*, 1887, House Exec. Doc. No. 1, 50th Cong., 1st sess., 1887–1888, Serial 2542, p. 763.

35. *Annual Report of the Commissioner of Indian Affairs*, 1887, reprinted in Prucha, *Americanizing the American Indians*, pp. 200–203.

36. *Annual Report of the Commissioner of Indian Affairs*, 1889, reprinted in Prucha, *Americanizing the American Indians*, p. 233; and "Instructions to Indian Agents in Regards to Inculcation of Patriotism in Indian Schools," *Annual Report of the Commissioner of Indian Affairs*, 1890, House Exec. Doc. 1, 51st Cong., 2nd sess., 1890–1891, Serial 2841, p. CLXVII.

37. For the belief system of U.S. history texts during this period see Ruth M. Elson, *Guardians of Tradition: American Schoolbooks of the Nineteenth Century* (Lincoln: University of Nebraska Press, 1964); and Laurence M. Hauptman, "Mythologizing Westward Expansion: Schoolbooks and the Image of the American Frontier before Turner," *Western Historical Quarterly*, 8 (July 1977), 269–282.

38. Quoted in *Annual Report of the Commissioner of Indian Affairs*, 1901, House Exec. Doc. 5, 57th Cong., 1st sess., 1901–1902, Serial 4290, p. 524.

39. Simmons, *Sun Chief*, p. 99.

40. *Southern Workman*, March 1892, p. 42.

41. Tzvetan Todorov, *The Conquest of America: The Question of the Other*, trans. Richard Howard (New York: Harper & Row, 1984).

42. Nineteenth-century images of the Indian are examined in Ray Allen Billington, *Land of Savagery, Land of Promise: The European Image of the American Frontier* (New York: W. W. Norton, 1981); Elemire Zolla, *The Writer and the Shaman: A Morphology of the American*

Indian (New York: Harcourt Brace Jovanovich, 1969), chaps. 4–7; Berkhofer, *The White Man's Indian*, pts. 1–3; Roy Harvey Pearce, *The Savages of America: A Study of the Indian and the Idea of Civilization* (Baltimore: The Johns Hopkins Press, 1965); Reginald Horsman, *Race and Manifest: The Origins of American Racial Anglo-Saxonism* (Cambridge: Harvard University Press, 1981), chaps. 6–10; and Thomas F. Gossett, *Race: The History of an Idea in America* (New York: Schocken, 1965), chaps. 3–4, 10.

43. Quoted in Pearce, *The Savages of America*, p. 155.

44. The philanthropic tradition in early federal Indian policy is treated in Bernard W. Sheehan, *Seeds of Extinction: Jeffersonian Philanthropy and the American Indian* (Chapel Hill: University of North Carolina Press, 1973); and Prucha, *The Great Father*, vol. 1, chapter 5.

45. Lewis Henry Morgan, *Ancient Society* (New York: Henry Holt & Co., 1877).

46. For a discussion of Morgan's ideas see Dwight W. Hoover, *The Red and the Black* (Chicago: Rand McNally, 1976), pp. 157–160; Berkhofer, *The White Man's Indian*, pp. 52–54; and Gossett, *Race*, pp. 248–251. The idea of social evolution also figured prominently in the works of sociologists Herbert Spencer and William Graham Sumner and historian Frederick Jackson Turner. However, in the hands of these writers there was little room for a happy resolution to the Indian story. See Richard Hofstadter, *Social Darwinism in American Thought* (Philadelphia: University of Pennsylvania Press, 1944; rpt. ed., Boston: Beacon Press, 1962), chaps. 2–3; David A. Nichols, "Civilization over Savage: Frederick Jackson Turner and the Indian," *South Dakota History*, 2 (Fall 1972), 383–405; and Robert F. Berkhofer, "Space, Time, Culture and the New Frontier," *Agricultural History*, 38 (January 1964), 21–30.

47. *Annual Report of the Commissioner of Indian Affairs*, 1881, House Exec. Doc. No. 1, 47th Cong., 1st sess., 1881–1882, Serial 2018, pp. 1–2.

48. Shurz, "Present Aspects of the Indian Problem," *North American Review*, No. 133 (July 1881): 7. See also *Annual Report of the Secretary of the Interior*, 1886, House Exec. Doc. No. 1, 49th Cong., 2nd sess., 1886–1887, Serial 2467, p. 4; and *Annual Report of the Commissioner of Indian Affairs*, 1888, House Exec. Doc. 1, 50th Cong., 2nd sess., 1888–1889, Serial 2637, p. 262. While reformers' statements on the possibility of Indian extinction may reflect the rising tide of social Darwinism, I would argue that they were much more rooted in the Jeffersonian tradition that hoped for a philanthropic resolution of the Indian question. For the impact of social Darwinism on American thought, see Hofstadter, *Social Darwinism in American Thought;* and Robert Bannister, *Social Darwinism: Science and Myth in Anglo-American Social Thought* (Philadelphia: Temple University Press, 1979). This is also an underlying theme in Stephen Jay Gould's *The Mismeasure of Man* (New York: W. W. Norton, 1981).

49. *Annual Report of the Commissioner of Indian Affairs*, 1891, House Exec. Doc. No. 1, 52nd Cong., 1st sess., 1891–1892, Serial 2934, p. 5.

50. *Proceedings of the Thirteenth Annual Meeting of the Lake Mohonk Conference of Friends of the Indian*, 1895, pp. 36–37.

51. *Proceedings of the Fourteenth Annual Meeting of the Lake Mohonk Conference of Friends of the Indian*, 1900, reprinted in Prucha, *Americanizing the American Indians*, p. 339. See also Herbert Welsh, *Four Weeks Among Some of the Sioux Tribes of Dakota and Nebraska Together with a Brief Consideration of the Indian Problem* (Philadelphia: Horace F. McCann, 1882), p. 21.

52. Welsh, "The Meaning of the Dakota Outbreak," *Scribner's Magazine*, April, 1891, p. 452. Welsh's anti-Catholicism came through in his efforts to end the government's support for contract schools (missionary schools supported by congressional funds) when Catholics began to capture an increasing percentage of appropriations. See Francis Paul Prucha, *The Churches and the Indian Schools, 1888–1912* (Lincoln: University of Nebraska Press, 1979), chap. 3.

53. *Annual Report of the Commissioner of Indian Affairs,* 1887, reprinted in Prucha, *Americanizing the American Indians,* p. 203.
54. *Annual Report of the Secretary of the Interior,* 18850, House Exec. Doc. No. 1, 49th Cong., 1st sess., 1885–1886, Serial 2378, p. 777.
55. *Annual Report of the Secretary of the Interior,* 1880, House Exec. Doc. No. 1, 46th Cong., 3rd sess., 1880–1881, Serial 1959, p. 7.
56. *Annual Report of the Commissioner of Indian Affairs,* 1879, House Exec. Doc. No. 1, 46th Cong., 2nd sess., 1879–1880, Serial 1910, p. 174.
57. *Annual Report of the Commissioner of Indian Affairs,* 1889, House Exec. Doc. No. 1, 51st Cong., 1st sess., 1889–1890, Serial 2725, p. 119.
58. *Reports of the Department of Interior,* 1909, Administrative Reports, Vol. II, p. 89. For selected aspects of the boarding school story see David Wallace Adams, "Schooling the Hopi: Federal Indian Policy Writ Small, 1887–1917," *Pacific Historical Review, 48* (August 1979), 335–356; Wilbert H. Ahern, "The Returned Indians: Hampton Institute and Its Indian Alumni, 1879–1893," *Journal of Ethnic Studies, 10* (Winter 1983), 101–124; Robert A. Trennert, "From Carlisle to Phoenix: The Rise and Fall of the Indian Outing System, 1878–1930," *Pacific Historical Review, 52* (August 1983), 267–291; Trennert, "Educating Indian Girls at Nonreservation Boarding Schools, 1878–1920," *Western Historical Quarterly, 13* (July 1982), 271–290; Margaret Connell Szasz, "Federal Boarding Schools and the Indian Child: 1920–1960," *South Dakota History, 7* (Fall 1977), 371–384; and Sally J. McBeth, *Ethnic Identity and the Boarding School Experience of West-Central Oklahoma American Indians* (Washington, DC: University Press of America, 1983).
59. McGillycuddy, *McGillycuddy, Agent: A Biography of Dr. Valentine T. McGillycuddy* (Stanford: Stanford University Press, 1941), pp. 205–206.
60. Hampton's Indian work is examined in Frances Greenwood Peabody, *Education for Life: The Story of Hampton Institute* (New York: Doubleday, Page and Co., 1918); David Wallace Adams, "Education in Hues: Red and Black at Hampton Institute, 1878–1893," *South Atlantic Quarterly, 76* (Spring 1977), 159–176; William H. Robinson, "Indian Education at Hampton Institute," in *Stony the Road: Chapters in the History of Hampton Institute,* ed. Keith L. Schall (Charlottesville: University of Virginia Press, 1977), pp. 1–33; and Joseph Willard Tingey, "Indians and Blacks Together: An Experiment in Biracial Education at Hampton Institute, 1878–1923," Ed.D. Diss., Teachers College, Columbia University, 1978.
61. *Southern Workman,* February, 1885, p. 20.
62. *Red Man,* March–April, 1893, p. 4.
63. See Wilcomb E. Washburn, "The Moral and Legal Justifications for Dispossessing the Indians," in *Seventeenth-Century America: Essays in Colonial History,* ed. James Morton Smith (Chapel Hill: University of North Carolina Press, 1959), pp. 15–32; and Arrell Morgan Gibson, "Philosophical, Legal, and Social Rationales for Appropriating the Tribal Estate, 1607 to 1980," *American Indian Law Review, 12* (1985), 3–37. The link between dispossession and education is briefly but perceptively analyzed by Lawrence A. Cremin in his *American Education: The National Experience, 1783–1876* (New York: Harper & Row, 1980), pp. 230–242.
64. Quoted in Gibson, "Philosophical, Legal, and Social Rationales," p. 14.
65. Quoted in Gibson, *The American Indian,* p. 272.
66. Berkhofer, *The White Man's Indian,* pp. 134–145.
67. Pancoast, *Impressions of the Sioux Tribes in 1882 with Some First Principles in the Indian Question* (Philadelphia: Franklin Printing House, 1883), pp. 6–7.
68. Thomas J. Morgan, "A Plea for the Papoose," reprinted in Prucha, *Americanizing the American Indians,* p. 249.
69. *Proceedings of the Third Annual Meeting of the Lake Mohonk Conference,* 1885, reprinted in Prucha, *Americanizing the American Indians,* pp. 33–34.

70. The literature on the Dawes Act is especially rich. See Prucha, *The Great Father,* vol. 2, chap. 26; Prucha, *American Indian Policy in Crisis,* chap. 8; Hoxie, *A Final Promise,* pp. 70–81, chap. 5; Priest, *Uncle Sam's Stepchildren,* pt. 4; D. S. Otis, *The Dawes Act and the Allotment of Indian Lands,* ed. Francis Paul Prucha (Norman: University of Oklahoma Press, 1973); Leonard A. Carlson, *Indians, Bureaucrats, and Land: The Dawes Act and the Decline of Indian Farming* (Westport, CT: Greenwood Press, 1981). Two excellent case studies are Donald J. Berthrong, *The Cheyenne and Arapaho Ordeal: Reservation and Agency Life in the Indian Territory, 1875–1907* (Norman: University of Oklahoma Press, 1976); and William T. Hagan, *United States–Comanche Relations: The Reservation Years* (New Haven: Yale University Press, 1976), chaps. 9–12.

71. In 1881, Indians owned 155,632,312 acres. By 1900, the number had dwindled to 77,865,373. Prucha, *American Indian Policy in Crisis,* p. 257.

72. *Proceedings of the Sixth Annual Meeting of the Lake Mohonk Conference of Friends of the Indian,* 1888, reprinted in *Annual Report of the Commissioner of Indian Affairs,* 1888, House Exec. Doc. No. 1, 50th Cong., 2nd sess., 1888–1889, Serial 2637, p. 780.

73. *Proceedings of the Fifth Annual Meeting of the Lake Mohonk Conference of Friends of the Indian,* 1887, reprinted in *Annual Report of the Commissioner of Indian Affairs,* 1887, House Exec. Doc. No. 1, 50th Cong., 1st sess., 1887–1888, Serial 2542, p. 959.

74. *Annual Report of the Commissioner of Indian Affairs,* 1889, reprinted in Prucha, *Americanizing the American Indians,* p. 237.

75. *Talks and Thoughts,* February, 1904, p. 4.

76. T. J. Jackson Lears, "The Concept of Cultural Hegemony: Problems and Possibilities," *American Historical Review, 90* (June 1985), 567–593.

77. "Instructions to Indian Agents in Regard to Inculcation of Patriotism in Indian Schools," p. CLXVII.

78. *The Red Man,* March, 1890, p. 5.

79. Quoted in Cora Folsom, "Memories of Old Hampton," Cora Folsom Papers, Hampton Institute.

80. While the focus of this paper is essentially on the meaning behind policymakers' assimilation efforts, it should be noted that students responded to these efforts in a variety of ways. While some cooperated with the educational program, others resisted. In the latter instance, arson, running away from school, and subtle forms of passive resistance all proved effective. Another response was to selectively embrace some aspects of the program while rejecting other strands, thereby constructing a kind of personal syncretic resolution of potentially conflicting value systems, all the while attempting to maintain a sense of personal and ethnic identity. The subject of student response is treated in Michael C. Coleman, "The Mission Education of Francis La Flesche: An Indian Response to the Presbyterian Boarding School in the 1860's," *American Studies in Scandinavia, 18* (1986), 67–82; Coleman, "The Responses of American Indian Children to Presbyterian Schooling in the Nineteenth Century: An Analysis through Missionary Sources," *History of Education Quarterly,* 1988; Sally J. McBeth, *Ethnic Identity and the Boarding School Experience of West-Central Oklahoma American Indians* (Washington, DC: University Press of America, 1983), esp. pp. 127–134; David Wallace Adams, "The Federal Indian Boarding School: A Study of Environment and Response, 1879–1918," Ed.D. Diss., Indiana University, 1975, chaps. 5–6; and Wilbert H. Ahern, "The Returned Indians: Hampton Institute and Its Indian Alumni, 1875–1893," *Journal of Ethnic Studies, 10* (Winter 1983), 101–124. An important perspective can be gained from consulting Indian autobiographies. Especially good are Luther Standing Bear, *My People the Sioux* (1928; rpt. Lincoln: University of Nebraska, 1975); Simmons, *Sun Chief;* Louise Udall, ed., *Me and Mine: The Life Story of Helen Sekaquaptewa* (Tucson: University of Arizona Press, 1965); Francis La Flesche, *The Middle Five: Indian Schoolboys of the Omaha Tribe* (Madison: University of Wisconsin Press, 1963); Jim Whitewolf, *The Life of a Kiowa Apache Indian,* ed. Charles Brandt (New York: Dover,

1969); and Harold Courlander, *Big Falling Snow: A Tewa-Hopi Indian's Life and Times and the History and Traditions of His People* (Albuquerque: University of New Mexico Press, 1978).

81. The text is reprinted in Wilcomb E. Washburn, ed., *The Indian and White Man* (Garden City: Anchor Books, 1964), pp. 128–130. Charles Burgess has used the Gast painting as a point of departure for his discussion of the late nineteenth-century compulsory school-attendance movement in "The Goddess, the School Book, and Compulsion," *Harvard Educational Review, 46* (May 1976), 199–216.

82. Washburn, *The Indian and the White Man*, p. 129.

The first two photographs in this article are provided courtesy of the National Archives. The third is provided courtesy of the Library of Congress.

Transitional Bilingual Education and the Socialization of Immigrants

■ ■ ■

DAVID SPENER

Controversy abounds in this country regarding the education of immigrant children in the public schools. Specifically, this controversy has centered upon the language, or languages, to be used in the instruction of language-minority students. Both advocates and opponents of bilingual education make many claims about the relative merits of English-only instruction versus the use of the students' mother tongue (Cummins, 1984; Gersten & Woodward, 1985; Hakuta, 1986; Ovando & Collier, 1985). Some light can be shed on this debate by looking beyond the immediate issue of language use in the classroom to the role of immigrants to the United States in general. This article will first examine the economic and social situation of immigrants and other minorities in the United States, and then, with this context established, will examine the role of transitional bilingual education in the socialization of immigrants and ethnolinguistic minorities.

Those concerned about how well public school students achieve their individual or familial goals in society cannot ignore the reverse side of educational policy: that is, how well the educational system prepares students to be able to perform tasks and occupy the social roles necessary to the social, political, and economic functioning of society. Educational policy at the macro level deserves scrutiny in conjunction with other aspects of governmental policy: By viewing the educational system as serving the needs of society instead of the individual student, we implicitly recognize that educational policy is not only related to, but is, in fact, largely determined by economic, social, and political factors.

Education is an integral part of the socialization process. It is future-oriented in that it prepares students to function productively in the niches of the social structures they will occupy as adults. As a part of the socialization process, education depends upon the features of the wider society — eco-

Harvard Educational Review Vol. 58 No. 2 May 1988, 133–153

nomic, technological, and political — for its direction. These features interact to form the *opportunity structure* of the society, that is, the array of social and economic positions open for a given individual to occupy on the basis of his or her particular socialization (Ogbu, 1978). How individuals confront society's opportunity structure may vary greatly, both in terms of starting position and degree of social mobility. How, then, immigrants to the United States confront its opportunity structure has important implications both for educational policy regarding immigrants and for their achievement levels in the educational system.

The Role of Minorities in the U.S. Economy

The notion of the existence of an opportunity structure in U.S. society assumes that in order for available social and economic slots to be filled by appropriately "qualified" individuals, the nature of the structure itself must somehow be communicated to society members. It is the job of the family and the school to equip youth with the skills, knowledge, attitudes, and personal attributes for both high- and low-status social roles as adults, so that all slots are filled and all necessary societal functions are served. Moreover, the skills, knowledge, attitudes, and personal attributes that determine a low-status position in this society must be differentiated from those suitable for a high-status position. Given this, and assuming that all the slots are in some sense "necessary," it follows that some individuals must be socialized to occupy high-status positions, while others must be socialized or adapted to fill low-status positions. Under these differential socialization processes certain groups can be specially socialized to occupy certain positions in society. Indeed, historically, it has been the case that individuals from racial, ethnic, and linguistic minority groups have tended to occupy low-status positions in our society.

The perceptions of both immigrant and majority groups concerning opportunities in U.S. society for immigrant groups who are also members of racial and ethnolinguistic minorities matter in two ways. First, how both parents and children perceive the opportunities open to them in society and the combination of knowledge, skills, and behaviors that must be acquired in order to take advantage of them has an effect on how children are trained. Levine (1967) has posited two hypotheses about how children acquire the attributes for upward social mobility within the opportunity structure. In one, he suggests that parents of socially mobile children train them to adopt the attributes of a "successful" person in the society, thus helping their children to gain access to high-status positions. In the other, he proposes that children develop accurate perceptions of the possibilities for social advancement in response to differing "messages" received from society and adapt their behavior accordingly. Both of these hypotheses assume that social mobility depends on an individual's ability to adapt to the norm for mobility (Levine, 1967, cited in Ogbu, 1978).

Secondly, the perceptions of the majority group in society regarding minority group members are important, because in a society such as the United States the members of the majority White group control the opportunity structure. In his book *Minority Education and Caste: The American System in Cross-Cultural Perspective,* John U. Ogbu (1978) discusses discrimination against minority groups in terms of their socialization through public education. He describes situations in which groups controlling the opportunity structure ascribe to members of different minority groups only those attributes specific to low-status social and economic situations. If such ascription is intense, it creates an invisible but effective job ceiling above which it may be extremely difficult to rise. Ogbu goes on to contrast the different kinds of minority groups that may be present in a society and the ways in which their relation to the opportunity structure may vary according to their relative ascribed status and their perception of that status. Additionally, he distinguishes between castelike minorities and immigrant minorities.

Castelike Minorities and Immigrant Minorities

According to Ogbu (1978), members of castelike minorities are perceived by the majority group to be inherently inferior in all aspects of intelligence and ability to carry out the tasks associated with high-status jobs. They "enjoy" a pariah status which sharply circumscribes their economic, political, and cultural participation in society. Members of castelike minorities do not compete freely with majority group members but, instead, are summarily excluded from certain jobs solely because of their caste status. Thus, they occupy the least desirable positions in society and face job ceilings which only a few may surmount. Children of caste-minority parents may be socialized for inferiority based on their parents' and their own perceptions of the adult statuses open to them. In addition, public schools may play subtle roles in educating and socializing caste-minority children for low-status positions as adults. Such "inferiorating" education can result from the following causes: negative teacher attitudes and expectations toward these children; teachers recruited from the majority group who are isolated from the minority community, thus inhibiting parent/teacher collaboration in the children's education; biased testing, misclassification of students as learning disabled, and ability group "tracking"; biased textbooks and curricula; use of clinical definitions of caste-minority children's academic problems which place the blame on the minority family for producing "inferior" children; and classroom dynamics that favor the more active participation of majority-group children (Cummins, 1984; McDermott, 1976; Ogbu, 1978). In addition to these factors are the more commonly cited problems of overcrowding, decaying facilities, and drug abuse found in many schools with primarily minority children.

In Ogbu's classification scheme, immigrant minorities may be treated by the majority group in the host society much the same as castelike minorities. That is, their political, economic, and social roles are circumscribed, and they face job ceilings similar to those for caste-minority members. Members of immigrant minorities, however, may react to the same opportunity structure in ways very different from castelike minorities. Since a common reason members of immigrant minorities come to this country is to improve their condition relative to what they experienced in their homelands, they come into contact with the opportunity structure voluntarily. One of their personal measures of success, then, is not whether they have achieved parity in status with the majority group of the host society, but whether their situation has improved materially by immigrating — in which case, the member of an immigrant minority may actually accept discrimination as the price for personal advancement.

Furthermore, as strangers who may have established their own separate communities in the host country, immigrants are not as likely as native-born minorities to internalize the host society's caste ideology. Consequently, members of immigrant minorities may hold instrumental attitudes toward the host society, seeing it as a means to an end while holding on to either the hope of steady relative advance within it, or an improved economic position upon returning to the home country (Ogbu, 1978). Parents' instrumentalist attitudes toward the society in general may carry over to their children in school, who may see more immediate value in their education than caste-minority students whose families may not expect to advance.

There are several problems with Ogbu's castelike versus immigrant minority dichotomy in describing the current situation for immigrants in the United States. First is the issue of race, which is noted but not fully developed in Ogbu's analysis. For Ogbu, the major castelike minority in the United States is, of course, Black people, who constitute a pariah group whose main identifying characteristic is race. But Ogbu does not explicitly discuss the racial background of immigrant minorities in his classification scheme. This is an important omission, since historical experience in the United States has demonstrated that assignments of immigrant groups to low-status positions in the opportunity structure have often been made primarily upon the basis of race. During past waves of immigration to this country from Europe, the outward ethnolinguistic markers of immigrant minorities have disappeared after one or two generations. But for current immigrants from the Third World, race will not escape them even after linguistic and cultural barriers to their advancement have been overcome. The vast majority of those currently immigrating to the United States are non-White people from Latin America, the Caribbean, and Asia (Cockcroft, 1986; Dulles, 1966; Moyers, 1985; U.S. English, 1985).

Many current immigrants, especially Latin Americans, are racially and linguistically "lumped" by the White majority with Chicanos and Puerto Ricans, who, along with the Chinese in some areas, have become castelike minorities by establishing themselves permanently in the United States over the course of several generations. For example, the experiences of Chicanos and Puerto Ricans show that, over time, immigrant minorities may become castelike minorities who share a pariah status with Black people based principally on their race. The phenomenon of "lumping" new immigrants with ethnically similar caste minorities undermines Ogbu's contention that the children of immigrants may have a better chance at higher rates of success in school on the basis of their purported instrumentalist attitudes toward education. Failure to look at the racial background of immigrants also ignores the relatively ascribed statuses among different groups of recent immigrants. Numerous reports appear in the press comparing "successful" immigrant groups with those in the process of becoming castelike minorities. Thus, "Korean-ness" may come to carry a positive racial stereotype, whereas "Mexican-ness" may come to be stigmatized (Matthews, 1985).

It is also important to consider other changes in the nature of immigration to this country. One difference is that a large number of new immigrants to the United States are coming not so much to better their economic situation as to escape war and physical repression in their native countries in Central America, Indochina, and the Caribbean. Because of their experience of violence and physical and emotional trauma, they may have different aspirations and adapt themselves to the opportunity structure here in ways that are quite different from both established caste minorities and traditional immigrant groups. How these new refugees are received also differs. Some are welcomed with open arms by the U.S. government, while others live under constant threat of deportation by the Immigration and Naturalization Service (INS). Indochinese refugees, for example, are clearly being sent a different message about the array of opportunities open to them in this society than are Central American or Haitian refugees. Indochinese (who are not policed by the INS, need not fear deportation, and are eligible for public assistance) are recognized as victims of Communist aggression and are welcome in this country, while Central Americans and Haitians (who are policed by the INS, have reason to fear deportation, and are not eligible for any kind of public assistance) are perceived as taking away jobs from U.S. citizens (MacEoin & Riley, 1982).

The nature of economically motivated immigration itself has also changed since the first part of this century. Earlier groups of immigrants, from Southern and Eastern Europe, came to the United States at a time of rapid industrial expansion and were actively recruited to work in nearly all segments of a burgeoning industry. They came at a time of very real labor shortage, and although exploited, had a relatively large array of opportunities for placement and advancement, at least *within* the working class. This relative mobility was possible not only because of the labor shortage, but also because quite a large percentage of the working class was drawn from the ranks of first- and second-generation immigrants (Dulles, 1966).

Current immigrants, from Asia and Latin America, are entering a post-industrial United States which faces economic stagnation, high levels of unemployment — especially among members of the industrial working class — and a shift in the economy away from the production of goods toward the provision of services. As such, the opportunities for these new non-White immigrants tend toward low-level employment in the expanding service sector, seasonal farm labor, or membership in the strata of the chronically unemployed or underemployed (Harrington & Levinson, 1985). If these, in fact, are the roles open to most new immigrants to the United States, then we might well expect that government policies, including educational policy, will work in favor of socializing immigrants for such roles.

The Role of "Illegal Aliens" in the U.S. Economy

Tove Skutnabb-Kangas of Denmark's Roskilde University has examined how the immigration and educational policies of several European countries relate to the roles played by immigrants in those countries. In her article "Guest Worker or Immigrant: Different Ways of Reproducing an Underclass" (1981), she analyzes post–World War II immigration to several Western European countries. Immediately following the war, these countries initiated guest worker programs to meet a severe labor shortage. Rapid post-war reconstruction and economic growth led the governments of these countries to recruit and hire, for a finite amount of time, unskilled and uneducated workers from Southern Europe and the Balkans to fill low-paying industrial and service jobs undesired by domestic workers.

Forty-plus years have passed since the end of World War II, and Europe has been rebuilt, but many guest workers have yet to return home, even though industrial production has slowed or been exported to the Third World, and high levels of unemployment have become chronic in the host countries. The continued residence of alien workers and their families in Western Europe with the tacit or official approval of the host countries has led Skutnabb-Kangas (1981) and others (Cockcroft, 1986; Dixon, Martinez, & McCaughan, 1982) to propose that immigrants have taken on a new function in modern, post-industrial nations. In the past, a host country would encourage immigration in order to meet labor shortages in an expanding economy. A primary role for immigrants in modern, post-industrial countries is to serve as a buffer between the domestic population, specifically the native-born working class, and the effects of periodic downturns in the economy. In essence, Skutnabb-Kangas sees immigrants as coming to constitute the modern caste minorities of Europe — the last hired, the first fired, the lowest status members of society. Nowhere does this view of the situation seem more real than in Great Britain today, where non-White immigrants compose the vast majority of the British underclass. If one accepts that the economies of the United States and Western European countries are similar, immigrants to the United States can be seen as additions to the ranks of castelike minorities historically represented by Blacks, Chicanos, Chinese, Native Americans, and Puerto Ricans.

Although Skutnabb-Kangas's model for the new role of immigrants in post-industrial societies sheds some light on the situation in the United

States, it does not directly address itself to one of the most provocative and controversial issues for U.S. immigration policy — the increasing presence of "illegal aliens" in the U.S. work force. Few public issues have generated as emotional a debate as the new wave of Hispanic immigration across our southern border. The alarm with which this migration has been treated in the press has fostered widespread misunderstanding of its nature and has fueled nativist and racist sentiments among large segments of the country's population. Even normally restrained and cautious public officials, such as former CIA Director William Colby, have expressed fears of the development of "a Spanish-speaking Quebec in the U.S. Southwest," and have viewed illegal immigration from Mexico as "a greater threat to national security than the Soviet Union" (Cockcroft, 1986, p. 39). Television specials present images of "an army of aliens waiting to move forth across the border when night falls," and reporters interview White workers who feel that the United States is "being invaded as surely as [if] we had an enemy dropping bombs on us" (Moyers, 1985).

Nonetheless, by using the tools of analysis developed by Skutnabb-Kangas and by Ogbu, illegal immigration can be viewed quite differently. Some leaders in this country are less alarmed and more rational about immigration, as illustrated by William French Smith, the Reagan administration's first attorney general. Smith commented that the administration's goal was not to stem the flow of foreign workers into this country, but rather to "reduce and regulate" the flow and to channel foreigners "into jobs where they are needed" (Cockcroft, 1986; p. 220).

As noted above, Skutnabb-Kangas has suggested that immigrant workers serve as a buffer between native-born workers and the effects of economic downturn in developed nations. The historian and political economist James Cockcroft, in his book *Outlaws in the Promised Land* (1986), develops this analysis more completely in examining the role of undocumented Mexican workers in the U.S. economy. Cockcroft argues that thousands of "bad" jobs in the U.S. economy need filling, and employers face an acute shortage of laborers willing to fill those jobs. For Cockcroft, a "bad" job is one that does not pay a worker an adequate living wage, does not provide health and life insurance benefits, and exposes a worker to unsafe working conditions and unhealthy hours. Furthermore, Cockcroft points out that often the difference between a "good" job and a "bad" job is not intrinsic to the nature of the work or the level of skill required to perform it. The large difference in wages and benefits between an auto worker and an assembler of calculator parts in Silicon Valley, for example, cannot be accounted for by differences in skills, since neither job requires an extended period of special education or training; essentially the work performed in both jobs is similar. The auto worker has a better job because the work force in the auto industry is organized and has benefited for decades from union contracts with the major auto firms. In other words, workers have the ability to organize collectively under certain free-labor conditions to transform low-paying, undesirable jobs into better paying positions that are relatively attractive and difficult to obtain. In reality, Cockcroft maintains, there is no shortage of unskilled workers in the U.S. economy. Instead, he argues, there is a shortage of employers willing to pay a living wage and provide decent working conditions for their employees.

If, for example, seasonal farm labor paid better, there would be no seasonal labor shortage to be filled by undocumented Mexican workers in California's Central Valley. Farm labor jobs pay poorly because the work force in the agricultural sector of the economy is unorganized. Native-born or naturalized citizens, who enjoy the protection of federal and state labor codes won by decades of union organizing and who are eligible for social services, have no interest in taking these "bad" jobs. It is the role of illegal immigrants — the "outlaws" whose lack of protection by U.S. laws renders them unable to organize to raise wages or improve working conditions — to fill the "bad" jobs in the U.S. economy (Cockcroft, 1986). Cockcroft argues that illegal immigrants are recruited on the basis of their special "illegal" status to fill low-status slots in the U.S. opportunity structure outlined by Ogbu.

By extrapolating from the work of Skutnabb-Kangas (1980), it can be said that undocumented workers in the United States are not significantly different from the guest workers of post-war Western Europe, although they may not be officially recognized as such. Guest workers serve at the pleasure of the host country and can be ordered to return to their country of origin at any time. Their legal status is that of a policed labor force tightly constrained by the host government. They are denied the right to make demands for higher wages or for the provision of social services from business or government. They are like the immigrant minorities of Ogbu's model in that, even under the most draconian conditions in the host country, they may "enjoy" a higher standard of living than in their home countries. Guest workers are brought into the host country to do its most menial work for lower wages than the native-born work force would accept. The presence of guest workers in a country can also serve to elevate the status and pay of native-born or naturalized workers. This is because guest workers contribute substantially to expanding the gross national product and pay taxes to the host country while drawing substandard wages and receiving only token government expenditures for social services (Skutnabb-Kangas, 1981). While there has not been an official government guest worker program in the United States for over twenty years, the continued participation of "illegal aliens" in the U.S. work force suggests a tacit government guest worker policy, although the benefits to the naturalized work force may not be as directly correlated as in Great Britain's guest worker program.

The immigration reform legislation that was recently signed into law (Immigration Reform and Control Act, 1986) by President Reagan has received much attention. On the surface, it appears to take strong measures to halt the influx of undocumented workers, who many citizens believe threaten the

DAVID SPENER

livelihoods of "legal" workers. The efficacy of the measures mandated by the bill must be questioned, however. Although sanctions against knowingly hiring undocumented workers may discourage some employers, enforcement of this provision may or may not be vigorous. Consider the Bracero Guest Worker Program, for example, in which the U.S. government imported Mexican workers to work in agriculture to meet labor shortages. The workers stayed well after the return to a peacetime economy. Many believe that the Bracero program survived because it preserved a docile, cheap labor force for U.S. agribusiness. The historical record shows that many regulations governing the import and employment of workers in this program generally went unenforced, allowing employers to violate them with impunity (Cockcroft, 1986).

In spite of the fact that vast new expenditures have authorized the INS to strengthen and expand law enforcement and investigative capabilities, most knowledgeable observers agree that the agency lacks the capability to close the border and prevent the employment of "illegals" in this country (Brinkley, 1986; Matthews, 1986). Finally, the inclusion of a guest worker program for seasonal farm labor gives an additional indication that many of those individuals presently working illegally in the United States are, in fact, needed economically. Cockcroft (1986) notes that in the past, mass importation of Mexicans as "guest workers" has occurred simultaneously with their mass deportation as "illegals." The new immigration law seems less likely to eliminate illegal aliens from the work force than to police their presence in order to keep the "bad" jobs filled.

The Effect of U.S. Economic Realities on Attitudes toward Minorities

If immigrants, guest workers, and "illegal aliens" are performing services that are important to the U.S. economy by filling undesirable jobs, contributing to the growth of the GNP, and paying taxes, and if the existence of an underclass artificially raises the status of the White working class, why should the United States be witnessing an outpouring of anti-immigrant sentiment from the White working class at this time? One explanation lies in the nature of the changes in the U.S. economy and its export of "good" jobs (as defined by Cockcroft) to other countries where wages and corporate taxes are lower than those in the United States. The greatest loss of jobs in the economy has been in those heavy-manufacturing industries which, because of unionization and high profits during the period between the end of World War II and the end of the U.S. involvement in the Vietnam War, had paid high hourly wages, provided good benefit packages for their workers, and had been regulated by the government for standards of worker health and safety (Harrington & Levinson, 1985). The greatest growth in jobs, on the other hand, has been in the so-called service sector, where jobs were traditionally filled by members of the underclass, and in the high-tech field, where most firms are non-union (Bluestone, 1987). Huge cuts in government expenditures on welfare, combined with the loss of "good" jobs in the economy, have forced many members of the White, native-English-speaking working class to seek lower status jobs in the growth sectors of the economy (Harrington & Levinson, 1985). For the first time, many majority group members are competing with members of castelike and immigrant minorities for suddenly scarce jobs (Bluestone, 1987). Traditionally, this competition has not existed, and it may be the perception of large numbers of White, native-born workers that such competition is unjust, especially when their chief competitors are not "Americans." Hostility toward foreigners from U.S. workers, however misplaced, should really come as no surprise under these conditions.

A second possible explanation concerns U.S. nationalism and its role in enhancing the self-perception of the domestic working class. The rise of the United States to the most powerful and economically successful nation in the world following World War II had the effect of raising the absolute status of all U.S. citizens in a world context, regardless of their relative status within the U.S. social hierarchy. Although mythical, this perceived status has had a powerful effect upon the psyche of U.S. workers. Another myth is that of the United States as a "melting pot," a nation of newcomers who have given up their old identities in order to assume the new, if somewhat vague, "American" identity. All newcomers then start at the bottom of the social ladder and climb in status as they progressively shed their foreign identities. As the economy is restructured, many assimilated Americans are experiencing a loss in relative status that forces them to work alongside and compete for jobs with foreign workers and other out-group members who, according to the myth, "belong" at the bottom of the social ladder because they are not Americanized. At this point, the fall in relative status is transformed into a fall in absolute status as the status of native-born within the United States falls to that of foreigners.

The perceived superior status of Americanized workers in the world might be preserved in several ways. One alternative, the deportation of foreigners so that the only workers remaining are culturally Americanized, is reflected in mounting pressures to stem the "tide" of illegal aliens entering the country and to deport those illegals already working. Another possibility is to drop the job ceiling for immigrant minorities even lower through intensified racial discrimination and violence. Consider the following recent events in Georgia, where the connection between anti-immigrant and non-English speakers has been used by lawmakers to prohibit the use of Spanish. In the small community of Cedartown, near the Alabama border, a meat-packing plant that was the town's largest source of jobs employed about one hundred Mexican workers alongside a large majority of White and Black employees. In 1985, many of the Anglo and Black workers walked off the job in a strike action organized by the Ku Klux Klan to protest the "discrimination" against U.S. workers by the company. The strike action followed the roadside slayings of two of the plant's Mexican employees in the previous three years by Klan members or associates ("Bill Pushes an Official State Prejudice," 1986). One of the Klan defendants was acquitted by an all-White jury ("Cedartown

Strike," 1986). In 1986, the Georgia General Assembly passed a resolution declaring English to be the state's official language in order to reinforce "the cultural fabric of one language" within the state. The *Atlanta Constitution* stated in an editorial that it could not be seen as coincidence that the measure was introduced into the state legislature by the senator whose district includes Cedartown:

> It is such an obvious slap at dozens of Mexicans who came to Cummings's northwest Georgia district to work in a local meat-packing plant, only to find themselves targets of intense hatred and violence by local yahoos, that one wonders at the short span of some of the lawmakers' memories. ("Bill Pushes an Official State Prejudice," 1986, p. 22A)

The legislators' action in this light can be seen both as an effort to bestow official blessing upon state residents who speak English, and a repudiation of those residents who do not. The rapid growth in the number of Hispanic immigrants from diverse national and racial backgrounds to this country has contributed to the perception of the Spanish language as a racial characteristic, since Spanish is virtually the only feature common to all Hispanic immigrants (though not to all Hispanic residents), and because most new immigrants to the United States are coming from Latin America. If one accepts the notion that speaking Spanish functions as a racial characteristic of Hispanics in this country, can one ignore the racist implications of Georgia's English-language resolution?

In a related case in California, where there is a long history of violent crimes against Hispanic migrant workers and union organizers, and where it is traditional for the perpetrators of such crimes to go unpunished (Cockcroft, 1986), voters in 1986 overwhelmingly passed a ballot initiative declaring the primacy of the English language in public discourse ("An Official Language for California," 1986). The measure is intended to curtail the use of Spanish in the state government bureaucracy and in public schools.

A third alternative for preserving the status of Americanized workers, and the one that has the greatest implication for educational policy, is to insist that the immigrants who are allowed to remain in the United States become full-fledged, Anglicized Americans at the earliest possible date. Advocates of this path, among them the most strident critics of bilingual education, seem to fear that the price of cultural pluralism is the loss of a cultural basis for nationalism. All three of these remedies, however contradictory, are being applied simultaneously in the United States in the mid-1980s. At times, they are even cloaked in the rhetoric of the civil rights movement. A recent article written by a Black columnist in the *Washington Post,* for instance, questioned whether or not the United States could compete with a "homogeneous society like Japan" unless it, too, took steps towards homogenization by moving faster towards assimilating ethnic and racial minorities into the mainstream (Rowan, 1986).

The Role of U.S. Educational Policy in Socializing Minorities for a Part in the Economy

Not surprisingly, current public demands to assimilate immigrant groups quickly, for their own good and for the good of the nation, have revolved around proficiency in the English language. English has become *the* public issue in the socialization of immigrant adults and children living in the United States. Increasingly, attempts are being made to ensure that mastery of the "standard" or "core" dialect of American English is represented as emblematic of an "American" identity. The public debate on the English language issue raised two concerns. First, it has always been true that millions of native-born U.S. citizens have never mastered Standard English as defined by school textbooks, and that, since its founding, the United States has been multilingual (Hakuta, 1986; Shor, 1986). Second, it is necessary to question the extent to which mastery of English is necessary to carry out the functions of the roles open to adult immigrants in the U.S. opportunity structure. If, as a consequence of the imposition of a job ceiling on the upward social mobility of their members, immigrant minorities are restricted to "immigrant" jobs which do not require high English proficiency, it may be unrealistic to expect that immigrants will ever master "Standard" English. A number of eminent linguists, most notable among them John Schumann, have hypothesized that individuals become proficient in a second language not so much due to the effects of formal instruction, but rather to the degree that second language proficiency serves their social and economic needs (Schumann, 1976, 1980). In this sense, proficiency in Standard English is not a causal variable in an individual's social status, but rather, is reflective of the individual's opportunities to participate in social settings where Standard English is the language of the participants (Schumann, 1980). The lack of proficiency in Standard English on the part of many Black and White working-class Americans, in spite of years of public schooling, bears witness to the predictive value of Schumann's hypothesis.

Respect for the U.S. public education system has rested on the belief that public education is a great upward equalizer, giving children of low-status families the chance to surpass their parents' status through achievement in school (Shor, 1986). This belief parallels the melting pot myth which links social advancement to the process of "Americanization." Both notions presume that the opportunity structure of U.S. society will always have a surplus of higher status jobs to be filled by individuals who have adopted the language, values, and beliefs of the dominant White majority as they pass through the educational system. The presumption of a surplus of "good" jobs in the United States is dubious at best. Nonetheless, the "excellence in education" movement, spearheaded by the presidential commission's report on the nation's public schools (National Commission on Excellence in Education, 1983) rests on just such an assumption, and advocates the adoption of national curriculum standards aiming at the "Americanization" of students from groups outside the cultural mainstream. A focus on mastery of Standard English is a major feature of the proposed new curriculum standards (Shor, 1986).

The "Excellence in Education" Movement

Educational curriculum theorists, including Ira Shor of the City University of New York, have extensively analyzed the proposals for restoration of "excellence" in the nation's schools. Shor has commented in particular on the curriculum standards heralded by excellence movement leader Albert Shanker, president of the American Federation of Teachers. Shanker was disturbed by tendencies towards "permissiveness" and "cultural relativism" in the schools in the 1960s and 1970s, and began to argue for the re-establishment of standards of academic excellence in public schools. The "core curriculum" formulated by Shanker is described by Shor as follows:

> This theme of a universal course of study embodying a singular dominant culture took shape as a "core curriculum." That core of knowledge emanated from the center of authority outward to the periphery. It is based in Standard English, a traditional reading list, and cleansed versions of history (the "American Heritage"). The "core curriculum" idea rejects the ideological diversity of the protest era. (Shor, 1986, p. 13)

Shor criticizes the concept of the "core curriculum" in general because, he says, it "transmits an official value system disguised as universal knowledge" (Shor, 1986, p. 23). He also criticizes the "core curriculum" for fostering a nationwide hysteria over an alleged "literacy" crisis in the United States based upon widespread lack of mastery of Standard English, which has been a linguistic reality among Black people, immigrant groups, and lower class Whites in this country almost since its founding (Dulles, 1966; Hakuta, 1986; Johansen & Maestas, 1983; McDermott; 1976; Ovando & Collier, 1985; Rodriguez, 1981; Sennett & Cobb, 1972). Shor writes: "Curriculum and civilization were defined in the Literacy Crisis as resting on the authority of the elite language; that language was posed as a universal standard of culture rather than as a class-specific form of expression" (Shor, 1986, p. 65). Shor contrasts the English achievement standards of the core curriculum with more tolerant views regarding language usage:

> [in 1973] the largest organization of English teachers, the National Council of Teachers of English, had voted in its policy on "Students' Rights to Their Own Language." This egalitarian document described Standard English as a privileged dialect, and as one dialect among many in a diverse culture. It is no secret that most people speak a form of English different from the language of teachers, of literature, and of the elite. (Shor, 1986, p. 65)

The call for excellence in education, including the demand for assimilation of immigrant and castelike minorities in the United States, is justified as necessary to raise the skills and productivity of the U.S. work force as the U.S. economy moves into new technological and trade frontiers in the twenty-first century. In spite of the fact that most evidence points to a *decrease* in the need for skilled laborers as the complexity of goods produced in the economy increases (Bluestone, 1987; Braverman, 1974), proponents of the excellence movement insist that the shortage of skilled, literate personnel in the labor market restricts U.S. ability to compete with the rest of the world. As evidence, they point to the declining productivity of workers and the falling academic test scores of students. The workers and students responsible for these declines are then seen as dragging down the rest of the society as it strives to enter a new age of high-tech prosperity. Members of immigrant and castelike minorities, who often score lower on measures of academic achievement both because of cultural and dialectal differences and decades of discrimination, are easily targeted for this criticism. Minorities have, in fact, been scapegoated on numerous occasions, as shown in this excerpt from the conservative journal *Heritage Today:*

> The most damaging blows to science and mathematics education have come from Washington. For the past 20 years, federal mandates have favored "disadvantaged" pupils at the expense of those who have the highest potential to contribute positively to society. . . . By catering to the demands of special interest groups — racial minorities, the handicapped, women and non-English speaking students — America's public schools have successfully competed for government funds, but they have done so at the expense of education as a whole. (Gardner, 1983, pp. 6–7)

The question of how the call for excellence in education is compatible with the decline in the number of "good" jobs available and skilled laborers needed in the U.S. economy is important if one accepts Shor's proposition that the educational system is "functional or dysfunctional to society at any instance to the degree it prepares student attitudes appropriate to the needs of an unequal social order" (Shor, 1986, p. 168). On the surface, it would seem that accepting the excellence program in the schools would lead to just the sort of dysfunction to which Shor alludes. Returning to Ogbu's job ceiling notion helps to reveal a way in which the imposition of new standards of excellence in the schools is highly functional.

In a sense, the United States is not experiencing a literacy crisis, but a crisis of an "overeducated" work force. Well-compensated, higher status jobs in the economy are in short supply relative to the number of workers "qualified" by their education and socialization to fill them (Bluestone, 1987; Cockcroft, 1896; Harrington & Levinson, 1985; Shor, 1986). As competition among workers for "good" jobs intensifies, employers can arbitrarily raise the qualifications a worker must have. The excellence movement seeks through its meritocracy to reward the "excellent" student who "excels" in the language and behaviors of the dominant elite, and to punish (through low grades and tracking) the "inferior" student who does not master the language and behaviors of the elite, the outcome of the movement will be to maintain a job ceiling for minorities. This serves to preserve the perceived superior status of the native-born White worker who is increasingly being called upon to accept employment in occupations formerly reserved for the underclass.

The United States offers immigrants an ambiguous social contact. It reads, more or less, as follows: "In order to participate in a non-marginal way in the U.S. economy, you must become an American by giving up your loyalty to your home country and language, and you must learn the language of the American elite. In order to become an American, you must meet certain standards. This country is in the process of raising its standards because, unfortunately, there are already too many Americans. If you aren't allowed to become an American, there's still plenty of room for you in this country — at the bottom." Due to catastrophic economic conditions in much of the rest of the world, there are millions of people ready to sign on. A Mexican woman waiting to sneak across the U.S. border at Tijuana put it this way: "We're sad about it, but what can we do? There is no opportunity in Mexico. Mexico is very poor, and the government doesn't help the people. . . . We are born to die. We know where we were born, but we don't know where we will end up" (Kelly, 1986).

Assimilation as a Goal of Immigrant Educational Policies

In spite of all the limitations on the social mobility of immigrants within the United States, the goal of almost any educational policy directed toward them will be assimilationist in some measure. The pace of the assimilation will vary as will the means of achieving it. The strategies that have been employed to implement immigrant educational policies in both the United States and Europe include so-called submersion, immersion, and transitional bilingual education programs. A question that must be raised at this point concerns the type of assimilation the United States aims to achieve through its educational policies. Is the goal to assimilate immigrant children into the dominant social group of the host society, or more to discourage their assimilation of the cultural and linguistic norms of their home country? In the United States, a long history of racism and the existence of a stratified opportunity structure combine to work against assimilation into the host society's higher status, dominant White group. What could be the rationale for assimilating immigrant children away from their own culture?

Ogbu's caste minority/immigrant minority model can provide some insight into this question. Ogbu (1978) noted that many immigrants hold instrumental attitudes toward the host society — by holding on to the hope of steady relative advancement within it or by an improved economic position upon returning to the home country. Viewing the host society instrumentally means concomitantly that immigrants view their stay as provisional, depending upon how they perceive their position in facing the opportunity structure. In Ogbu's view, it is the unassimilated status of immigrant minorities, best illustrated by the possibility of ultimately returning to the home country, that qualitatively distinguishes them from caste minorities. (A number of authors have studied the situation of immigrants standing at the crossroads between assimilation and return: See Ekstrand, Foster, Olkiewicz, and Stankovski [1981].) That unassimilated status means that immigrants may hold onto attitudes, values, and behaviors that are incompatible with occupying a traditional caste-minority position with the U.S. opportunity structure.

The education of immigrant children enters the picture here in a most profound way. In order to prepare students for caste-minority status in the host society, whether in the United States or Europe, several things must be accomplished. First, children must let go their instrumentalist attitudes that view school and the host country as a means of personal advancement. Second, they must internalize the caste ideology of the host society. That is, they must not have a value system and a way of life independent of that of the society at large. Finally, they must be denied the possibility of returning to their home country should prospects for advance in the host country dim. How can schooling accomplish these aims? Official indoctrination might be one way. Another more politically acceptable way is to take away the immigrant child's language and culture and replace them with some form more suited to the social roles he or she can be expected to occupy as an adult in the host society. All three strategies mentioned earlier — submersion, immersion, and transitional bilingual education — can be effective means of achieving both assimilation and a progressive disengagement from the home language and culture. They may also play a role in educating immigrant children for low-status roles as adults.

The aim of educational approaches which prohibit mother-tongue instruction for immigrants is unquestionably and strongly assimilationist. The so-called submersion approach, which places limited-English-proficient children in English-only classrooms in the hope that they will somehow learn the new language and adapt themselves to the new culture, has been shown to have devastating consequences on the average immigrant child's cognitive development and academic achievement (California State Department of Education, 1982; Hakuta, 1986; Ovando & Collier, 1985). The immersion approach is also English-only, though the academic outcomes of immersion programs in the United States have only recently begun to be studied (Gersten & Woodward, 1985). The few programs in the United States that do use some degree of mother-tongue instruction and that have been implemented on a large scale are transitional bilingual education (TBE) programs. Since bilingual education is currently embroiled in controversy, an examination of how it may function as an agent of socialization for immigrant children is worthwhile.

The goal of federally funded TBE programs in the United States has never been the "production" of bilingual, biliterate, bicultural adults capable of functioning competently in two languages and cultures. If this were the case, there would have to be numerous programs that promote the development of academic skills in immigrant students' native languages in all school subjects through the end of high school. Virtually no such programs exist in this country. Since the 1974 reauthorization of Title VII of the Elementary and Secondary Education Act, the primary aim of such programs has been to raise the English proficiency of non-English-speaking children such that they may be able to participate "effectively" in classrooms where English is the sole medium of instruction (Ovando & Collier, 1985). Transitional bilingual education programs typically last only two to three years. The mother tongues of children in such transitional programs are used as necessary to introduce content material and to begin to develop the literacy competencies that will presumably help children learn to read and write in English. English instruction focuses on the development of students' oral command of the language as well as communicative competencies in English. After three years, or when students are deemed sufficiently proficient in English (whichever comes first), they are "mainstreamed" into regular English-only classrooms (Ovando & Collier, 1985). With formal instruction in the mother tongue completely terminated both as the medium of instruction in the mother tongue completely terminated both as the medium of instruction and as a content subject very early on in students' education, they may be put on the road to *limited bilingualism.*

Limited bilingualism, that is, less than native-like proficiency in either the mother tongue or the second language, has been associated with impeded cognitive development and lowered academic achievement in a number of studies (California State Department of Education, 1982; Cummins, 1981; Hakuta, 1986). Research into bilingualism as a cognitive phenomenon has shown that second-language acquisition is most successful when there is a strong foundation in the mother tongue, and that conversational skills in a second language are learned earlier than the ability to use the language for academic learning (Hakuta, 1985). Research has also indicated that in order for bilingual children to match their monolingual peers' levels of cognitive and academic achievement, they must first attain a minimum linguistic threshold of near native proficiency in at least one of their two languages (Cummins, 1981, 1984; Skutnabb-Kangas, 1979). Cummins (1981) has gone further to suggest that it takes at least three to four years of formal schooling to attain such a threshold.

It is now widely accepted among researchers studying language acquisition that there are two dimensions of language proficiency (California State Department of Education, 1982; Hakuta, 1986; Ovando & Collier, 1985). The first dimension has to do with those skills associated with casual conversational use of the language, what Cummins has called BICS — basic interpersonal communicative skills. The second dimension concerns more formal intellectual understanding of the language and the ability to use it for intellectual or academic purposes. Cummins has called this dimension CALP — cognitive academic learning proficiency. Proficiency in one dimension, however, does not necessarily correlate positively with proficiency in the other. Moreover, it is generally believed that the BICS dimension is acquired before the CALP dimension (California State Department of Education, 1982; Cummins, 1984; Hakuta, 1986). The minimum linguistic threshold includes the development of CALP-level skills in a formal academic setting (Cummins, 1981, 1984).

Transitional Bilingual Education Programs

Bilingualism research findings have important implications for transitional bilingual education programs. The overriding goal of TBE programs is to mainstream students into English-only classrooms. As a result, a major component of such programs is the development of English proficiency in the students. Unfortunately, most of the programs last only two to three years, not long enough for children to build up CALP level skills in either their mother tongue or English. Such children may be mainstreamed into English-only classes before they have attained the minimum linguistic threshold necessary to ensure their ability to carry out cognitively demanding academic tasks in English. Additionally, two to three years at the elementary level is regarded as insufficient time to allow for the development of CALP skills in the mother tongue. Students mainstreamed after only two to three years in bilingual classrooms will generally not be able to rely on a cross-language transfer of academic skills from their mother tongue to English to compensate for their CALP deficit in English. Consequently, language-minority students who are mainstreamed out of transitional bilingual programs may not be sufficiently prepared to participate and compete in English-only classrooms where English is the mother tongue of the majority of their peers.

The consequences of mainstreaming limited-English-proficient children into English-only classrooms extend beyond the cognitive and the personal. The social consequences include defining the terms of competition and social ranking in the public schools and influencing the perceptions that English mother-tongue students and teachers have of immigrant children in their classes. Immigrant children (as well as children of native-born linguistic minority parents) mainstreamed into regular classrooms from transitional bilingual programs may be presented before their teachers and classmates not as equal-but-different representatives of another language and culture, but rather as imperfect or inferior members of the domestic culture (Skutnabb-Kangas, 1981). The differences most noted may be the immigrants' imperfect use and understanding of English, their poorer academic performance, and the color of their skin.

The process of mainstreaming limited bilingual students may potentially reinforce the racist stereotypes in U.S. society that limit the advancement of caste or castelike minorities. The majority of recent immigrants to this country are non-White, and members of the White majority may consciously or subconsciously associate the cognitive deficits linked to poor educational policies with particular races and nationalities, particularly if transitional bilingual education programs are viewed in the same light as other forms of compensatory education. Intellectual inferiority would then be ascribed to immigrant groups on the basis of ascribed characteristics, since their school performance would still be perceived as deficient, even after they have received several years of special help in school. Blaming the victim, especially Black Americans, has been established as a given in the United States (Ogbu, 1978).

Research on bilingualism seems to indicate that early mainstreaming, the legal goal of short-term TBE programs, is flawed as a compensatory educational strategy for immigrant students (California State Department of Education, 1982; Cummins, 1981, 1984; Hakuta, 1985, 1986). It seems likely that many TBE programs are, in fact, turning out students whose CALP-dimension proficiency in both the mother tongue and English is inadequate for participation in English-only classrooms. On the surface, at least, it is on this issue that bilingual education is attacked. On another level, however, TBE may be an appropriate way for society to educate the children of immigrants.

If U.S. society needs to recruit and prepare new candidates for a growing number of low-status, poorly compensated slots in the opportunity structure, transitional bilingual education programs for non-English-speaking immigrants may be construed by the majority as part of a "reasonable" set of educational policies for the nation. If political and social considerations dictate that Black and other non-White and/or foreign-born people bear a greater share of the hardships, poverty, and unemployment in the U.S. economy, it is "reasonable" to expect the educational system to reflect such considerations. Black people and many new immigrants are already separated by means of race as they confront the opportunity structure. Educational policy can serve to reinforce caste distinctions in the society by providing, more or less intentionally, non-White people with an inferior education. In doing so, the educational system plays a role in creating a pool of adults who are "qualified" to be economically exploited, unemployed, or underemployed.

Reagan's Department of Education has vigorously attacked TBE programs because, it is claimed, they hinder non-English-speaking students' acquisition of English and keep them separated from mainstream students for too long. In fact, the criticism of TBE programs from within the government began under the Carter administration. Consider this statement by a former Secretary of Health, Education and Welfare, Joseph Califano: "[In bilingual programs] too little attention was paid to teaching English, and far too many children were kept in bilingual classes long after they acquired the necessary proficiency to be taught in English" (Califano, 1981). Further, Ronald Reagan did not wait long after entering the White House to begin to speak out against bilingual school programs:

It is absolutely wrong and against American concept to have a bilingual education program that is now openly, admittedly dedicated to preserving their native language and never getting them adequate in English so they can to out into the job market. (quoted in Hakuta, 1985, p. 207)

The attacks on transitional bilingual education are not consistent with the available research evidence on bilingualism, but they can be seen as consistent with trends toward the further lowering of the job ceiling for immigrants in the United States. New regulations governing the expenditure of funds for bilingual education promulgated by William Bennett, the Secretary of Education, seek to discourage the use of languages other than English in instruction and to encourage the early "mainstreaming" of students out of bilingual programs. Furthermore, the aim of native-language instruction under the new regulations is not to provide for children's overall academic success, but rather, to foster the acquisition of English. To this end, the Department of Education hopes to renegotiate many districts' compliance with the civil rights provisions of Title VII legislation (Orum, 1985). The National Council of La Raza, a national Hispanic American civil rights organization, has commented that the Secretary of Education seems to believe that instruction in English as a Second Language alone is a sufficient educational remedy to meet the department's civil rights obligations as set by the *Lau v. Nichols* Supreme Court case of 1974 (Orum, 1985).

The provisions of the Department of Education's proposed new rules governing bilingual education programs receiving Title VII monies are as follows:

- DOE will provide for "maximum flexibility" on the part of local districts in designing programs to meet the needs of limited-English-proficient students. (In practice, this means that the native component of such programs may be eliminated.)
- Bilingual education programs will use native language instruction only to the extent necessary to achieve competence in English and to meet grade promotions and graduation requirements.
- No minimum amount of time or instruction is to be established to meet the standards of achieving English competence and meeting grade promotion and graduation requirements. (In other words, early mainstreaming of students is permissible.)
- The Secretary will fund proposals only if they can demonstrate the ability, financial or otherwise, to continue the project after Title VII monies are exhausted. Increased local responsibility for funding programs will be a priority. (U.S. Department of Education, 1985)

The last provision is of particular interest because of its implications for the many bilingual education programs located in poor districts. It appears that the Department of Education will fund only those projects in districts that can afford bilingual programs after federal start-up monies are spent.

It is conceivable, then, that many districts will be denied federal bilingual education funds not because there is no demonstrable need for a bilingual program, but because the economically marginal status of the populations served cannot manage to foot the bill for the programs (Crawford, 1986). In relation to this point, Navarro (1985) notes that the rollback of bilingual education programs in the state of California is largely attributable to the real powerlessness of Hispanics there. In addition, he says that it is increasingly true that those who have a direct interest in public education policy are the disenfranchised, impoverished ethnic and racial minorities, while members of the dominant majority group in society are less and less willing to pay for such educational programs.

It is interesting to look at how the new DOE-proposed regulations define a "program of transitional bilingual education." According to the department, TBE refers to programs designed to meet the educational needs of limited-English-proficient students and provide "structured English language instruction, and, to the extent necessary to allow a child to achieve competence in the English language, instruction in the child's native language . . ." (U.S. Department of Education, 1985). Clearly, the goal of such a program in this scheme — and the one criterion used to evaluate its success or failure (as well as the success or failure of the students participating in it) — is the acquisition of English as a badge of American identity. The insights gained from sociological and linguistic investigation seem to show that this goal serves the interest of society at the expense of the needs of language-minority students.

It remains to be seen whether or not TBE programs produce results in terms of student academic achievement. The research to date in bilingualism indicates, however, that in both the cognitive and affective domains, maintenance bilingual programs or two-way enrichment programs of longer duration (at least six years) would be far superior to transitional bilingual programs. Bilingual advocates need to consider whether or not they are preserving the essence of quality bilingual education when they seek to promote bilingual education through the defense of existing programs. If, in so doing, they defend compensatory programs whose graduates are consistently outperformed by their monolingual peers, they may inadvertently play a role in the negative stereotyping of the language and immigrant minorities whose cause they champion.

Finally, those who believe that compensatory educational programs for immigrants and language minorities play an important role in the advancement of minority civil rights need to be wary. The analysis presented in this article suggests that the existence of low-status social roles is necessary to U.S. society in some sense and that someone must fill those roles. Compensatory education assumes that low-status people suffer low status because of their lack of school success, and that if they were to become successful in school, their status would rise. In the United States, where race and ethnicity frequently form the basis of low status, such an assumption does not hold true. Educational advocates for immigrants and language minorities must look beyond strictly academic themes and examine the adult roles open to these students, in order to determine whether such programs do indeed facilitate both their advancement and mobility in our society.

References

An official language for California. (1986, October 2). *New York Times,* p. A23.

Barreto, J., Jr. (1986, August 9). English isn't the only language we speak. *Washington Post,* p. A19.

Bill pushes an official state prejudice [Editorial]. (1986, February 18). *Atlanta Constitution,* p. 22A.

Bluestone, B. (1987). *The De-Industrialization of America.* New York: Basic Books.

Braverman, H. (1974). *Labor and monopoly capital.* New York: Monthly Review Press.

Brinkley, J. (1986, June 26). U.S. set to act on border drug flow. *New York Times,* p. 1.

Califano, J. (1981). *Governing America: An insider's report from the White House and the Cabinet.* New York: Simon & Schuster.

California State Department of Education, Office of Bilingual and Bicultural Education. (1982). *Basic principles for the education of language-minority students: An overview.* Sacramento: Author.

Cedartown Strike. (1986, February 15). *Mundo Hispanico,* Atlanta, p. 10A.

Cockcroft, J. D. (1986). *Outlaws in the promised land: Mexican immigrant workers and America's future.* New York: Grove Press.

Crawford, J. (1986, February 12). Bennett's plan for bilingual overhaul heats up debate. *Education Week,* p. 1.

Cummins, J. (1981). The role of primary language development in promoting educational success for language minority students. *Schooling and language minority students: A theoretical framework.* Evaluation, Dissemination, and Assessment Center, California State University at Los Angeles.

Cummins, J. (1984). *Bilingualism and special education: Issues in assessment and pedagogy.* San Diego: College Hill Press.

Cummins, J. (1986). Empowering minority students: A framework for intervention. *Harvard Educational Review, 56,* 18–36.

Dixon, M., Martinez, E., & McCaughan, E. (1982, March). *Chicanas and Mexicanas within a transnational working class.* Paper presented at the Chicana History Project and Symposium, University of California at Los Angeles.

Dulles, F. R. (1966). *Labor in America: A history.* Arlington Heights, IL: AHM Publishing.

Ekstrand, L. H., Foster, S., Olkiewicz, E., & Stankoviski, M. (1981). Interculture: Some concepts for describing the situation of immigrants. *Journal of Multilingual and Multicultural Development, 2,* 269–295.

Gardner, E. (1983). What's wrong with math and science teaching in our schools. *Heritage Today, 3* (May–June), 6–7.

Georgia General Assembly. (1985). *Georgia State House of Representatives Bill Number 717.*

Gersten, R., & Woodward, J. (1985). A case for structured immersion. *Educational Leadership, 43,* 75–84.

Hakuta, K. (1985, September 27). Generalizations from research in second language acquisition and bilingualism. Testimony presented before the House Education and Labor Committee, Washington, DC.

Hakuta, K. (1986). *Mirror of language: The debate on bilingualism.* New York: Basic Books.

Harrington, M., & Levinson, M. (1985, September). The perils of a dual economy. *Dissent,* pp. 417–426.

Johansen, B., & Maestas, R. (1983). *El Pueblo: The Gallegos family's American journey, 1503 to 1980*. New York: Monthly Review Press.

Kelly, P. (1986, November 19). American bosses have jobs; Mexican need work. *The Guardian*, New York, p. 11.

Levine, R. A. (1967). *Dreams and needs: Achievement and motivation in Nigeria*. Chicago: University of Chicago Press.

MacEoin, G., & Riley, N. (1982). *No promised land: American refugee policies and the rule of law* Boston: Oxfam America.

Matthews, J. (1985, November 14). Asian-American students creating a new mainstream. *Washington Post*, p. A1.

Matthews, J. (1986, November 16). Few employers fear new immigration law: Threat of sanctions greeted with a shrug. *Washington Post*, p. A3.

McDermott, R. P. (1976). Achieving school failure: An anthropological approach to illiteracy and social stratification. In H. Singer & R. B. Russel (Eds.), *Theoretical models and processes of reading* (pp. 389–424). Newark, DE: International Reading Association.

Moyers, B. (1985, September). *Whose America is it?* Television documentary aired on CBS.

National Commission on Excellence in Education. (1983). *A nation at risk: The imperative for educational reform*. Washington, DC: U.S. Department of Education.

Navarro, R. (1985). The problems of language education and society: Who decides? In E. Garcia & R. V. Padilla (Eds.), *Advances in bilingual education research* (pp. 289–312). Tucson: University of Arizona Press.

Ogbu, J. U. (1978). *Minority education and caste: The American system in cross-cultural perspective*. New York: Academic Press.

Orum, L. S. (1985, October 31). Secretary Bennett's bilingual education initiative: Historical perspectives and implications. *Perspectivas Publicas*, a newsletter published by the National Council of La Raza, Washington, DC.

Ovando, C., & Collier, V. (1985). *Bilingual and ESL classrooms: Teaching in multicultural contexts*. New York: McGraw-Hill.

Rodríguez, R. (1981). *Hunger of memory: The education of Richard Rodríguez*. Boston: David R. Godine.

Rowan, C. T. (1986, October 7). The real issue Nakasone raised. *Washington Post*, p. A17.

Schumann, J. H. (1976). Second language acquisition: The Pidginization hypothesis. *Language Learning, 26*, 391–408.

Schumann, J. H. (1980). Affective factors and the problem of age in second language acquisition. In K. Croft (Ed.), *Readings on English as a second language*, 2nd ed. Cambridge, MA: Winthrop.

Sennett, R., & Cobb, J. (1972). *Hidden injuries of class*. New York: Random House.

Shor, I. (1986). *Culture wars: School and society in the conservative restoration, 1969–1984*. Boston: Routledge & Kegan Paul.

Skutnabb-Kangas, T. (1979). *Language in the process of cultural assimilation and structural incorporation of linguistic minorities*. Rosslyn, VA: National Clearinghouse for Bilingual Education.

Skutnabb-Kangas, T. (1981). Guest worker or immigrant: Different ways of reproducing an underclass. *Journal of Multilingual and Multicultural Development, 2*, 89–113.

U.S. Department of Education. (1985, November 22). Notice of proposed rule-making for bilingual program implementation and general provisions. *Federal Register, 50* (226), 48352–48370.

U.S. English. (1985). *A kind of discordant harmony: Issues in assimilation*. Pamphlet, Washington, DC.

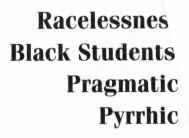

Racelessnes
Black Students
Pragmatic
Pyrrhic

■ ■ ■

SIGNITHIA F

In recent years, a major change appears to have occurred in the aspirations of Black Americans toward social mobility. Previous generations of Black Americans felt a great deal of pride and satisfaction when one member of the community "made it." For example, when Thurgood Marshall, Ralph Bunche, Lena Horne, and Jackie Robinson became "The First" Black Americans to break the color barrier in their chosen careers, most Black Americans saw their accomplishments as signs of the weakening of racial barriers and evidence that there would be less resistance to the efforts of other members of the group who wanted to pursue similar careers. These generations of Black Americans defined success for one Black person as success for all Black people.

Increasingly, however, today's Black Americans are rejecting the older generation's attitude toward social mobility: they do not view the accomplishments of individual members of the group as evidence of the advancement of the entire group; instead, they more often define Black achievement in terms of the collectivity (Dizard, 1970). Success now means that Blacks must succeed *as a people,* not just as individual Blacks. In other words, contemporary Black Americans are opting for a more inclusive view of success.

Black children who grow up in predominantly Black communities, then, are raised in the collective view of success, an ethos that is concerned with the Black community as a whole. But since an individualistic rather than a collective ethos is sanctioned in the school context, Black children enter school having to unlearn or, at least, to modify their own culturally sanc-

Harvard Educational Review Vol. 58 No. 1 February 1988, 54–84

behavioral styles and adopt those styles rewarded
f they wish to achieve academic success.[1]

this paper is the struggle that Black adolescents face in
ose" between the individualistic ethos of the school — which
flects the ethos of the dominant society — and the collective
heir community. I will describe and analyze one strategy for achiev-
ccess that high school students (as well as adults) utilize: that is, the
enomenon of becoming raceless. Specifically, this paper examines the
complex relationship between Black adolescents' racial identity and their
school performance, and the role that the larger social structure plays in that
relationship. I argue that, despite the growing acceptance of ethnicity and
strong ethnic identification in the larger American society, school officials
appear to disapprove of a strong ethnic identity among Black adolescents,
and these contradictory messages produce conflict and ambivalence in the
adolescents, both toward developing strong racial and ethnic identities and
toward performing well in school. My assertions lead to this question: Is
racelessness among Black adolescents a pragmatic strategy or Pyrrhic victory?

This article is divided into five sections. The first section explains the
concept of fictive kinship, the dominant cultural system that exists in Black
communities, and its relation to the formation of an oppositional social
identity (Fordham, 1981, 1982, 1985; Fordham & Ogbu, 1986). The second
section of the article introduces the phenomenon of racelessness and the
efficacy of utilizing it as a strategy for vertical mobility. The third section of
the article describes the research setting. The fourth section presents and
analyzes my research data, which suggest that Black students must develop
a raceless persona in order to achieve academic success. The final section of
the paper concludes with implications of racelessness and suggestions for
minimizing the need for such a strategy for social mobility and academic
excellence among Black adolescents.

The findings emerging from this research are not necessarily gener-
alizable to all Black adolescents. The data were derived from a small segment
of the larger group of "Black adolescents," and from a school located in a
poor Black community. Thus, in order to formulate a general theory of Black
adolescent school achievement, research must be conducted in a variety of
settings, such as middle-class Black schools, predominantly White private
schools, and parochial schools, and with Black adolescents who represent a
cross-section of cultural backgrounds and socioeconomic classes. The signifi-

---

[1] I hypothesize that this response is prevalent not only among Americans of African descent
but also among most subordinated populations in the United States. The desire to succeed — as
defined by the dominating population — causes subordinated peoples to seek social distance
from the group with which they are ethnically or racially identified. However, efforts at dissociation or disidentification are often characterized by conflict and ambiguity about both the individual's value and identity. Because it is virtually impossible to eliminate all traces of the markers
associated with one's indigenous cultural systems, efforts at dissociation are often only marginally
successful.

cance of this research is that it identifies a social phenomenon that must be examined if we are to fully understand the Black adolescent school experience in the United States.

Fictive Kinship and Oppositional Social Identity

In studying the social identity and cultural frame of reference among Black Americans, I have found the anthropological concept "fictive kinship" useful (Fordham, 1982, 1983, 1985a). It refers to a kinship-like connection between and among persons in a society, not related by blood or marriage, who have maintained essential reciprocal social or economic relationships (Bloch, 1971; Brain, 1972; Folb, 1980; Fortes, 1969; Freed, 1973; Hale, 1982; Liebow, 1967; Norbeck & Befu, 1958; Pitt-Rivers, 1968, 1973; Stack, 1974; Staples, 1975, 1981). Among Black Americans the connection extends beyond the social and economic, and includes a political function as well. The term conveys the idea of "brotherhood" and "sisterhood" of *all* Black Americans; thus, a sense of peoplehood or collective social identity. This sense is evident in the various kinship terms that Black Americans use to refer to one another, such as "brother," "sister," and "blood" (Folb, 1980; Liebow, 1967; Sargent, 1985; Stack, 1974).

As used here, the term "fictive kinship" denotes a cultural symbol of collective identity among Black Americans, and is based on more than just skin color. The term also implies the particular mind-set, or world view, of those persons who are considered to be "Black," and is used to denote the moral judgment the group makes on its members (Brain, 1972). Essentially, the concept suggests that merely possessing African features or being of fan descent does not automatically make one a Black person or a member in good standing of the group. One can be black in color, but choose not to seek membership in the fictive-kinship system. One can also be denied membership by the group because one's behavior, attitudes, and activities are perceived as being at variance with those thought to be appropriate and group-specific, which are culturally patterned and serve to delineate "us" from "them." An example is the tendency for Black Americans to emphasize *group loyalty* in situations involving conflict or competition with Whites.

Only Black Americans are involved in the evaluation of group members' eligibility for membership in the fictive-kinship system; thus, they control the criteria used to judge one's worthiness for membership. That is, the determination of the criteria for membership in the fictive-kinship system rests solely within the Black community. Furthermore, criteria for fictive kinship have a special significance for Black people, because they are regarded as the ideal by which members of the group are judged. This judgment is also the medium through which Black Americans distinguish "real" from "spurious" members of the community (Williams, 1981a, 1981b).

Additionally, as I view it, the fictive-kinship system described here has another important function. It symbolizes Black Americans' sense of peoplehood in opposition to White American social identity. In fact, the system was developed partly in response to two types of mistreatment from Whites: the economic and instrumental exploitation by Whites during and after slavery, and the historical and continuing tendency of White Americans to treat Black Americans as an undifferentiated mass of people, indiscriminately ascribing to them certain inherent strengths and weaknesses (Anderson, 1975; Bullock, 1970; Drake & Cayton, 1970; Myrdal, 1944; Spivey, 1978). Black Americans have generally responded to this mistreatment by inverting the negative stereotypes and assumptions of Whites into positive and functional attributes (Fordham, 1982; Holt, 1972; Ogbu, 1983). Thus, Black Americans may have transformed White people's assumptions of Black homogeneity into a collective identity system.

An example of collective treatment by White Americans is evident in one event that occurred following Nat Turner's "insurrection" in Southampton, Virginia, in 1831. Prior to Turner's insurrection, the general practice in Washington, DC, was to allow Black children to attend Sunday school with the White residents in the city. After that incident, Whites restricted the movement of Blacks into the predominantly White community and limited contact among Blacks themselves as well, regardless of their place of residence or personal involvement in the insurrection (Haley, 1976; Styron, 1966). Black children were forbidden to attend Sunday School with White children, although local Whites knew that the Black children had no part in the insurrection. What was well understood by Black people in Southampton, Virginia, in Washington, DC, and elsewhere in the country, was that the onus for Turner's behavior was extended to all Black Americans solely on the basis of their being Black. Numerous arbitrary mistreatments of this kind, coupled with a knowledge that they were denied true assimilation into the mainstream of American life, encouraged Black Americans to develop what DeVos (1967) calls "ethnic consolidation," a sense of peoplehood expressed in fictive-kinship feelings and language (Green, 1981).

Black children learn the meaning of fictive kinship from their parents and peers while they are growing up. It appears, moreover, that they learn it early enough, and well enough, so that they even tend to associate their life chances and "success" potential with those of their peers and other members of the community. The collective ethos of the fictive-kinship system is challenged by the individual ethos of the dominant culture when the children enter school, and when the children experience the competition between the two for their loyalty. For many Black adolescents, therefore, the mere act of attending school is evidence of either a conscious or semiconscious rejection of the indigenous Black American culture (Weis, 1985a, 1985b). Thus, in order to reinforce their belief that they are still legitimate members of the Black community, these students, wittingly and unwittingly, "create" (Weis, 1985b) an environment — for example, through the use of "Black English" — that reinforces the indigenous culture from which they are separated through the process of schooling. In recreating their indigenous culture in the school context, Weis (1985a, 1985b) argues, they inadvertently ensure their "failure" (see also MacLeod, 1987; Willis, 1981). Conversely, those students who minimize their connection to the indigenous culture and assimilate into the school culture improve their chances of succeeding in school. Unlike the students who seek to maintain their identification and affiliation with the indigenous culture, students who assimilate seek to maximize their success potential by minimizing their relationship to the Black community and to the stigma attached to "blackness." These students attempt to develop a raceless persona in order to succeed in school and in life. Racelessness, then, is the desired and eventual outcome of developing a raceless persona, and is either a conscious or unconscious effort on the part of such students to disaffiliate themselves from the fictive-kinship system described above.

Racelessness as a Strategy for Vertical Mobility

> I am a Black. . . . I suppose I still believe that there is a place in space or time where the pigmentation of my skin might be of only incidental relevance — where it could be possible to give a socially meaningful description of who I am and what I've done without using the word black at all. I have abandoned the belief that somewhere or someone will turn out to be here and now. So, for all practical purposes, I accept a belief that I have taken to calling "achromism" (from the Greek a-, meaning "not" and chroma, meaning "color"), which is that within the context of the society to which I belong by right — or misfortune — of birth, nothing I shall accomplish or discover or earn or inherit or buy or sell or give away — nothing I shall ever do — *will outweigh the fact of my race in determining my destiny* [emphasis added]. (Bradley, 1982, pp. 58–59)

This self-description, quoted from David Bradley, the author of *The Chaneysville Incident,* asserts the critical importance of race, and places it as one of the most formidable obstacles in the lives of Black Americans. The practice of becoming raceless appears to have emerged as a strategy both to circumvent the stigma attached to being Black, and to achieve vertical mobility. In an effort to minimize the effects of race on their aspirations, some Black Americans have begun to take on attitudes, behaviors, and characteristics that may not generally be attributed to Black Americans. Out of their desire to secure jobs and positions that are above the employment ceiling typically placed on Blacks, they have adopted personae that indicate a lack of identification with, or a strong relationship to, the Black community in response to an implicit institutional mandate: Become "un-Black." The following examples from the world of corporate America illustrate this phenomenon.

In an article about the achievements of a Black disc jockey in Washington, DC, Gaines-Carter (1984) describes him in the following manner:

The voice is quiet thunder. Seductive. He stretches words, rolls them around in his mouth. Because his voice is neither black nor white and favors no geographical region, there has been some confusion about his racial identity. "I've had people look at me like I'm a ghost," says the 30-year-old disc jockey. "Some of them were expecting a white person. I hate for people to say I sound white. I don't. It's a matter of speaking properly, and anyone can do that." (Gaines-Carter, 1984, p. 6)

In a similar vein, Max Robinson, a Black reporter and one of three anchors on the ABC national news during the early 1980s, notes with bitter irony how his White superior's perception of him as a raceless person was influential in his achieving vertical mobility within that organization:

One of the problems I have is that we tend to separate everything, so at ABC Roone [Arledge; the director in charge of hiring news personnel] . . . mentioned on three occasions, he said, "I told you when I hired you, I didn't think you were black, or I didn't think of you as a black man." That's an incredible statement. I mean, I must be the funniest looking white man in this country. And the fact is, what he was trying to say, "I am going to give you credit. I admire you greatly, so therefore I will not think of you as black." (Transcript, *The Oprah Winfrey Show,* January 23, 1987, p. 4)

A third example of becoming "un-Black" can be found in the political arena. Here, particular Black candidates, in order to broaden their political base, often actively seek to minimize their allegiance to the Black community. This is evident in political elections in which the candidate is seeking election to a statewide or national office. MacPherson (1986) describes how Doug Wilder, a Black man who ran for the lieutenant-governor's seat in Virginia, won that election:

In the state with the lowest percentage of blacks (17) of any southern state, he [Wilder] announced his candidacy in front of a picture of Harry Byrd and downplayed race until "people never perceived a Black candidate running." A statewide trek, backed up with television ads that included an archetypal white deputy sheriff endorsing Wilder, paid off. Wilder undid his tie and rolled up his sleeves in front of Confederate flags at country stores. Instant press, statewide and local, at every stop. (MacPherson, 1986, p. 4)

Although the examples above concern Black men adapting to the dominant ethos, Black women are also affected negatively by the phenomenon of racelessness. This is shown in a recent article discussing the success of Oprah Winfrey, television's latest talk-show host, who, the author claims, has very little emotional attachment to the Black community. Richman (1987) describes her as having suffered as a college student in a predominantly Black college in Tennessee because "she was uninterested in the compelling black issues of the day" (p. 56).

They [the students at Tennessee State] all hated me — no, they resented me. I refused to conform to the militant thinking of the time. I hated, hated, hated college. Now I bristle when somebody comes up and says they went to Tennessee State with me. Everybody was angry for four years. It was an all-black college, and it was in to be angry. Whenever there was any conversation on race, I was on the other side, maybe because I never felt the kind of repression other black people are exposed to. I think I was called "nigger" once, when I was in fifth grade. (Richman, 1987, p. 56)

Perhaps no example more clearly typifies the tensions endemic to the racelessness issue in the work arena than the suicide of Leanita McClain, a journalist and the first Black American female to be elected to the Board of Directors of the *Chicago Tribune*. Having grown up in a predominantly Black community in Chicago, and subsequently having achieved enormous success in a White-dominated profession, McClain's sense of belonging and self-confidence were seriously undermined. To her White colleagues at the *Tribune*, McClain appeared raceless, indistinguishable from them.

Klose (1984) suggests that McClain was committed both to the development of a raceless persona and to racial integration as a social reality, and that she denied the existence of racism as an endemic feature of the social system in the United States. He cites as evidence a passage from a brief essay McClain wrote as a teenager:

Why is there so much hate and contempt among people? I have never been blocked from anything because of my color, and I'm not ashamed of it either. My great-grandfather was Caucasian and so was my great-grand-mother. . . . Why can't people just be people and live in peace and harmony? Maybe I'm in search of the perfect world. Or maybe I'm just me. That's it. I'm me. But to be me is to be nothing — to be nothing is to be me. And I love all people. Even pink polka-dotted ones with olive ears. (Klose, 1984, p. C2)

After having achieved the success she sought. McClain notes the personal transformation and the attendant anguish she feels:

I am burdened daily with showing whites that blacks are people. I am, in the old vernacular, a credit to my race . . . my brothers' keeper, and my sisters', though many of them have abandoned me because they think that I have abandoned them. . . . I assuage white guilt. I disprove black inadequacy and prove to my parents' generation that their patience was indeed a virtue. (McClain, cited in Klose, 1984, p. C3)

As she rose within the ranks of journalism, her commitment to the ideals espoused by the larger American society was constantly challenged, especially during and immediately after the election of Harold Washington, the first Black mayor of Chicago. Although McClain had previously denied the existence of racism, she slowly began to realize that it is a critical component of Black Americans' social reality that adversely affects all facets of their lives. This realization led to what she described as "hellish confusion" (McClain, 1983). Apparently, accepting this reality proved to be too burdensome for her.

Campbell (1982) further documents racelessness as a strategy used by Black Americans who choose, or who are chosen, to work in settings that historically have been off-limits to them. She notes the duality of their existence in such settings, and the resulting feelings of alienation and isolation.

> They consciously choose their speech, their walk, their mode of dress and car; they trim their hair lest a mountainous Afro set them apart. They know they have a high visibility, and they realize that their success depends not only on their *abilities* [emphasis added], but also on their white colleagues' feeling comfortable with them. (Campbell, 1982, p. 39)

Black Americans who gain entry into these predominantly White institutions are likely not only to experience enormous stress and feelings of isolation and ambivalence, but also to be viewed suspiciously by other Black people who are not themselves working in such institutions and who tend to view these members of the Black community as "un-Black" people.

> Many times, other blacks feel that these strange creatures with three-piece suits and briefcases have sold out. "A black manager can have a multi-million dollar deal on his mind," explains Dr. [Ronald] Brown of San Francisco. "But when he passes that black janitor, he knows that he'd better remember to speak; otherwise, he'll be labeled as 'acting white.'" (Campbell, 1982, p. 100)

Given the situation I have just presented, it is not surprising that many Black adolescents are keenly aware of the stigma associated with being successful in school, since school is seen as an agent of the dominant society. Based on the data gathered from my own research (which will be presented in the next section of the paper), I posit that *ambivalence* and *conflict* about academic effort appear to be at the center of Black students' — especially the high achievers' — responses to school and schooling. Hence, they develop complex strategies that enable them to resolve, or, at least cope with, the ambivalence they experience. One such strategy is intended to minimize the influence and impact that the schooling process might have on their relationships to peers and to the community; the strategy follows what some researchers have termed the "anti-achievement ethic" (Granat, Hathaway, Saleton, & Sansing, 1986). Students who utilize this strategy, unfortunately, tend to fare poorly in school. The strategy that seems to be used frequently by adolescents who succeed in school is the phenomenon that I describe as developing a raceless persona.

Students who adopt a raceless persona do so with some risk of losing their feelings of belonging and of group membership:

A black teenager in Prince George's County [a suburban community outside Washington, DC] says many black kids "think if you succeed, you're betraying your color." Adds a friend: "The higher you get, the fewer blacks there are. You can succeed, but you feel like an outcast." (Granat et al., 1986, p. 166)

Recently, several articles in the press have illuminated the particularly painful consequences of being a successful student. In a headline story reported in *Newsweek*, Sylvester Monroe, a high-achieving prep school student, describes the attempts made by his school to separate and isolate him from his peers and indigenous community and to transform him from a group-centered Black person to a raceless "American."

One of the greatest frustrations of my three years at St. George's [a predominantly White private school in New England] was that people were always trying to separate me from other black people in a manner strangely reminiscent of a time when slave owners divided blacks into "good Negroes" and "bad Negroes." Somehow, attending St. George's made me a good Negro, in their eyes, while those left in Robert Taylor [the housing project where he and his parents lived in Chicago] were bad Negroes or, at the very least, inferior ones. . . . Another St. George's teacher was surprised at my reaction when he implied that I should be grateful for the opportunity to attend St. George's, far away from a place like the Robert Taylors. How could I be, I snapped back, when my family, everyone that I cared most about were still there? But you're different, he continued. That's why you got out. . . . I'm not different, I insisted. I'm just lucky enough to have been in the right place at the right time. (Monroe, 1987, p. 57)

Monroe also talks about the alienation he experienced as a result of well-intended, yet implicitly racist, efforts on the part of school officials to integrate him into the school environment.

Looking back on it, I was pleased to show what black boys were capable of. Yet, there was a faint disquiet. What bothered me was that some people found it easier to pretend I was something else. "We're colorblind here [at St. George's]," a well-meaning faculty member once told me. "We don't see *black* students or *white* students, we just sees students." But black was what I was; I wasn't sure he saw me at all. . . .

The disquiet that Monroe describes is centered around the raceless persona he felt pressure to assume in order to be accepted at St. George's. Moreover, Monroe's description suggests that he had to become something other than an individual from the Black community. He had to become, instead, a "racial symbol," someone who embodies all the noble qualities necessary for a Black American to "make it" in the larger society (Trescott, 1977).

Morgan (1985) provides another example of how the school, as an institution that reproduces the dominant cultural values, pressures a seventeen-year-old student named Ellis to minimize his racial identity in order to achieve some measure of success. Ellis delineates the dual reality that confronts him in his predominantly White school in a suburban community outside Charlotte, North Carolina.

> Last year, the student council president, who was black, wanted to set aside a day to honor [Dr.] Martin Luther King. A lot of blacks said it was a good thing to do, but a lot of whites said it was a waste of time and was not fair. . . . I felt hurt that they [my White friends] would accept me as a black person but would not accept the idea of honoring a black person. . . . One of my white friends said, "I don't see you as a black friend, but as a friend." But I want them to look at me for what I am. *I am a black person* [emphasis added]. (Morgan, 1985, pp. 34–35; 90–92, 96–100)

The experiences of both Black males indicate the necessity of negotiating the duality, and the resulting ambiguities, of their existence.

In order to achieve academic success and, ultimately, vertical mobility, some Black students consciously choose risking membership in the fictive-kinship system to which, at one level, all persons socially defined as Black are "eternally bound." The following examples are illustrative cases:

> They [my friends and family] don't want [me] to change. They want me to be just like them. . . . I'm trying very hard to get away from black people. When I was in that all [Black] school, of course, my friends were all [Black]. But I don't have any more [Black] friends right now. I live in an all [Black] area, but I don't even talk to anybody who lives near me. I wanted to find out what white people were all about. So when I went to high school, I tried to make new friends and get away from the [Black] people as much as possible. . . . I've tried to maintain an image of myself in the school — getting away from those people. I work, and I buy my own clothes, and I study hard. In fact, I have all As in my classes and I'm in many of the white activities, like Speech — the only [Black person] in the whole group. . . ." (cited in Petroni & Hirsch, 1971, pp. 12, 20)

Similarly, Gray (1985) poignantly describes her largely unsuccessful efforts at disguising her racial identity, what she identifies as playing her "un-Black" role:

> During my pompous period, I dealt with my insecurities by wearing a veil of superiority. Except around my family and neighbors, I played the role — the un-Black. . . . To whites, I tried to appear perfect — I earned good grades and spoke impeccable English, was well-mannered and well-groomed. Poor whites, however, made me nervous. They seldom concealed their contempt for blacks, especially "uppity" ones like me. . . . To blacks, I was all of the above and extremely stuck up. I pretended not to see them

on the street, spoke to them only when spoken to and cringed in the presence of blacks being loud in front of whites. The more integrated my Catholic grammar school became, the more uncomfortable I was there. I had heard white parents on TV, grumbling about blacks ruining their schools; I didn't want anyone to think that I, too, might bring down Sacred Heart Academy. So I behaved, hoping that no one would associate me with "them" [other Black Americans]. (Gray, 1985, pp. E1, E5)

The common theme in all of the examples presented here is the conflict and ambivalence experienced by Black Americans in both school and work settings, and the persistent questioning of how they are accepted by both Black and White people. Not surprisingly, the conflict and ambivalence appear to be more pronounced and debilitating among those Black Americans who achieve the greatest degree of success as defined by the dominant society, and relative to the success of peers in their indigenous communities.

The Research Setting: The Capital High Community

Capital High is a public high school located in a predominantly poor Black neighborhood of Washington, DC.[2] As is typical of such urban neighborhoods, the main thoroughfare near the school, Hunter Avenue, is lined with fast food chain restaurants like McDonald's and Kentucky Fried Chicken, various Catholic and Protestant churches, and a variety of corner stores. On the side streets there are detached single-family homes, similar to those on The Avenue, but with small, well-cared-for front yards. During the spring, many of these yards are adorned with begonias, petunias, tulips, and other blooming plants, strongly contrasting with the brick and cement of the major thoroughfares in the neighborhood.

The Physical Structure

The school itself is located on a large plot of land in the middle of the block on a major thoroughfare. One section of the building was completed during the early 1960s; the other was completed during the academic year 1970–1971. The lapse in time between construction of the two sections is clearly evident in the amenities featured in the two structures. For example, in the new section there is both a basement and sub-basement level; this is not the case in the original structure. The new section is completely air-conditioned, while the older section of the building is not.

The school's cafeteria, auditorium, and gymnasium are all located in the original section of the school. Since the addition of the new section allowed the enrollment to double, the gymnasium, cafeteria, and auditorium are no longer large enough to accommodate the student population.

---

[2] The name of the school and names of individuals used in this article are fictitious.

219

Nowhere is this problem of space more apparent than in the auditorium. The lack of adequate space means that there is never an assembly of the entire student body at one time. Moreover, this structural limitation appears to have justified the administration's decisions to limit assembly attendance primarily to students who are taking courses in the Advanced Placement program at the school. In addition to the lack of adequate space, there is also limited accessibility to the building for students who are physically disabled.

In spite of the relative newness of the physical plant, during the period of my research, it was not in the best condition. Some areas of the building, such as the cafeteria, were in critical need of repair. When it rained, there was always a possibility of seeing trash barrels sitting in the middle of the cafeteria floor to prevent the rain from soaking the floor and flooding the hallways. Yet in spite of the state of disrepair, the building was spotless. The fastidiousness of Mr. McGriff, the current principal, was apparent everywhere; he believed that cleanliness and the ability to decipher educational symbols were inextricably commingled. Consequently, he constantly picked up paper and other debris in the halls and on the streets adjacent to the school. Moreover, he regularly admonished the students to keep the building clean by following his example, and constantly urged teachers and other school personnel to remind the students of the importance of keeping the building clean.

Because of the layout of the building, herculean efforts were necessary to maintain departmental and organizational integrity at the school. Although it was not always easy to discern why certain departments and programs were placed where they were in the building, it was apparent that enormous effort was made to keep them in proximity according to academic discipline. The exceptions to this were made to insure that students with handicapping conditions, particularly those in wheelchairs, had access to certain basic courses. So, for example, even though most courses in the mathematics department were taught on the second floor of the building, three were taught on the first floor.

The Students

According to official statistics of the District of Columbia Public Schools, Capital had a total enrollment of 1,886 students (at the start of the 1982–1983 school year), with Blacks constituting 99 percent of the student body. During the regular fall registration, 490 students enrolled; there were 130 discharges by the third week of November. There were 476 graduates in the class of 1982, representing 75 percent of the twelfth graders. Most of the students come from one-parent homes, many of them live in public or low-income housing, and approximately one-fourth of the student body is eligible for the reduced-cost lunch program.[3]

[3] As stated previously, the community is beset by poverty and other effects of structural inequality. Thus, many — though not all — of the students from the community who attend

The School Personnel

There was a total of 172 school personnel at Capital. Of this total, 130 were teachers, including four special education teachers, one transition teacher (who helped students bridge the gap between junior and senior high), and two math and reading skills teachers. Most of the teachers were tenured, and most had between six and ten years of classroom teaching experience. The administrative staff consisted of a principal, four assistant principals, five counselors, and two librarians (although the school was without a certified librarian until after the spring break of 1983). The support staff was made up of ten cafeteria workers, five clerical aides, two community aides, twelve custodians (including the engineering staff), and one school nurse.

The racial composition of the personnel reflected that of the student body: It was predominantly Black. The English department had the largest number of White teachers, but most departments, including Special Education, had at least one White member. Interestingly, the White teachers taught the more advanced or "difficult" courses, such as Chemistry, Physics, Government, and the Advanced Placement classes. They were also the ones who served as sponsors for academically oriented activities such as the club "It's Academic" and the Chess Club.

The Curriculum

Capital High offered students a wide range of courses and programs of study. The academic programs included Advanced Placement courses and basic and advanced computer courses; woodshop, printing, auto mechanics, and stage and television productions were offered in the non-academic curriculum. In other words, the "shopping mall" concept of schooling (Powell, Farrar, & Cohen, 1985) was part and parcel of the educational landscape at Capital High.

The school had a four-tier curricular structure that consisted of two special programs (Advanced Placement and Humanities), the regular curriculum in which most of the students were placed, and a program for students in need of special education. Where there were areas of overlap in the regular curriculum and the two special programs, students were grouped according to performance on standardized examinations, and were either permitted or required to take the appropriate courses for their skill levels.

In the school's regular curriculum, the norm appeared to be for students to take *only* the courses that were required for graduation. The counselors, however, urged the students to take courses in subjects the students generally believed to be difficult, such as math, science, and foreign languages, and

Capital High are poor. High school students in the District of Columbia School System are allowed to attend the schools of their choice; therefore, many parents from other communities throughout the District encourage their children to attend Capital because of the wide range of courses offered there. Hence, although the student body is best characterized as poor, it includes working-class and middle-class students.

to remain in them even though they might experience some difficulty. The students, however, did not generally follow the suggestions of their counselors; instead, they dropped the so-called difficult courses once they had been given a "Letter of Understanding" apprising them of what courses they had to take in order to meet graduation requirements. In the rare instance in which a senior student did not reject the suggestion of his/her counselor, and remained in the difficult course, the student resorted to behaviors that made him or her "appear to but not to": 1) he or she continued in the course, but rarely attended class, thus virtually assuring failure; or 2) he or she took the body to class but left the mind somewhere outside the classroom.

Students who are assigned courses or who sign up for more courses than they need for graduation are generally thought of as "strange" or "crazy." However, those few students are usually able to convince their peers that they are unable to get out of the class or classes by attributing their deviation from the norm to the intractability of their counselors: "Man, Mr. Collins would not let me drop this class."

Unlike students in the regular curriculum, students in the special academic programs, although few in number (the larger of the two programs included just over 400 of the nearly 2,000 students enrolled in the school), were exposed to a curriculum whose minimal requirements far exceeded those of the regular curriculum. They were required to complete a math course and a science course at each grade level and to take two years of a foreign language.[4] Moreover, class assignments included an additional time period (so that these students took seven courses instead of the six taken by those in the regular curriculum), and a flexible curriculum that enabled students to spend longer periods of time in some classes.

The students in the two academic programs were provided special academic and support services intended to enhance their school experience and to improve their chances for academic success. These students were assigned teachers who had the most prestigious credentials and who were regarded as the most skilled in their particular subject areas. They were advised by a special counselor whose primary responsibility was to help them achieve their goals. she provided students with the specific information they needed in order to make the appropriate educational and career choices and organized specialized courses in test-taking and other auxiliary skills to help them perform as well as mainstream White students on standardized measures of academic success. Furthermore, these students were even transported to and from school, and were not allowed to be employed after school during the academic year because, it was argued, work interfered with their homework and extracurricular academically oriented activities.

---

[4] It should be noted that this list of requirements changed during the second year of the study, but they were in place during the base year of the research and had been for several years.

How the Study Was Conducted

I gained entry to Capital High as an ethnographer at the start of the fall semester of 1982, and the data were collected over a two-year period. During the first year, formal and informal interviews were conducted with students, teachers, counselors, and parents. Observations of students were made both inside and outside of the classrooms. Out-of-class observations took place at school and at other places such as churches, work sites, recreation centers, and sports events. The second year of the study was devoted to the administration of a 55-page, 201-item questionnaire to 600 students from all the grades, and findings were compared to those obtained in the first year.

The sample for the first year of the study was selected from a pool of students referred by both teachers and counselors. The teachers and counselors were asked to identify eleventh-grade high achievers and underachievers who they thought would be willing to participate in this intensive and time-consuming study, and whose parents would approve of their participation. I verified the claims of the teachers and counselors by analyzing the cumulative folder of each student. Thirty-three students participated in the study; twenty-one of them were identified as underachievers; twelve of them were identified as high achievers, and constituted the primary sample. In this paper, data on six of the high-achieving students — three males and three females — will be presented and analyzed.

Racelessness at Capital High

Racelessness and school success appear to be linked at Capital High. This is evident in many aspects of the lives òf the students and in their responses to questions regarding Black life and culture. Also, racelessness appears to be more prevalent among the high-achieving students, although the verbal responses of both high- and under-achieving students indicate a tendency to disaffiliate themselves from other Black Americans. Essentially, the high-achieving students' responses indicate a strong belief in the dominant ideology of the American social system: equality of opportunity for all, regardless of race, color, creed, or national origin; and merit as the critical factor in social mobility. Some examples from my research are illustrative.

The Female High-Achieving Students

The most salient characteristic shared by the female members of the research sample is their unequivocal commitment to the values of the dominant social system. Unlike the male students, whose "duality of socialization" is clearly evident in both their behaviors and responses, the female students appear to be much less victimized by the fact that they are required to live in two worlds concurrently. Indeed, they appear to be more unanimously committed to the ideology and values of the larger society than they are to the norms and values of the existing fictive-kinship system. The following three examples are illustrative of how the female students' commitment to racelessness as a strategy for vertical mobility structures their behavior and performance in the school context.

Rita

Rita is one of the highest achieving female students in the sample group. She is a sixteen-year-old student who takes most of the courses available to eleventh graders from the Advanced Placement program at Capital. She is also the student with the highest score on the verbal component of the PSAT this academic year (1982–1983). The best adjectives to describe Rita are: intelligent, creative, hostile, sarcastic, assertive, garrulous, comedic, and manipulative. It is also appropriate to describe her as kind, caring, complex, clever, confused, and troubled. She often challenges the values and rules of the school with conviction, vacillating between demanding total adherence to these ideals on the part of her teachers and other school administrators, and discounting and disparaging these same values and rules herself in ways that display a blatant disregard for and arrogance toward their sanctity and value.

These characteristics appear to make Rita a very unfeeling and thoughtless person. Yet times is not an accurate picture. Admittedly, she is confused and angry, and she does not know how to focus her anger; however, she is also a very sensitive person whose "hellish confusion" (McClain, 1983) is the result of her efforts to cope with the disparaged economic and social conditions of Black Americans. Her confusion is so intense and so rampant that she told me on more than one occasion that she is often flabbergasted when people ask her if she views herself as a White person:

> Some — a lot of times I have people ask me that — "Do you think you are a white person?"! But I don't know, maybe it's me. Maybe I don't carry myself like a Black person. I don't know. But I'm Black. And I can't go painting myself white or some other color, it's something that I have to live with. So it's the way it is, and it's not like having herpes or something — it's not *bad*. It's — I think it's just the same as being white, as far as I'm concerned — everybody's equal. (Formal Interview, May 4, 1983)

However, despite her verbal claims that she does not view being Black in America as a negative factor, her constant disparagement of those activities and events generally associated with Black Americans negates her claims, suggesting, instead, a preference for those activities her family and some of her friends view as "White activities." She insists that her mother and sisters view her as an antisocial person because she does not like to do the things they like to do, such as going to shows at Constitution Hall and the Capital Center and attending cabarets and other places frequented by Black Washingtonians.

. . . They [my family] go to all the shows, go out to the Capital Center and all that crap, and listen to all that trash — as far as I'm concerned. But I don't really like going out [there], you know, but if I ask them to go see the Washington Philharmonics with me, they won't go. "Is that opera?" [they want to know]. . . . And they don't go to the museums with me either, 'cause they don't think, they'd go crazy, they'd rather go to the movies to see Eddie Murphy in "48 Hours" than to go see "To Fly" at the Air and Space Museum, and so. . . . (Formal Interview, January 12, 1983)

Rita's desire to dissociate herself from the Black community is even more evident in her response to a question about the kind of music she listens to and the kind of albums she buys:

Black music is meaningless to me. . . . The lyrics, I mean, they, "Oh, it got a nice beat, so it must be good," you know, but that's not always, you now, like that. And so . . . oh, well . . . you know . . . it's just meaningless, you know. You listen to the lyrics sometime, and Black artists, you know, just into meaningless music. And I think I listen to Stevie Wonder because, you know, all of his records usually have, you know, some sort of meaning, like his "Hotter Than July" album, you know, like — what is it? — "Happy Birthday," "Hotter Than July" . . . it's meaningful. But Vanity 6, "Nasty Girls," I mean, what's that, really? It's not — it's just trash . . . as far as I'm concerned. . . . So I start[ed] listening to WPGC [a contemporary non-Black music format] . . . instead of OK-100 [a station which plays music sung primarily by Black artists]. (Formal Interview, January 12, 1983)

There are other, even stronger, indicators of Rita's desire to dissociate herself from the fictive-kinship system prevalent in the Black community. This is particularly apparent in her response to a question about her identification with Black people:

I identify with Blacks and whites alike — I don't — see, that's one thing I don't go for: I don't like when people ask me do I identify with Black people or do I identify with white people? I identify with *people*. People are people, Black or white, Spanish, red, white or blue, we're all the same. (Formal Interview, May 4, 1983)

However, the tone of her voice when she responded to the above question conveyed to me much more than her idealistic response ever could. She was clearly offended by my question and felt personally attacked by my inquiry. I apologized, but felt compelled to try and understand the latent feelings this young woman has about her identity as a Black American. Apparently, she subordinates her identity as a Black American to her identity as an American, hoping that a raceless persona will mitigate the harsh treatment and severe limitations in the opportunity structure that are likely to confront her as a Black American.

Despite Rita's assertions that she does not feel any pressure to separate from Black Americans, her response to the large amount of literature she has begun to receive from various colleges since her PSAT scores were posted is clearly indicative of her ambivalence and confusion about racial identity. She has been forced to acknowledge that distinctions between people based on race are quite rampant, and that they are even found in the "halls of ivy." Rita's racelessness was directed at the core of the ideology for the American social system that maintains that differences of race, religion, and national origin are not important. However, her belief in this ideology was constantly tested when she was forced to acknowledge — or others around her constantly reminded her — that such distinctions not only exist but are critically important in the dominant American society. The literature she received from colleges, indicating that special consideration is given to Black and other "minority" students, was a case in point.

> I mean — okay, this college sent me a Third World — I mean, they said, "We have a Third World Club" — place for Blacks! I mean, the audacity! To even *think* that I would go to a college that has a club for Blacks! I was. . . . Okay, Middlebury — I went to the college — but they sent me this little pamphlet that said, "Minorities at Middlebury" — like, "Do they exist?" or something like that. . . . I mean, it's like — "well, we put them aside in some other place," or something — I don't care. I say, well, I mean, I *suppose* minorities go there — I mean, I guess at least a *few* of them — there *were* only twenty-five there, out of the whole school. But, nevertheless, I *know* they're there by you sending me this pamphlet. I don't appreciate it! (Formal Interview, May 4, 1983)

Rita is convinced that if only people — Black and White — would seriously begin to discount race as a factor in their interactions with each other, discrimination and other invidious distinctions would disappear. She does not view racism in America as an institutionalized phenomenon. It is in connection with this belief system that she has built the raceless persona she presents in the school and non-school context. Her commitment to the ideology of the dominant social system is what structures her academic effort and performance in the school context, motivating her to strive for academic excellence.

Katrina

Katrina presents another example of racelessness as a factor in the academic achievement of high-achieving females. She had the highest grade-point average of any student in the research sample and she graduated as the valedictorian of the Class of 1984. Her best performance was in math and math-related subjects such as computer science; her weakest performance was in the humanities and social sciences. Her performance on the math component of the PSAT was at the 95th percentile. Only one other student scored higher than she, and only one other student had a score that was comparable to hers. Her overall score on the PSAT was higher than that of most of her class- and schoolmates.

Katrina admits that she has had to put brakes on her academic performance in the school context in order to minimize the stress she experiences. In most instances she is much better at handling the subject matter than her peers are, but, like many of the other high achievers, she tries not to be conspicuous.

> Junior high, I didn't have much [of a] problem. I mean, I didn't have — there were always a lot of people in the classroom who did the work, so I wasn't like, the only one who did this assignment. So — I mean, I might do better at it, but I wasn't the only one. And so a lot of times, I'd let other kids answer — I mean, not *let* them, but. . . . All right, I *let* them answer questions [laughter], and I'd hold back. So I never really got into any arguments, you know, about school and my grades or anything. (Formal Interview, February 8, 1983)

The important point to keep in mind is that, although she was extremely fearful of what might happen to her if she acted in ways which were not sanctioned by her peer group, she was, and still is, unwilling to give up on her desire to do well in school. Hence, she chose to "go underground," to become a visible yet invisible person. By using this technique, she did not draw attention to herself, thereby minimizing the possibility of appearing to be different from those around her. Katrina constantly worries, even today, about appearing to be over-confident. An example from one interview session with her supports this observation. The "It's Academic" club is perhaps the most "intellectual" extracurricular activity at the school. In order to participate on the three-person team, students must compete by answering correctly a "test" the school sponsor has prepared for the participants. The students obtaining the three highest scores are identified and are then eligible to participate on the team representing the school on television. Katrina was unable to avoid taking the test because of her relationship with the club's sponsor, who was her physics teacher. However, she established certain preconditions for participation in the qualifying activity: she would take the test, but even if she earned a score that would make her eligible for participating on the school's team, she was not to be selected to participate on television. Having obtained the consent of the club's sponsor and her counselor to these preconditions, she took the qualifying test. As a result of her score on the qualifying exam (she scored higher than all the other participants), she was obviously one of the three students eligible to participate on the school's team. However, since she had made it quite clear to the club's advisor and all other interested parties that she was not to be chosen as one of the team's members, she was made an alternate. She found this arrangement quite satisfying for several reasons: 1) it allowed her to display her knowledge to her teachers and some of her supportive friends, thereby validating her academic capabilities; 2) at the same time, she was able to retain her invisibility as a high achiever, a much-desired status on her part; and 3) she satisfied, at least in part, her teacher's request that she compete for one of the most highly sought academic honors at the school (Formal Interview, March 7, 1983). Katrina was pleased with herself because she had proved herself capable of out-performing most of her peers at the school — even those students who were twelfth graders. At the same time, she was able to remain anonymous and invisible in the school context. Her invisibility had made it so much easier to pursue her goal of academic excellence.

In comparison with Rita, Katrina's personality seems dull. Nevertheless, she, too, is insightful and fun to be with. She also has the kind of personality that makes it easy for those who interact with her to do so comfortably. Like Rita, she is able to perform well on school measures of success, both in the classroom context and on standardized measures. Also like Rita, Katrina is not sure that Black Americans have a viable cultural system. Her uncertainty stems from her lack of attention to the issue rather than some strongly held view on the matter. When I insisted that she describe for me what she thinks of when she thinks of Black culture, she sighed and finally responded by saying: "Music. Dance." Like Rita, Katrina does not like contemporary Black music and avoids those radio stations that are most often identified with the Black community. She views the music played on those stations as being too "rowdy"; she also does not like the regular TV serials, preferring old movies, especially the ones with such stars as Doris Day, Fred Astaire, and Ginger Rogers. The fact that both she and Rita tend to eschew Black music is an important aspect of their raceless personae, given the symbolic significance of indigenous music in the Black community.[5]

Like many of the other student members of the research sample, Katrina believes in the democratic ideals of the nation, and wants Black and White Americans to live peaceably and contentedly together. In fact, she opposes any effort on the part of Black Americans to separate themselves from the majority culture. Her belief in the fairness and openness of the opportunity structure is primarily responsible for her commitment to school norms and academic achievement.

Katrina's responses to the questions about Black life and culture, and her explanation for the massive poverty in the Black community, suggest that she is not the least bit certain about the answers she offers. What is more

[5] The findings emerging from this study regarding Black music and other forms of indigenous entertainment in the Black community indicate that they are critical symbols of group unity and solidarity. Consequently, students who do not identify with these aspects of Black American culture are perhaps unwittingly avoiding an important symbol of membership in the fictive-kin-ship system and shared behavioral patterns.

important, her responses indicate that she has not given much thought to the nature and configuration of the social organization of the Black community. She has not given much thought to these questions, in part because they are rarely discussed in the school context as part of the core curriculum. This has had a negative effect on her perception of her racial group membership and her sense of herself as an individual. Moreover, the lack of a strong attachment to the Black community in her home environment and a limited focus on the value of that membership in the school context have led her to embrace a raceless persona so as to minimize the harm that is likely to result from an acknowledgment that she is Black.

Katrina also admits that she has no real preference for how she should be identified, racially or ethnically. The fact that she has no preference suggests a desire to appear raceless, or non-Black. Like Rita, she believes that hard work on the part of Black Americans is the key to the elimination of economic and social differences between Black and White Americans, and, as noted above, she holds Black Americans primarily responsible for their present lower-class status because, in her mind, Black Americans are basically lazy. Her acceptance of the widely held stereotypical image of Black Americans motivates her to try to be an exception to the rule. She does not want other people to view her in the same way; in other words, as a lazy person. This persistent negative perception of Black Americans motivated her to develop the kind of raceless persona which is so much a part of the person she is today. Because she has defined success as going "to college, and graduate in the highest percentile . . . a nice steady job [which] pays well . . . travel . . . and friends," she constantly seeks to dissociate herself from the negative stereotypes which are so much a part of the daily social reality of Black Americans.

Katrina has been able to maintain a high level of proficiency on school measures of success while at the same time muting the hostility of her peers and classmates who might otherwise use boundary-maintaining mechanisms to limit her efforts at social mobility. She has done this by developing a persona which makes her appear virtually raceless in the school context. Among her schoolmates and peers, Katrina's raceless persona is characterized by her inconspicuousness and seeming invisibility; to her teachers and other representatives of the dominant society, her racelessness is evident in her strong commitment to the values and norms condoned in the school context and the larger society, as well as her disavowal of those features of the Black community which are rejected by the school and the larger social system (for example, speaking non-standard English, commitment to group advancement rather than individual mobility, and so on). Racelessness as a strategy for social mobility is also evident in her willingness to put forth the effort necessary to excel in those arenas and aspects of the school curriculum which have traditionally been defined as the purview of White Americans.

Maggie

Maggie is the third example of how high-achieving females work to develop a raceless persona. She is a seventeen-year-old student with a high GPA who scheduled her core courses from the regular curriculum. Choosing regular courses instead of Advanced Placement courses is not a particularly unproductive strategy for Maggie, since her mother and maternal family members provide her with a strong support system for academic achievement. Her mother, who forms the base of this support system, is uncompromising in her insistence on behavior befitting a "young lady" and the appropriate grades at this level of schooling. In fact, the support system is so strong that it tends to have many unintended consequences, at least from Maggie's perspective.

Maggie does not consider herself to have a lot of friends, either at school or in her immediate neighborhood. Indeed, she insists that she has virtually no contact with the people who live near her; that all her friends are either fellow students or, in a more limited number, people she knows from church. She claims to know no one from her neighborhood, despite the fact that she has lived with her parents in the same single-family townhouse for more than ten years. She insists that her knowledge of the people in the neighborhood is so severely limited because her parents, particularly her mother, are afraid that she will start using drugs and engage in other undesirable behaviors if she becomes too familiar with the neighborhood residents. They, therefore, demand that she avoid such relationships. This avoidance of the people who are constantly around her has taught her to view herself as being different from those people, despite the fact that racially they are the same: they too are Black Americans.

Perhaps the most contradictory component of Maggie's life — both in and outside the school context — is reflected in her efforts to come to grips with being Black in a country where being Black is devalued. This reality has led to the development of identity problems for her; problems which are exacerbated by her lighter skin color. She admits that her fairer skin color is not as problematic today as it was when she was in elementary and junior high school, where she was frequently referred to as "yellow." This description of her was so pervasive when she was in elementary school that she came to see herself as being raceless, neither Black nor White. When asked to choose one of the various labels used to identify Black Americans ("Black," "Negro," "Colored," "Afro-American," and so forth), she responded in the following manner:

> I wouldn't consider myself as none of them. When I was small, people used to say I was yellow, right?, so I thought — I really thought I was yellow. I didn't think I was Black. I thought I was a Mongoloid. So all these — all this time I've been — well, not *recently* — I thought I was yellow until I got into — maybe around the sixth, seventh grade. Then my mother told me I wasn't yellow, 'cause on the papers when we used to fill out, I used to put

"Yellow" on it, you know, for "Black, White or Other"? . . . I would put "Other" or put "Yellow" on it, 'cause people used to call me "yellow." And my mother told me that I was Black.

. . . I kind of felt different. I felt like a different person. I said, "All this time I thought I was yellow. And now I'm Black. . . ." (Formal Interview, February 25, 1983)

The residual effect of this misidentification is still a part of Maggie's identity structure, aiding and abetting her conscious and unconscious desire to be an "exception to the rule." Part of the reason for her reluctance to be identified as a Black American stems from the fact that, perhaps unwittingly, she accepts many of the popular negative stereotypes regarding the behavior and lifestyles of Black Americans, magnifying her desire to dissociate herself from the larger Black community. As with most of the other female high achievers, her family reinforces her perception of being different. In the school context, this perception is supported by her teachers and other school officials, who constantly reassure her that her willingness to work at achieving school success is evidence of her lack of affiliation with her peers and other Black Americans. The juxtaposition of her desire to disaffiliate from her eternal and unbreakable bond and her obligation to the Black community (Taylor, 1973) exacerbates her uncertainty and confusion regarding racial loyalty.

In summary, racelessness among the female students described in this analysis is a strategy for social mobility both in and out of the school context. These young women tend to internalize the values, beliefs, and ideals taught and learned in school, making them a part of their behavior pattern in their family and community environments. In this way, racelessness becomes a definite part of their lives, creating enormous stress and anxiety. Moreover, this raceless response to the duality of their existence puts social distance between them and their less successful peers, enabling them to pursue goals and objectives that, under the scrutiny and careful eyes of their peers, might be severely criticized. Also, as this analysis shows, the female high-achievers vacillate between inconspicuousness among their less successful peers and carefully constructed racelessness in the presence of their teachers and other representatives of the dominant society. The raceless personae they present appear to be mandated by the school — the price they pay if they desire to achieve vertical mobility. These students appear to understand that the school and their teachers expect them to distance themselves from the "Black" aspects of their home, peers, and immediate community in ways that suggest an individualistic orientation toward success and social mobility.

The Male High-Achieving Students

A common theme in the responses — verbal and behavioral — of the male high-achieving students is their commitment to the ideology of the American social system, and the sense of conflict and uncertainty about their dual relationship with the larger dominant society and the indigenous fictive-kinship system of the Black community. This uncertainty and the resultant conflict force them to question their identity repeatedly, leading to a response pattern that highlights their relationship to the dominant society while at the same time maintaining their relationship to the Black community and the existing fictive-kinship system. Hence, the male high achievers differ from their female counterparts in that they appear to be much more victimized in the school context by the "double consciousness" attendant on the dual socialization pattern that appears to be an endemic feature of the childrearing practices prevailing in the Black community. In other words, presenting a raceless persona appears to be much more difficult for the male students in the sample group. Nevertheless, as in the female high achievers, racelessness appears to be a quality which enhances the academic potential of the male students in the research sample. Some examples from my research are instructive of how the development of a raceless persona enables them to succeed in the school context. Kent is a case in point.

Kent

Kent is one of the most unusual students at Capital High in that he appears to be unaffected by his peers' perception or acceptance of him. He appears to be both adult- and goal-oriented. He was the male valedictorian of his junior high school graduating class. He makes good grades and never cuts class.

> I haven't missed a day of school ever since I was in seventh grade. And it's just come to me now, if I miss a day — I don't want to miss a day. Sometime my mother say, "Stay home. You deserve to stay home, relax and everything." I say, "I can't do that, I gotta go to school." And I want to stay home, but it's hard for me now that I've become adjusted to that and everything. And it's like when I'm going to bed the night sometime — I used to go to bed something like nine o'clock. Now I don't go to bed till about two, two-thirty, or three o'clock [A.M.]. . . . 'Cause I'm used to staying up studying and everything and thinking about my plans for tomorrow, and it just became a habit. I just kept on doing it and kept on doing it. (Formal Interview, February 23, 1983)

Kent loves track and could probably earn a track scholarship were he to participate in that sport at Capital; however, he recently resigned from the track team because he concluded that it interfered with his ability to complete his math homework when he went home after practice.

> I wasn't doing that well in math at first, but because I wanted to run track, and I was practicing and everything . . . when you taking Algebra II, Trig, you cannot be tired going home. You cannot be tired and study at the same time, 'cause if you do, you won't comprehend that algebra and stuff. So

now, this third advisory and everything, I got hundreds on all my math tests, 'cause I quit track, for one thing, and I told myself I'm gonna get my work, my work come first and everything. . . . (Formal Interview, February 23, 1983)

Kent's teachers generally consider him to be a hardworking and serious young man. He is often asked to introduce guests or make oratorical presentations at school assemblies. As a tenth grader, he won First Place in the citywide and regional Science Fair competitions, and was a finalist at the national level. He also took first honors in the citywide History Fair for a project he undertook on the relationship between the Japanese and American automobile industries. He attends the Upward Bound program at Georgetown University on Saturdays on his own initiative. No one demands that he attend this program, nor does he get extra credit for doing so. It is an activity he enjoys, and it reinforces his desire to "be somebody." His commitment to the value of schooling is unquestioned. He is convinced that if an individual does well in school, he will succeed in the larger society.

Kent's explanations for the poverty conditions experienced by Black Americans, like those of most of the high-achieving males participating in this study, are ambivalent and contradictory. He attributes the widespread poverty to inadequate schooling caused by Black Americans' general resistance to investing great effort in education. He identifies effort as an important factor in an individual's achieving his or her goal.

Interestingly, however, Kent camouflages his scholastic efforts and the importance placed on education as a vehicle for success by developing a comedic persona. This transformation minimizes negative or hostile reactions from his peers. From his description of his behavior and interactions in the school situation, one can perceive his strong commitment to the "achievement ideology" (MacLeod, 1987). Evidence from his interview and my observations shows that he uses humor as a strategy to diffuse the emergence of a raceless persona in the classroom when interacting with the teacher as well as in bantering with his classmates during class time:

> . . . I start saying some of my jokes . . . and make the class laugh and get things moving or something. Like, if [the teacher] might . . . say he was talking to us about some kind of bonds, chemical bonds and he spelled out this word wrong on the board. So he look[ed] at it and he said, "I can't spell today," and I say, "Yes, you can, Doc — it's t-o-d-a-y. My little brother can spell that." And he wasn't talking about that. He was talking about his word on the board he messed up. And everybody thought that was so funny. I do — sometimes I do things like that. (Formal Interview, February 23, 1983)

Although Kent has decided to put the values, beliefs, and ideology of the larger society over those of the indigenous fictive-kinship system when these values collide, he has been able to minimize his peers' perception of his emerging raceless persona. Many of them see him as somewhat "strange," but a nice fellow, nonetheless. Not surprisingly, he is constantly juggling his various personae in order to minimize the risks associated with the pursuit of school success. Hence, Kent feels the conflict between the two cultural systems competing for his loyalty. His efforts to dissociate himself from the fictive-kinship system and the Black community have negative consequences for him.

Wendell

Wendell is another example of a Black male who develops a persona to achieve academic excellence and acceptance in the dominant society. Wendell prides himself on his achievement of excellent grades in school while preserving the appearance of commitment to the Black community. He has maintained the balance because, until this point in his schooling, he rarely had to study to receive good grades.

> . . . I think that I catch on quick. . . . That's how I got academic — not smart, you know. I don't consider myself smart. . . . When people think smart, like, they know *everything*. I think people who are academic know some things, but, you know, to a certain point. That's how I think. (Formal Interview, March 23, 1983)

Wendell indicates the extent of his ambivalence about the relationship between academic excellence and his identity as a Black American male student, pointing specifically to the conflict he experienced around the issue of being separated from his friends and those with whom he identifies.

> I would have been in [the Advanced Placement courses], but they kept pressing me. . . . They [school officials] kept on — like, almost begging me to be in the [AP courses]. . . . I wouldn't do it 'cause they kept . . . pressing. They kept on. They almost was trying to *make* me get in [the AP courses]. I would have got in, too. Like when I was doing my grades, they looked, and my grades checked. "Oh, he goin' be in [the AP courses]." I said, "No, I'm not." They said, "Put him down for [the AP courses]," they was *telling* me I was going to be [in those courses]. I was in junior high. And they was *telling* me. All through the summer they kept calling me, "You want to be in [the AP courses]?" "No, that's all right." So that's why I didn't get in [the AP courses]. And they — some things they don't let you do [if you take the AP courses], either. You know, like sports-wise and stuff. I don't like that. They almost run your life. (Formal Interview, March 23, 1983)

Apparently this conflict stems from Wendell's desire to be identified in a way that allows him to be acceptable to both school officials and to his friends.

Prior to attending Capital High School, Wendell envisioned a career as a chemist in a major corporation; his excellent grades in junior high school earned him the title of valedictorian of his ninth-grade class. Belatedly, he now realizes that his decision to forego his assignment to the AP courses at the school has undermined his attempts to convince his teachers that he is not dumb. In high school, unlike the way he felt before, he is confused and uncertain about whether to pursue academic excellence. In junior high school, Wendell was able to achieve school success without much effort and without being differentiated by the school officials from his less successful peers and friends. At the high school level, where the distinctions between successful and not-so-successful students are sharper, it is more difficult for him to bridge these two groups.

His decision not to attend the National Honor Society induction ceremony at his school illustrates Wendell's ambivalence about his academic role. When asked why he chose not to participate in the ceremony honoring his achievements during his first year (tenth grade) and the first semester of his second year at the school, he simply shrugged his shoulders, indicating that he did not have an acceptable response. A later response to a question about the meaning of the term "brainiac" provides insight into his behavior. He admitted that most of the students at the school seek to avoid being so labeled even though they might earn grades that, given the definition of the term, warrant such a label. Wendell stated that he himself is in such an undesirable position. I asked him to tell me why most students do not want to be identified as brainiacs.

> Because they think people won't like them, if they smart. Like, my French teacher was saying that — well, my — she said — she was saying that I'm good and everything, right? — in class, around her, want everybody to act like me. And I tried to say, "No! Don't say *that!*" you know, 'cause I know people get mad at me and stuff. So — it seem like sometime you want to have your friends. . . . [when brainiac is considered a negative term, it is intended to say,] like, when you're — like, you're [out]cast, since you're smart. Outcast. . . . [T]hey say, "Since he smart, you know, he think he *too* smart. You know, we don't want to deal with him." Like that. (Formal Interview, March 29, 1983)

Wendell admits that he does not want to be identified as being different from his peers, but the pressure of trying to live up to the expectations associated with being "smart" while at the same time trying to minimize the social distance between him and his peers is overwhelming.

From the discussion above we see that Wendell's earlier belief in the efficacy of school and the attendant commitment to racelessness are undergoing a precipitous change. Prior to the second semester of this, his eleventh-grade year, he has consistently earned above-average grades in school. The present change in his perception of the value of school and schooling can be linked to his changing perception of what it means to be a young Black American male and of the importance of school credentials for the adult roles he believes are available to males who share his ethnic and racial background. Wendell's emerging disillusionment is so severe that it points up the critical need for future research to address the question: "Are Black male adolescents who become racially conscious in the high school context likely to respond in a negative way to school-sanctioned norms?" There is limited evidence to support a positive answer to this question, but the sample represented in this study is too small to offer unequivocal proof (Reeves, 1972).

Wendell began to pursue academic excellence in response to the persistence of stereotypical myths that suggest that Black Americans, as a social group, are "ignorant." As the son of an unmarried woman whose major means of supporting her children is through public assistance (AFDC), Wendell, throughout his school experience, has fought to minimize the stereotypes frequently attributed to such families: lazy, unproductive, underachieving in the school context, and so forth. The primary strategy available to him is to minimize his identity as a Black person, because — as he is quick to point out — the best way Black people can enhance their potential for success is to remember: "Don't be looked upon as Black" (Formal Interview, May 20, 1983, p. 98). In Wendell's mind, doing well in school is a good way to make a political statement about himself and his family and similarly economically disadvantaged families. Hence he is driven to do well in school. Insofar as the children of welfare recipients are subjected to a more pronounced stigma than Black children whose parents are not on welfare, he felt compelled to disavow his resemblance to those with whom he was racially and economically identifiable.

Because Wendell has recently begun to see his future as being intimately linked to his racial group affiliation, his academic effort has diminished considerably. He no longer seeks to distinguish himself from his peers in the one way in which he had sought distinction prior to senior high school: getting high grades without much effort. He has come to this stage of his development primarily because his perception of the opportunity structure is governed less by the official ideology of the dominant social system than it is by the informal rules and regulations that operate in the present fictive-kinship system. He has come to believe that a raceless persona is not all he had thought it to be. Hence, the only distinction he made between himself and his peers — obtaining good grades in school — is no longer a worthwhile option for him, especially since he must now put forth effort in order to receive grades comparable to those he received in elementary and junior high school.

Martin

Martin is another example of how male high achievers seek to distinguish themselves from their peers by the development of a repertoire of skills and behaviors that are generally attributed to non-Black students. Although Martin maintains that he is in many ways different from his peers at Capital,

236

primarily because he earns good grades in school and "care[s] about what people think of [him]," he also notes with unintended anguish his efforts to cloak a raceless persona. Because he earns good grades in school, he is constantly mindful of being labeled "brainiac" or "pervert."

> A pervert is like a brainiac . . . a pervert won't have his mind on girls or [on] nothing but his schooling, that's it! He'll come to school, do this work, won't say nothing to nobody, and leave. . . . That's all I know *he'll* do. (Formal Interview, March 23, 1983)

Martin believes it is important for a male high-achieving student at Capital High to be protective of his image and to cloak it in other activities to minimize the harm that is likely to follow from being known as a brainiac. Moreover, he says that there are persistent rumors that some of the male students who take all or a large number of the Advanced Placement courses at the school are gays, or "perverts."

> *Interviewer:* Are there many "perverts" or squares or brainiacs at this school?
>
> *Martin:* In [the Advanced Placement courses], yes. . . . [For example,] I know one guy, he call boys "Egberts" — 'cause a guy named Egbert he knew one time was very smart. I call them — some of them — well, I hate to say it about some of them, but some of them be acting like gays. (Formal Interview, March 23, 1983)

To minimize the possibility of being known as a brainiac and thereby bringing their manhood into question, high-achieving male students who are doing well in school often resort to "lunching" — behaviors suggestive of clowns or comedians or some other unconventional personalities.

Martin's perception of Black Americans is full of conflicts and contradictions. For example, he identifies discrimination and prejudice as being widely practiced by White Americans, thus limiting Black Americans' ability to improve their economic, political, and social conditions. At the same time, he believes they (Black people) "don't care."

> Like I said, they [Black Americans] don't care. That's what I say. They don't care. . . . I mean, they'll stand on the corner, smoke marijuana, and all that. I don't know why . . . they won't get [themselves] together, but I think they just don't care. (Formal Interview, March 23, 1983)

Martin sees himself as being different from most other Black Americans in that he "care[s] what people think of [him]. [He] always tr[ies] to [make] a good impression on people. [He] always care[s] . . ." (Formal Interview, March 23, 1983). His view of himself as being different from the masses of Black people is a factor to a limited extent in his commitment to school achievement. His commitment to "impression management," as well as to dispelling persistent negative stereotypes associated with Black Americans, motivates him to work at the development of a raceless persona.

Summary and Implications

In this article I have tried to capture the endemic tensions and conflicts experienced by Black high-achieving students as they seek to define their dual relationship to the indigenous Black American cultural system and the individualistic, impersonal cultural system of the dominant society. Because the individualistic ethos predominates in the school context, high achievers often make choices that either put social distance between them and their peers or undermine group solidarity. They do not appear to believe — nor does their experience support — the idea that they can truly be bicultural and actualize what Edwards (1987) describes as their "crossover dreams" — the widely touted dreams of wealth, fame, and fortune. Instead, their experiences, both in and out of school, support the value of appearing raceless to their teachers and other adults in the school context.

Indeed, various indicators at Capital High suggest that a raceless persona is valued in school. The structure of the curriculum that separates the "winners" from the "losers" is the primary example. Although not perceived by either the parents or the students as having the malevolent intentions overwhelmingly attributed to most tracking systems, the Advanced Placement courses form a subtle track that fosters a distinctive individualistic ideology within those students selected to enroll in them. Furthermore, the school implicitly weakens the collective ethos in the Capital High community — an extension of the collective ethos of the fictive-kinship system prevailing in the Black community — by enticing students who display signs of having only a marginal relationship to the collectivity into participating in the special programs. Separating students in this manner isolates them from the masses in ways comparable to the experiences reported earlier in this article (Campbell, 1982; Gray, 1985; McClain, 1983; Monroe, 1987; Petroni & Hirsch, 1971). In short, the high achievers described in this paper have learned the value of appearing to be raceless — a clear example of internalizing oppression — in their efforts to "make it."

Because the high-achieving students believe firmly in the "American dream" they willingly, and in some instances not so willingly, seek to distance themselves from the fictive-kinship system in the Black community. The organizational structure of the school rewards racelessness in students and thus reinforces the notion that it is a quality necessary for success in the larger society. As a result, the students are also led to believe in the view of racism and discrimination as the practices of individuals rather than as part and parcel of institutionally sanctioned social policies.

What high-achieving students often forfeit in their development toward becoming raceless, however, is strong allegiance to the Black community and connection to the fictive-kinship system. This trade-off becomes problematic because many of their less successful peers do not share the value of becoming raceless. Consequently, many of the successful students find themselves juggling their school and community personae in order to minimize the conflicts and anxieties generated by the need to interact with the various competing constituencies represented in the school context.

My analysis also demonstrates that racelessness among the Black adolescents at Capital High may be influenced by gender, with the female high-achieving students appearing to be more willing to be closely identified with the values and beliefs of the dominant social system than their male counterparts. When compared with the female students, the high-achieving males appear to be less committed to the cultural system of the larger society and far more confused and ambivalent about the value of forsaking their indigenous beliefs and values. Hence, the high-achieving male students mask their raceless personae to a far greater degree than their female counterparts in the school context. In spite of these differences, both male and female students do believe that school and schooling are the primary means of achieving vertical mobility for Black Americans in the existing social system.

The resistance of high-achieving students to identifying too strongly with the Black community parallels that of Black adults in the work force who have achieved some measure of success above the existing job ceiling. In other words, successful students, like their successful adult counterparts, seek to minimize the discomfort experienced by members of the dominant society who evaluate them as they enter institutions that are governed by dominant group norms and standards. If they are not successful in minimizing their ethnic group membership — that is, appearing raceless — their chances of achieving vertical mobility are seriously diminished, despite clear evidence of academic excellence on standardized measures of success.

The critical question this paper addresses, therefore, is whether the development of raceless personae by the high-achieving students at Capital High in order to achieve academic excellence is a pragmatic strategy or a Pyrrhic victory. The answer to this question is complex. At the individual level, the high-achieving student's attainment of his or her self-defined goals appears to be enhanced by the development of a raceless personae. At the level of the individual, then, racelessness appears to be a pragmatic strategy.

This is true, in part, because at Capital High, and perhaps in other schools, the message conveyed to Black adolescents is that they cannot be culturally different and, at the same time, achieve success as defined by the dominant society. This is an important observation because, unlike many other ethnically distinctive markers, Blackness is a barrier that limits and inhibits vertical mobility in the larger American society. As Aplin-Brownlee (1984, p. D5) notes, it is difficult for White Americans, when interacting with Black Americans, to "get past the look of blackness to actually hear what's being said."

Yet, given the Black community's penchant for the collectivity, what kind of support from peers can be expected by Black adolescents whose behaviors and values in the school context appear to be at odds with the indigenous social organization of Black people? At Capital High School there is not much support for students who adopt the individualistic ethos, because succeeding in school is invariably associated with movement away from the community and is seen as a sign of having been co-opted by the dominant society. Hence, even those high achievers who camouflage their efforts at academic excellence are viewed with suspicion, and are tested constantly by their less successful peers to determine whether their appearance of being "drylongso" (Gwaltney, 1980) is in fact who they are. This surveillance helps the group to maintain established cultural boundaries, ensuring the survival of the group as well as its cultural integrity (Staiano, 1980). Unfortunately, this constant surveillance of the behaviors of members of the school community — both high- and under-achieving — drains the energy of students which might be devoted to the pursuit of academic excellence and other creative endeavors. Thus, while the development of a raceless persona is a prerequisite for success in the Advanced Placement curriculum of the school, it is equally the case that the development of such a persona is marked by conflict and ambivalence.

In my analysis, the larger questions are directed to the Black community. It is imperative that Black Americans, particularly parents, ask themselves the following questions to determine what they can give up in order for their children to achieve academic success: 1) Are we willing to have our children defined as successful even though they display very little commitment to the Black community? 2) Or are we more committed to the integrity of the existing cultural system in the Black community and, therefore, willing to sublimate our individual goals for the collective advancement of our people? Another equally compelling question must be directed to school officials: Are you willing to modify existing school curricula to incorporate a more group-centered ethos, thereby enabling Black students to "seek self-realization through personal effort in service to the group" (LeVine & White, 1986, p. 103). The answer to each of these questions has important, and drastically different, implications for Black adolescents' school performance and the continued integrity of the existing fictive-kinship system in the Black community.

As my analysis suggests, within the school structure, Black adolescents consciously and unconsciously sense that they have to give up aspects of their identifies and of their indigenous cultural system in order to achieve success as defined in dominant-group terms; their resulting social selves are embodied in the notion of racelessness. Hence, for many of them the cost of school success is too high; it implies that cultural integrity must be sacrificed in order to "make it." For many Black adolescents, that option is unacceptable. For the high achievers identified in this paper, achieving school success is not marked only by conflict and ambivalence, as noted earlier, but with the need to camouflage efforts directed at behaviors that the group identifies as "acting White." Moreover, Black Americans' changed perceptions of what it means to be successful in America will dictate to some degree how Black adolescents respond to the system of schooling in this country. The ethos that values the collectivity over individual mobility has an important impact on the academic efforts and perceptions of Black adolescents.

Given the continued domination of the individualistic ethos in public schooling in the United States, if the Black community continues to sanction group rather than individual mobility, Black adolescents' academic achievement is likely to remain unchanged. But if Black Americans as a people are willing to have their children evince behaviors and attitudes that suggest a lack of connectedness to the larger Black community, then racelessness is a pragmatic strategy that more Black Americans should embrace, and not a Pyrrhic victory. The issue of pragmatic strategy or Pyrrhic victory can and should be determined only by Black Americans. Although further research is clearly indicated, it is imperative that Black Americans define explicitly their relationship to the larger society, and hence their expectations for their children in the school context.

References

Anderson, J. D. (1975). Education as a vehicle for the manipulation of Black workers. In W. Feinberg & H. Rosemont, Jr. (Eds.), *Work, technology, and education: Dissenting essays in the intellectual foundations of American education.* Chicago: University of Illinois Press.

Aplin-Brownlee, V. (1984, July 8). July 4 reminds me . . . : Blacks and Whites still talk to each other through masks. *Washington Post,* p. C4.

Bloch, M. (1971). The moral and tactical meaning of kinship terms. *Man, 6,* 79–87.

Bradley, D. (1982, May). Black and American, 1982. *Esquire,* pp. 58–64, 69.

Brain, J. J. (1972). Kinship terms. *Man, 7,* 137–138.

Bullock, H. A. (1970). *A history of Negro education in the South: From 1619 to the present* (2nd ed.). New York: Praeger.

Campbell, B. M. (1982, January 17). Black executives and corporate stress. *New York Times Magazine,* pp. 1–42.

DeVos, G. A. (1967). *Japan's invisible race: Caste in culture and personality.* Berkeley: University of California Press.

Dizard, J. (1970). Black identity, social class, and Black power. *Psychiatry, 33,* 195–202.

Drake, S. C., & Cayton, H. R. (1970). *Black metropolis: A study of Negro life in a northern city* (Vols. 1 and 2). New York: Harcourt Brace Jovanovich.

Edwards, A. (1987). Crossover dreams: For Blacks, the cost of corporate success too often is bicultural stress. *Essence, 17,* pp. 53–68.

Folb, E. (1980). *Runnin' down some lines: The language and culture of Black teenagers.* Cambridge, MA: Harvard University Press.

Fordham, S. (1981, October 24). *Differential schooling in internally colonized social systems: A cultural ecological perspective.* Paper presented at the 24th Annual Meeting of the African Studies Association, Bloomington, IN.

Fordham, S. (1982, December 3–7). *Cultural inversion and Black children's school performance.* Paper presented at the 81st Annual Meeting, American Anthropological Association, Washington, DC.

Fordham, S. (1983, November 17–20). *Afro-Caribbean and native Black American school performance.* Paper presented at the 82nd Annual Meeting, American Anthropological Association, Chicago.

Fordham, S. (1985). *Black student school success as related to fictive kinship: An ethnographic study in the Washington, DC, Public School System* (Final report). Washington, DC: National Institute of Education.

Fordham, S., & Ogbu, J. (1986). Black students' school success: "Coping with the burden of 'acting White.'" *Urban Review, 18,* 176–206.

Fortes, M. (1969). *Kinship and the social order: The legacy of Lewis Henry Morgan.* Chicago: Aldine.

Freed, S. A. (1973). Fictive kinship in a northern Indian village. *Ethnology, 2,* 86–103.

Gaines-Carter, P. (1984, June 17). Quiet thunder: On a roll with Donnie Simpson. *Washington Post Magazine,* pp. 6–7.

Granat, D., Hathaway, P., Saleton, W., & Sansing, J. (1986). Blacks and Whites in Washington: How separate? How equal? A special report. *The Washingtonian, 22,* pp. 152–182.

Gray, J. (1985, March 17). A Black American princess: New game, new rules. *Washington Post,* pp. E1, E5.

Green, V. M. (1981). Blacks in the United States: The creation of an enduring people? In G. P. Castile & G. Kushner (Eds.), *Persistent peoples: Cultural enclaves in perspective.* Tucson: University of Arizona Press.

Gwaltney, J. L. (1980). *Drylongso: A self-portrait of Black America.* New York: Random House.

Hale, J. (1982). *Black children: Their roots, culture and learning styles.* Provo, UT: Brigham Young University Press.

Haley, A. (1976). *Roots: The saga of an American family.* Garden City, NY: Doubleday.

Holt, G. S. (1972). "Inversion" in Black communication. In T. Kochman (Ed.), *Rappin' and stylin' out.* Urbana: University of Illinois Press.

Klose, K. (1984, August 5). A tormented Black rising star dead by her own hand: Leanita McClain: A pioneer at the racial frontier who lost her way. *Washington Post,* pp. C1, C2.

LeVine, R., & White, M. (1986). *Human conditions: The cultural basis of educational development.* New York: Routledge & Kegan Paul.

Liebow, E. (1967). *Tally's corner: A study of Negro street-corner men.* Boston: Little, Brown.

MacLeod, J. (1987). *Ain't no makin' it: Leveled aspirations in a low-income neighborhood.* Boulder, CO: Westview Press.

MacPherson, M. (1986, February 2). Doug Wilder. *Washington Post,* pp. G1–G2.

McClain, L. (1983, July 24). How Chicago taught me to hate Whites. *Washington Post,* pp. C1, C4.

Monroe, S. (1987, March 23). Brothers: A vivid portrait of Black men in America. *Newsweek,* pp. 55–86.

Morgan, T. (1985). The world ahead: Black parents prepare their children for pride and prejudice. *New York Times Magazine,* pp. 34–35, 90–92, 96–100.

Myrdal, G. (1944). *An American dilemma: The Negro problem and modern democracy.* New York: Harper.

Norbeck, E., & Befu, H. (1958). Informal fictive kinship in Japan. *American Anthropologist, 60,* 102–117.

Ogbu, J. (1983, October 21–22). *Crossing cultural boundaries: A comparative perspective on minority education.* Paper presented at a Symposium on "Race, Class, Socialization and the Life Cycle," in Honor of Allison Davis. University of Chicago, Chicago.

The Oprah Winfrey Show. (1987, January 23). Prejudice against Black men. Transcript.

Petroni, F. A., & Hirsch, E. A. (1971). *Two, four, six, eight, when you gonna integrate?* New York: Behavioral Publications.

Pitt-Rivers, J. (1968). Pseudo-kinship. In D. L. Sills (Ed.), *The international encyclopedia of social sciences.* New York: Macmillan.

Pitt-Rivers, J. (1973). The kith and kin. In J. Goody (Ed.), *The character of kinship.* New York: Cambridge University Press.

Powell, A., Farrar, E., & Cohen, D. (1985). *The shopping mall high school: Winners and losers in the educational marketplace.* Boston: Houghton Mifflin.

Reeves, D. (1972). *Notes of a processed brother.* New York: Pantheon Books.

Richman, A. (1987). Oprah Winfrey: The best talker on TV (and a movie star to boot). *People Weekly, 27*(2), 48–50, 55–56, 58.

Robinson, M. (1987, January 23). Prejudice. Transcript, *The Oprah Winfrey Show.*

Sargent, E. (1985, February 10). Freeing myself: Discoveries that unshackle the mind. *Washington Post,* pp. D1, D4.

Spivey, D. A. (1978). *Schooling for the new slavery: Black industrial education, 1868–1915.* Westport, CT: Greenwood Press.

Stack, C. (1974). *All our kin: Strategies for survival in a Black community.* New York: Harper and Row.

Staiano, K. V. (1980). Ethnicity as process: The creation of an Afro-American identity. *Ethnicity, 7*(1), 27–33.

Staples, R. (1975). To be young, Black and oppressed. *Black Scholar, 6,* 2–9.

Staples, R. (1981). The Black American family. In C. H. Mindel and R. W. Habenstein (Eds.), *Ethnic families in America: Patterns and variations.* New York: Elsevier.

Styron, W. (1966). *The confessions of Nat Turner.* New York: Random House.

Taylor, S. A. (1973). Some funny things happen on the way up. *Contact, 5*(1), 12–17.

Trescott, J. (1977, April 1). Anchorman-reporter Ed Bradley: Like it or not, a symbol. *Washington Post,* pp. B1, B3.

Weis, L. (1985a). *Between two worlds: Black students in an urban community college.* New York: Routledge & Kegan Paul.

Weis, L. (1985b). Without dependence on welfare for life: Black women in the community college. *Urban Review, 17*(4), 233–255.

Williams, M. D. (1981a). *On the street where I lived.* New York: Holt, Rinehart & Winston.

Williams, M. D. (1981b). Observations in Pittsburgh ghetto schools. *Anthropology and Education Quarterly, 12*(3), 211–220.

Willis, P. (1977). *Learning to labor: How working-class kids get working-class jobs.* Lexington, MA: D. C. Heath.

Caswell County Training School, 1933–1969: Relationships between Community and School

—■—■—■—

EMILIE V. SIDDLE WALKER

W hen court-ordered school desegregation plans were announced in 1969 for rural Caswell County, North Carolina, the local newspaper recorded the reaction of one White parent:

> We have no animosity toward the Board. They have done all they can to stall. However, we now feel that this reorganization of our public schools will destroy our high standard of education, depriving our children of the quality of education they deserve and what we all want.

What they wanted, the parent continued, "was the highest standard of education in [the] county" ("Eighteen-Member Board," 1969).

That parent's implicit denigration of the county's one Negro school was ironic.[1] The county high school for Negro children, the Caswell County Training School (CCTS), was a three-story, immaculately kept brick structure that included a gymnasium and a 722-person-capacity auditorium with a balcony.[2] The principal, Nicholas Longworth Dillard, who held a master's degree from the University of Michigan, was esteemed locally by both Black and White educational leaders for his knowledge of national educational

---

[1] The terms "Negro," "colored," "Black," and "African American" are used interchangeably in this article. In general, the term used reflects the appropriate label given to those of African descent during the particular era being discussed.

[2] During the last decade of segregation, the name of the school was changed to Caswell County High School, even though it continued to maintain an elementary department for the local township until 1967. In the early years, it was referred to as the Yanceyville School and, after integration, the name was changed to Dillard Junior High School. For purposes of consistency, this article consistently refers to the facility as Caswell County Training School, the name by which it was known for the longest period of time.

Harvard Educational Review Vol. 63 No. 2 Summer 1993, 161–182

issues. By 1954, 64 percent of the school's teachers had graduate training beyond state recertification requirements, and during Dillard's thirty-six-year tenure from 1933 to 1969, the school offered more than fifty-three extracurricular clubs and activities to enhance student leadership and development. Moreover, the school's educational programs had been on the approved list of the Southern Association of Colleges and Schools since 1934, and were formally accredited in 1955 after that agency began accrediting Negro schools. In contrast, the area high school for White children was smaller, older, had fewer facilities, and was not accredited.

Yet this White parent's belief that White educational systems were superior to Black, and that Negro educators could have nothing to offer White children, is an accurate reflection of many White Americans' perception, both during that era and into the present. Indeed, the history of U.S. education documents so well the inequities African American children experienced during the pre-integration era — specifically the lack of resources, the substandard facilities, and the poor response of school boards to the needs of schools (see Anderson, 1988; Brown, 1960; Clark, 1963; Clift, Anderson, & Hullfish, 1962; Kluger, 1977; Newbold, 1935) — that these images of uniform deprivation have become the dominant picture at the center of most thinking about the segregated schooling of African American children.

This perception of inequality, while not totally inaccurate, is, however, one-sided. It highlights the need and struggle for equality, but overlooks any suggestion that not all education for African American children during segregation was inferior. Sowell (1976), for example, in his description of six "excellent" historically Black high schools and two elementary schools, lists some traits common to these good schools. These traits include, but are not limited to, the commitment and educational levels of the teachers and principals, and the support, encouragement, and rigid standards that characterize the schools' atmospheres. Similarly, in Jones's *A Traditional Model of Educational Excellence* (1981), the segregated school environment is described as "one's home away from home, where students were taught, nurtured, supported, corrected, encouraged, and punished" (p. 2). These and other studies (Adair, 1984; Foster, 1990; Irvine & Irvine, 1984) suggest the presence of a positive sociocultural system in which "uniquely stylized characteristics" reflective of the student population developed independently of White control (Irvine & Irvine, 1984, p. 416), and in which African American youth were successful because of the school environment in which they were taught.

The degree to which such descriptions of segregated Black schooling might also apply to other undocumented cases is further suggested by the numerous voices in southern African American communities, which today speak forcefully of the "goodness" of their pre-integration schools. These voices do not speak of test scores and/or any measured success of school graduates in defining "goodness." Rather, they fondly recall a time when, in the words of one eighty-year-old grandmother, "colored children learnt something in school." Cecelski (1991) has captured some of this appreciation as he chronicles a little-known political struggle in which Negro parents and students boycotted their school system for a year, rather than sacrifice their schools in a locally proposed desegregation plan. Though other voices remain undocumented, the fact that they are heard so frequently in many small-town communities suggests that schooling that was valued by parents, students, and school personnel may have been more common than has been realized.

However, little is known about these unidentified good community schools. Even the paucity of literature that exists on pre-integration Black schooling focuses almost exclusively on good urban high schools, so defined because of their success with standardized test scores, the number of doctoral degrees earned by graduates, or some other easily measured outcome variables. Educators understand little of the emic perspective — that is, how and why communities considered their schools to be good. Educators also do not understand the nature of the schooling in those community-defined good schools. This lack of knowledge not only denies that there are valuable lessons to be learned from principals and teachers who successfully schooled African American children in the past (Foster, 1990), but it also ignores the fact that the communities were pleased with that education. Perhaps more significantly, this lack of knowledge also results in ahistorical approaches to school reform that deprive reformers of important contextual information that could directly impact the success or failure of select school programs. Such oversight could well decrease opportunities for African American children to succeed in today's schools.

I premise this article on the idea that segregated schools that were valued by their communities did exist, and that understanding more about the nature of those schools is important for historical accuracy and for educational reform. As I discuss below, I believe that understanding the history of education in these schools, as well as the types of parent and community participation that were present, will facilitate our ability to ask the right questions as we tackle current reform issues. This is preferable to focusing on questions that are premised on negative assumptions about African American communities.

With this in mind, I present the case of CCTS, the segregated Negro school described earlier. Situated in North Carolina's rural Caswell County, CCTS was a self- and community-defined "good" school. The belief that their school provided a good environment for learning was shared by its graduates, parents, and teachers. This belief is documented in the school's written and oral history, and remains generally consistent throughout most of its existence. In this article, I accept the community's evaluation of CCTS as a good school. I make no effort to argue that by traditional criteria, such as test scores or college attendance rates, CCTS represents the best in segregated schools in the South, or even in its region. Importantly, my description of why CCTS was perceived as a good school is not meant to validate the

inequities or minimize the discrimination that existed in this and other segregated schools, where parents were overly burdened to create for themselves the educational facilities and opportunities school boards often denied them (Anderson, 1988; Bullock, 1967). Rather, I offer this case as
representative of the many other southern African American schools whose
communities were also pleased with their schools, but whose histories have
been lost and whose value is understood now only by former teachers, principals, parents, and students.

This case, ethnographically approached, uses eighty open-ended interviews with former teachers, students, parents, and administrators, to uncover
the themes of the school's goodness, and also to explore the nature of the
relationships within the school environment that explain that goodness.[3] To
reduce the influence of interviewee nostalgia, school documents such as
yearbooks, school newspapers, handbooks, and so forth, as well as newspaper
accounts, minutes of school board meetings, Southern Association reports,
and other archival materials are used to corroborate emerging themes. The
knowledge base derived from a triangulation of documents with interviews
is used in this article to analyze one area little explored in segregated schooling — that is, the nature of the relationship between community and school.
Within the context of this discussion, "community" refers to all of the African
American adults who lived within the forty-square-mile county and who
shared a real or imagined bond with CCTS. While some of the adults lived
within the town in which the school was located, and thereby had more than
the usual informal contact with the principal and teachers at the churches,
stores, and other incidental meetings places, this discussion is not confined
to their relationship with the school. It also incorporates the feeling of relationship and perspective of those adults who lived outside the town. Thus,
the community was not defined by physical proximity. In this article, I focus
specifically on the ways in which this community and CCTS supported each
other. I further explore the significance of these activities, both in their
historical context and in their implications vis-à-vis current advocacy for
more involvement of African American parents in their children's education.

The Case in Historical Context: African Americans in Traditional
Modes of Support

CCTS did not always boast the facilities or programs it enjoyed in 1969, the
year it ceased to operate as a high school. Indeed, like most other segregated
schools, its history was one of financial struggle, broken promises, delayed
response from White school authorities, and financial burdens on its stu-

---

[3] "Open-ended interviews" is a term used to describe a questioning format that allows the
researcher to ask for facts about the matter under discussion, as well as to ask the interviewee's
opinion about the facts. This method was used in conjunction with Spradley's (1979) suggestions
for the "ethnographic interview," which describes specific procedures to tap the knowledge base
of a participant in a culture scene. Interviews lasted usually from 60 to 90 minutes; participants
represented varying regions of the community and varying degrees of involvement in the school.

dents and parents. It began as a small elementary school in a two-story house purchased by several prominent Negro citizens in 1906.[4] In the 1924–1925 school year, it expanded to a four-room "Rosenwald" structure, which teachers and community patrons had contributed $800 to complete.[5] Having previously been denied permission to expand the school beyond the seventh grade, community patrons, under the leadership of newly arrived Principal Dillard, were able in 1934 to add a high school attended by seventy-seven students, many of whom had to travel twenty miles to school on an open-air truck. The truck was donated by a parent, Ulysses Jones, who operated it at a loss for two years, before finally donating it to the state as collateral for the new truck the PTA promised to supply. Meanwhile, another parent, T. S. Lea, paid the electric bill, and others who had dug an unauthorized well were not reimbursed by the school board for their expenses.

Although by 1938 the over-crowded school housed six hundred children in fewer than ten rooms, and a "colored citizen [had] offered to donate to the county nine-and-a-half acres of land as a site for a new school" (Newbold, 1935), the community was forced to wait thirteen years before the new facility was completed.[6] This delay can be attributed in part to the school board's self-description of being "hindered in the making and completing of their plans by lack of sufficient funds" (School Board Minutes, November 3, 1941). However, the minutes also suggest that the county was initially unwilling to use local resources for the building of a Negro school. Further, even after local resources were appropriated, the building needs of the Negro children were merged with those of two other schools for White children.

In the meantime, while the school board passed four resolutions affirming its commitment to build a new school, Negro parents continued to provide resources for the twenty-two teachers and 735 pupils who were part of the school by the 1948–1949 school year. The 1949 yearbook notes that "while the building does not yet satisfy our patrons, they are proud of its equipment." This equipment included modern tablet arm chairs; instructional supplies, including audio-visual aids such as radios, a movie projector, a

[4] Under a fund set up by Julius Rosenwald in 1917, Negro patrons received matching funds for any monetary or other contributions they could make towards the building of schools for Negro children. Records indicate that Caswell County school patrons participated in this program, and that their school, like the 5000 others built in the South before 1948, was known as a "Rosenwald" school. This name, of course, detracts attention from the numerous contributions made by Negro parents and educators. This emphasis on the program rather than the parents is more fully discussed by Anderson (1988).

[5] Although I refer here to the first known building, the education of Negro children in the area precedes the purchase of a school building in Yanceyville in 1906. The North Carolina Session of 1897, for example, notes the incorporation of the "Yanceyville Colored Graded School" for the education of the colored children. Moreover, the oral history records the existence of church schools throughout the area in the late 1800s.

[6] This information is based upon a letter recorded in the school board minutes from N. C. Newbold, director of the Negro Division of Education, to Holland McSwain, Superintendent of Caswell County Schools. The letter itself is dated August 29, 1938; the letter is recorded in the school board minutes under the meeting for September 5, 1938.

35-mm projector, and a wire recorder; and other items they considered important for education, but which the school board refused to supply. The academically oriented school curriculum was complemented by an award-winning debate team, a band (the first in any Caswell County high school), a newspaper, and other student organizations (Caswell County, 1949).

In March of 1951, when the students and teachers finally moved into the twenty-seven-room facility described by the local paper as "modern in every respect," the new building reflected the tremendous community support that was part of its history. While the county contributed $80,000 toward the cost of the $325,000 state-funded project, the Negro citizens themselves added close to $8,000 in equipment, almost a tenth of the cost the county expended, to create the kind of facility they had envisioned in 1949 — "a physical plant second to none in the state" (Caswell County, 1949). Among the items added were an $1,800 stage curtain and colored footlights, $3,000 worth of venetian blinds for the windows, a $400 time clock to regulate classes automatically, and a $2,000 public-address system ("Dedication," 1951). The money for these items was contributed by students, parents, and other community supporters.

Between 1951 and 1969, parents continued to support the financial needs of CCTS, supplying such items as band uniforms and instruments, science equipment, a piano, and workbooks. While they engaged in many fundraising activities during those years, the most consistent and most remembered was the Popularity Contest. In this annual event, each high school class nominated a king and queen; members of the class, with the participation of parents and other community leaders, then raised money to support their nominees. In the heyday of this event, records indicate that the winning class alone contributed as much as $1,410.35 to support the school. In February of 1969, however, things began to change: Principal Dillard died unexpectedly in the midst of planning desegregation, and that fall the school was reorganized as a fully integrated junior high. After these two events, Negro parents ceased all such financial assistance to the school.

Considering a rural community where, in 1953, 58 percent of the parents were farmers, 23 percent homemakers, 6 percent laborers, and 8 percent service and domestic workers, there is a temptation to view the CCTS community's financial contributions to the school as exceptional. Their self-reliance, sacrifice, and sense of community responsibility not only created ongoing support for the school, but also provided their children with a model for the role interested parents should play. Their commitment insured that continuous resources would be provided for the education of Black children, despite the lack of adequate support from the all-White school board. Yet, the sacrifices, self-help, and support of these CCTS patrons were typical of Negroes in many communities in the South during this era. This story of self-help for segregated schools has been most notably described and analyzed by Anderson (1988), who emphasizes the fact that, although such help was helpful in improving school conditions, it also was oppressive in that it imposed a "double taxation" on Negro citizens. According to Anderson, "rural Blacks in particular were victims of [this] taxation without representation" (p. 156). They were often forced to "take from their meager annual incomes and contribute money to the construction and maintenance of public schools for the Black child because southern state and local governments refused to accept responsibility for Black public education" (p. 176). In other words, Black parents paid taxes for services they did not receive. The history of CCTS lends additional evidence to Anderson's thesis.

What has been less often discussed, however, are the other avenues of parental support that existed in segregated school environments. Although CCTS grew significantly between 1933 and 1969, the nature of the relationship between school and community remained consistent. In addition to providing financial support, parents at CCTS 1) maintained a physical presence in the school, primarily through the Parent Teachers Association (PTA) and other events to which they were invited; 2) played an "advocacy" role for the school in soliciting funds from the school board; and 3) provided invisible home-based support for the principal and teachers.

Parents in the School: Other Avenues of Community Support

In the CCTS environment, the PTA functioned as an umbrella organization that took the lead in providing financial contributions to the school, and also provided other opportunities for parental involvement in school activities. Perhaps the most obvious facet of this involvement was parents' attendance at PTA meetings. While exact attendance figures are not available, former teacher Helen Beasley remembers:

> I don't know how many folks we *didn't* have at PTA! Good gracious. If the auditorium wasn't filled up, it was maybe like three-fourths. That great big auditorium would be three-fourths full with the mamas and daddies and the brothers and the sisters and the grandmamas and the aunts, and the uncles and whoever.

Though not all informants are as enthusiastic in their memories of the number of people attending and often focus instead on whether there should have been even more, they do report that the auditorium was frequently filled to capacity as Beasley relates. In absolute numbers, PTA attendance was less in earlier years, when parents were more likely to sit around a pot-bellied stove rather than gather in a formal setting; nevertheless, participation was reportedly high, especially given the distance parents had to travel and the lack of automobiles. When parents did not attend, it was usually because of transportation problems or conflicting work schedules. Lack of interest in the school or a feeling of alienation were seldom the reasons given for their absence.

Several activities were consistently part of the business portion of the PTA meeting. First, parents received reports about the school's financial and educational status. Since one of the PTA's primary missions was to help supply the school's needs, the financial report often involved the president or the principal outlining the most pressing needs. Based on these reports, parents organized collaborative plans of action with teachers and the principal, and actively engaged in completing the projects. These activities typically included overseeing a teacher's homeroom activities and reporting on that class's participation, or joining in a parent-teacher basketball game. Parents who were not active in planning often provided support by attending an event, and supplying or buying items on sale there.

The principal also regularly used a portion of the meeting to report to the parents about education, what was going on in the school such as problems drivers were having on buses, or ways in which parents could help their children succeed academically. He also reviewed his expectations for the children, the school policies, and the events planned for the year. Parents who recall Dillard's PTA reports remember how interested he was in the children. Says one parent: "[Having every child succeed] — that was his main priority."

Dillard also shared with parents his experiences at any national or regional meetings he had attended. His teachers, who were required to join their professional organization and urged to attend non-local meetings, were also expected to report to parents during this segment of PTA meetings. Today CCTS parents describe little about the educational trends that were discussed during those times, but they still remember the jokes Dillard was famous for collecting and sharing with them.

In addition to the PTA business reports and discussions, parents could also expect entertainment and refreshments. This entertainment came from various high school groups or elementary classes, who were assigned a time in the school year to make a presentation to the PTA. Teachers often repeated for the PTA the assembly programs they were periodically scheduled to have in Chapel.[7] Since few parents saw these programs during Chapel, they usually played to a new audience. The refreshments that were served afterward to cast, teachers, and parents were supplied by the PTA.

When the formal portion of the PTA meetings ended, the informal talk between teachers and parents began. According to parent Dorothy Graves, these informal talks, during which the parents could find out how their children were doing in school, were one of the primary reasons they went to PTA. She explains:

> You didn't go to the schools during the day or after school to talk about your children. You didn't go in unless there was a problem and the principal called you in. The time during the school day was allotted for the

[7] Chapel was a weekly gathering of the principal, teachers, and students, where student talent was showcased and where the principal used the time to talk to the students about pressing issues, such as life, discipline, or any other topic he felt compelled to address. While religious services were not the focus of the gathering, talk often emphasized moral values that were consistent with the values held by the community.

teaching of the student. Parents just didn't go in to school and disturb a teacher. [The teachers would say], tell your parents to come to PTA.

These informal conversations between teachers and parents sometimes took place in the classrooms, at other times in different areas of the auditorium. Most conversations began with the parent's single question: "How is my child doing?" If the teacher responded "fine," little else would be said, other than the parent perhaps saying, "Now you let me know if there's a problem." Or if there was a problem, the teacher might consult her rollbook and say, "Jeff is doing fine in English; however, he needs to work on his math." Such informal conversations continued until each parent had the opportunity to speak to every teacher he or she wished to see. Since teachers were required to attend PTA meetings, said one parent, "there was never any worry that [your child's teacher] wouldn't be there."

Besides attending the regular monthly meetings, some PTA members implemented planned tasks, such as preparing appreciation dinners for the teachers or continuing their ongoing fundraising activities. They referred to this as "working along with the teachers," and valued the time as an opportunity to get to know each other. Parents also attended major school functions, filling the auditorium for the concerts held by the high school choir and band every Christmas and spring, and the annual "operettas" held by the primary and upper elementary schools. A few parents were also involved in some classroom functions, such as providing food and setting up for a class Christmas or end-of-year party, supervising the Maypole dances in preparation for field day, or, in the case of at least one teacher, assisting in classroom instruction by playing educational games with the children. Reports indicate that parents on all socioeconomic levels were likely to participate in the events, if they were asked.

What is central to the nature of this parental presence at CCTS is the key phrase, "if asked." For example, Nellie Williamson, the teacher who had parents play educational games with the children, emphasizes that "not many did this"; those who did, she says, did so "because she had a conversation with them individually." Thus, parents who helped in the classroom or assisted with other events were responding to teachers' notes or oral invitations. PTA meetings and student performances were other events to which parents had invitations. Says Janie Richmond, a former student and later an elementary school teacher, "the parents supported the school" and came whenever you asked them, but they didn't schedule parent-teacher conferences, or volunteer to assist with tutoring, or concern themselves with other areas of classroom instruction. Long-time English teacher Chattie Boston concurs that "parents left curricula concerns to the teachers." The data suggest both are correct, as parents never describe themselves as having initiated visits to the school to observe or to discuss any curricular concerns. Some parents, however, did assume a political role that might be termed "working for the school." This role of advocate was historically associated with the PTA leaders. These advocates positioned themselves between the school's needs and the oversight of the school board, and on numerous occasions lobbied for additional funding for the school. No records indicate that the White school board was hostile to the Negro patrons who sought their assistance; they were generally polite, even as they postponed and denied repeated requests for funding.[8]

The leadership role these parent advocates took in going before the board to lobby for the school is termed "working" for the school because the teachers and principal seldom appeared before the board. In the political climate of the era, those employed by the school system could expect to lose their jobs if they involved themselves in questions of equity. As one parent advocate recalls, "Dillard himself couldn't afford to come out. He was a very smart leader who knew how far they would let him go." A second parent recalls, "Mr. Dillard provided prompting on preparation, who to speak to. He would give you an idea. Usually [men] would go. They would go as a group and usually have one spokesman." This behind-the-scenes prompting most often occurred with farmers who owned their own land, preachers, or private business owners. While in the earlier years these were primarily men, documents and interviews from later periods indicate that women also assumed an advocacy role. What all advocates generally had in common was that they relied on other Negroes for their income, and thus did not need to fear repercussions from the White school board.

The role of parent advocates also extended beyond the county level. Records indicate that these citizens, like Dillard, made numerous trips to the state capital to seek assistance when their requests were denied on the local level. This was particularly true of their efforts in the early years of CCTS to see that a high school be established, and later, that a new one be built. In response to these visits, and as a part of his push to get the county to build a new school, the Director of the Division of Negro Education wrote the Caswell County school board requesting that an "adequate brick building be supplied" for the Negroes. He freely admitted that his urging was the result of having been "approached by a group of very intelligent colored citizens from [Caswell] County."[9]

The importance of this advocacy role over the years was recognized and appreciated not only by other parents, but also by the students. Consider

---

[8] The board's receptivity did, as may be expected, increase in the 1950s and 1960s. This may be attributed in part to the aftermath of the *Brown* decision, when the county sought to be certain that all its Negro schools were "equal." However, the parents also credit the efforts of a new superintendent, Thomas Whitley, who they characterized as a "fair" man who was willing to go "as far as he could go" to promote equity.

[9] In 1921, the Negro Division of Education was established by Legislative Act in the state of North Carolina. Although headed by a White agent, the director, N. C. Newbold, has been credited with helping to "set in motion the development and standardization of secondary schools" in North Carolina (Brown, 1960, p. 49). The school board minutes in Caswell County indicate that through both letters and meetings with the board, Newbold was instrumental in pressuring the county to address the needs of the Negro community.

their commendation of three parents in the opening pages of the 1960 year-book:

> The annual certainly would be incomplete if the seniors failed to salute the successful efforts of these three patrons in obtaining a modern physical education building for the school. Over a three year period they continuously appeared before the Board of Education in behalf of a new physical education building. Time and time again they made appeals and, needless to say, at times they were disappointed, but not enough to ever cease their efforts. Soon, thanks to them, this facility will be available. The students and patrons of C.C.T.S. shall ever remember with gratitude their untiring efforts. Again we salute you, Mrs. Bigelow, Mrs. Saylor, and Mrs. Little. Words will never express our appreciation.

The passage is accompanied by a portrait of the three women. While other CCTS yearbooks do not contain such elaborate expressions of appreciation, special thank you's to parents for their assistance frequently appeared in dedications and in class histories.

Perhaps the most consistent way parents supported the school — even those who never participated in PTA or related activities or assumed the role of advocate — was accomplished without the parents ever leaving home. They instilled in their children a respect for teachers, which carried with it an expectation of obedience. Says parent Nannie Evans, "I would always tell my child, 'when you go to school, remember you are supposed to obey your teachers just like you obey me at home.'"

These attitudes about obedience led students to believe that if they were punished at school for an offense, they could expect additional punishment at home. In the words of one student: "I knew not to get sent home for anything. If I did, I knew my daddy was going to whoop me good — not spank — but whoop me. I knew not to try to get into trouble." And if a child did get into trouble at school, the parent's likely response to the teacher was, "Well, if he doesn't do well, you just let me know again."

This "home training," as southern African Americans are likely to call their parents' expectations of them, reinforced school policies and provided a solid mechanism of invisible support. While the disciplinary skills of the CCTS principal and teachers will not be discussed in this article, I will point out that demands on their disciplinary skills were lessened by this seldom-articulated, yet forceful parental support. Thus, parent and school were united in their expectations of the students. As one student described the relationship: "My mommy and daddy are pushing me and my teachers are pushing me . . . oh well, I got to do good."

School Supports Community

CCTS parents provided financial and physical support, advocacy, and home-front support. From the vantage point of current advocates of parental involvement (see, for example, Henderson 1987, 1988; Rich, 1987), the parents' degree of activity might not be considered unusual. However, given the current lack of involvement of many African American parents in schools (Henderson, 1987), the degree of their support is exceptional. To what might their level of involvement be attributed?

Several explanations are possible. As Lightfoot (1978, 1981) has noted, African Americans have traditionally believed in the importance of education, and have made sacrifices to be certain that their children had opportunities to achieve in school. That parents valued education and therefore contributed to the support of CCTS is corroborated by records from other elementary schools scattered throughout Caswell County, where parents were also active in PTA and other school events. Thus, the parental response at CCTS might well have been the public manifestation of the parents' private beliefs about the importance of education. Another equally compelling reason for the relationship between CCTS and parents in later years might relate to existing community ties. As many parents point out, they had known Principal Dillard themselves as children, when they attended school under his leadership; they had also gone to school with some of the teachers. Therefore, school personnel were not strangers, but rather people with whom they already had a relationship.

Though parents' belief in education and the existence of community ties are both important factors in understanding the parents' relationship to the school, they offer an insufficient explanation for the levels of support provided by parents. Teachers who had not grown up in the county, for example, were equally accepted, supported, and welcomed by parents, as was Dillard, even in his early years. According to Inez Blackwell, a parent and former student, this was because new teachers quickly made themselves known to the community. "They were never stuck up," she says. "Within months," Blackwell notes, "it seemed like they had been here all the time." Thus, teachers who had previous ties with the community had little advantage over those who came into the county. Moreover, though African American parents today still believe in the power of education, their belief does not evoke the responses described at CCTS. Perhaps a more compelling explanation for the consistency of support from parents at CCTS lies in the manner in which the school reached out to and supported the parents.

For example, in his weekly Chapel talks with the students, Principal Dillard was heard to say on more than one occasion: "I'm not going to let you come up here and wear your mama and daddy's clothes out and they're out there working hard for you and you're up here doing nothing." The band director, Leonard Tillman, recalls the admonishments students received in the classroom:

> I used to tell my kids — Miss Ann doesn't need anyone to cook for them anymore. ["Miss Ann" was a term used by Negroes to describe White women who had servants.] They got frozen foods. All they got to do is throw them in the oven. Don't you think you need to stay here and get this education?

In their talks with students, the principal and teachers assumed the posture of protectors of the parents' sacrifices, and their frequent reminders of the need to get an education echoed parents' aspirations for their children.

The school also actively assisted parents. For students who wanted to go on to college, this assistance included helping them fill out forms, providing financial aid, traveling with students to campuses, and in some cases giving advice on what would be expected in college. As Aleane Rush, a former student and later president of the state teachers' association, remembers:

> [Mr. Dillard] would try to help students. . . . He would refer them person-ally to college contacts, friends; he was very helpful in trying to see that they would leave Caswell County with the appropriate kind of clothing. Remember I said he knew his students. So, he would not feel intimidated, nor would the student if he said, "Now Vanessa, you can not go to Shaw with those kind of shoes on. . . . You will be in college and you are coming from CCTS, remember that. And you've got to represent yourself, your family, and your community." And when he spoke of community, he was speaking of Caswell County. And parents of those students were very, very appreciative.

In some cases, as in that of teacher and former student Deborah Fuller, the principal actually accompanied the student and parents on their first trip to a campus, functioning as mediator between the family's aspirations and the unknown expectations of college admissions. Teachers also engaged in these sorts of supportive activities, providing financial assistance through their teachers' clubs and, more frequently, offering the encouragement a student needed to go to college. Irvine and Irvine (1984) have characterized this behavior most succinctly:

> Black schools served as the instrument through which professional educa-tors discharged their responsibility to their community. Black educators labored to help students realize their achievement goals. In this role both principals and teachers were mere but profound extensions of the interests of the Black community. (p. 417)

In effect, the authors note, parents and school had a "collective stake in the educational process of the youth in the community" (p. 419).

But the school's support was not only available for college-bound students. The principal and teachers also assumed responsibility for students who were having difficulty in school by working with the child and contacting parents about any problems. One parent remembers Principal Dillard telling her about her son's school behavior: "Well, he just loves to sometimes stand out in the hall and have a chance to go uptown." ("Uptown" is a local slang term used to refer to the town's small business district, which was located approxi-mately one mile from the school.) Of Dillard's disciplinary approach and contact with her, this parent says, "I felt good because I felt like he was there with him and he was paying attention [to my child]." After describing the events of mischievousness that accompanied her son through his school years, she concludes, "But anyway, he finally finished . . . and I felt like Mr. Dillard had a great hand in that."

The school's protectiveness toward the children — going the extra mile to see that students succeeded — instilled in parents an adamant conviction that the teachers and principal really "cared about those children." In the words of Rachel Long, a farming parent who sent nine children through high school and college, "I think all those teachers were really close to those students. I know they were to my children." Her conviction echoes the sentiments of many. A former student, the Reverend Cephaus Lea, remembers Principal Dillard:

> He was never too busy to talk with you about your problems. Not only was he interested in you in school, he was interested when you left school. He knew all the children by name. He wasn't like some other people I've known. He loved people and he was concerned about you. And that's the kind of principal Mr. Dillard was.

While the influence of the school's ethic of caring is a story that I cannot explore fully in this discussion, I must note that parents' belief that the school cared about the success of their children might help explain the "respect" and "trust" that parents had toward CCTS and their support of it. In essence, in supporting the institution, the parent were directly supporting those responsible for the success of their children.

Principal Dillard's particular style of interacting with parents is another way that parents were drawn to CCTS. In effect, Dillard created a sense of "us" that helped to forge the collaboration between school and community. Though he was clearly the visionary, "he did not boast [about] what he did," says one parent. "He used to always say, 'we're working together. See what we can do if we work together.' But he never did say what *he* did." This style of interaction was probably carefully chosen. In the traditional African American community, the "educated" are often viewed with suspicion if they are perceived as "above" the other members of the community; thus Dillard's approach represented an important way of reaching out, and conveyed to community members his respect for their contributions.

Perhaps the most striking way in which the school reached out was in its willingness to meet the parents on their own turf. Dillard, for example, was an avid member of community organizations and would often walk to town after school was out and take the time to talk with farmers gathered on the corner. He sang in the local choir, attended both the Methodist and Baptist churches, and frequently visited the rural churches and the homes of parents who lived out in the country. Says one parent:

> He visited my home a lot of times. He would get around. Then another thing he would do — if his children's [relatives] or somebody passed, he

would try to make it to the churches to the funerals. He had a closeness to people.

Valuing community members apparently was an important part of Dillard's philosophy. Even "from the beginning, he worked with the community," reports teacher and former student Janie Richmond, whose mother worked actively in the creation of the first PTA. "Whatever project they put on, he was very diligent in working with them — picnics, fishing trips, etc. His being present helped to draw other people."

It is important to note that Dillard also used his visits in the community as opportunities to communicate. Often when invited to speak in area churches, he would speak about his belief in the value of education. Thus, parents were apprised of the goals of the school and the needs of the children in their own communities, churches, and homes. These visits and talks were supplemented by frequent notes that children brought home with information about school events or classroom needs.

Dillard expected no less community involvement from his teachers. "I would hope you would be broad enough to attend some of the area churches," he was known to tell new faculty members. In essence, he expected that if they worked in the community, they should make themselves known and become part of it. He wanted teachers who were accessible to the average parent. He also expected teachers to visit the students' parents in their homes, whether or not a disciplinary problem had arisen. "If you could see the circumstances out of which the children have come," many teachers remember him saying, "you would understand better how to teach them."

And the teachers did go — both to the churches and the homes. Fifth-grade teacher Betty Royal remembers telling parents who opened the door to her knock, "I just happened to have been in the area and I thought I would just stop by and say hello." The parents generally responded positively to these unannounced visits, having been told to expect them at PTA meetings.

Reaching out to support parents occurred in other ways, too. The school offered adults classes in agriculture, typing, and sewing, and provided guidance and counseling for adults. The school also ranked itself highly on "providing community use of the school and facilities" (CCTS Faculty, 1950). From the parents' perspective, however, the school's interest in their children's development and the teachers' community visits are the ways of reaching out that are most remembered and most valued.

Significance of School and Community Interactions in the Historical Context

Long-time residents of this Caswell County community who participated in the CCTS culture remember the interaction between school and community as a collaborative relationship, a kind of mutual ownership in which the community and school looked out for each others' needs — the parents depended on the school's expertise, guidance, and academic vision, and the school depended on the parents' financial contributions, advocacy, and home-front support. They were united in a common mission to provide a quality education for their children.

This relationship provides several important ideas to consider. While school and community members moved easily in and out of each other's domain, the participants were clear about the boundaries of their relationships. The parents' role was to attend school events, to reinforce discipline at home, and to get their children to school. They also made economic sacrifices to allow their able-bodied offspring to go to school rather than keeping them home to help "take in the crop." When the students went home in the afternoon, parents made sure the children had time to do their lessons. As one student remembers, "[Our] parents didn't have any education, but after you finished your work and chores, they knew to tell you to sit down and get your lesson." The teachers' and principal's reciprocal role was to exercise authority in the school environment and address issues of curriculum and instruction.

The strength of the respect for these boundaries was reinforced by its presence across economic and class lines. For example, even teachers who had children in the classrooms of other teachers did not discuss curriculum or help their children with homework. In fact, the attitude that the teacher was completely in charge of the child once in the classroom was reflected in private conversations with their coworkers. Said one teacher, "I've got my classroom to see to. If anything happens, you do the punishing. I don't have anything to do with it." Like other parents, these teachers did support the punishment given by their child's teacher by reinforcing discipline at home. However, they did not interfere with the teacher or class activities within the school.

Unlike current situations in which parents and schools disagree about how they should support one another (Henderson, 1987), in the CCTS environment, participants shared common expectations. The distinct roles minimized conflict between school and community, as all interaction was defined by mutually accepted boundaries of authority.

Also significant are the opportunities for, and the positive nature of, the communication that was possible in the CCTS environment — unlike interaction today, in which talk between teachers and parents is almost uniformly negative, and parents indicate that they only hear from the school when there is a problem (Lightfoot, 1978; Swap, 1987). The school's fund-raising activities, for example, created opportunities for parents, the principal, and teachers to discuss how to achieve their common goals. Moreover, during some fund-raising activities, opportunities existed for role-reversal between administration and members of the school community. For example, if parents were assigned to oversee participation in a particular classroom, it meant that the teacher looked to the parents for assistance. This created a sense of teamwork and reinforced the idea that parents and teachers could both be authorities — even if they exercised power in different domains. Thus, the creation of teamwork between teacher and parent was a direct outcome of the fund-raising activity.

Also important to the school-community relationship were the informal interactions maintained outside of school. When teachers visited the churches, parents were likely to invite them to other services, such as a revival or church homecoming, and teachers in turn used these opportunities to invite parents to particular activities at the school. Students' work was not necessarily discussed in these incidental interactions.

The opportunity to engage in dialogue both in the school environment and in the community was important to the community-school relationship, but it would not have succeeded had not the principal and teachers known how to talk to the parents. Parent Marie Richmond confirms this:

> I heard [Mr. Dillard] say it so many times. He would say, "When you are in a situation, you don't go in there using a lot of big words and you know the people can't understand you.". . . He wasn't one of these people that kept so high up that he couldn't get in where a person was and understand him. I think that's why people loved him so. You could relate to him. But when you go into a place . . . and are so high and mighty, parents would stay away from you, because they feel like you think you are better than they are because maybe they didn't get any schooling. But if you know how to mix, and they feel comfortable with you, they will work with you.

The ability to adapt his language to the demands of a situation is a talent for which Dillard is consistently credited; he told his son he learned it in his job as an insurance salesman after graduating from college. Of the teachers, parents also said, "They knew how to talk to you, and that made a big difference."

The "difference" was that, when parents had the opportunity to talk with teachers and the principal, both in and out of school, they were positive exchanges in which teachers and principal communicated with language parents could appreciate and respect. That is, they used the language of the parent, adopting informal forms of language and styles of communication that created an atmosphere in which parents did not feel intimidated to speak.

This atmosphere of respect also created a positive environment for handling more sensitive problems. Teachers or the principal could begin a difficult discussion with positive comments about a child, because they knew the children so well, understood their family circumstances, and likely had some interaction with someone in the family. Moreover, because of the opportunities for positive informal talk and the school's proactive role in its relationship with parents, the parents did not view the teacher or principal as always being the bearer of bad news about their child, which diminished the potential for hostility or animosity.

The nature of the community-school relationship, strengthened by the principal's personal characteristics, eased tensions when differences did occur. English teacher Chattie Boston recalls that, if a parent came in upset over a perceived injustice done to his or her child, "Mr. Dillard didn't get excited. If the parent was excited, Mr. Dillard listened and let them talk. He let them get it off their chest." Then, she says, "he would explain the situation and when [the parent] left, everybody would be buddy-buddy."

This personal style of settling conflicts was impossible when the disagreement involved larger concerns, such as choosing a location for the new school. Such differences were resolved through an open meeting where both sides had opportunities to air their concerns, and the final decision was made by voting. But even when the community-school relationship was not completely tranquil, the dissonance did not destroy their working relationship or the individual respect between parents, the teachers, and the principal.

Segregation in Retrospect: Issues and Challenges for Today

The nature of the relationship I have described between CCTS and its community suggests some valuable lessons for education today. One suggestion is a possible change in the definition of parental involvement. Although parental involvement has been defined by researchers in a number of ways (Henderson, 1987, 1988; Rich, 1987; Swap, 1987), for purposes of this discussion, consider a definition offered by Hoover-Dempsey, Bassler, and Brissie (1987), who define parent involvement in their child's school as including: 1) parent-teacher conferences; 2) parent involvement in classroom volunteer work; 3) parent involvement in tutoring at home, such as assisting with homework; and 4) parent involvement in carrying out home-instruction programs designed or suggested by teachers to supplement regular classroom instruction (p. 423). In each of these cases, parents initiate and/or are involved in complementing the curriculum and instruction provided by the teacher.

Current definitions of parent involvement, however, do not explain the kind of support the CCTS parents demonstrated. They did not have formal parent-teacher conferences as they are now defined; they did not volunteer unless they were specifically asked; and they did not tutor at home or carry out home-instruction programs.

By current definitions, these parents could be deemed failures. One wonders, then, if African American parents and White teachers and school leaders are operating out of different frameworks for parental involvement. Perhaps schools apply dominant cultural definitions of good parental involvement, such as those described by Hoover-Dempsey, Bassler, and Brissie (1987), while African American parents lean towards more traditional perceptions and modes of interaction, such as those practiced at CCTS.

To explore this possibility, consider the comment of Dorothy Graves, a Black parent who observed the CCTS parents when they first attended PTA meetings after court-ordered integration began in Caswell County in the fall of 1969:

> You just didn't see any teachers hardly. What few teachers came said, "you don't walk up to teachers and ask how your child is doing; you have a conference." They said we were not supposed to ask about any [concerns] about our children [in the presence of] anyone else. We were used to when we were there at the PTA meeting, we could just talk.

This parent further explains that PTA meetings after integration seemed to focus more on bringing in resource people than dealing with the problems of the students. She notes that before integration, the students were the primary focus for PTA meetings — either discussing their needs and jointly devising plans of action, and/or watching their performances before the PTA. After integration, she remembers that less attention was paid to students and that there was more of a focus on procedures. She sums up the differences by adding, "I guess this was their method. [It seems] when we integrated we went into using their pattern and not our pattern."

This difference in handling the PTA meetings suggests that after integration a cultural mismatch occurred between school personnel and parents on at least two levels. First, for parents accustomed to using the PTA to talk informally with teachers, the absence of many teachers and the directives by those present to schedule a conference represented a system for interacting with teachers that was not familiar to Black parents. While the data are not available to document the response of Black parents to this new system, it is worth noting that Dorothy Graves, the parent quoted above, recalls scheduling only one conference after integration, as compared to monthly meetings with teachers before integration.

In addition to creating new expectations of the appropriate way to relate to teachers, the focus of the PTA in the integrated system also was perceived by Black parents to change. At the segregated PTA meetings, parents expected to discuss the needs of the school and to see their children perform — both activities that contributed to the importance of attending PTA meetings. In the integrated system, they describe a system where "your part was already outlined and you just went through the procedure." PTA was thus transformed from a parent-school gathering where meaningful input was expected, to meetings that became the "contrived occasions" that Lightfoot (1978) describes.

The data are not available to argue that the failure of African American parents today to volunteer, to schedule parent/teacher conferences, and so forth is the result of historical differences in definitions of involvement. However, the forms of support demonstrated at CCTS suggest that it is at least possible that historical models of parental involvement may differ from current definitions, and that this may be one area to consider in efforts to understand African American parents' failure to conform to expectations about school involvement. The failure to consider the possible influence of conflicting expectations about roles may result in parents, especially African American parents, being labeled deficient and uncaring.

Consider further the current literature on parental involvement, which emphasizes the parents' desire to be involved in school decisionmaking. According to Henderson (1987), "Educators tend to relegate parents to insubstantial bake sale roles, leaving parents feeling frustrated, belittled, and left out" (p. 2). Yet the CCTS parents did not express a desire to have input in the school's curriculum decisionmaking. The same is true in Sowell's (1976) descriptions of other historically Black schools:

> The interest of the teachers in the students was reciprocated by the interest of the parents in supporting the teachers and the school. . . . Parental involvement was of this supportive nature rather than an actual involvement in school decision making (p. 36).

Sowell's finding is consistent with the type of support CCTS parents offered, and their parallel lack of discussion of curricular matters. This is not to say that parents should not now be involved in such decisionmaking. However, making decisions on curricular matters may not be a traditional parental role valued within the African American community, where community and school shared similar values and where parents trusted the teachers and principal to create the best learning environments for their children.

Moreover, while the current literature on parental involvement denigrates the bake sale and the ritualistic PTAs (Henderson, 1987, 1988), CCTS parents found comfortable avenues of support through such activities. Perhaps the value of these activities, especially their ability to create ownership and pride in the school, should be explored before they are unilaterally dismissed as trivial functions. Swap (1987) has advocated having refreshments at PTA meetings and using children in the program as examples of incentives that schools might use to help initiate parental involvement in school functions. Both of these activities made useful contributions to the CCTS PTA meetings, so perhaps the CCTS examples suggest extending the parent-school relationship beyond some current practices.

Two other ideas should also be briefly considered. The data suggest that the community-school relationship is a two-way process, that involvement should not be defined simply as how to bring the parents into the school, but also how the school can be "in" the community. It was CCTS's outreach to the community that prompted the parents to "reach in" to the school. While some studies have considered the positive results of home visits (Olmstead, 1983, cited in Tangri & Moles, 1987), too little has been done to create schools with positive attitudes toward the community, both in terms of the school's general outreach and the attitude of individual teachers. School reform leaders might do well to remember the CCTS example, and to consider ways that teachers and principal can become advocates for, rather than adversaries in, their students' communities.

Schools might also consider the benefits of implementing activities that communicate to parents a sense of caring about their children. The response of CCTS parents to their school should not be considered atypical; people generally respond well to those they believe are concerned about their loved ones. When people, or communities, perceive that this caring is no longer present, they respond with mistrust. Thus, it should not be surprising that many African American parents are now distrustful of schools in which their offspring are the ones most often punished, most frequently on the lower tracks (Braddock, 1995), most likely to have the least successful teachers (Darling-Hammond, 1995), and most likely to feel alienated and drop out of school. This care ethic would seem to be as crucial to conversations about how to induce parental involvement as is advocacy for parental voice on curricular matters.

Can all ideas applied at CCTS transfer simply and easily to today's schools? Indeed they cannot. CCTS functioned in a uniquely closed society in which the school for the Black community was one of the two major social, cultural, and educational centers, the church being the other. Together these centers served to counteract the effects of racism in a segregated society. Since that era, the nature of problems confronting children has changed, as has the structure of families. The 1990 U.S. Census Bureau, for example, indicates that Black children are less likely to live with two parents today than they were in 1967, and that families are now more likely to be polarized between the well-educated and the poor. Moreover, crack, AIDS, and guns are the serious issues confronting school personnel, as compared with alcohol, smoking, and truancy during the era of CCTS.

What we can gain from the case of CCTS is a deeper understanding of what African Americans valued in their schools during legal segregation, an understanding of the community-school relationships that allowed for the school's successful operation, and a series of ideas about school-community interaction that might spur thinking on how to achieve similar ends in new contexts. Moreover, the CCTS case provides an important framework within which to consider current problems of school reform. For example, understanding the various possibilities for parental involvement may lead to more appropriate questions when considering how to link schools and communities. A question asked frequently about African American parents in reform meetings I have attended is, "How can we get them to become involved with the school?" a question that suggests that parents have never been involved and are generally uninterested. Yet, as the evidence demonstrates, these poor, rural parents were very much involved, when one applies their definition of involvement. They only ceased to be so when the schools integrated. Thus, perhaps a more appropriate question is, "Why did they stop supporting schools and what can be done to eliminate the barriers so they will come back?" These different questions suggest a variety of different answers and strategies. Only by asking the right questions, however, are we likely to find answers that will result in meaningful and lasting solutions.

The CCTS case also suggests an agenda for new research questions: for example, how do African American parents currently view the schools? Are there still "invisible" ways they support the school that are generally unknown and unappreciated? Are African American parents and schools operating from the same expectations about appropriate community-school interactions? To what extent has the advocacy role ceased, or is it operative in other ways? For example, at the school level, do African American parents have a mode of advocacy that creates dissonance, rather than collaboration, between parents and administrators? Is it possible that the level at which they protest treatment of their children has moved from the school board to the teachers and principal in the school itself?

Serious consideration of these and other questions about the relationship between African American parents and their children's schools is important for enlightened educational policy and agendas. Seeking answers to these questions is also important in restoring voice to African American educators and parents, whose knowledge has been devalued and whose opinions have been silenced since the onset of integration (Foster, 1990; Irvine & Irvine, 1984). Most importantly, documenting the nature of community-school relationships in the segregated school is important because it begins to correct the commonly held misperception that those schools were without any merit, and that educators have nothing to learn from them. The correction of this misperception is long overdue.

References

Adair, A. A. (1984). *Desegregation: The illusion of black progress*. Lanham, MD: University Press of America.

Anderson, J. D. (1988). *The education of blacks in the south*. Chapel Hill: University of North Carolina Press.

Brown, H. V. (1960). *A history of the education of Negroes in North Carolina*. Raleigh, NC: Irving Swain Press.

Braddock, J. H. (1995). Tracking, literacy, and minority status. In V. Gadsden & D. Wagner (Eds.), *Literacy among African-American youth: Issues in learning, teaching, and schooling*. Norwood, NJ: Ablex.

Bullock, H. A. (1967). *A history of Negro education in the south*. Cambridge, MA: Harvard University Press.

Caswell County Training School PTA: 1924–1948. (1949). In *Caswell County Training School Yearbook, 1949*.

CCTS Faculty. (1950). *Evaluative criteria* (Washington Cooperative Study of Secondary School Standards).

Cecelski, D. (1991). *The Hyde County School boycott: School desegregation and the fate of black schools in rural south, 1954–1969*. Unpublished doctoral dissertation, Harvard University, Cambridge, MA.

Clark, K. B. (1963). *Prejudice and your child*. Boston: Beacon Press.

Clift, V., Anderson, A., & Hullfish, H. (1962). *Negro education in America*. New York: Harper.

Darling-Hammond, L. (1995). Teacher quality and equality: Implications for literacy among black youth. In V. Gadsden & D. Wagner (Eds.), *Literacy among African-American youth: Issues in learning, teaching, and schooling*. Norwood, NJ: Ablex.

Dedication of new Caswell County school will take place tomorrow. (1951, March). *Caswell Messenger*, p. 5.

Eighteen-member board of trustees named to direct private schools. (1969, February). *Caswell Messenger*, p. 1.

Foster, M. (1990). The politics of race: Through African-American teachers' eyes. *Journal of Education, 172*(3), 123–141.

Henderson, A. T. (1987). *The evidence continues to grow: Parent involvement improves student achievement.* Columbia, MD: National Committee for Citizens in Education.

Henderson, A. T. (1988). Parents are a school's best friends. *Phi Delta Kappan, 70,* 148–153.

Hoover-Dempsey, O., Bassler, J., & Brissie, J. (1987). Parent involvement: Contributions of teacher efficacy, school socioeconomic status, and other school characteristics. *American Educational Research Journal, 24,* 417–435.

Irvine, R., & Irvine, J. (1984). The impact of the desegregation process on the education of black students: Key variables. *Journal of Negro Education, 52,* 410–422.

Jones, F. (1981). *A traditional model of educational excellence.* Washington, DC: Howard University Press.

Kluger, R. (1977). *Simple justice.* New York: Random House.

Lightfoot, S. L. (1978). *Worlds apart.* New York: Basic Books.

Lightfoot, S. L. (1981, Spring). Toward conflict and resolution: Relationships between families and schools. *Theory into Practice, 20,* 97–104.

Newbold, N. (1935). *Report of the governor's commission for the study of problems in the education of the Negro in North Carolina* (Publication No. 183). Raleigh, NC: State Superintendent of Public Instruction.

Rich, D. (1987). *Teachers and parents: An adult to adult approach.* Washington, DC: National Education Association.

Sowell, T. (1976). Patterns of black excellence. *The Public Interest, 43,* 26–58.

Spradley, T. P. (1979). The ethnographic interview. New York: Holt, Rinehart & Winston.

Swap, S. M. (1987). *Enhancing parent involvement in schools: A manual for parents and teachers.* New York: Teachers College Press.

Tangri, S., & Moles, O. (1987). Parents and the community. In V. Richardson-Kolher (Ed.), *Educator's handbook: A research perspective* (pp. 519–550). New York: Longman.

This research was supported through a Spencer Post-Doctoral Fellowship from the National Academy of Education. The author also acknowledges early research support provided by the Graduate School of Education at the University of Pennsylvania and continuing support provided by the University Research Committee at Emory University. Research assistants Trudy Blackwell and Evelyn Lavizzo aided in the data collection and processing.

Cultivating a Morality of Care in African American Adolescents: A Culture-Based Model of Violence Prevention

—■ ■ ■—

JANIE V. WARD

In response to the rising tide of youth violence, educators have developed a number of school- and community-based violence prevention programs for children and youth. Although social science researchers point to the importance of cultural factors that can either augment or attenuate the likelihood of a violent response to problem-solving, for the most part, violence prevention programs tend either to ignore, over-simplify, or devalue the influence of these factors. Far too often, cultural differences are seen solely as the impetus for intergroup conflict; discussions of culture are then singled out and addressed only in prejudice reduction and anti-bias training. It is clear from the paucity of programs designed to address the cultural specifics of violence prevention that at present, race, culture, and social-class factors are not deeply understood.

I propose that we bring culture forward and design violence prevention programs that attend to specific cultural concerns and incorporate cultural traditions, values, norms, and beliefs that have, over time, served to mitigate interpersonal violence and promote care and compassion in individuals. I maintain that the core values of care and practices of compassion and interdependence are culturally determined. I will demonstrate that the increase in violence in African American communities reveals a breakdown in the tradition of caring behavior, and that efforts to strengthen a morality of care in Black youth can reduce interpersonal violence and nurture a sense of care and connection in the Black adolescent's relational world.

Harvard Educational Review Vol. 65 No. 2 Summer 1995, 175–188

Traditions of Caring in African American Communities

Black people have a long tradition of caring. Studies of African philosophy and worldviews reveal a focus on interdependence, collective survival, and the value of cooperation among tribal and community members (Nobles, 1976; White & Parham, 1990). The Black ethic of care is also embodied in the extended family and in the kinship patterns of tribal Africa that emphasized cooperation and respect toward others. Such an extension of concern beyond the family unit to others considered connected to oneself led to the development of intricate mutual aid networks that provided assistance to family and other kin as required. African slaves brought with them to the New World this strong communalistic orientation. Despite the degradation and horrors of chattel slavery, the values and practices of interdependence constituted a cultural and psychological resource that helped slaves retain a sense of personhood and dignity in the face of relentless oppression (Gutman, 1976).

The end of slavery, however, did not mean the end of oppression. Following emancipation, Black people, still considered inferior, continued to be denied equality in education, housing, employment, health care, and social services. Caring for one another was not only an action of compassion and benevolence; it was often literally a matter of survival, as the community came together over crises and personal hardships such as death or illness, or loss of jobs or shelter (Height, 1989). Thus, the harsh conditions faced by Black people in the United States reinforced African cultural codes of care and communalism.

The Black church in the United States is probably the most familiar example of an indigenous cultural institution engaged in care-giving activities. It was typically a social hub, the central organizing institution of mutual aid networks. In addition to material aid and a sense of community, the church provided its members with a deep inner faith that sustained them and a moral code to guide daily living (Paris, 1985). The communalistic orientation transported from Africa was reinforced by Christianity's guiding principles, such as the Golden Rule and similar injunctions to extend oneself through acts of charity and caring for others. Moreover, traditional codes of caring in African American communities have tended to encompass a political agenda of social activism. Black service providers and community activists alike have long recognized that their own destiny was inextricably linked to the destiny of other Blacks, and that in forging ties of mutual support, collective survival and racial progress would be achieved. The community-based social and economic programs of such organizations as the NAACP, the National Urban League, the Black Women's Services Clubs, and Black fraternities and sororities similarly attest to this creed.

For Black folks raised within the Christian tradition, church work, such as visiting the sick and shut-in, and participation in communal celebrations such as the preparation and distribution of holiday food baskets provided a

270

multitude of opportunities for children to engage in acts of giving and sharing. Even during times of extreme hardship, children were taught that being poor was no reason to be selfish nor an excuse for a lack of care.

As Dorothy Height, President of the National Council of Negro Women, maintains in writing about the traditional self-help efforts of African Americans prior to the elimination of legalized segregation:

> Since the end of the slave era, Black people have had to provide services for one another in every conceivable way: feeding and clothing the destitute; tending the sick; caring for orphaned children and the aged; establishing insurance companies, burial societies, travelers' accommodations when hotels were segregated — the list goes on. (1989, p. 136)

Over the last thirty years, however, the traditional values of care and connectedness that have served to support and sustain Black people during the worst of times have been undermined by a number of powerful sociocultural, economic, and political forces. These forces are the pervasive effect of systemic racial and economic oppression; a national preoccupation with consumption, excessive autonomy, and individualism at the expense of connectedness to the group; and the increasing cynicism of many Black teenagers toward a social system that professes an ideology of social justice, yet offers little more than illusions of equality. The breadth of this erosion extends to virtually all of the social and economic determinants of African American life, including income maintenance, education, health care, and family and community social structure. With each downturn of the U.S. economy, African Americans, particularly low-income and working-class Blacks, have suffered not only measurable economic losses but social losses as well (National Research Council, 1989). The complex structure of interdependence referred to by McCray (1980), Billingsley (1972), and Stack (1974), among others, has been largely supplanted by a relationship of dependence (on sources of income maintenance and on the provision of social welfare services in particular) outside the Black community. These sources have proven inadequate to cope with the problems they were designed to alleviate and, at times, have even contributed to a worsening of those problems.

In this connection, Jewell (1984, 1988) points out that the interdependent nature of traditional mutual aid networks, in both the Black church and the Black extended family, fostered a mutuality of care between the recipient and the caregiver. In contrast, government welfare programs are characterized by bureaucratic impersonality and by a provider-client relationship that encourages a sense of subservience and powerlessness (Jewell, 1988). An example of adversive governmental intervention occurred in the late 1950s, when many states, in attempting to reduce Black welfare recipiency, adopted punitive administrative policies that required a man, regardless of his relationship to the family, to be absent from the home in order for a mother and her children to receive financial assistance (Trattner, 1994).

Over time, this policy resulted in a progressive erosion of parental and economic stability in low-income Black families (Trattner, 1994, pp. 310–311). While public assistance programs serve an essential support role in the lives of many in need, they have, in some cases, replaced traditional care-giving functions of the family and the community. For example, some teenage mothers who receive public aid leave the family home to rear their children alone, receiving more assistance from social workers than from the extended family.

The decline in these kinds of traditional self-help community supports can be seen as a loss of self-reliance and a shift to dependence on others. Years of eroded opportunity and increasing reliance on government programs have fostered the belief among many Blacks that the government can better deal with their problems than they can. The gradual loss of interpersonal connection and the traditions and practices of care in the African American culture are particularly troubling when we consider the effect of this loss on the lives of youth today.

The quotes that appear throughout this article were shared with me in 1991 by Black adolescent males and females, all of whom voluntarily participated in a study investigating the intergenerational process of racial socialization in African American families. In conducting this study, I was particularly interested in the acquisition and transmission of race-related morals and values developed by African Americans in response to our social condition of racial discrimination and victimization (see Ward, 1991). During the in-depth interviews, the adolescents reflected on social, moral, and political judgments about being Black in White America. In the words of one student:

> WHAT ABOUT BLACK PEOPLE MAKES YOU FEEL PROUD? What makes me glad . . . are the ones that's trying to do something to help us out here. What makes me ashamed? Seeing drugs . . . and to see Black people turn on Black people. I hate that real bad. (Jamal, age 16)

Violence is clearly not an issue exclusive to African Americans or even to urban cities — it is epidemic in all parts of this country, and no one is immune to its effects. In fact, homicide is now the second leading cause of death by injury among children across all ethnic groups and ages (Rodríguez, 1990). In the interviews, however, the incursion of violence into the lives of Black adolescents in the nation's urban, suburban, and rural areas of the northeastern, southern, and southwestern regions where I conducted my research was chilling and profound. The research participants, in speaking about the ravaging effects of violence in Black communities, alluded to abandoned traditions and misplaced values. As I listened to these interviews, it became clear that it is senseless to discuss morality (one's system of conduct based on principles such as right or wrong, just or caring) without attending to issues of violence and violent behavior, and senseless to discuss violence without addressing morality.

Violence and Relational Breakdown

In 1989, former Secretary of Health and Human Services Lewis W. Sullivan drew national attention when he pronounced violence a public health issue. Sullivan named joblessness, homelessness, and substance abuse as prime causes of the increase in violence. Since then, others, such as Howard University Professor of Political Science Ronald Walters, have objected to the characterization of violence as a public health issue, arguing instead that it is a social, not a health, concern (Douglas, 1994).

The victimization rate of residents in inner cities — twice that of suburban areas — has led many experts to agree with Dr. Sullivan. As a result, they too call youth violence a deadly and insidious public health hazard, particularly in Black and low-income communities. Among African Americans in the fifteen- to twenty-four-year-old age group, homicide is the leading cause of death (Gibbs, 1989). Over 95 percent of the Blacks who perish in this way are killed by other Blacks, often youths (Ward, 1988). While the rate of participation in violence by females is increasing (Sommers & Baskin, 1994), males are most often both the primary victims and the perpetrators of violence. Women, however, are increasingly the indirect victims of violence; that is, behind the male homicide statistics is a mother who has lost a son, a wife who has lost a husband, a little girl who has lost a father.

When viewed from the perspective of interpersonal relations, the escalation of intraracial violence among Blacks, especially among young people, reflects a serious breakdown of care and connection in the African American community, and in the United States in general. The kinship principle embedded in the African heritage of Black people regards the self as an extended self, a self that exists primarily in relation to others. Violence destroys the underlying interrelatedness and interdependence not only of its perpetrators and victims, but of the community at large.

From the perspective of the teen who is growing up in an ambiance of violence, life often seems cheap. With the increasing availability of guns, there is a heightened feeling of threat and danger, leaving many young people with a sense of never being safe in the world:

> I'm worried that just because my mother can afford to give [my brother] a nice jacket and some other kid can't, they're going to stab him for it. (Cheri, age 15)

Cheri's fear that her brother's new jacket may put him at risk of violence reveals her recognition that for some teenagers, the acquisition of material possessions overrides relational concerns. Within this charged atmosphere of gang vendettas, drug wars, and "cut-throat" morality, there is recognition among the kids themselves that if you are a Black male, the chances are good that you will die young.

Children are barraged with media messages that glorify violence, often portraying it as the primary means of conflict resolution. While few teenagers are actually committed to a violent lifestyle, many struggle with the strong feelings associated with adolescence and with uncertainty about how to mediate anger and frustration. For those teens who are particularly "at risk" for experiencing the combined effects of factors such as low income, racial minority status, school failure, and family stress, the temptation to resort to violence can be frighteningly powerful.

Stereotypic negative images of Black adolescent violence, relentlessly perpetrated by the electronic and print media, often view these youngsters as lawless, morally depraved, beyond hope and redeemability, and, thus, outside the social order. Once consigned to this marginal status, such adolescents often are considered beyond the responsibility of society. Social scientists traditionally have shaped our perceptions by locating the problem of violence either in the individual, citing intrapsychic deficits, or in the environment, stressing adverse socioeconomic influences such as racism, blocked opportunities, high unemployment, and poor prospects for the future (Bandura, 1973; Gibbs, 1989; Oliver, 1989; Parke & Slaby, 1983; Straus, Gelles, & Steinmetz, 1980; Wolfgang & Ferracuti, 1967).

For years, many scholars have interpreted acts of violence among poor Black males as maladaptive efforts to gain a sense of self-efficacy and personal power in a society that limits their opportunities. In the minds of many male teenagers, acts of violence are still seen as a means of proving their manhood. For example, criminologist William Oliver (1989) points out that low-income Black males, denied opportunity to equal access, may opt for one of two stereotypic male roles: "tough guy" or "player-of-women" (p. 258). While providing the illusion of control, both of these roles are, in fact, dysfunctional adaptations to racial and economic oppression. For young men, both roles can readily lead to scenarios of violence. The tough guy may resort to violence in an effort to exert his dominance and control over others. For the player-of-women, competition with male rivals may lead to physical confrontations, and jealousy and distrust of women may result in violent acts against the women themselves.

When we view the current explosion of crime and violence as meaningless acts perpetrated by uncontrollable teenagers who lack conscience or care for other human beings, we paint a dire picture that offers few solutions and little hope. On the other hand, when we see moral misbehavior as a way of "acting out a moral claim" (Blakeney & Blakeney, 1991), this reframing of the meaning of violence in the lives of Black teens allows us to move toward constructive solutions. As philosopher Cornell West argues,

> most young Black people have been fundamentally shaped by the brutal side of American society. Their sense of reality is shaped on the one hand by a sense of coldness and callousness, and on the other hand by a sense of passion for justice, contradictory impulses which surface simultaneously. (hooks & West, 1991, p. 11)

Today's adolescents came of age in the 1970s and 1980s — decades of economic expansionism and the excessive individualism of the "me generation." The rampant materialism in the larger society fueled an extraordinary level of competition for personal acquisition. Identity for both adults and adolescents became increasingly equated with ownership, goods came to convey status, and teenagers murdered one another over high-priced pairs of running shoes. Constant exposure to violence in the media inures young people to its concrete reality. For example, an emergency room physician recently remarked that a fourteen-year-old male patient, suffering from a gunshot wound, expressed shock that the bullet actually hurt (Prothrow-Stith, 1991). Now, in the 1990s, economic insecurity, heightened competition and self-centeredness, and the increased presence of physical danger contribute to a pervasive meanness in our society that is reflected in the lives of many Black youth.

Issues of justice and fairness have been powerfully intertwined with the history of African Americans and the experience of being Black in a White America. From our earliest beginnings in this nation, the effects of injustice have circumscribed our lives, while the unifying vision of justice has inspired and energized our struggle for equality. The heightened consciousness of social injustice engendered during the civil rights era increased hope and raised the level of expectation for Blacks and Whites alike. Twenty years later, however, the Reagan/Bush years dashed the hopes of many, as a shift to more conservative beliefs brought a dismantling of many of the social welfare programs, community supports, and civil rights gains of the 1960s. Under their administrations, Congress reduced spending for unemployment insurance, child nutrition, Food Stamps, and AFDC programs, and slowly chipped away at a number of the Affirmative Action programs and policies (Karger & Stoesz, 1994). Despite these changes, Black adolescents today, no less than in the past, grow up with a passion for justice. Unfortunately, even though their lives are tied to the promise of justice, over 45 percent of today's Black children are born into and grow up in poverty (Children's Defense Fund, 1994). For them, the promise has been broken; the incongruities of justice confront them every day: unsafe streets and under-funded schools, a youth unemployment rate that is double that for White youth (Children's Defense Fund, 1994), police unresponsiveness to calls for help, criminals returned to neighborhoods to further victimize citizens, and victims' rights repeatedly ignored. Black adolescents are acutely aware of the gap between what society promises and the reality of the many injustices they experience (Ward, 1991).

For example, in her interview with me, Ayesha recounts the discriminatory and disrespectful treatment she often receives in her local department store:

> Because a lot of times people in the stores, they stare you down, they stay on your tail, they'll watch you the whole time that you're in the store. You don't see them walking around following White people walking around in

stores. But you will see them follow the Black person when they walk around the stores.

Rather than helpful assistance, Ayesha and countless other African American adolescents quickly discover that their presence in public spaces is met with suspicion and distrust. Such everyday indignities mirror a social reality in which Blacks find themselves the victims of degrading double standards.

Examining the phenomenon of violence from a relational perspective enables us to begin to formulate a broader understanding of its dynamics. Through my research, I encountered the following stories of violence which reveal a series of relational breakdowns. In Philadelphia, a young teenage woman is stabbed outside her high school gymnasium, murdered by another youngster for an expensive pair of gold earrings. Such a tragedy reveals an utter and absolute relational breakdown. The murderer's only relationship is to the object he wants to acquire. The chilling and senseless brutality seen in this example arises out of a cold and callous social climate in which excessive individualism leads to indifference and human disconnection.

A seventeen-year-old Los Angeles boy, reacting to what he believes is a false accusation, grabs a gun and roams the streets looking to defend his honor and avenge this personal attack. Both his perception that he had been wronged and his urge to retaliate arise out of a deep-seated "passion for justice." His impulse to seek revenge, or justice as he would see it, is dangerously misguided, however: it is out of proportion to the incident that prompted it. It goes beyond the law and the social order; it eclipses human connection and it may risk lives.

The African American teenager coming of age in this divisive economic, social, and political climate far too often sees a systematic devaluation of Black lives. The stereotypic characterizations of Black males as violent and predatory serve to create a climate in which even Blacks treat each other in ways that support these demonic archetypes. Moreover, African American teens frequently receive the message, embedded within the current discourse of race relations outside the Black community, that they shouldn't have any particular affinity to other Blacks, as such attachments are seen as separatist and run counter to principles of racial and social integration.[1]

Crime feeds on elements of self-denigration, the fraying of social bonds, and the loss of a shared sense of community. The "nihilist threat of meaninglessness, hopelessness, and lovelessness" that West (1992, p. 40) suggests contributes to destructive behavior, elucidates interpersonal violence as a relational break, and, in so doing, allows us to reinterpret and find new meaning in the disturbing acts of the violent few. Black adolescents, seeing themselves ignored and marginalized in the general society and feeling they cannot find justice anywhere else in their lives, may be viewed as attempting to take justice into their own hands.

As Martin Luther King eloquently stated, "Injustice anywhere is a threat to justice everywhere. We are caught in an inescapable network of mutuality, tied in a single garment of destiny. Whatever affects one directly, affects all indirectly" (1963, p. 79). What has been lost to the violent Black teenager is an awareness that aggression against the other, particularly other Blacks, is aggression against the self — a violation of the care and connectedness implicit in the notion of racial identity. In contrast, a consciousness of care and connection through racial identity protects the self from psychological destruction and despair, and fortifies the larger community against moral nihilism and collective alienation.

During adolescence, the need to identify strongly with a sense of people-hood is heightened for African Americans by a consciousness of belonging to an ethnically and culturally distinct group that has a shared experience of racial discrimination and social oppression (Ward, 1989). Thus, their racial identity is comprised of an awareness of shared group characteristics and history, as well as by the experience of shared racial discrimination and oppression. To have such a collective identity is to know that one is not alone, that one is inextricably connected to others and embedded in a network of interdependent relationships within the African American community.

Adolescents caught up in struggles of wounded pride and vengeance seek justice for themselves, yet they fail to grasp the larger significance of the need for justice for all. While a narrow perspective on adolescent violence sees it as arising merely out of interpersonal conflict, the broader picture reveals a sociopolitical backdrop in which moral codes of justice and equity are frequently violated, as in the Rodney King beating and subsequent trials.

Efforts at violence prevention for African American youth should be designed to focus on the two essential psychosocial tasks of adolescence — identity formation and moral development. By tapping into and building upon these natural developmental processes, we can engage African American teens on a cognitive and affective level. This would both speak to the adolescents' hunger for identity, meaning, and self-worth (West, 1992), and serve to develop systems of culturally based values that guide just and caring social behavior.

Resisting Detachment: Moral Development and Racial Identity

Engaged in the process of identity formation and self-creation, adolescents are passionately concerned with moral values and principles (Kohlberg & Gilligan, 1971). Past research in moral development has highlighted justice and care as the prevailing moral principles most often brought to bear on moral encounters. Studies of these two moral orientations suggest that individuals, in organizing their moral thinking and feelings, tend to emphasize either issues of unfairness (justice) or problems of disconnection (care) in their narratives of real-life moral conflict and choice. Though people have recourse to both justice and care orientations, researchers have found that individuals "tend to lose sight of one perspective or silence one set of concerns in arriving at decisions or in justifying choices they have made" (Gilligan, 1988, p. xix). As objects of both injustice and a lack of care from the general society, African American adolescents may be especially interested in the content of these principles.

In my 1986 investigation of how teens who reside in a large U.S. city make sense of the violence that surrounds them, I asked a group of low-income, ethnically diverse but predominately African American urban adolescents (N=51) to reflect upon their own real-life experiences with violence (Ward, 1988). I asked them to tell me about a violent situation or a situation in which someone was being hurt.

In the ninety-three separate narratives of real-life violent events, justice reasoning (either alone or in combination with care reasoning) was used to justify and explain violence far more often than any other type of moral consideration. The teens were willing and able to apply justice principles, particularly retributive justice, as an organizing moral orientation. More striking, however, was that in the context of this study, care reasoning appeared to mitigate violence far more often than justice reasoning. This association with nonviolent responses to violence and with restraint against invoking a violent response suggests, then, that care reasoning is an important and desirable moral orientation, one that we need to nurture and sustain more deeply in adolescents.

Detachment in human relationships is a moral problem. At the same time, the ability to perceive relational detachment is a prerequisite to care. Yet, I maintain that care as a moral orientation has cultural dimensions. If culture defines who we are, as well as the requisite moral and social knowledge that frames our relationships to one another, then the importance of cultural constructions of identity and relationship become central considerations in understanding care. When we turn our attention to the moral development of African American youth, we must look at how cultural norms affect the differential experiencing, valuing, and construction of caring. In addition, we must focus on those elements that are inextricably related to moral development, such as racial identity, which forms the basis for African Americans' sense of self and connection to others. Thus, solutions to violence may lie in strengthening racial identity and traditional values of caring in Black adolescents. As one of the adolescents I interviewed expressed it:

What really bothers me? We're hurting our own people and we're already going down as a whole. There's things that we need to do to bring our race back up, and then to fight each other when we should be helping out each other, that bothers me. (Stephanie, age 18)

The research on African American traditions of caring can be found in a number of scientific disciplines, including psychology (Nobles, 1976), anthropology (Gwaltney, 1980), and sociology (Collins, 1990). Toinette Eugene's (1989) study of the subjugation and exploitation of Black women suggests an ethic of care that has been forged out of their experiences. In her study of the return migration of African Americans to rural southern "homeplaces," sociologist Carol Stack (1991) noted both justice and care orientations in interviews with adults and pre-adolescent children. Stack found a collective social conscience wherein individuals perceived their obligations "within the context of a social order and anchored to others, rather than in an individual focus on their own personal welfare" (p. 25). Stack's research underscores how moral reflection occurs within a framework that includes the context of people's historical period and life history.

Racial Identity and Connectedness

Youth and delinquency. I wish they'd realize that they are going to need the people they are hurting now. (Alan, age 16)

For Alan, and many of the other African American teens I've interviewed and talked with, moral values related to self-definition and values related to other Blacks are embedded in their sense of racial identity, which illuminates connection between culture and care. Racial identity concerns the psychological implications of belief systems that evolve in response to perceived racial group membership (Helms, 1990, p. 3). Through racial identity, the group's way of understanding and organizing experience is transmitted to and internalized by the child (Barnes, 1972). Phinney and Rotherdam's 1987 review of the existing literature on ethnic and racial identity development concludes that four unifying themes prevail: 1) ethnic group differences in appearance, behaviors, attitudes, and values have a significant impact on development; 2) the impact of ethnicity varies with a child's age; 3) ethnic socialization has different implications depending on the particular group to which children belong; and 4) the role of ethnicity in development is influenced by the immediate environment and the sociocultural and historical context. Psychologists maintain that a stable concept of self, both as an individual and as a member of the Black race, is essential to the healthy growth and development of a Black self (Comer & Poussaint, 1975; Ladner, 1978). Development of a positive Black identity involves synthesis of internal and external experiences within the context of cultural, familial, societal, and historical influences (Cross, 1991).

The process of healthy and successful identity development for Black youth is largely about moving beyond internalization of racial denigration to internalization of racial pride — that is, a repudiation of unacceptable roles and a rebirth, or affirmation, of the self in one's own terms (Ward, 1989). As racial identity research has shown, racial pride can be enhanced through lessons culled from Black history, as well as from lessons of struggle and resistance, pride and self-help. With regard to intragroup dynamics, enhancing racial identity can influence the attitudinal components of images Black teens hold of one another, thereby repudiating negative images of the self (both personal and group) and allowing Black adolescents to uncover commonalities and strengthen connections (Cross, 1978, 1991).

Emancipatory Possibilities

A sense of belonging and pride in one's heritage lays the groundwork for establishing a healthy sense of self. African American adolescents appear to be more certain of who they are *not,* and less clear of who they are. Racial identity helps Black youth to understand who they are. A strong and positive racial identity can empower African American youth by building on their sense of belonging to a group whose very survival has been dependent on their collective ability to resist social and psychological annihilation. Developing such a racial identity in Black youth helps them to understand who they are; nurturing an ethic of care helps them to honor their connections to one another.

For centuries, the Black church has been a foundation upon which African Americans have maintained their hopes and dreams of liberation. From the earliest articulations of moral judgments against slavery, to Martin Luther King Jr.'s pronouncements that Blacks have a moral right to disobey unjust laws, our morality of justice has emphasized social and political activism and the fight against oppression. Violence prevention programs should encourage Black teens to develop and act in accord with their developing ethical principles of a justice that struggles against injustice and inequality for African Americans and other disenfranchised groups. Such programs should also build on adolescents' sense of care to encourage their personal response for prosocial conduct toward other Blacks within the community and to an ever-widening range of recipients outside of the Black community.

Adults have a role to play in helping adolescents of color make sense of the injustice in their lives and in guiding them toward moral solutions that acknowledge their own and others' rights and relational experiences. Parents, teachers, and youth workers can join with teenagers in their efforts to identify, critically assess, and build upon indigenous cultural values that can be transformed to have meaning in daily life. For example, adults can help Black teens come to see that they have the power to influence the welfare of others by developing their capacity to give of themselves for the benefit of others. Community service programs and church work are examples of areas in which Black teens can be encouraged to strengthen their ties to our cultural traditions of service and mutual aid. In our schools, African American teens can be encouraged to participate in the leadership opportunities afforded in school government, particularly those that emphasize political advocacy, social commitment, and democratic change. Finally, the adults in the lives of African American youth can work to counter negative values like excessive individualism by instilling cultural values that link individual advancement to group advancement and, in turn, recognize group advancement as a source of individual hope. Historian Lerone Bennett has argued that Black folks "must return to the rich soil of our traditions and dig there for the spreading roots of a love that slavery and segregation couldn't kill"

(1989, p. 121). I maintain that once African American youths have recovered their relationship with our history and cultural traditions and solidified a sense of renewed identity, they may then go forward, joining efforts with other groups to work toward such common goals as social justice. By this example, adolescents are helped to an understanding of how the principles of caring and justice may be applied to the larger human community.

References

Bandura, A. (1973). *Aggression: A social learning analysis.* New York: Holt, Rinehart & Winston.

Bennett, L. (1989). The ten biggest myths about the Black family. *Ebony, 45*(1), 114–121.

Billingsley, A. (1972). *Children of the storm: Black children and American child welfare.* New York: Harcourt, Brace & Jovanovich.

Blakeney. R., & Blakeney, C. (1991). Understanding and reforming moral misbehavior among behaviorally disordered adolescents. *Behavioral Disorders, 16*(21), 120–126.

Children's Defense Fund. (1994). *Progress and peril: Black children in America.* Washington, DC: Author.

Collins, P. (1990). *Black feminist thought.* Boston: Unwin-Hyman.

Cross, W. (1978). Models of psychological nigrescence: A literature review. *Journal of Black Psychology, 5,* 13–31.

Cross, W. (1991). *Shades of black: Diversity in African American identity.* Philadelphia: Temple University Press.

Comer, J., & Poussaint, A. (1975). *Black child care.* New York: Simon & Schuster.

Douglas, L. (1994, December 15). Is violence a public health issue? *Black Issues in Higher Education,* p. 20.

Eugene, T. (1989). Sometimes I feel like a motherless child: The call and response for a liberational ethic of care by Black feminists. In M. Brabeck (Ed.), *Who cares: Theory, research and educational implications of the ethic of care* (pp. 45–62). New York: Praeger.

Gelles, R. (1974). *The violent home.* Beverly Hills: Sage.

Gibbs, J. (1989). Black American adolescents. In J. Gibbs, A. Huang, & Associates, *Children of color: Psychological interventions with minority youth* (pp. 179–223). San Francisco: Jossey Bass.

Gilligan, C. (1982). *In a different voice.* Cambridge, MA: Harvard University Press.

Gilligan, C. (1988). Adolescent development reconsidered. In C. Gilligan, J. Ward, & J. Taylor, *Mapping the moral domain: A contribution of women's thinking to psychological theory and education* (pp. vii–xxxix). Cambridge, MA: Harvard University Press.

Gutman, H. (1976). *The Black family in slavery and freedom.* New York: Pantheon.

Gwaltney, J. (1980). *Drylongso: A self portrait of Black America.* New York: Random House.

Height, D. (1989, July 24-31). Self-help: A Black tradition. *The Nation,* pp. 136–138.

Helms, J. (Ed.). (1990). *Black and White racial identity: Theory, research and practice.* Westport, CT: Greenwood Press.

hooks, b., & West, C. (1991). *Breaking bread: Insurgent Black intellectual life.* Boston: South End Press.

Jewell, K. (1984). Use of social welfare programs and the disintegration of the Black nuclear family. *Western Journal of Black Studies, 8,* 192–198.

Jewell, K. (1988). *Survival of the Black family: The institutional impact of U.S. social policy.* New York: Praeger.

Karger, H., & Stoesz, D. (1994). *American social welfare policy: A pluralist approach.* New York: Longman.

King, M. (1963). *Why we can't wait.* New York: Harper & Row.

Kohlberg, L., & Gilligan, C. (1971). The adolescent as a philosopher. *Daedalus, 100,* 1051–1086.

Ladner, J. (1978). *Mixed families: Adopting across racial boundaries.* New York: Doubleday.

McCray, C. (1980). The Black woman and family roles. In L. Rodgers-Rose (Ed.), *The Black woman* (67–78). Beverly Hills, CA: Sage.

National Research Council. (1989). *A common destiny: Blacks and American society.* Washington, DC: National Academy Press.

Nobles, W. (1976). Extended self: Rethinking the so-called Negro self-concept. In *Journal of Black Psychology, 2*(2), 15–24.

Oliver, W. (1989). Black males and social problems: Prevention through afrocentric socialization. *Journal of Black Studies, 20*(1), 15–39.

Parke, R., & Slaby, R. (1983). The development of aggression. In P. H. Mussen (Ed.), *Handbook of Child Psychology* (Vol. 4, 4th ed.). New York: Wiley.

Paris, P. (1985). *The social teaching of the Black churches.* Philadelphia: Fortress Press.

Phinney, J., & Rotherdam, M. (1987). Children's ethnic socialization: Themes and implications. In J. Phinney & M. Rotherdam, *Children's ethnic socialization* (274–292). Beverly Hills, CA: Sage.

Prothrow-Stith, D. (1991). *Deadly consequences: How violence is destroying our teenage population and a play to begin solving the problem.* New York: Harper Collins.

Rodríguez, J. (1990). Childhood injuries in the United States. *American Journal of Diseases of Childhood, 144,* 627–646.

Somers, I., & Baskin, D. (1994). Factors related to female adolescent initiation into violent street crime. *Youth and Society, 25,* 468–489.

Stack, C. (1974). *All our kin.* New York: Harper & Row.

Stack, C. (1991). Different voices, different visions: Gender, culture and moral reasoning. In F. Ginsburg & A. Tsing, *Uncertain terms: Negotiating gender in American culture* (pp. 19–26). Boston: Beacon Press.

Straus, M., Gelles, R., & Steinmetz, S. (1980). *Behind closed doors: Violence in the American family.* New York: Anchor Press.

Trattner, W. (1994). *From poor law to welfare state: A history of social welfare in America* (5th ed.). New York: Free Press.

Ward, J. (1989). Racial identity formation and transformation. In C. Gilligan, N. Lyons, & T. Hamner (Eds.), *Making connections: The relational worlds of adolescent girls at Emma Willard School* (pp. 215–232). Cambridge, MA: Harvard University Press.

Ward, J. (1988). Urban adolescents' conceptions of violence. In C. Gilligan, J. Ward, & J. Taylor (Eds.), *Mapping the moral domain* (pp. 175–200). Cambridge, MA: Harvard University Press.

Ward, J. (1991). Eyes in the back of your head: Moral themes in African American narratives of racial conflict. *Journal of Moral Education, 20,* 267–281.

West, C. (1992). Nihilism in Black America. In G. Dent (Ed.), *Black popular culture: A project by Michele Wallace* (pp. 37–47). Seattle: Bay Press.

White, J., & Parham, T. (1990). *The psychology of Blacks: An African American perspective* (2nd ed.). Englewood Cliffs, NJ: Prentice Hall.

Wolfgang, M., & Ferracuti, F. (1967). *The subculture of violence: Towards an integrated theory of criminology.* London: Tavistock.

This article was supported by a grant from the Lilly Endowment Research Grants Program in Youth and Caring. I wish to thank Tracy Robinson for her assistance in this project, and Lynn Hamilton, Deborah Tolman, and Coleman Herman for their editorial support. I am deeply grateful to the adolescents and parents who participated in these studies.

PART THREE

▪ ▪ ▪

The Practice of Anti-Racism

The academy is not paradise. But learning is a place where paradise can be created. The classroom, with all its limitations, remains a location of possibility. In that field of possibility we have the opportunity to labor for freedom, to demand of ourselves and our comrades, an openness of mind and heart that allows us to face reality even as we collectively imagine ways to move beyond boundaries, to transgress. This is education as the practice of freedom.

— bell hooks, *Teaching to Transgress:*
Education as the Practice of Freedom

The last section reflects our hope that teachers, students, and communities can conquer racism by transforming classrooms into sites where we practice freedom and openness towards each other. We present the following six articles, each of which is a testimony to the commitment and successful efforts of educators to move beyond racism and towards anti-racism in their ideologies and pedagogies.

In "Reading the World of School Literacy: Contextualizing the Experience of a Young African American Male," Arlette Ingram Willis engages the reader in a dialogue about the hidden cultural assumptions of literacy programs. Drawing on her experiences as a teacher educator, concerned mother, and African American, she provides a richly textured discussion of the struggles experienced by her elementary-school-aged son Jake in writing about his culturally shaped experiences. She frames her son's struggles within the historical and cultural context of racism that has affected the lives of culturally and linguistically diverse school children throughout U.S. history. Part of her solution to institutionalized racism is to expand teachers' understandings of the various cultures that children represent. Toward this end, Willis provides examples from her own pre-service teacher education course in which she successfully brings her students to an awareness of their racial heritages and the assumptions they bring to the classroom about the cultures of others.

In "Because You Like Us: The Language of Control," Cynthia Ballenger takes us into her own process of recognizing the role that culture — her own and that of her Haitian preschool students — played in her pedagogy. Her experiences exemplify the kinds of conversations that Lisa Delpit identified in Part One as being central to cross-cultural understandings in the classroom. Examining conversations between Haitian teachers and their students, Ballenger reveals how Haitian culture emphasizes group membership and responsibilities, as opposed to the individuality stressed by her own North American culture. Her exploration of her own values throughout the process poignantly reflects the transformative capacities of honest dialogue across difference.

Beverly Daniel Tatum also addresses the problematic neutrality accorded to White culture in "Talking about Race, Learning about Racism: The Application of Racial Identity Development Theory in the Classroom." Noting that conversations about racism are often missing from discussions of multiculturalism, Tatum brings together two models of racial identity development, her experiences as a university professor of psychology, and journal excerpts from her students to illustrate how her college classroom has become a key starting point for Whites and people of color to understand racism as a salient aspect of U.S. social institutions. Her work suggests that the classroom can be a crucial site for personal and institutional change toward anti-racist thought and behaviors.

Jim Cummins, in "Empowering Minority Students: A Framework for Intervention," views the academic experiences of racial and language minority students relationally; that is, he considers the relationships between teachers and students, institutions and communities, and dominant and dominated social groups as key factors in how schools can promote or obstruct academic success for all students. As Cummins argues, new programs and policies have resulted in little change in the educational underachievement of minority students because teachers and institutions have maintained dominant/dominated power relationships with minority communities. Examples of empowering relationships found in selected bilingual and compensatory education programs highlight the personal and political redefinitions facing educators and policymakers who earnestly want to bring about educational reform.

One of the trends requiring such a redefinition is the increasing disparity in the cultural makeup of the U.S. teaching and student populations: Over 90 percent of prospective teachers are White European American, while the population of schoolchildren is becoming increasingly racially diverse. This disparity is problematic, given that research has shown that teachers are most effective in educating students who resemble them in culture and race. In "Uncertain Allies: Understanding the Boundaries of Race and Teaching," Marilyn Cochran-Smith points out the need for teacher educators to "open up the unsettling discourse of race" in the pre-service curriculum (p. 374) in order for them to increase their effectiveness and understanding in working with students from different racial backgrounds. By documenting the written and spoken reactions of her pre-service teachers to notions such as White privilege, Afrocentric curricula, racial identity development, and the culture of power, and by critically interrogating her own pedagogy and intentions, Cochran-Smith demonstrates how profound a process it is for many educators to understand teaching as a political endeavor. An important contribution of this article is that it brings to our attention many of the uncertainties that teachers encounter when questioning the ostensibly "normative" constructions of education.

Reading the World of School Literacy: Contextualizing the Experience of a Young African American Male

—■—■—■—

ARLETTE INGRAM WILLIS

L et me share a conversation that I had with my nine-year-old son, and the context in which it occurred:

It's a cold, frosty winter morning, and everyone has left for work or school except my youngest son Jake and me. I am busy applying last-minute touches to my makeup and encouraging Jake, in the next room, to "step it up." I wonder why he is dragging around; school starts in ten minutes and we haven't yet left the house. Jake knows the routine; I wonder if something is troubling him. So, I peek around the corner and find him looking forlorn — you know, a scowl on his face, a look of growing despair and sadness. I forget about the clock and attend to him.

"Jake, what's wrong? Why are you so unhappy?" I ask.

"We have the Young Authors [writing] Contest today, and I don't have anything to write about."

"Sure you do. There are lots of things you can write about," I encourage him. (I believe people write best about those subjects they know and care about.) *"Why don't you write about baseball or soccer?"*

"No," he replies. "A kid at our school wrote about cancer last year, and the story went all the way to the next state [regionals]."

"Well," I answer, "maybe you should write about something funny — like when you go to the barbershop. You and your brothers are always talking about your trips there."[1]

[1] Going to the barbershop and getting a haircut is a bimonthly occurrence for many African American males. A number of Jake's classmates differed in their definition of what constituted a "part"; however, the other African American children in his class have a similar cultural understanding of the term.

Harvard Educational Review Vol. 65 No. 1 Spring 1995, 30–49

"Oh no, Mom, they wouldn't understand. When I just get my haircut, they always ask me, 'Why do you have that line in your hair?' 'It's not a line, it's a part,' I try to tell them. I can't write about the barbershop. They won't understand."

"Well," I say, trying to clarify what I really mean, "I don't mean write about getting a haircut. I mean writing about all the funny people that come in and the things that happen while you are at the barbershop. You and your brothers always come home tellin' a funny story and laugh about it for the rest of the week. That's what I mean by writing about the barbershop."

"No, Mom. They won't understand," he insists.

"What do you mean, 'they won't understand?' Who is this 'they'?" I ask.

"The people in my class," he replies, somewhat frustrated.

Jake continues, "You should read this story that M. wrote. It is a mystery story and it's really good. I can't beat that story. I'll bring you a copy of it if I can. I know it will win." (Sadder now that he has had time to consider his competition, Jake turns and walks toward his room.)

Wanting him to participate in the contest, I ask, "How do you know M.'s story is good?"

"She read it in class. Everybody said it's really good," he responds.

"Well, I still think you should try. You are a really good writer. Look at all the 'good stuff' you wrote in Mrs. S.'s room. You could rewrite some of it and turn it in."

Finally he answers, "I'll think about it," and we go off to school.

As I remember the conversation, Jake's tone of voice hinted at both frustration and defensiveness. I interpreted his use of phrases like "they always ask" and "I try to tell them" to mean that since he gets his hair cut every two weeks, it gets pretty tiresome answering the same questions from his classmates so frequently.[2] Furthermore, I interpreted his intonation to mean that he has had to stand his ground with other children who either do not agree with his definition of a "part," or who try to define its meaning for him.

I believe that Jake cannot bring this aspect of his life and culture into the classroom because he doesn't feel that it will be understood by his classmates and teacher. When Jake says "They won't understand," I interpret his words to mean that if his classmates cannot understand the simplest action in getting a haircut — the barber taking less than ten seconds to place a part in his hair — how can he expect them to understand the context and culture that surround the entire event. Also, I see Jake's reluctance to share something as commonplace in his home and community life as a haircut as a way of distancing this portion of his life from the life he leads at school. It seems that he has come to understand that as an African American he must con-

[2] As a Writing Workshop parent volunteer in his class, I know that Jake's class consists of ten European American boys, nine European American girls, four African American boys, two African American girls, and one Asian American girl. The class is taught by a European American woman with over twenty years of experience. Also, during this school year, there have been three student teachers (all European American women) and several other parent volunteers (also European American women).

stantly make a mediating effort to help others understand events that appear to be commonplace on the surface, but are in fact culturally defined.

Several interwoven incidents have helped me to understand the conversation with Jake. I will briefly describe them to provide the context for my understanding of the subtle, yet ever-present and unquestioned role of cultural accommodation that occurs in the school literacy experiences of children from diverse backgrounds. I have been teaching courses in multicultural literature at my university for several years. After my fall 1993 course, I reflected, using journal writing, on my growing experience teaching multicultural literature courses.[3] Teaching these courses has led me to a more informed understanding of how, in the practice of school literacy, there are many culturally defined moments of conflict that call daily for cultural understanding, knowledge, and sensitivity from teachers. These "moments" also challenge non-mainstream students to choose between cultural assimilation and accommodation, or resistance. My journal entries centered on my readings, research, and, most importantly, my daily conversations about school life with my three sons, who range in age from nine to seventeen. In my classes, I have often shared my sons' school experiences and my reactions to them in an effort to help my students understand how teachers' daily subtle and seemingly inconsequential decisions can affect the learning of the children they teach.

A striking example of a teacher's unintentional disregard for the cultural history, understanding, experiences, and voice of a student occurred when my oldest son struggled to meet the requirements of a national essay contest entitled, "What it means to be an American." One of the contest's restrictions was that students should not mention the concept of race. My son thought this was an unfair and impossible task to complete, since his African American identity is synonymous with his being American. Yet, his efforts to articulate the difficulty of the task to his English teacher were frustrated by her response that, although she was empathic, she did not have the authority to change the rules. I intervened and spoke with the teacher at length about my son's values, beliefs, and his unwillingness to compromise himself in order to compete in an essay contest in which he had little or no interest other than a grade.

My second son also had a similar experience involving unintentional cultural insensitivity. He is a member of the school band, which was having its fall concert. While attending, I noticed that all the music the band played was composed by Europeans or European Americans. I spoke with one of the band directors, and asked rhetorically if there were any songs that the band members could perform that were composed by people of color. She responded that she had never considered the choices she made as nonrepre-

<hr/>

[3] In the fall of 1993 I taught a pilot course, which included multicultural education, reading methods for grades six–twelve, and literature for grades six–twelve with special emphasis on multicultural literature.

sentative of all the students who had to learn them, while I could see little else than the absence of cultural diversity. I was pleased when the winter concert included some Hanukkah tunes. It was a start.

Reflections

Though my conversation with Jake is now months old, it has continued to haunt me. I have been deeply concerned about a noticeable shift in my son's attitude toward writing. Jake's early writing experiences in kindergarten and first grade revealed that he found writing to be a natural outlet for self-expression. He often wrote for pleasure and has kept all of his drafts. Jake learned the process approach to writing in first grade and treasures his portfolio, which he had originally developed in that class. I have found him in his room revisiting a piece he had written earlier. However, this past year I have noticed a change in his level of production. Jake no longer writes detailed accounts. Instead, he spends a great deal of time thinking about what to write and how to say it. While I believe these are laudatory traits of a good writer, his teachers often accuse him of being under-productive.

Reflecting on our conversation, I sense that Jake believes (understands?) that his perceived audience will neither value nor understand the cultural images and nuances he wishes to share in his writing. Jake is a child wrestling with an internal conflict that is framed by the sociohistorical and sociocultural inequities of U.S. society. He is trying to come to grips with how he can express himself in a manner that is true to his "real self," and yet please his teacher and audience of readers who are, in effect, evaluating his culture, thinking, language, and reality.

Jake's perception of an unaccepting audience is not unique. Several researchers have expressed similar concerns about the narrowly defined culture of acceptable school literacy and the growing literateness of culturally and linguistically diverse children (Delpit, 1986, 1991, 1993; Gutierrez, 1992; Heath, 1983; Labov, 1972; Ovando & Collier, 1985; Reyes & Molner, 1991; Sawyer & Rodriguez, 1992).[4] Why is it clearer to children than to adults that there are systematic, institutional inequalities in the decisions teachers make about the "appropriate" methods and materials used to enhance their students' literacy development?

Like millions of culturally and linguistically diverse people, Jake understands the unstated reality of schooling in U.S. society: It is built upon a narrow understanding of school knowledge and literacy, which are defined and defended as what one needs to know and how one needs to know it in order to be successful in school and society. As Barrera (1992) explains:

---

[4] To me, "growing literateness" means an understanding of how language, reading, and writing fit into the communication patterns of home and school life. It can also mean the development of literate behaviors, the adoption of literate attitudes, and the confidence that allows one to define oneself as a reader and a writer.

The school culture can be seen to reflect the dominant class and, so too, the cultures of literacy and literature embedded within the school culture. For this reason, the teaching of literacy and literature are considered to be neither acultural nor neutral, but cultural and political. (p. 236)

The real question is, why do we as educators continue this "sin of omission" — that is, allowing the cultural knowledge of culturally and linguistically diverse children to be ignored, devalued, and unnurtured as valid sources of literacy acquisition? Excerpts from the writings of five noted African Americans help to illustrate my point.

The Past Revisited

The problem of defining one's literary self is not a new one. As noted scholar W. E. B. DuBois argued in 1903:

After the Egyptian and Indian, the Greek and Roman, the Teuton and Mongolian, the Negro is a sort of seventh son, born with a veil, and gifted with second-sight in this American world, — a world which yields him no true self-consciousness, but only lets him see himself through the revelation of the other world. It is a peculiar sensation this double-consciousness, this sense of always looking at one's self through the eyes of others. . . . One ever feels his twoness, an American, a Negro; two souls, two thoughts, two unreconciled strivings; two warring ideals in one dark body, whose dogged strength alone keeps it from being torn asunder. The history of the American Negro is the history of this strife, — this longing to attain self conscious manhood, to merge his double self into a better and truer self. (1903/1965, pp. 214–215)

Similarly, historian Carter G. Woodson (1933/1990) stated:

In this effort to imitate, however, those "educated people" are sincere. They hope to make the Negro conform quickly to the standard of the whites and thus remove the pretext for the barriers between the races. They do not realize, however, that if the Negroes do successfully imitate the whites, nothing new has thereby been accomplished. You simply have a larger number of persons doing what others have been doing. The unusual gifts of the race have not thereby been developed. (p. 4)

Poet Langston Hughes (1951) expressed a similar notion:

I guess being colored doesn't make me not like
the same things other folks like who are other races.
So will my page be colored that I write?
Being me, it will not be white.
But it will be
a part of you, instructor.
You are white —
yet a part of me, as I am a part of you.

That's American.
Sometimes perhaps you don't want to be a part of me.
Nor do I often want to be a part of you.
But we are, that's true!
As I learn from you,
I guess you learn from me —
although you're older — and white —
and somewhat more free. (pp. 39–40)

Novelist Ralph Ellison (1952) writes:

> I am invisible, understand, simply because people refuse to see me. Like the bodiless heads you see sometimes in circus sideshows, it is as though I have been surrounded by mirrors of hard, distorting glass. When they approach me they see only my surroundings, themselves, or figments of their imagination — indeed, everything and anything except me. (p. 3)

And, finally, Toni Morrison (1992) refers to the phenomenon of double consciousness as "writing for a white audience" (p. xii). She asks:

> What happens to the writerly imagination of a black author who is at some level *always* conscious of representing one's own race to, or in spite of, a race of readers that understands itself to be "universal" or race-free? In other words, how are "literary whiteness" and "literary blackness" made, and what is the consequence of these constructions? (p. xii)

Like other culturally and linguistically diverse people before him (including myself and every other person of color with whom I have shared this incident), Jake has encountered the struggle of literary personhood.

Questions and concerns flood my mind: Where, I wonder, has he gotten the idea of a "White" audience — that is, the sense that his classmates and others who read his writing will not appreciate what he has to share? When did his concept of a "White" audience arise? My questions persist: How long has Jake known, intuitively perhaps, that his school literacy experiences have been tempered through a mainstream lens? Will Jake continue to resist "writing for a white audience?" When do culturally and linguistically diverse children learn that they must choose between selfhood and accommodation?[5] When do they learn that "the best way, then, to succeed — that is, to receive rewards, recognition . . . is to learn and reproduce the ways of the dominant group?" (Scheurich, 1992, p. 7). Must there be only one acceptable culture reflected in current school literacy programs? What thoughts, words, and language is Jake replacing with those of the dominant culture in order to please his audience? Will he ever be able to recapture his true literate self after years of accommodation?

---

[5] Selfhood, as used in this article, means the awareness of oneself as a person, in particular as a person who belongs to a specific culturally and linguistically distinct group.

As a third grader, Jake is writing, but not for pleasure. Whereas once he wrote as a way of expressing himself or as a hobby, now he does not. He only writes to complete assignments. Much of the "joy" he experienced in writing for pleasure seems to have waned. I recently read some of his writings and noted that he concentrated on topics that do not reflect African American culture. For example, his most recent entries are about his spoon collection, running track, rocks, and football — pretty generic stuff.

My fears are like those of all parents who believe they have prepared their child, having done all that they have read and know a parent should do, yet see their child struggling with a history, a tradition, that is much larger than they can battle.[6] What can I do to help my son and children like him enjoy the freedom of writing and reading? How can I help them value the culturally relevant events in their lives? How can school literacy programs begin to acknowledge, respect, and encourage the diverse cultural knowledge and experiences that children bring to school?

In this article, I am speaking as a teacher educator and parent. This article is an attempt to begin conversations with my colleagues that will address cultural complexities so often ignored in literacy research and practice. For too long, the only perspective published was European Americans' understanding of literacy events. Over the past few years, other cultural perspectives have been published and, more recently, a few have questioned the connection between the theoretical notions of literacy and the historical, and daily, reality of institutionalized inequalities.

As a scholar, I can begin conversations with my colleagues about reexamining theories of literacy to include the role of culture and linguistic diversity. Moreover, teachers and teacher educators like myself can then extend these conversations to reinterpret literacy development, school literacy programs, and teacher education methods and materials to include the experiences of nonmainstream cultures. Finally, I can further extend these conversations into rethinking how we teach and practice school literacy.

Broadening the Scope

Several contemporary positions on literacy serve to enlighten our understanding of how literacy is defined in the field and how it is defined in practice. In this section, I will offer a brief look at several definitions. First, Cook-Gumperz (1986) describes two competing definitions of school literacy

---

[6] Cose's (1993) book, *The Rage of a Privileged Class*, gives examples of the frustration experienced by other middle-class African Americans who believed that by doing everything according to plan they would reap just rewards. For example, Cose quotes Darwin Davis, senior vice president of Equitable Life Assurance Society: "They [young Black managers] have an even worse problem [than I did] because they've got M.B.A.'s from Harvard. They did all the things that you're supposed to do . . . and things are supposed to happen" (p. 76).

By "history," I mean how the inequalities that exist in schools reflect a much greater history of institutionalized inequalities. By "tradition," I mean teachers' tendency to teach how they were taught. Whether history or tradition is the overriding factor in this instance, I am not sure.

that are useful in framing this discussion. She states that "inherent in our contemporary attitude to literacy and schooling is a confusion between a prescriptive view of literacy, as a statement about the values and uses of knowledge, and a descriptive view of literacy, as cognitive abilities which are promoted and assessed through schooling" (p. 14). Second, a more expansive definition of how literacy is conceptualized is offered by Freire and Macedo (1987). They suggest that "literacy becomes a meaningful construct to the degree that it is viewed as a set of practices that functions to either empower or disempower people. In the larger sense, literacy is analyzed according to whether it serves a set of cultural practices that promotes democratic and emancipatory change" (p. 141). Further, they clarify their position on literacy by noting that "for the notion of literacy to become meaningful it has to be situated within a theory of cultural production and viewed as an integral part of the way in which people produce, transform, and reproduce meaning" (p. 142). Third, more general discussions of literacy define literacy as functional, cultural, or critical. Each of these concepts also refers to very different ways of thinking about literacy. *Functional literacy* refers to mastery of the skills needed to read and write as measured by standardized forms of assessment. This view of literacy is similar to Cook-Gumperz's (1986) notion of a descriptive view of literacy. The functional view promotes literacy as a cognitive set of skills that are universal, culturally neutral, and equally accessible through schooling, and is based on a positivistic ideology of learning. Further, this view is heavily dependent on the use of standardized testing measures as a proving ground for literacy acquisition. Most basal reading series and programmed reading approaches embrace the functional/descriptive view of literacy.

Cultural literacy is a term that is most often associated with E. D. Hirsch's 1987 book, *Cultural Literacy: What Every American Needs to Know.* Hirsch defines cultural literacy as "the network of information that all competent readers possess. It is the background information, stored in their minds, that enables them to take up a newspaper and read it with an adequate level of comprehension, getting the point, grasping the implications, relating what they read to the unstated context which alone gives meaning to what they read" (p. 2). Cook-Gumperz (1986) has labelled this form of literacy "prescriptive." In effect, this form of cultural literacy validates language forms, experiences, literature, and histories of some and marginalizes or ignores the language forms, experiences, literature, and histories of others. In the United States, the prescriptive view can be seen in the use of standard English, Eurocentric ways of knowing and learning, a Eurocentric literary canon, and a conventional unproblematic rendering of U.S. history. This form of the cultural/prescriptive view marginalizes the pluralistic composition of U.S. society by devaluing the language, contributions, and histories of some groups. Traditional or conventional approaches to school-based literacy take this form. McLaren (1987) argues that there is a second form of cultural literacy. He writes that this form of cultural literacy "advocates using the language standards and cultural information students bring into the class-room as legitimate and important constituents of learning" (p. 214). Cultural literacy, thus described, suggests that the language and experiences of each student who enters the classroom should be respected and nurtured. This form of cultural literacy recognizes that there are differences in language forms, experiences, literature, and histories of students that will affect literacy learning. Social constructivist theories fall into this prescriptive/cultural literacy category. These approaches to literacy emphasize the active engagement of learners in making meaning from print, the social context of literacy learning, and the importance of recognizing individual and cultural differences.

Critical literacy refers to the ideologies that underlie the relationship between power and knowledge in society. The work of Brazilian educator Paulo Freire has been influential to U.S. efforts to adopt a critical literacy position. Freire, among others, suggests that literacy is more than the construction of meaning from print: Literacy must also include the ability to understand oneself and one's relationship to the world. Giroux's (1987) discussion is worth quoting here at length:

> As Paulo Freire and others have pointed out, schools are not merely instructional sites designed to transmit knowledge; they are also cultural sites. As sites, they generate and embody support for particular forms of culture as is evident in the school's support for specific ways of speaking, the legitimating of distinct forms of knowledge, the privileging of certain histories and patterns of authority, and the confirmation of particular ways of experiencing and seeing the world. Schools often give the appearance of transmitting a common culture, but they, in fact, more often than not, legitimate what can be called a dominant culture. (p. 176)

Giroux goes on to state that:

> At issue here is understanding that student experience has to be understood as part of an interlocking web of power relations in which some groups of students are often privileged over others. But if we are to view this insight in an important way, we must understand that it is imperative for teachers to critically examine the cultural backgrounds and social formations out of which their students produce the categories they use to give meaning to the world. For teachers are not merely dealing with students who have individual interests, they are dealing primarily with individuals whose stories, memories, narratives, and readings of the world are inextricably related to wider social and cultural formations and categories. This issue here is not merely one of relevance but one of power. (p. 177)

Similarly, Apple (1992) has argued for nearly a decade that "it is naive to think of the school curriculum as neutral knowledge. . . . Rather, what counts as legitimate knowledge is the result of complex power relations and struggles among identifiable class, race, gender, and religious groups" (p. 4).

Critical literacy draws attention to the historical, political, cultural, and social dimensions of literacy. Most importantly, this form of literacy focuses on power relations in society and how knowledge and power are interrelated. Educationalists, practitioners in particular, have not yet fully grasped this position on literacy. The other forms of literacy, functional/descriptive and cultural/prescriptive, do not include, among other things, the notion of power relations in literacy instruction.

Philosophically, social constructivist notions (a form of prescriptive/cultural literacy) may be seen as comparable to those espoused by critical literacy. From the schema theorists of the early 1980s to the social constructivist theories of the 1990s, literacy development is understood to be a "meaning making process" — that is, socially mediated (Meek, 1982). Drawing primarily on the work of Halliday (1975), Vygotsky (1978), and Goodman (1989), a number of literacy researchers have stressed the universality of language learning. For example, Goodman's (1989) discussion of the philosophical stance of whole language is that:

> At the same time that whole language sees common strengths and universals in human learning, it expects and recognizes differences among learners in culture, value systems, experience, needs, interests and language. Some of these differences are personal, reflecting the ethnic, cultural, and belief systems of the social groups pupils represent. Thus teachers in whole-language programs value differences among learners as they come to school and differences in objectives and outcomes as students progress through school. (p. 209)

However, I argue that the role of culture in the social constructivist theories is not as well defined as it needs to be in a pluralistic or multicultural society. While it is fair to say that unidimensional views of culture would not be supported by social constructivists, it is also fair to say that the multilayered complexity of culture, especially the cultures of historically oppressed groups, is not explicitly addressed by them either. By way of example, I will examine the prescriptive/cultural literacy foundation of whole language. Goodman (1986) argues that "language begins as means of communication between members of the group. Through it, however, each developing child acquires the life view, the cultural perspective, the ways of meaning particular to its own culture" (p. 11). But this definition fails to acknowledge that in addition to acquiring culturally "neutral" knowledge, some children must also acquire a Eurocentric cultural perspective to be successful in school. It is not sufficient to suggest that the language and culture of every student is welcomed, supported, and nurtured in school without explicitly addressing the power relations in institutions, social practice, and literature that advantage some and hinder others (Delpit, 1988; Reyes, 1992). School-based literacy, in its varying forms, fails to acknowledge explicitly the richness of the cultural ways of knowing, forms of language other than standard English, and the interwoven relationship among power, language, and literacy that silences kids like Jake.[7] To fail to attend to the plurality and diversity within the United States — and to fail to take seriously the historic past and the social and political contexts that have sustained it — is to dismiss the cultural ways of knowing, language, experiences, and voices of children from diverse linguistic and cultural backgrounds. This is not to imply that programs based on such theories need to be scrapped. It does mean that social constructivist theories need to be reworked to include the complexities of culture that are currently absent. It will also mean that teacher education will need to: 1) make explicit the relationship among culture, language, literacy and power; and 2) train teachers to use cultural information to support and nurture the literacy development of all the students who enter their classrooms.

When taken at face value, social constructivist theory would lead one to assume that new holistic approaches to literacy are culturally validating for all students. An examination of Jake's home and school contexts for his developing understanding of literacy illustrates that this is not always true. That is, we need to understand where he acquired language and his understanding of culture, as well as his history of literacy instruction, to understand how he is "reading the world" of school literacy and how his experiences with a variety of school literacy forms, including holistic approaches, have not addressed his cultural ways of knowing, experiences, language, and voice.

Literacy Contexts

Home Context

Literacy acquisition does not evolve in one context or through one type of event; rather, it is a complex endeavor that is mediated through culture. Jake's home literacy environment began with our preparations for him as a new baby. He was brought into a loving two-parent home in which two older brothers were awaiting his arrival. Jake also entered a print- and language-rich environment. He was read to when only a few months old, and continues to share reading (and now writing) with family members. Like the homes of many other middle-class children, Jake's is filled with language, and a range of standard and vernacular languages is used. Our talk centers around family issues, but also includes conversations about world events, neighborhood and school concerns, and personal interests. There are stories, prayers, niceties (manners), verbal games, family jokes, homework assignments, daily

[7] Silencing, as used by Michelle Fine (1987), "constitutes a process of institutionalized policies and practices which obscure the very social, economic and therefore experiential conditions of students' daily lives, and which expel from written, oral, and nonverbal expression substantive and critical 'talk' about these conditions. . . . Silencing constitutes the process by which contradictory evidence, ideologies, and experiences find themselves buried, camouflaged, and discredited" (p. 157).

Bible reading and discussion, as well as family vacations and excursions to museums, zoos, concerts, and ball parks. Daily routines include reading and responding to mail, making schedules, appointments, grocery and chore lists, and taking telephone messages, all of which include opportunities for shared conversations. There is also a family library that consists of adult fiction, nonfiction, and reference materials. Conversations flow constantly and with ease as we enjoy sharing with each other.

Prior to Jake's entering school, we enjoyed music, games, songs, fingerplay, writing notes on unlined paper with lots of different writing tools, long nature walks, as well as trips to the store, library, barbershop, and church.[8] All these activities were accompanied by lots of talk to expand understanding and draw connections. In addition, Jake and his brothers all have their own bedroom library in which they keep their favorite books, collected since early childhood. Jake's written communications include telephone messages, calendar events, schedules, notes, recipes, invitations, thank-you notes, game brackets (Sega or Nintendo), and occasionally letters and poems.

Jake has a special interest in his collections of stickers, stamps, coins, puzzles, board games, maps, newspaper clippings, and baseball, football, and basketball cards. He also enjoys reading his bedtime story books, magazines (especially *Sports Illustrated for Kids*), and the newspaper (his favorite parts are the sports page, the comics, and the weather map).

What makes Jake's understanding of language and literacy so culturally different from his school's, although both are apparently based on middle-class standards, is that his home literacy events have been culturally defined and are mediated through his cultural understanding. Jake's world is African American; that is, his growing understanding of who and what he is has consciously and unconsciously been mediated through an African American perspective. We select our artwork, magazines, novels, television programs, music, videos, and movies to reflect interests in African American life and society.

School Context

Like most parents, I inquired about the kindergarten's literacy program before enrolling Jake in school.[9] I wanted to have some idea of how his teachers viewed literacy development and how they planned to conduct literacy instruction. My primary question was, "What approach to literacy will you use?" Jake's private, full-day kindergarten was founded by three Jewish women, two of whom taught the kindergarten class, while the third served as school administrator. The teachers informed me that they had taught for many

[8] "Fingerplay" is a term often used to describe actions made with the fingers as children sing a song. For example, the motions used with the song "The Itsy Bitsy Spider" are fingerplay.

[9] During my years as a classroom teacher, many parents asked what type of reading program I planned to use. While most parents do not use the term "literacy programs" or inquire about writing programs per se, they do inquire about reading. I have also found that parents are interested in the methods used to teach spelling and vocabulary.

years and were aware of the modern trends. They had therefore designed a program that included what they considered to be the strong points of several programs. Jake's classmates included twelve European Americans (eight were Jewish) and two African American children. His teachers tried to provide all the children with what they thought the children would need to know in order to be successful readers and writers in grade one. As a result, the classroom was colorful and full of print. Labels were placed on cubbyholes, activity centers, children's table chairs, and charts.[10] The reading material was an eclectic mix of basals, trade books, and a small library of children's classics.

In first grade, Jake attended a public elementary school. This classroom was a mixed-age group (grades one and two) of twenty-three children, including seventeen European Americans, four African Americans, and two Asian Americans. His teacher described her literacy program as literature-based, and she stressed reading and writing. This teacher read to the children, who also read individually or in small groups. The reading materials included recipients of the Caldecott award and other award-winning books, stories, and poems by children's favorite authors, classics of children's literature, and writing "published" by the students. The children especially liked to read folk tales. As they gained reading and writing skills, the children coauthored, published, and shared their own work. Students were also encouraged to read and write for pleasure. In all these works, I recall that very few were written about or authored by people of color, except for a few on the Caldecott list.

Jake attended a different elementary school for second grade. I eagerly met his new teacher and asked my standard question about literacy. She informed me that she used the basal approach, which she believed ensured that all the "skills" needed to be a successful reader would be covered. The particular basal series she used included "universal" themes and contained illustrations of various racial/ethnic groups but made little reference to the culture of the people. There were several "ethnic" stories, but I consider their authorship suspect, at best.[11] The series also included isolated skill development, vocabulary regulated text, several thematically organized stories, informational selections, and limited writing opportunities. This class of twenty-eight children included twenty European Americans, five African Americans, and three Asian Americans.

Not wishing Jake to repeat this basal approach in grade three, I spoke with other mothers in the neighborhood, soliciting information about the "good"

[10] Activity centers are areas set aside for special activities. For example, the science center, math center, etc., all have activities specifically designed for children interested in learning more about a selected topic.

[11] Many stories contained in basals, like the one Jake used in second grade, are written by teams of authors seeking to control vocabulary or teach specific skills. Basal stories are often abridged or edited versions of original works, and in some instances, such as folk tales, legends, and fairy tales, are translations or a retelling of the original.

third-grade teachers. After much prayer, I informed the principal of my choice. Now in third grade, Jake is experiencing what his teacher refers to as a whole language approach to literacy, which includes lots of reading and writing for meaning, working in cooperative groups, process writing, and having sustained time for reading and writing. Writing is a daily activity, and Thursday mornings are designated as Writing Workshop mornings with parent volunteers who assist students in a variety of ways, from brainstorming topics to editing their writing. The teacher allows time for individual and small group readings of trade books on a daily basis. Since my conversation with Jake, I have learned his teacher had selected the books she planned to use during the school year, ahead of time, and the children were allowed only to choose which of these books to read. All of the books were written by European American authors. Even the folk tales from other countries were rewritten by European Americans. Very few books by or about U.S. minorities have been read to students by the teacher, student teachers, or in the reading groups.

I cannot account for the moment-by-moment decisions Jake's teachers have had to make each day. However, I can review the philosophies behind the programs they use. Theoretically, each literacy program purports to be culturally neutral and not mediated by any dominant view of language, when, in fact, a Eurocentric, mainstream cultural view dominates. Darder (1991) argues that it is important to understand the historicity of knowledge:

> The dominant school culture functions not only to support the interests and values of the dominant society, but also to marginalize and invalidate knowledge forms and experiences that are significant to subordinate and oppressed groups. This function is best illustrated in the ways that curriculum often blatantly ignores the histories of women, people of color, and the working class. (p. 79)

Having held a conference with each of Jake's teachers and observed each class setting on several occasions, I can say without hesitation that each teacher believed that she was doing her best to meet the needs of each child in her classroom. That is, she was trying to foster a growing sense of literacy competence in each child. Yet, I don't believe that any of Jake's teachers were aware that they were also narrowly defining the cultural lens through which all children in the classroom were expected to understand literacy.

Thus, in four short years Jake has experienced a wide range of philosophies, approaches, and instruction in literacy, and, at the same time, a narrow ethnocentric view of school literacy. All of his teachers have meant to encourage his growth and development as a literate person. Why, then, have they failed to acknowledge an important part of who he is and what he *culturally* brings to the school literacy program? Reyes (1992) argues that teachers often fail to make adjustments in their approaches to literacy for culturally and linguistically diverse learners because the majority of [teachers] are members of the dominant culture, implementing programs designed primarily for mainstream students. Teachers implementing these programs tend to treat students of color as exceptions to the norm, as students who should be assimilated into the dominant group, rather than accommodated according to their own needs. (p. 437)

Some theorists, researchers, and teachers may suggest the counter argument; that is, that elements of the mainstream culture are apparent in all "parallel cultures" and that it is easiest to teach to the mainstream (Hamilton, 1989).[12] I would argue that to ignore, consciously or not, the culture and language that each child brings to the literacy table is to mis-educate him or her. As the research by Au (1993), Morrow (1992), and Reyes and Laliberty (1992), among others, has shown, when cultural and linguistic adjustments are made to school literacy programs, all children benefit.

You may wonder if I have tried to inform Jake's teachers of the narrowness of the literacy lens through which they seem to be defining literacy development and instruction. I admit that I have failed miserably to take a strong stand. Rather than confront them about the lack of culturally responsive literacy instruction, I have expressed my concerns for Jake's personal literacy growth. For example, I have shared multicultural book lists with Jake's teachers and offered to serve as a resource. I have honestly wanted to inform Jake's teachers of two things: one, the need to be more sensitive in their approach to the language and cultural experiences that children bring to the classroom; and two, the need to incorporate more books written by people of color to legitimize the contributions of all literate people. Yet I have also believed that expressing my thoughts might jeopardize Jake's educational future with some kind of backlash.

A Status Report

While literacy theorists, researchers, and practitioners continue to suggest that school literacy is culturally neutral, Jake's literacy experiences offer an intimate and compelling argument that, as currently practiced, school literacy has been and still is narrowly defined in terms of culture. Only the packaging is new.

Descriptions of my conversation with Jake have met with lots of head nodding and similar stories from many of my non-White students. Delpit (1988) has shared similar insights into what she correctly describes as the "silenced dialogue." The commonsense response among some people of

[12] Recently, Hamilton (1989) used the term "parallel cultures" to refer to the historical experiences of domestic minorities in the United States. "Parallel" conveys a sense of coexistence with the more dominant European American culture so loosely referred to as American culture. The term "domestic minorities" is used to refer to minority groups that have a long history in this country (African Americans, Asian Americans, etc.) but whose forefathers and foremothers lived elsewhere — except in the case of Native Americans.

color to school literacy (and schooling in general) has been to take a "way things are" attitude. Many people of color understand that there are inequalities in the educational system; however, we also understand that little can be done without massive school reform. So, to be educated in our current system requires accepting that "this is the way things are. If you want to advance you must learn to play the game." That is, institutionalized racism is something we all know, but see as an unavoidable part of education in U.S. society.

In sharing my analysis with my graduate students, several European Americans have questioned why I refer to Jake's school literacy experiences as being narrowly defined and inquired what is so "acultural" about his literacy education. They ask, "Aren't literature-based and whole language programs built upon notions of constructivist theory that embrace notions of culture?" Of course, my students' understanding is correct: Current holistic school literacy programs support constructivist theory. I guess that's what is so frightening.

While the rhetoric of school literacy programs suggests that culture is part of the theoretical framework, "culture" has been narrowly defined to mean middle-class European American culture. The tacit assumption is, then, that all children are being well served by the new literacy programs that are built on the "natural" language acquisition of middle-class European American children. However, natural language acquisition is mediated through the particular culture in which the child lives. The reality, then, as shared in this article, is that theoreticians, researchers, teacher educators, practitioners, and publishers of literacy approaches and programs are frequently unaware of their assumptions.

Some may truly believe that they are delivering on their promise to build on the culture and language of the child, but what they have been unable, or unwilling, to acknowledge is that school literacy, as it exists, is not universal or reflective of the language and culture of many children. They claim that current school literacy programs and practices are acultural. These programs, however, clearly put some children at a disadvantage, while giving an advantage to others. It is clear, even to a nine-year-old, that school literacy is narrowly defined.

Discussion

In order to meet the needs of our U.S. society, which is rapidly becoming more culturally diverse, our literacy programs should offer more than sensitivity training, human relations, or attitudinal shifts to issues of culture and linguistic diversity. Programs are needed that will also help teachers transform their thinking about the role of language and culture in literacy development. It is simply not enough to inform teachers of what they do not know. Teachers need to question "cultural bumps," or mismatches in expectations of performance in literacy development (Garcia, 1994, personal communication). As Barnitz (1994) states, "Teachers must recognize difference as manifestations of cultural discourse which can be expanded rather than interrupted or suppressed" (p. 587).

What I see is an institutionalized racism that is grounded in the theories used to discuss literacy and to inform and educate teachers and teacher educators. I believe that we need to enhance pre-service teacher curricula and education. The current method of dispersing concepts of diversity, inclusivity, or multiculturalism across several courses, hoping students will synthesize these issues into a workable whole, has been ineffective. Pre-service teachers also need intensive education in understanding the dynamic role that culture plays in language and literacy development and in defining school literacy.

In a pre-service teacher education course I teach, I use literature authored by domestic minority men and women as a starting point for pre-service teachers to begin to reflect on their cultural assumptions about how they "read the word and the world" (Freire, 1985). The method has been effective in helping many students face their own, heretofore unvoiced, assumptions of their own culture and the cultures of other groups.

Most of my students are in their early twenties and have never really concerned themselves with issues of race. Even the students who are members of U.S. minority groups prefer not to discuss race, ethnicity, or culture openly. At the opening of class, for example, many of my students think that their cultural understanding will not affect the students they teach. They believe that their most important concern should be the subject matter and how to transmit effectively a love for their subject to their students. Some of my students also have difficulty understanding the notion of institutionalized racism in U.S. public education. It is at this point in the course that I begin to share the daily occurrences in the lives of my children. Further, some of my European American students see themselves only as "American" and do not wish to deal with their heritage. They want to minimize any tie to Europe and only concentrate on their "Americanness." Some students believe that most U.S. minority group members are poor people, and that most poor people (from all racial groups, but especially those seen most frequently in the media — African Americans and Latinos) really don't care about their children's education. Some also think that children from minority groups don't care about their own education. Most of my students have not even considered how to prepare to teach in multicultural or multilingual classrooms. They tend to live under the false assumption that they can get jobs in homogeneous, suburban school districts.

As in most pre-service teacher education courses nationwide, my students are predominantly European American women. However, in each of my classes, I have had at least one U.S. minority group member. The presence of members from these groups has helped give voice to the concerns of their various communities. My courses are elective, which I believe is important, because it means that the students in my class are interested in issues of diversity. In the best of all worlds, all students would be so inclined, but they are not.

One of the first things I do to help my students become aware of their own cultural understandings is to have them write an autobiographical essay. The essay requires them to trace their ancestry over four or five generations, and to explain their families' use of language, food traditions, and other interesting cultural habits. The essays are shared first in small groups and then with the whole class. In this way, students can readily understand that everyone is a product of their culture, knowingly or not. I too share my cultural and ethnic background. As a person of African, Native, and European American descent, yet who looks only African American, I use my background and life as a springboard for discussions of students' cultural diversity and the limited conception of "culture" in most schools. Since this is a semester-long course, we have the time to engage in many activities, such as community and faculty presentations, videos, and readings by U.S. minority members. However, I believe that some of the most productive work occurs in the small group discussions my students have with each other as they respond to literature written by U.S. minority group members. For example, recently we read a number of novels written by Asian Americans. Many of my students had not heard of the internment of Japanese Americans during World War II.

After my students and I have reflected upon the cultural assumptions from which we perceive our world (and those worlds that might differ from our own), we begin to address teachers' roles and how their cultural assumptions affect the decisions they make, their interactions with students, and their selection of teaching materials. I then give the students opportunities to use their growing understanding of cultural knowledge in lessons they design and teach. My students are all required to teach two literacy lessons during the semester. Many of them choose activities that require participants to work together in cooperative learning groups. Four examples come to mind. One student asked each of us to recall an event using the Native American concept of a "skin story" — drawing on animal pelts — to create pictograph symbols to relate that event. Another student separated class members by attributes they could not control (gender, hair color, size of feet). The "minority" group members (men in this case) were seated in the front of the classroom and were the only students the leader of the exercise asked to respond to her questions. In a third example, a student distributed a series of photographs to small groups and had each group classify the people in the photos, rating them on attributes such as who appeared most intelligent, most successful, and nicest. Finally, a student asked us to read current newspaper articles about war-torn countries and write a diary entry or letter to a government official from the perspective of someone in the country.

Through such exercises and activities, my students have learned that culture is a complex issue, one that cannot be taken lightly. They learn to think and act reflectively and become predisposed to considering issues of race, class, gender, age, and sexual preference. Moreover, they understand that their decisions must be based on more than theory; they must also consider the interrelationship of power and knowledge.

I also design in-class lessons around students' responses to the authentic texts they have read. Throughout their field experiences, I have been impressed by the culturally responsive approach to literacy and literature that many of my students have taken with them into the field. For example, one of my students invited recent Asian immigrants to her eighth-grade class to be interviewed by her students. She believed that the face-to-face interactions her students had during the interviews allowed them to understand better the hardships endured by the new U.S. citizens. Another student taught *Huckleberry Finn.* She began the lesson by sharing the historical context in which the novel was written, a model I insist each student use in my class. When confronted by an African American student about the use of the word "nigger" in the novel, she was able to facilitate a group discussion on the use of derogatory terms. She believed that membership in my class enabled her to deal openly with the student and the offensive term. Her experience demonstrates that it is possible to create multicultural learning communities within classrooms that are based on critical literacy theory that validates and legitimizes all learners.

Conclusion

In this article, I have argued that for school literacy to begin to move beyond its "neutral" conception of culture, educators at all levels must acknowledge the role and importance of more than one culture in defining school literacy. Educators have not effectively built upon the culture and language of every child, and have set arbitrary standards of acceptance and defined them as normative. I have also argued for the reconceptualization and program development of school literacy, not to dismantle, but to strengthen, literacy frameworks. We can and must do a better job of inviting all students to the literacy table and including them in conversations on school literacy.

I had initial misgivings about sharing my conversation with Jake, as I feared that my thinking would be misinterpreted. My fears lay with the "predictable inability" (West, 1993) of some European Americans to consider honestly the shortcomings of programs they espouse as universal. In addition, I was concerned that my colleagues would view the conversation as one isolated event, ignoring the fact that there are countless instances of narrow cultural constructions of literacy in the daily lives of culturally and linguistically diverse children. I was also reluctant to give such an intimate look into my private world. Therefore, I hope that sharing the incident opens conversations about reconceptualizing and reforming school literacy. When I wonder if I've done the right thing, I recall Jake saying to his older brothers, "I want to share a picture of my real self."

References

Apple, M. (1992). The text and cultural politics. *Educational Researcher, 21*(7), 4–11, 19.

Au, K. (1993). *Literacy instruction in multicultural settings.* Fort Worth, TX: Harcourt Brace Jovanovich.

Barnitz, J. (1994). Discourse diversity: Principles for authentic talk and literacy instruction. *Journal of Reading, 37,* 586–591.

Barrera, R. (1992). The cultural gap in literature-based literacy instruction. *Education and Urban Society, 24,* 227–243.

Cook-Gumperz, J. (Ed). (1986). *The social construction of literacy.* Cambridge, Eng.: Cambridge University Press.

Cose, E. (1993). *The rage of a privileged class.* New York: Harper Collins.

Darder, A. (1991). *Culture and power in the classroom: A critical foundation for bicultural education.* New York: Bergin & Garvey.

Delpit, L. (1986). Skills and other dilemmas of a progressive Black educator. *Harvard Educational Review, 56,* 379–385.

Delpit, L. (1988). The silenced dialogue: Power and pedagogy in educating other people's children. *Harvard Educational Review, 58,* 280–298.

Delpit, L. (1991). A conversation with Lisa Delpit. *Language Arts, 68,* 541–547.

Delpit, L. (1993). The politics of teaching literate discourse. In T. Perry & J. Fraser (Eds.), *Freedom's plow: Teaching in the multicultural classroom* (pp. 285–295). New York: Routledge.

DuBois, W. E. B. (1965). *The souls of Black folks.* New York: Bantam. (Original work published in 1903)

Ellison, R. (1952). *Invisible man.* New York: Random House.

Fine, M. (1987). Silencing in public schools. *Language Arts, 64,* 157–174.

Freire, P. (1985). Reading the world and the word: An interview with Paulo Freire. *Language Arts, 62,* 15–21.

Freire, P., & Macedo, D. (1987). *Literacy: Reading the world and the word.* South Hadley, MA: Bergin & Garvey.

Giroux, H. (1987). Critical literacy and student experience: Donald Graves' approach to literacy. *Language Arts, 64,* 175–181.

Goodman, K. (1986). *What's whole in whole language?* Portsmouth, NH: Heinemann.

Goodman, K. (1989). Whole-language research: Foundations and development. *Elementary School Journal, 90,* 207–221.

Gutierrez, K. (1992). A comparison of instructional contexts in writing process classrooms with Latino children. *Education and Urban Society, 24,* 244–262.

Halliday, M. (1975). *Learn how to mean.* London: Edward Arnold.

Hamilton, V. (1989). Acceptance speech, Boston Globe-Horn Book Award, 1988. *Horn Book, 65*(2), 183.

Heath, S. (1983). *Ways with words: Language, life and work in the communities and classrooms.* Cambridge, Eng.: Cambridge University Press.

Hirsch, E. (1987). *Cultural literacy: What every American needs to know.* Boston: Houghton Mifflin.

Hughes, L. (1951). Theme for English B. In L. Hughes, *Montage of a dream deferred* (pp. 39–40). New York: Henry Holt.

Labov, W. (1972). The logic of nonstandard English. In R. D. Abrahams & R. C. Troike (Eds.), *Language and cultural diversity in American education* (pp. 225–261). Englewood Cliffs, NJ: Prentice-Hall.

McLaren, P. (1988). Culture or canon? Critical pedagogy and the politics of literacy. *Harvard Educational Review, 58,* 213–234.

Meek, M. (1982). *Learning to read.* Portsmouth, NH: Heinemann.

Morrison, T. (1992). *Playing in the dark: Whiteness and the literary imagination.* Cambridge, MA: Harvard University Press.

Morrow, L. (1992). The impact of a literature-based program on literacy achievement, use of literature, and attitudes of children from minority backgrounds. *Reading Research Quarterly, 27,* 251–275.

Ovando, C., & Collier, V. (1985). *Bilingual and ESL classrooms: Teaching in multicultural contexts.* New York: McGraw-Hill.

Reyes, M. de la Luz. (1992). Challenging venerable assumptions: Literacy instruction for linguistically different students. *Harvard Educational Review, 62,* 427–446.

Reyes, M. de la Luz, & Laliberty, E. (1992). A teacher's "Pied Piper" effect on young authors. *Education and Urban Society, 24,* 263–278.

Reyes, M. de la Luz, & Molner, L. (1991). Instructional strategies for second-language learners in content areas. *Journal of Reading, 35,* 96–103.

Sawyer, D., & Rodriguez, C. (1992). How native Canadians view literacy: A summary of findings. *Journal of Reading, 36,* 284–293.

Scheurich, J. (1992). Toward a White discourse on White racism. *Educational Researcher, 22*(8), 5–10.

West, C. (1993). *Race matters.* Boston: Beacon Press.

Woodson, C. (1990). *The mis-education of the Negro.* Nashville, TN: Winston-Derek. (Original work published 1933)

Vygotsky, L. (1978). *Mind in society.* Cambridge, MA: Harvard University Press.

Because You Like Us:
The Language of Control

—■—■—■—

CYNTHIA BALLENGER

T his article is the result of a year spent in conversations about teaching — difficult conversations in which I, a seasoned teacher and fledgling sociolinguist, was only rarely the informed party.[1] Mike Rose, in *Lives on the Boundary* (1989), uses the metaphor of "entering the conversation" to describe the process of learning to participate in academic discourse. In my case, there was a multitude of different conversations I was trying to enter, and in each I had a different role to play.

During that same time I was teaching preschool, as I have done for most of the past fifteen years. The school was in the Haitian community in Dorchester, Massachusetts, and primarily served the children of Haitian immigrants. I went there because in my previous work as an early childhood special education teacher I had noticed that more and more Haitian children were being referred to my class. These children were arriving attended by all kinds of concerns from the educational professionals: they were "wild," they had "no language," their mothers were "depressed." There were certainly some children I saw who had genuine problems, and yet time and time again I found that, after a period of adjustment, they were responsive, intelligent children; their mothers were perhaps homesick and unhappy in a strange, cold country, but generally not clinically depressed. During that period, however, we did make many mistakes, and I became interested in learning the Haitian culture and language in order to see the children more

[1] Earlier versions of this work have been presented at the Penn Ethnography in Educational Research Forum in February 1991 and the Brookline Teacher-Researcher Seminar in June 1990. My research was carried out as a member of that seminar with teachers and children at my school. In this article, all teachers' and children's names have been changed.

Harvard Educational Review Vol. 62 No. 2 Summer 1992, 199–208

clearly. After a period of graduate school studying sociolinguistics, I took a position as a preschool teacher in a bilingual school where both Haitian Creole and English were spoken and where, as I came to understand, Haitian culture was quite central. I was the only teacher at this school who was not Haitian and, although by this time I spoke Creole, I was still getting to know the culture.

During that time I was one of two instructors of a course in child development that a local college offered for Haitian people who wished to work in day-care centers. My Haitian co-instructor and I designed this course based on the model of a conversation about child rearing — a dialogue between Haitians and North Americans about their attitudes on the subject. I was also a new member of the Brookline Teacher-Researcher Seminar (BTRS), a group of public school teachers and academic researchers who are attempting to develop a common language and a shared set of values with which to approach classroom issues (Michaels & O'Connor, in press; Phillips, 1991). As a graduate student in sociolinguistics, I had done research; as a teacher, I had thought about teaching; I was now involved in trying to approach issues in ways that incorporated both of these perspectives. The work that I will report on here was part of these conversations. I will try to let the reader hear some of the different voices that I heard.

In this article, I will discuss the process I went through in learning to control a class of four-year-old Haitian children. Researchers who regard language as the principal vehicle by which children are socialized into their particular family and culture have consistently regarded control and discipline as central events — events where language patterns and cultural values intersect in visible ways (Boggs, 1985; Cook-Gumperz, 1973; Watson-Gegeo & Gegeo, 1990). When, as in my case, the adult does not share the same cultural background and the same experience of socialization as the children, one becomes very aware of learning how to enter and manage the relevant conversation. Although it can be argued that my participation in the events I relate here was in some ways informed by sociolinguistic theory, I present this more as a story than as a research report. This is my attempt to discuss this experience in a way that will not deny access to the conversation to those who helped form my understanding of it. I must stress, however, that all of these conversations would not have been possible if there hadn't been room in the preschool day for talk — the school was run jointly by the teachers and we spent considerable time each day together — and if there had not been some financial support for the Brookline Teacher-Researcher Seminar (Phillips, 1991). This support, in the form of small stipends, photocopying, money for an occasional day off to reflect, and a sense of being valued, combined with the nature of the school where I was teaching, made my situation luxurious compared with that of many teachers faced with problems similar to mine.

The Problem

Having had many years of experience teaching in early childhood programs, I did not expect to have problems when I came to this Haitian preschool three years ago. However, I did. The children ran me ragged. In the friendliest, most cheerful, and affectionate manner imaginable, my class of four-year-olds followed their own inclinations rather than my directions in almost everything. Though I claim to be a person who does not need to have a great deal of control, in this case I had very little — and I did not like it.

My frustration increased when I looked at the other classrooms at my school. I had no notice that the other teachers, all Haitian women, had orderly classrooms of children who, in an equally affectionate and cheerful manner, *did* follow directions and kept the confusion to a level that I could have tolerated. The problem, evidently, did not reside in the children, since the Haitian teachers managed them well enough. Where then did it reside? What was it that the Haitian teachers did that I did not do?

The group of Haitian preschool teachers whom I was teaching in the child-development course recognized the problem in their own terms. As part of the course, they were all interning in various day-care centers, some with me at the Haitian school, the majority in other centers. Many of the teachers in the other centers were extremely concerned about behavior problems. What they told me and each other was that many of the children in their centers were behaving very poorly; many felt that this was particularly true of the Haitian children. They felt that the way in which they were being instructed as teachers to deal with the children's behavior was not effective. One woman explained to me that when she was hit by a four-year-old, she was instructed to acknowledge the anger he must be feeling, then to explain to him that he could not hit her. She told me that, from her point of view, this was the same as suggesting politely, "Why don't you hit me again?"

When I talked with Haitian parents at my school, I again heard similar complaints. From the point of view of many of the people I talked with, the behavior tolerated in their neighborhood schools was disrespectful; the children were allowed to misbehave. A common refrain in these conversations was, "We're losing a generation of children"; that is, the young children here now, who were not brought up first in Haiti, were not being brought up with the same values. However, when I asked for specific advice about things I might do to manage the children better, the teachers and I could never identify any behaviors of mine that I could try to change.

I took my problem to the Brookline Teacher-Researcher Seminar. The members of BTRS have come to share a focus on language — the language of instruction; children's language in a wide variety of situations; the language of science talk, of book talk, of conflict; and so on. Thus, in our conversations, the BTRS group encouraged me to approach my problem by discovering what it was that the Haitian teachers *said* to the children in situations where directions were being given. The Seminar members have also come to believe that an important part of a research project is examining where a particular research question comes from in one's own life — why it seems important, what its value is to the teacher-researcher. In many cases, this is a matter of investigating one's own socialization, a kind of self-reflection that became an important part of my investigation.

Situations as Texts

I began to write down what the Haitian teachers said to the children in situations where the children's behavior was at issue. I then carried these texts to the various conversations of which I was a part: the Haitian teachers in the child development course, the North American teachers in the Brookline Seminar, and the parents and teachers at the school where I was teaching. I will present here some texts that I consider typical in their form and content, and then share some of the responses and the thinking engendered by these texts among the people with whom I had been conversing.

I present first Clothilde's account of an event at her day-care center. Clothilde is a middle-aged Haitian woman and a student in the child-development course. She has a great deal of experience with children — both from raising her own and from caring for other people's — and many of her classmates turn to her for advice. The text below is from a conversation in which she had been complaining to me about the behavior of the Haitian children in the day-care center where she was student teaching. She felt that the North American teachers were not controlling the children adequately.

One day, as Clothilde arrived at her school, she watched a teacher telling a little Haitian child that the child needed to go into her classroom, that she could not stay alone in the hall. The child refused and eventually kicked the teacher. Clothilde had had enough. She asked the director to bring her all the Haitian kids right away. The director and Clothilde gathered the children into the large common room. The following is the text of what she told me she said to the children:

> *Clothilde:* Does your mother let you bite?
>
> *Children:* No.
>
> *Clothilde:* Does your father let you punch kids?
>
> *Children:* No.
>
> *Clothilde:* Do you kick at home?
>
> *Children:* No.
>
> *Clothilde:* You don't respect anyone, not the teachers who play with you or the adults who work upstairs. You need to respect adults — even people you see on the streets. You are taking good ways you learn at home and not bringing them to school. You're taking the bad things you learn at school and taking them home. You're not going to do this anymore. Do you want your parents to be ashamed of you?

According to Clothilde, the Haitian children have been well-behaved ever since. Other Haitian teachers with whom I have shared this text have confirmed that that was what the children needed to hear. However, they also said that Clothilde will have to repeat her speech because the children won't remain well-behaved indefinitely without a reminder.

The next text involves an incident at my school. Josiane, who has taught for many years both here and in Haiti, was reprimanding a group of children who had been making a lot of noise while their teacher was trying to give them directions:

Josiane: When your mother talks to you, don't you listen?

Children: Yes.

Josiane: When your mother says, go get something, don't you go get it?

Children: Yes.

Josiane: When your mother says, go to the bathroom, don't you go?

Children: Yes.

Josiane: You know why I'm telling you this. Because I want you to be good children. When an adult talks to you, you're supposed to listen so you will become a good person. The adults here like you, they want you to become good children.

Finally, we have Jérémie's father speaking to him. Jérémie is a very active four-year-old, and the staff had asked his father for help in controlling his behavior:

Father: Are you going to be good? (Jérémie nods at each pause)

Are you going to listen to Miss Cindy?

Are you going to listen to Miss Josiane?

Because they like you.

They love you.

Do it for me.

Do it for God.

Do you like God?

God loves you.

Reflecting

The content and the form of these texts are different from what I, and many other North American teachers, would probably have said in the same circumstances. I shared these and other texts and observations with many parents and teachers, both Haitian and North American. I asked them to reflect with me on how these conversations were different and what underlay them. What follows is a blend of many people's observations and self-reflections, including my own. Here I want to note that I am assuming that the North American teachers, including myself, shared similar training and enculturation. Although we differed in many ways, I would characterize our culture — as Heath does in *Ways with Words* (1983) — as "mainstream culture." The Haitian teachers also shared some, although not all, values and assumptions. Although I am trying to distill these conversations in order to identify "typical" practices of Haitian or North American teachers, I do not mean to imply that all North American or all Haitian teachers are the same.

The Haitian preschool teachers had clear insights into behavior characteristic of North American teachers. Clothilde commented that the North American teachers she knows frequently refer to the children's internal states and interpret their feelings for them; for example, "you must be angry," "it's hard for you when your friend does that," and so on. Clothilde pointed out to me that in her speech she makes no reference to the children's emotions; other Haitian teachers I have observed also do not do this as a rule.

Rose, another Haitian teacher, also commented that North American teachers often make reference to particular factors in the child's situation that, in the teacher's opinion, may have influenced his or her behavior. For example, Michel, whose mother had left him, was often told that the teachers understood that he missed his mother, but that he nevertheless needed to share his toys. When a child pushes or pinches another child sitting next to him or her, many North American teachers will suggest that, if the child does not like people to sit so close, he or she should say so rather than pinch. Rose felt, and from my observation I concurred, that Haitian teachers rarely do this. Josiane suggested further that if she were concerned about an individual child and his or her particular problems, instead of articulating them for him or her, her goal would be "to make him or her feel comfortable with the group." If the child were misbehaving, she felt she would say, "You know I'm your friend," and then remind him or her that "we don't do that." In fact, I have seen her do exactly that many times, with excellent results.

These examples suggest to me a difference in focus between the North American and Haitian teachers. It seems that North American teachers characteristically are concerned with making a connection with the individual child, with articulating his or her feelings and problems. On the other hand, Clothilde, Josiane, and the many other Haitian people I spoke with and observed, emphasize the group in their control talk, articulating the values and responsibilities of group membership. For example, we have seen that both North American and Haitian teachers make reference to the family, but in different ways. North American teachers are likely to mention particular characteristics of a child's family, characteristics that are specific to that family and are seen as perhaps responsible for the child's individual actions. The Haitian teachers emphasize instead what the families have in common. The families do not differ in their desire that the children respect adults, that the children behave properly, and that their behavior not shame them.

The children's answers, when they are given in unison as in Josiane's text above, present a vivid enactment of the sort of unity the Haitian teachers' approach may engender.

Another difference the Haitian teachers noted is the use of consequences. North American teachers typically present the particular consequences of an act of misbehavior. For example, I often say something like, "He's crying because you hit him," or, "If you don't listen to me, you won't know what to do." Haitian teachers are less likely to differentiate among particular kinds of misbehavior; they condemn them all, less in terms of their results than as examples of "bad" behavior. Clothilde is typical of the Haitian teachers in that the immediate consequences are not made explicit; she does not explain why she is against biting or punching. She instead refers to such behavior as "bad," and then explains to the children the consequences of bad behavior in general, such as shame for the family. Jérémie's father simply tells Jérémie to be good, to be good for those who love him. Josiane, too, tells the children to be good because the people who like them want them to be good. I have heard other Haitian teachers refer to the impression that bad behavior would create in a passer-by, or to the necessity of modeling good behavior for younger children. But Haitian teachers rarely mention the specific consequences of particular acts, a clear difference from North American teachers.

In the Haitian texts, one has the impression that the children share the adult's understanding of what bad behavior is. Clothilde's series of rhetorical questions, like "Do your parents let you kick?", is an example of the form that many Haitian teachers adopt when addressing children about their behavior. The children understand their role without difficulty; they repeat the expected answers in choral unison. The choice of this form — that is, questions to which the answer is assumed — emphasizes the fact that the children already know that their behavior is wrong.

In the North American control situation, on the other hand, the child often appears to be receiving new information. If there is a consensus about behavior — certain behavior is bad, certain other behavior is good — we don't present it this way. North Americans frequently explain the consequences of particular actions as if they were trying to convince the child that there was a problem with his or her behavior. As presented in school, misbehavior is considered wrong not because of anything inherent in it, but because of its particular consequences, or perhaps because the behavior stems from feelings that the child has failed to identify and control.

These differences, as I came to recognize them, seemed significant enough to account for some of the difficulties I had been experiencing in my classroom. But what to do about them?

Practice

With the overwhelming evidence that these children were used to a kind of control talk other than what I had been providing, I have since begun to adopt some of the style of the Haitian teachers. I assume that I am not very good at it, that I have no idea of the nuances, and I continue to include many of the ways I have typically managed behavior in my teaching. Nevertheless, I have developed a more or less stable melange of styles, and my control in the classroom has improved significantly. In addition, I find that I love trying out this Haitian way. I was struck by an experience I had the other day, when I was reprimanding one boy for pinching another. I was focusing, in the Haitian manner, on his prior, indisputable knowledge that pinching was simply no good. I also used my best approximation of the facial expression and tone of voice that I see the Haitian teachers use in these encounters. I can tell when I have it more or less right, because of the way that the children pay attention. As I finished this particular time, the other children, who had been rapt, all solemnly thanked me. They were perhaps feeling in danger of being pinched and felt that I had at last been effective. This solemn sort of response, which has occurred a few other times, gives me the sense that these situations are very important to them.

The following anecdote may suggest more about the way in which these interactions are important to the children. Recently I was angrily reprimanding the children about their failure to wait for me while crossing the parking lot:

Cindy: Did I tell you to go?

Children: No.

Cindy: Can you cross this parking lot by yourselves?

Children: No.

Cindy: That's right. There are cars here. They're dangerous. I don't want you to go alone. Why do I want you to wait for me, do you know?

"Yes," says Claudette, "because you like us."

Although I was following the usual Haitian form — rhetorical questions with "no" answers — I had been expecting a final response based on the North American system of cause and effect, something like, "Because the cars are dangerous." Claudette, however, although she understands perfectly well the dangers of cars to small children, does not expect to use that information in this kind of an interaction. What, then, *is* she telling me? One thing that she is saying, which is perhaps what the solemn children also meant, is that, from her point of view, there is intimacy in this kind of talk. This is certainly the feeling I get from these experiences. I feel especially connected to the children in those instances in which I seem to have gotten it right.

The Larger Context

North American teachers generally think of reprimands — particularly of young children who are just learning to control their behavior — as put-downs, and are reluctant to give them. North American preschool teachers, in particular, will take great pains to avoid saying "no" or "don't." In contrast, I have learned from working with Haitian children and teachers that there are situations in which reprimands can be confirming, can strengthen relationships, and can, in a sense, define relationships for the child, as seems to have been the case for Claudette in the example given above.

Such an opportunity may be lost when we go to great lengths to avoid actually telling a child that he is wrong, that we disagree or disapprove. When we look at the difference between the ways in which things are done at home and at school, and the negative consequences that may result from these mismatches for children coming from minority cultural backgrounds, the area of misbehavior and the way it is responded to seem particularly important because it affects so directly the nature of the relationship between child and teacher.

I was not unaware when I began that this subject was a hotbed of disagreement: North Americans perceive Haitians as too severe, both verbally and in their use of physical punishment, while Haitians often perceive North American children as being extraordinarily fresh and out of control.[2] Haitian immigrant parents here are at once ashamed and defiantly supportive of their community's disciplinary standards and methods. In order to represent the views of Haitians I spoke with independent of my process of understanding, I asked them to reflect again on our two cultures after they had heard my interpretations.

People, of course, offered many varied points of view, yet everybody emphasized a sense of having grown up very "protected" in Haiti, of having been safe there both from getting into serious trouble and from harm. This sense of being protected was largely based on their understanding that their entire extended family, as well as many people in the community, were involved in their upbringing. Haitian families in the United States, some pointed out, are smaller and less extended. The community here, while tight in many ways, is more loosely connected than in Haiti. This change in social structure was bemoaned by the people I spoke with, especially with reference to bringing up children. They attributed to this change their sense that this generation of children, particularly those born here, is increasingly at risk. They

---

[2] It must be stated that the consequences of this disagreement are, of course, vastly more painful for the powerless. Contact with schools, with social service institutions, with the police, is in many cases highly problematic for Haitian families. The Haitian family, in these situations, is frequently met with a lack of understanding that leads easily to a lack of respect. Mainstream assumptions about "proper" ways of talking and dealing with children's behavior often stand in the way of distinguishing a functioning family, for example, from a dysfunctional one, in distinguishing a child whose parents are strict in order to help him or her succeed from one whose family simply does not want to deal with the child's problems. Such assumptions often stand in the path of appropriate help as well. The school where I taught was often called upon to discuss cultural differences with social service groups, hospitals, and other schools. Occasionally, we were asked to provide some assistance for particular cases. But, of course, there were countless instances in which Haitian families were involved with these various powerful institutions and the families were without such aid.

are at risk not only of falling away from their parents' culture, but also, and consequently, of falling prey to the drugs, crime, and other problems of urban life that they see around them.

And yet everyone I spoke with also recalled some pain in their growing up, pain they relate to the respect and obedience they were required to exhibit to all adults, which at times conflicted with their own developing desire to state their opinions or make their own choices. This pain was nevertheless not to be discarded lightly. For many of the Haitian people with whom I spoke, religious values underlie these twin issues of respect and obedience; respect for parents and other adults is an analogue for respect and obedience to God and God's law.

Many people seemed to agree with the ambivalence expressed by one Haitian lawyer and mother who told me that, while she had suffered as a child because of the uncompromising obedience and respect demanded of her in her family, she continued to see respect as a value she needed to impart to her children. She said to me, "There must be many other ways to teach respect." She was one of many Haitians who told me of instances where a child from a poor family, a child with neither the clothes nor the supplies for school, had succeeded eventually in becoming a doctor or a lawyer. In these accounts, as in her own case, it is in large measure the strictness of the family that is regarded as the source of the child's accomplishment, rather than the talent or the power of the individual.

Presumably, there is some tension in all societies between individual and community. In these accounts is some suggestion of the form this tension sometimes takes within Haitian culture. For my part, I am struck and troubled by the powerful individualism underlying the approach I characterize as typical of me and many North American teachers. It appears that North Americans do speak as if something like the child's "enlightened self-interest" were the ultimate moral guidepost. In comparison to the language used by the Haitian teachers, North American teachers' language seems to place very little emphasis on shared values, on a moral community.

The process of gaining multicultural understanding in education must, in my opinion, be a dual one. On the one hand, cultural behavior that at first seems strange and inexplicable should become familiar; on the other hand, one's own familiar values and practices should become at least temporarily strange, subject to examination. In addition to the information I have gained that helps me to manage and form relationships with Haitian children in my classroom, I also value greatly the extent to which these conversations, by forcing me to attempt to empathize with and understand a view of the world that is in many ways very different from my customary one, have put me in a position to reexamine values and principles that had become inaccessible under layers of assumptions.

I am not teaching Haitian children this year, although I continue to visit them. Next year I expect to have a classroom with children from a wide range of backgrounds. It is difficult to say how my last experience will illuminate the next — or, analogously, how my experience can be of use to teachers in different kinds of classrooms. I do believe that teachers need to try to open up and to understand both our own assumptions and the cultural meaning that children from all backgrounds bring to school. It seems to me that accommodation must be made on all sides so that no group has to abandon the ways in which it is accustomed to passing on its values. I have been fortunate that the knowledge and collaboration of so many people, Haitian and North American, were available to help me begin to understand my own experience. All of these conversations have been their own rewards — I have made new friends and, I believe, become a better teacher.

References

Boggs, S. (1985). *Speaking, talking and relating: A study of Hawaiian children at home and at school.* Norwood, NJ: Ablex.

Cook-Gumperz, J. (1973). *Social control and socialization.* London: Routledge & Kegan Paul.

Heath, S. B. (1983). *Ways with words.* Cambridge, Eng.: Cambridge University Press.

Michaels, S., & O'Connor, M. C. (in press). *Literacy as reasoning within multiple discourses: Implications for policy and educational reform.* Newton, MA: Education Development Center.

Phillips, A. (February, 1991). *Hearing children's stories: A report on the Brookline Teacher-Researcher Seminar.* Paper presented at the Penn Ethnography in Educational Research Forum, Philadelphia, PA.

Rose, M. (1989). *Lives on the boundary.* New York: Penguin.

Watson-Gegeo, K., & Gegeo, D. (1990). *Disentangling: The discourse of conflict and therapy in the Pacific Islands.* Norwood, NJ: Ablex.

Talking about Race,
Learning about Racism:
The Application of Racial Identity
Development Theory in the Classroom

—■—■—■—

BEVERLY DANIEL TATUM

s many educational institutions struggle to become more multicultural in terms of their students, faculty, and staff, they also begin to examine issues of cultural representation within their curriculum. This examination has evoked a growing number of courses that give specific consideration to the effect of variables such as race, class, and gender on human experience — an important trend that is reflected and supported by the increasing availability of resource manuals for the modification of course content (Bronstein & Quina, 1988; Hull, Scott, & Smith, 1982; Schuster & Van Dyne, 1985).

Unfortunately, less attention has been given to the issues of process that inevitably emerge in the classroom when attention is focused on race, class, and/or gender. It is very difficult to talk about these concepts in a meaningful way without also talking and learning about racism, classism, and sexism.[1] The introduction of these issues of oppression often generates powerful emotional responses in students that range from guilt and shame to anger and despair. If not addressed, these emotional responses can result in student resistance to oppression-related content areas. Such resistance can ultimately interfere with the cognitive understanding and mastery of the material. This resistance and potential interference is particularly common when specifically addressing issues of race and racism. Yet, when students are given the opportunity to explore race-related material in a classroom where both

---

[1] A similar point could be made about other issues of oppression, such as anti-Semitism, homophobia and heterosexism, ageism, and so on.

Harvard Educational Review Vol. 62 No. 1 Spring 1992, 1–24

their affective and intellectual responses are acknowledged and addressed, their level of understanding is greatly enhanced.

This article seeks to provide a framework for understanding students' psychological responses to race-related content and the student resistance that can result, as well as some strategies for overcoming this resistance. It is informed by more than a decade of experience as an African American engaged in teaching an undergraduate course on the psychology of racism, by thematic analyses of student journals and essays written for the racism class, and by an understanding and application of racial identity development theory (Helms, 1990).

Setting the Context

As a clinical psychologist with a research interest in racial identity development among African American youth raised in predominantly White communities, I began teaching about racism quite fortuitously. In 1980, while I was a part-time lecturer in the Black Studies department of a large public university, I was invited to teach a course called Group Exploration of Racism (Black Studies 2). A requirement for Black Studies majors, the course had to be offered, yet the instructor who regularly taught the course was no longer affiliated with the institution. Armed with a folder full of handouts, old syllabi that the previous instructor left behind, a copy of *White Awareness: Handbook for Anti-racism Training* (Katz, 1978), and my own clinical skills as a group facilitator, I constructed a course that seemed to meet the goals already outlined in the course catalogue. Designed "to provide students with an understanding of the psychological causes and emotional reality of racism as it appears in everyday life," the course incorporated the use of lectures, readings, simulation exercises, group research projects, and extensive class discussion to help students explore the psychological impact of racism on both the oppressor and the oppressed.

Though my first efforts were tentative, the results were powerful. The students in my class, most of whom were White, repeatedly described the course in their evaluations as one of the most valuable educational experiences of their college careers. I was convinced that helping students understand the ways in which racism operates in their own lives, and what they could do about it, was a social responsibility that I should accept. The freedom to institute the course in the curriculum of the psychology departments in which I would eventually teach became a personal condition of employment. I have successfully introduced the course in each new educational setting I have been in since leaving that university.

Since 1980, I have taught the course (now called the Psychology of Racism) eighteen times, at three different institutions. Although each of these schools is very different — a large public university, a small state college, and a private, elite women's college — the challenges of teaching about racism in each setting have been more similar than different.

In all of the settings, class size has been limited to thirty students (averaging twenty-four). Though typically predominantly White and female (even in coeducational settings), the class make-up has always been mixed in terms of both race and gender. The students of color who have taken the course include Asians and Latinos/as, but most frequently the students of color have been Black. Though most students have described themselves as middle class, all socioeconomic backgrounds (ranging from very poor to very wealthy) have been represented over the years.

The course has necessarily evolved in response to my own deepening awareness of the psychological legacy of racism and my expanding awareness of other forms of oppression, although the basic format has remained the same. Our weekly three-hour class meeting is held in a room with movable chairs, arranged in a circle. The physical structure communicates an important premise of the course — that I expect the students to speak with each other as well as with me.

My other expectations (timely completion of assignments, regular class attendance) are clearly communicated in our first class meeting, along with the assumptions and guidelines for discussion that I rely upon to guide our work together. Because the assumptions and guidelines are so central to the process of talking and learning about racism, it may be useful to outline them here.

Working Assumptions

1. Racism, defined as a "system of advantage based on race" (see Wellman, 1977), is a pervasive aspect of U.S. socialization. It is virtually impossible to live in U.S. contemporary society and not be exposed to some aspect of the personal, cultural, and/or institutional manifestations of racism in our society. It is also assumed that, as a result, all of us have received some misinformation about those groups disadvantaged by racism.

2. Prejudice, defined as a "preconceived judgment or opinion, often based on limited information," is clearly distinguished from racism (see Katz, 1978). I assume that all of us may have prejudices as a result of the various cultural stereotypes to which we have been exposed. Even when these preconceived ideas have positive associations (such as "Asian students are good in math"), they have negative effects because they deny a person's individuality. These attitudes may influence the individual behaviors of people of color as well as of Whites, and may affect intergroup as well as intragroup interaction. However, a distinction must be made between the negative racial attitudes held by individuals of color and White individuals, because it is only the attitudes of Whites that routinely carry with them the social power inherent in the systematic cultural reinforcement and institutionalization of those racial prejudices. To distinguish the prejudices of students of color from the racism of White students is *not* to say that the former is acceptable and the latter is not; both are clearly problematic. The distinction is important, how-

ever, to identify the power differential between members of dominant and subordinate groups.

3. In the context of U.S. society, the system of advantage clearly operates to benefit Whites as a group. However, it is assumed that racism, like other forms of oppression, hurts members of the privileged group as well as those targeted by racism. While the impact of racism on Whites is clearly different from its impact on people of color, racism has negative ramifications for everyone. For example, some White students might remember the pain of having lost important relationships because Black friends were not allowed to visit their homes. Others may express sadness at having been denied access to a broad range of experiences because of social segregation. These individuals often attribute the discomfort or fear they now experience in racially mixed settings to the cultural limitations of their youth.

4. Because of the prejudice and racism inherent in our environments when we were children, I assume that we cannot be blamed for learning what we were taught (intentionally or unintentionally). Yet as adults, we have a responsibility to try to identify and interrupt the cycle of oppression. When we recognize that we have been misinformed, we have a responsibility to seek out more accurate information and to adjust our behavior accordingly.

5. It is assumed that change, both individual and institutional, is possible. Understanding and unlearning prejudice and racism is a lifelong process that may have begun prior to enrolling in this class, and which will surely continue after the course is over. Each of us may be at a different point in that process, and I assume that we will have mutual respect for each other, regardless of where we perceive one another to be.

To facilitate further our work together, I ask students to honor the following guidelines for our discussion. Specifically, I ask students to demonstrate their respect for one another by honoring the confidentiality of the group. So that students may feel free to ask potentially awkward or embarrassing questions, or share race-related experiences, I ask that students refrain from making personal attributions when discussing the course content with their friends. I also discourage the use of "zaps," overt or covert put-downs often used as comic relief when someone is feeling anxious about the content of the discussion. Finally, students are asked to speak from their own experience, to say, for example, "I think . . ." or "In my experience, I have found . . ." rather than generalizing their experience to others, as in "People say . . ."

Many students are reassured by the climate of safety that is created by these guidelines and find comfort in the nonblaming assumptions I outline for the class. Nevertheless, my experience has been that most students, regardless of their class and ethnic background, still find racism a difficult topic to discuss, as is revealed by these journal comments written after the first class meeting (all names are pseudonyms):

The class is called Psychology of Racism, the atmosphere is friendly and open, yet I feel very closed in. I feel guilt and doubt well up inside of me. (Tiffany, a White woman)

Class has started on a good note thus far. The class seems rather large and disturbs me. In a class of this nature, I expect there will be many painful and emotional moments. (Linda, an Asian woman)

I am a little nervous that as one of the few students of color in the class people are going to be looking at me for answers, or whatever other reasons. The thought of this inhibits me a great deal. (Louise, an African American woman)

I had never thought about my social position as being totally dominant. There wasn't one area in which I wasn't in the dominant group. . . . I first felt embarrassed. . . . Through association alone I felt in many ways responsible for the unequal condition existing in the world. This made me feel like shrinking in a hole in a class where I was surrounded by 27 women and 2 men, one of whom was Black and the other was Jewish. I felt that all these people would be justified in venting their anger upon me. After a short period, I realized that no one in the room was attacking or even blaming me for the conditions that exist. (Carl, a White man)

Even though most of my students voluntarily enroll in the course as an elective, their anxiety and subsequent resistance to learning about racism quickly emerge.

Sources of Resistance

In predominantly White college classrooms, I have experienced at least three major sources of student resistance to talking and learning about race and racism. They can be readily identified as the following:

1. Race is considered a taboo topic for discussion, especially in racially mixed settings.
2. Many students, regardless of racial-group membership, have been socialized to think of the United States as a just society.
3. Many students, particularly White students, initially deny any personal prejudice, recognizing the impact of racism on other people's lives, but failing to acknowledge its impact on their own.

Race as Taboo Topic

The first source of resistance, race as a taboo topic, is an essential obstacle to overcome if class discussion is to begin at all. Although many students are interested in the topic, they are often most interested in hearing other people talk about it, afraid to break the taboo themselves.

One source of this self-consciousness can be seen in the early childhood experiences of many students. It is known that children as young as three notice racial differences (see Phinney & Rotheram, 1987). Certainly pre-schoolers talk about what they see. Unfortunately, they often do so in ways that make adults uncomfortable. Imagine the following scenario: A White child in a public place points to a dark-skinned African American child and says loudly, "Why is that boy Black?" The embarrassed parent quickly responds, "Sh! Don't say that." The child is only attempting to make sense of a new observation (Derman-Sparks, Higa, & Sparks, 1980), yet the parent's attempt to silence the perplexed child sends a message that this observation is not okay to talk about. White children quickly become aware that their questions about race raise adult anxiety, and as a result, they learn not to ask questions.

When asked to reflect on their earliest race-related memories and the feelings associated with them, both White students and students of color often report feelings of confusion, anxiety, and/or fear. Students of color often have early memories of name-calling or other negative interactions with other children, and sometimes with adults. They also report having had questions that went both unasked and unanswered. In addition, many students have had uncomfortable interchanges around race-related topics as adults. When asked at the beginning of the semester, "How many of you have had difficult, perhaps heated conversations with someone on a race-related topic?", routinely almost everyone in the class raises his or her hand. It should come as no surprise then that students often approach the topic of race and/or racism with both curiosity and trepidation.

The Myth of the Meritocracy

The second source of student resistance to be discussed here is rooted in students' belief that the United States is a just society, a meritocracy where individual efforts are fairly rewarded. While some students (particularly students of color) may already have become disillusioned with that notion of the United States, the majority of my students who have experienced at least the personal success of college acceptance still have faith in this notion. To the extent that these students acknowledge that racism exists, they tend to view it as an individual phenomenon, rooted in the attitudes of the "Archie Bunkers" of the world or located only in particular parts of the country.

After several class meetings, Karen, a White woman, acknowledged this attitude in her journal:

> At one point in my life — the beginning of this class — I actually perceived America to be a relatively racist free society. I thought that the people who were racist or subjected to racist stereotypes were found only in small pockets of the U.S., such as the South. As I've come to realize, racism (or at least racially orientated stereotypes) is rampant.

An understanding of racism as a system of advantage presents a serious challenge to the notion of the United States as a just society where rewards are based solely on one's merit. Such a challenge often creates discomfort in students. The old adage "ignorance is bliss" seems to hold true in this case; students are not necessarily eager to recognize the painful reality of racism.

One common response to the discomfort is to engage in denial of what they are learning. White students in particular may question the accuracy or currency of statistical information regarding the prevalence of discrimination (housing, employment, access to health care, and so on). More qualitative data, such as autobiographical accounts of experiences with racism, may be challenged on the basis of their subjectivity.

It should be pointed out that the basic assumption that the United States is a just society for all is only one of many basic assumptions that might be challenged in the learning process. Another example can be seen in an interchange between two White students following a discussion about cultural racism, in which the omission or distortion of historical information about people of color was offered as an example of the cultural transmission of racism.

"Yeah, I just found out that Cleopatra was actually a Black woman."

"What?"

The first student went on to explain her newly learned information. Finally, the second student exclaimed in disbelief, "That can't be true. Cleopatra was beautiful!" This new information and her own deeply ingrained assumptions about who is beautiful and who is not were too incongruous to allow her to assimilate the information at that moment.

If outright denial of information is not possible, then withdrawal may be. Physical withdrawal in the form of absenteeism is one possible result; it is for precisely this reason that class attendance is mandatory. The reduction in the completion of reading and/or written assignments is another form of withdrawal. I have found this response to be so common that I now alert students to this possibility at the beginning of the semester. Knowing that this response is a common one seems to help students stay engaged, even when they experience the desire to withdraw.

Following an absence in the fifth week of the semester, one White student wrote, "I think I've hit the point you talked about, the point where you don't want to hear any more about racism. I sometimes begin to get the feeling we are all hypersensitive." (Two weeks later she wrote, "Class is getting better. I think I am beginning to get over my hump.")

Perhaps not surprisingly, this response can be found in both White students and students of color. Students of color often enter a discussion of racism with some awareness of the issue, based on personal experiences. However, even these students find that they did not have a full understanding of the widespread impact of racism in our society. For students who are targeted by racism, an increased awareness of the impact in and on their lives is painful, and often generates anger.

Four weeks into the semester, Louise, an African American woman, wrote in her journal about her own heightened sensitivity:

Many times in class I feel uncomfortable when White students use the term Black because even if they aren't aware of it they say it with all or at least a lot of the negative connotations they've been taught goes along with Black. Sometimes it just causes a stinging feeling inside of me. Sometimes I get real tired of hearing White people talk about the conditions of Black people. I think it's an important thing for them to talk about, but still I don't always like being around when they do it. I also get tired of hearing them talk about how hard it is for them, though I understand it, and most times I am very willing to listen and be open, but sometimes I can't. Right now I can't.

For White students, advantaged by racism, a heightened awareness of it often generates painful feelings of guilt. The following responses are typical:

After reading the article about privilege, I felt very guilty. (Rachel, a White woman)

Questions of racism are so full of anger and pain. When I think of all the pain White people have caused people of color, I get a feeling of guilt. How could someone like myself care so much about the color of someone's skin that they would do them harm? (Terri, a White woman)

White students also sometimes express a sense of betrayal when they realize the gaps in their own education about racism. After seeing the first episode of the documentary series *Eyes on the Prize*, Chris, a White man, wrote:

I never knew it was really that bad just 35 years ago. Why didn't I learn this in elementary or high school? Could it be that the White people of America want to forget this injustice? . . . I will never forget that movie for as long as I live. It was like a big slap in the face.

Barbara, a White woman, also felt anger and embarrassment in response to her own previous lack of information about the internment of Japanese Americans during World War II. She wrote:

I feel so stupid because I never even knew that these existed. I never knew that the Japanese were treated so poorly. I am becoming angry and upset about all of the things that I do not know. I have been so sheltered. My parents never wanted to let me know about the bad things that have happened in the world. After I saw the movie (*Mitsuye and Nellie*), I even called them up to ask them why they never told me this. . . . I am angry at them too for not teaching me and exposing me to the complete picture of my country.

Avoiding the subject matter is one way to avoid these uncomfortable feelings.

"I'm Not Racist, But . . ."

A third source of student resistance (particularly among White students) is the initial denial of any personal connection to racism. When asked why they have decided to enroll in a course on racism, White students typically explain their interest in the topic with such disclaimers as, "I'm not racist myself, but I know people who are, and I want to understand them better."

Because of their position as the targets of racism, students of color do not typically focus on their own prejudices or lack of them. Instead they usually express a desire to understand why racism exists, and how they have been affected by it.

However, as all students gain a better grasp of what racism is and its many manifestations in U.S. society, they inevitably start to recognize its legacy within themselves. Beliefs, attitudes, and actions based on racial stereotypes begin to be remembered and are newly observed by White students. Students of color as well often recognize negative attitudes they may have internalized about their own racial group or that they have believed about others. Those who previously thought themselves immune to the effects of growing up in a racist society often find themselves reliving uncomfortable feelings of guilt or anger.

After taping her own responses to a questionnaire on racial attitudes, Barbara, a White woman previously quoted, wrote:

> I always want to think of myself as open to all races. Yet when I did the interview to myself, I found that I did respond differently to the same question about different races. No one could ever have told me that I would have. I would have denied it. But I found that I did respond differently even though I didn't want to. This really upset me. I was angry with myself because I thought I was not prejudiced and yet the stereotypes that I had created had an impact on the answers that I gave even though I didn't want it to happen.

The new self-awareness, represented here by Barbara's journal entry, changes the classroom dynamic. One common result is that some White students, once perhaps active participants in class discussion, now hesitate to continue their participation for fear that their newly recognized racism will be revealed to others.

> Today I did feel guilty, and like I had to watch what I was saying (make it good enough), I guess to prove I'm really *not* prejudiced. From the conversations the first day, I guess this is a normal enough reaction, but I certainly never expected it in me. (Joanne, a White woman)

This withdrawal on the part of White students is often paralleled by an increase in participation by students of color who are seeking an outlet for what are often feelings of anger. The withdrawal of some previously vocal White students from the classroom exchange, however, is sometimes interpreted by students of color as indifference. This perceived indifference often serves to fuel the anger and frustration that many students of color experience, as awareness of their own oppression is heightened. For example, Robert, an African American man, wrote:

> I really wish the White students would talk more. When I read these articles, it makes me so mad and I really want to know what the White kids think. Don't they care?

Sonia, a Latina, described the classroom tension from another perspective:

> I would like to comment that at many points in the discussions I have felt uncomfortable and sometimes even angry with people. I guess I am at the stage where I am tired of listening to Whites feel guilty and watch their eyes fill up with tears. I do understand that everyone is at their own stage of development and I even tell myself every Tuesday that these people have come to this class by choice. Some days I am just more tolerant than others. . . . It takes courage to say things in that room with so many women of color present. It also takes courage for the women of color to say things about Whites.

What seems to be happening in the classroom at such moments is a collision of developmental processes that can be inherently useful for the racial identity development of the individuals involved. Nevertheless, the interaction may be perceived as problematic to instructors and students who are unfamiliar with the process. Although space does not allow for an exhaustive discussion of racial identity development theory, a brief explication of it here will provide additional clarity regarding the classroom dynamics when issues of race are discussed. It will also provide a theoretical framework for the strategies for dealing with student resistance that will be discussed at the conclusion of this article.

Stages of Racial Identity Development

Racial identity and racial identity development theory are defined by Janet Helms (1990) as

> a sense of group or collective identity based on one's *perception* that he or she shares a common racial heritage with a particular racial group . . . racial identity development theory concerns the psychological implications of racial-group membership, that is belief systems that evolve in reaction to perceived differential racial-group membership. (p. 3)

It is assumed that in a society where racial-group membership is emphasized, the development of a racial identity will occur in some form in everyone. Given the dominant/subordinate relationship of Whites and people of color in this society, however, it is not surprising that this developmental process will unfold in different ways. For purposes of this discussion, William Cross's (1971, 1978) model of Black identity development will be described along with Helms's (1990) model of White racial identity development theory. While the identity development of other students (Asian Latino/a, Native American) is not included in this particular theoretical formulation, there is evidence to suggest that the process for these oppressed groups is similar to that described for African Americans (Highlen, et al., 1988; Phinney, 1990).[2] In each case, it is assumed that a positive sense of one's self as a member of one's group (which is not based on any assumed superiority) is important for psychological health.

Black Racial Identity Development

According to Cross's (1971, 1978, 1991) model of Black racial identity development, there are five stages in the process, identified as Preencounter, Encounter, Immersion/Emersion, Internalization, and Internalization-Commitment. In the first stage of Preencounter, the African American has absorbed many of the beliefs and values of the dominant White culture, including the notion that "White is right" and "Black is wrong." Though the internalization of negative Black stereotypes may be outside of his or her conscious awareness, the individual seeks to assimilate and be accepted by Whites, and actively or passively distances him/herself from other Blacks.[3]

Louise, an African American woman previously quoted, captured the essence of this stage in the following description of herself at an earlier time:

> For a long time it seemed as if I didn't remember my background, and I guess in some ways I didn't. I was never taught to be proud of my African heritage. Like we talked about in class, I went through a very long stage of identifying with my oppressors. Wanting to be like, live like, and be accepted by them. Even to the point of hating my own race and myself for being a part of it. Now I am ashamed that I ever was ashamed. I lost so much of myself in my denial of and refusal to accept my people.

In order to maintain psychological comfort at this stage of development, Helms writes:

> The person must maintain the fiction that race and racial indoctrination have nothing to do with how he or she lives life. It is probably the case that

[2] While similar models of racial identity development exist, Cross and Helms are referenced here because they are among the most frequently cited writers on Black racial identity development and on White racial identity development, respectively. For a discussion of the commonalities between these and other identity development models, see Phinney (1989, 1990) and Helms (1990).

[3] Both Parham (1989) and Phinney (1989) suggest that a preference for the dominant group is not always a characteristic of this stage. For example, children raised in households and communities with explicitly positive Afrocentric attitudes may absorb a pro-Black perspective, which then serves as the starting point for their own exploration of racial identity.

the Preencounter person is bombarded on a regular basis with information that he or she cannot really be a member of the "in" racial group, but relies on denial to selectively screen such information from awareness. (1990, p. 23)

This de-emphasis on one's racial-group membership may allow the individual to think that race has not been or will not be a relevant factor in one's own achievement, and may contribute to the belief in a U.S. meritocracy that is often a part of a Preencounter worldview.

Movement into the Encounter phase is typically precipitated by an event or series of events that forces the individual to acknowledge the impact of racism in one's life. For example, instances of social rejection by White friends or colleagues (or reading new personally relevant information about racism) may lead the individual to the conclusion that many Whites will not view him or her as an equal. Faced with the reality that he or she cannot truly be White, the individual is forced to focus on his or her identity as a member of a group targeted by racism.

Brenda, a Korean American student, described her own experience of this process as a result of her participation in the racism course:

I feel that because of this class, I have become much more aware of racism that exists around. Because of my awareness of racism, I am now bothered by acts and behaviors that might not have bothered me in the past. Before when racial comments were said around me I would somehow ignore it and pretend that nothing was said. By ignoring comments such as these, I was protecting myself. It became sort of a defense mechanism. I never realized I did this, until I was confronted with stories that were found in our reading, by other people of color, who also ignored comments that bothered them. In realizing that there is racism out in the world and that there are comments concerning race that are directed towards me, I feel as if I have reached the first step. I also think I have reached the second step, because I am now bothered and irritated by such comments. I no longer ignore them, but now confront them.

The Immersion/Emersion stage is characterized by the simultaneous desire to surround oneself with visible symbols of one's racial identity and an active avoidance of symbols of Whiteness. As Thomas Parham describes, "At this stage, everything of value in life must be Black or relevant to Blackness. This stage is also characterized by a tendency to denigrate White people, simultaneously glorifying Black people. . . ." (1989, p. 190). The previously described anger that emerges in class among African American students and other students of color in the process of learning about racism may be seen as part of the transition through these stages.

As individuals enter the Immersion stage, they actively seek out opportunities to explore aspects of their own history and culture with the support of peers from their own racial background. Typically, White-focused anger dissipates during this phase because so much of the person's energy is directed toward his or her own group- and self-exploration. The result of this exploration is an emerging security in a newly defined and affirmed sense of self.

Sharon, another African American woman, described herself at the beginning of the semester as angry, seemingly in the Encounter stage of development. She wrote after our class meeting:

> Another point that I must put down is that before I entered class today I was angry about the way Black people have been treated in this country. I don't think I will easily overcome that and I basically feel justified in my feelings.

At the end of the semester, Sharon had joined with two other Black students in the class to work on their final class project. She observed that the three of them had planned their project to focus on Black people specifically, suggesting movement into the Immersion stage of racial identity development. She wrote:

> We are concerned about the well-being of our own people. They cannot be well if they have this pinned-up hatred for their own people. This internalized racism is something that we all felt, at various times, needed to be talked about. This semester it has really been important to me, and I believe Gordon [a Black classmate], too.

The emergence from this stage marks the beginning of Internalization. Secure in one's own sense of racial identity, there is less need to assert the "Blacker than thou" attitude often characteristic of the Immersion stage (Parham, 1989). In general, "pro-Black attitudes become more expansive, open, and less defensive" (Cross, 1971, p. 24). While still maintaining his or her connections with Black peers, the internalized individual is willing to establish meaningful relationships with Whites who acknowledge and are respectful of his or her self-definition. The individual is also ready to build coalitions with members of other oppressed groups. At the end of the semester, Brenda, a Korean American, concluded that she had in fact internalized a positive sense of racial identity. The process she described parallels the stages described by Cross:

> I have been aware for a long time that I am Korean. But through this class I am beginning to really become aware of my race. I am beginning to find out that White people can be accepting of me and at the same time accept me as a Korean.
>
> I grew up wanting to be accepted and ended up almost denying my race and culture. I don't think I did this consciously, but the denial did occur. As I grew older, I realized that I was different. I became for the first time, friends with other Koreans. I realized I had much in common with them.

This was when I went through my "Korean friend" stage. I began to enjoy being friends with Koreans more than I did with Caucasians.

Well, ultimately, through many years of growing up, I am pretty much in focus about who I am and who my friends are. I knew before I took this class that there were people not of color that were understanding of my differences. In our class, I feel that everyone is trying to sincerely find the answer of abolishing racism. I knew people like this existed, but it's nice to meet with them weekly.

Cross suggests that there are few psychological differences between the fourth stage, Internalization, and the fifth stage, Internalization-Commitment. However, those at the fifth stage have found ways to translate their "personal sense of Blackness into a plan of action or a general sense of commitment" to the concerns of Blacks as a group, which is sustained over time (Cross, 1991, p. 220). Whether at the fourth or fifth stage, the process of Internalization allows the individual, anchored in a positive sense of racial identity, both to proactively perceive and transcend race. Blackness becomes "the point of departure for discovering the universe of ideas, cultures and experiences beyond blackness in place of mistaking blackness as the universe itself" (Cross, Parham, & Helms, 1991, p. 330).

Though the process of racial identity development has been presented here in linear form, in fact it is probably more accurate to think of it in a spiral form. Often a person may move from one stage to the next, only to revisit an earlier stage as the result of new encounter experiences (Parham, 1989), though the later experience of the stage may be different from the original experience. The image that students often find helpful in understanding this concept of recycling through the stages is that of a spiral staircase. As a person ascends a spiral staircase, she may stop and look down at a spot below. When she reaches the next level, she may look down and see the same spot, but the vantage point has changed.[4]

White Racial Identity Development

The transformations experienced by those targeted by racism are often paralleled by those of White students. Helms (1990) describes the evolution of a positive White racial identity as involving both the abandonment of racism and the development of a nonracist White identity. In order to do the latter,

___

[4] After being introduced to this model and Helms's model of White identity development, students are encouraged to think about how the models might apply to their own experience or the experiences of people they know. As is reflected in the cited journal entries, some students resonate to the theories quite readily, easily seeing their own process of growth reflected in them. Other students are sometimes puzzled because they feel as though their own process varies from these models, and may ask if it is possible to "skip" a particular stage, for example. Such questions provide a useful departure point for discussing the limitations of stage theories in general, and the potential variations in experience that make questions of racial identity development so complex.

he or she must accept his or her own Whiteness, the cultural implications of being White, and define a view of Self as a racial being that does not depend on the perceived superiority of one racial group over another. (p. 49)

She identifies six stages in her model of White racial identity development: Contact, Disintegration, Reintegration, Pseudo-Independent, Immersion/ Emersion, and Autonomy.

The Contact stage is characterized by a lack of awareness of cultural and institutional racism, and of one's own White privilege. Peggy McIntosh (1989) writes eloquently about her own experience of this state of being:

As a white person, I realized I had been taught about racism as something which puts others at a disadvantage, but had been taught not to see one of its corollary aspects, white privilege, which puts me at an advantage. . . . I was taught to see racism only in individual acts of meanness, not in invisible systems conferring dominance on my group. (p. 10)

In addition, the Contact stage often includes naive curiosity about or fear of people of color, based on stereotypes learned from friends, family, or the media. These stereotypes represent the framework in use when a person at this stage of development makes a comment such as, "You don't act like a Black person" (Helms, 1990, p. 57).

Those Whites whose lives are structured so as to limit their interaction with people of color, as well as their awareness of racial issues, may remain at this stage indefinitely. However, certain kinds of experiences (increased interaction with people of color or exposure to new information about racism) may lead to a new understanding that cultural and institutional racism exist. This new understanding marks the beginning of the Disintegration stage.

At this stage, the bliss of ignorance or lack of awareness is replaced by the discomfort of guilt, shame, and sometimes anger at the recognition of one's own advantage because of being White and the acknowledgment of the role of Whites in the maintenance of a racist system. Attempts to reduce discomfort may include denial (convincing oneself that racism doesn't really exist, or if it does, it is the fault of its victims).

For example, Tom, a White male student, responded with some frustration in his journal to a classmate's observation that the fact that she had never read any books by Black authors in any of her high school or college English classes was an example of cultural racism. He wrote, "It's not my fault that Blacks don't write books."

After viewing a film in which a psychologist used examples of Black children's drawings to illustrate the potentially damaging effect of negative cultural messages on a Black child's developing self-esteem, David, another White male student, wrote:

I found it interesting the way Black children drew themselves without arms. The psychologist said this is saying that the child feels unable to control his environment. It can't be because the child has notions and beliefs already about being Black. It must be built in or hereditary due to the past history of the Blacks. I don't believe it's cognitive but more biological due to a long past history of repression and being put down.

Though Tom's and David's explanations seem quite problematic, they can be understood in the context of racial identity development theory as a way of reducing their cognitive dissonance upon learning this new race-related information. As was discussed earlier, withdrawal (accomplished by avoiding contact with people of color and the topic of racism) is another strategy for dealing with the discomfort experienced at this stage. Many of the previously described responses of White students to race-related content are characteristic of the transition from the Contact to the Disintegration stage of development.

Helms (1990) describes another response to the discomfort of Disintegration, which involves attempts to change significant others' attitudes toward African Americans and other people of color. However, as she points out,

> due to the racial naivete with which this approach may be undertaken and the person's ambivalent racial identification, this dissonance-reducing strategy is likely to be met with rejection by Whites as well as Blacks. (p. 59)

In fact, this response is also frequently observed among White students who have an opportunity to talk with friends and family during holiday visits. Suddenly they are noticing the racist content of jokes or comments of their friends and relatives and will try to confront them, often only to find that their efforts are, at best, ignored or dismissed as a "phase," or, at worst, greeted with open hostility.

Carl, a White male previously quoted, wrote at length about this dilemma:

> I realized that it was possible to simply go through life totally oblivious to the entire situation or, even if one realizes it, one can totally repress it. It is easy to fade into the woodwork, run with the rest of society, and never have to deal with these problems. So many people I know from home are like this. They have simply accepted what society has taught them with little, if any, question. My father is a prime example of this. . . . It has caused much friction in our relationship, and he often tells me as a father he has failed in raising me correctly. Most of my high school friends will never deal with these issues and propagate them on to their own children. It's easy to see how the cycle continues. I don't think I could ever justify within myself simply turning my back on the problem. I finally realized that my position in all of these dominant groups gives me power to make change occur. . . . It is an unfortunate result often though that I feel alienated from friends and family. It's often played off as a mere stage that I'm going

through. I obviously can't tell if it's merely a stage, but I know that they say this to take the attention off of the truth of what I'm saying. By belittling me, they take the power out of my argument. It's very depressing that being compassionate and considerate are seen as only phases that people go through. I don't want it to be a phase for me, but as obvious as this may sound, I look at my environment and often wonder how it will not be.

The societal pressure to accept the status quo may lead the individual from Disintegration to Reintegration. At this point the desire to be accepted by one's own racial group, in which the overt or covert belief in White superiority is so prevalent, may lead to a reshaping of the person's belief system to be more congruent with an acceptance of racism. The guilt and anxiety associated with Disintegration may be redirected in the form of fear and anger directed toward people of color (particularly Blacks), who are now blamed as the source of discomfort.

Connie, a White woman of Italian ancestry, in many ways exemplified the progression from the Contact stage to Reintegration, a process she herself described seven weeks into the semester. After reading about the stages of White identity development, she wrote:

> I think mostly I can find myself in the disintegration stage of development.
> . . . There was a time when I never considered myself a color. I never
> described myself as a "White, Italian female" until I got to college and
> noticed that people of color always described themselves by their
> color/race. While taking this class, I have begun to understand that being
> White makes a difference. I never thought about it before but there are
> many privileges to being White. In my personal life, I cannot say that I have
> ever felt that I have had the advantage over a Black person, but I am aware
> that my race has the advantage.
>
> I am feeling really guilty lately about that. I find myself thinking: "I
> didn't mean to be White, I really didn't mean it." I am starting to feel angry
> towards my race for ever using this advantage towards personal gains. But
> at the same time I resent the minority groups. I mean, it's not our fault
> that society has deemed us "superior." I don't feel any better than a Black
> person. But it really doesn't matter because I am a member of the domi-
> nant race. . . . I can't help it . . . and I sometimes get angry and feel like
> I'm being attacked.
>
> I guess my anger toward a minority group would enter me into the next
> stage of Reintegration, where I am once again starting to blame the victim.
> This is all very trying for me and it has been on my mind a lot. I really
> would like to be able to reach the last stage, autonomy, where I can accept
> being White without hostility and anger. That is really hard to do.

Helms (1990) suggests that it is relatively easy for Whites to become stuck at the Reintegration stage of development, particularly if avoidance of people of color is possible. However, if there is a catalyst for continued self-examination, the person "begins to question her or his previous definition of Whiteness and the justifiability of racism in any of its forms . . ." (p. 61). In my experience, continued participation in a course on racism provides the catalyst for this deeper self-examination.

This process was again exemplified by Connie. At the end of the semester, she listened to her own taped interview of her racial attitudes that she had recorded at the beginning of the semester. She wrote:

> Oh wow! I could not believe some of the things that I said. I was obviously in different stages of the White identity development. As I listened and got more and more disgusted with myself when I was at the Reintegration stage, I tried to remind myself that these are stages that all (most) White people go through when dealing with notions of racism. I can remember clearly the resentment I had for people of color. I feel the one thing I enjoyed from listening to my interview was noticing how much I have changed. I think I am finally out of the Reintegration stage. I am beginning to make a conscious effort to seek out information about people of color and accept their criticism. . . . I still feel guilty about the feeling I had about people of color and I always feel bad about being privileged as a result of racism. But I am glad that I have reached what I feel is the Pseudo-Independent stage of White identity development.

The information-seeking that Connie describes often marks the onset of the Pseudo-Independent stage. At this stage, the individual is abandoning beliefs in White superiority, but may still behave in ways that unintentionally perpetuate the system. Looking to those targeted by racism to help him or her understand racism, the White person often tries to disavow his or her own Whiteness through active affiliation with Blacks, for example. The individual experiences a sense of alienation from other Whites who have not yet begun to examine their own racism, yet may also experience rejection from Blacks or other people of color who are suspicious of his or her motives. Students of color moving from the Encounter to the Immersion phase of their own racial identity development may be particularly unreceptive to the White person's attempts to connect with them.

Uncomfortable with his or her own Whiteness, yet unable to be truly anything else, the individual may begin searching for a new, more comfortable way to be White. This search is characteristic of the Immersion/Emersion stage of development. Just as the Black student seeks to redefine positively what it means to be of African ancestry in the United States through immersion in accurate information about one's culture and history, the White individual seeks to replace racially related myths and stereotypes with accurate information about what it means and has meant to be White in U.S. society (Helms, 1990). Learning about Whites who have been antiracist allies to people of color is a very important part of this process.

After reading articles written by antiracist activists describing their own process of unlearning racism, White students often comment on how helpful it is to know that others have experienced similar feelings and have found ways to resist the racism in their environments.[5] For example, Joanne, a White woman who initially experienced a lot of guilt, wrote:

> This article helped me out in many ways. I've been feeling helpless and frustrated. I know there are all these terrible things going on and I want to be able to do something. . . . Anyway this article helped me realize, again, that others feel this way, and gave me some positive ideas to resolve my dominant class guilt and shame.

Finally, reading the biographies and autobiographies of White individuals who have embarked on a similar process of identity development (such as Barnard, 1985/1987) provides White students with important models for change.

Learning about White antiracists can also provide students of color with a sense of hope that they can have White allies. After hearing a White antiracist activist address the class, Sonia, a Latina who had written about her impatience with expressions of White guilt, wrote:

> I don't know when I have been more impressed by anyone. She filled me with hope for the future. She made me believe that there are good people in the world and that Whites suffer too and want to change things.

For White students, the internalization of a newly defined sense of oneself as White is the primary task of the Autonomy stage. The positive feelings associated with this redefinition energize the person's efforts to confront racism and oppression in his or her daily life. Alliances with people of color can be more easily forged at this stage of development than previously because the person's antiracist behaviors and attitudes will be more consistently expressed. While Autonomy might be described as "racial self-actualization, . . . it is best to think of it as an ongoing process . . . wherein the person is continually open to new information and new ways of thinking about racial and cultural variables" (Helms, 1990, p. 66).

Annette, a White woman, described herself in the Autonomy stage, but talked at length about the circular process she felt she had been engaged in during the semester:

---

[5] Examples of useful articles include essays by McIntosh (1988), Lester (1987), and Braden (1987). Each of these combines autobiographical material, as well as a conceptual framework for understanding some aspect of racism that students find very helpful. Bowser and Hunt's (1981) edited book, *Impacts of Racism on Whites,* though less autobiographical in nature, is also a valuable resource.

If people as racist as C. P. Ellis (a former Klansman) can change, I think anyone can change. If that makes me idealistic, fine. I do not think my expecting society to change is naive anymore because I now *know* exactly what I want. To be naive means a lack of knowledge that allows me to accept myself both as a White person and as an idealist. This class showed me that these two are not mutually exclusive but are an integral part of me that I cannot deny. I realize now that through most of this class I was trying to deny both of them.

While I was not accepting society's racism, I was accepting society's telling me as a White person, there was nothing I could do to change racism. So, I told myself I was being naive and tried to suppress my desire to change society. This is what made me so frustrated — while I saw society's racism through examples in the readings and the media, I kept telling myself there was nothing I could do. Listening to my tape, I think I was already in the Autonomy stage when I started this class. I then seemed to decide that being White, I also had to be racist which is when I became frustrated and went back to the Disintegration stage. I was frustrated because I was not only telling myself there was nothing I could do but I also was assuming society's racism was my own which made me feel like I did not want to be White. Actually, it was not being White that I was disavowing but being racist. I think I have now returned to the Autonomy stage and am much more secure in my position there. I accept my Whiteness now as just a part of me as is my idealism. I will no longer disavow these characteristics as I have realized I can be proud of both of them. In turn, I can now truly accept other people for their unique characteristics and not by the labels society has given them as I can accept myself that way.

While I thought the main ideas that I learned in this class were that White people need to be educated to end racism and everyone should be treated as human beings, I really had already incorporated these ideas into my thoughts. What I learned from this class is being White does not mean being racist and being idealistic does not mean being naive. I really did not have to form new ideas about people of color; I had to form them about myself — and I did.

Implications for Classroom Teaching

Although movement through all the stages of racial identity development will not necessarily occur for each student within the course of a semester (or even four years of college), it is certainly common to witness beginning transformations in classes with race-related content. An awareness of the existence of this process has helped me to implement strategies to facilitate positive student development, as well as to improve interracial dialogue within the classroom.

Four strategies for reducing student resistance and promoting student development that I have found useful are the following:

1. the creation of a safe classroom atmosphere by establishing clear guide-lines for discussion;
2. the creation of opportunities for self-generated knowledge;
3. the provision of an appropriate developmental model that students can use as a framework for understanding their own process;
4. the exploration of strategies to empower students as change agents.

Creating a Safe Climate

As was discussed earlier, making the classroom a safe space for discussion is essential for overcoming students' fears about breaking the race taboo, and will also reduce later anxieties about exposing one's own internalized racism. Establishing the guidelines of confidentiality, mutual respect, "no zaps," and speaking from one's own experience on the first day of class is a necessary step in the process.

Students respond very positively to these ground rules, and do try to honor them. While the rules do not totally eliminate anxiety, they clearly communicate to students that there is a safety net for the discussion. Students are also encouraged to direct their comments and questions to each other rather than always focusing their attention on me as the instructor, and to learn each other's names rather than referring to each other as "he," "she," or "the person in the red sweater" when responding to each other.[6]

The Power of Self-Generated Knowledge

The creation of opportunities for self-generated knowledge on the part of students is a powerful tool for reducing the initial stage of denial that many students experience. While it may seem easy for some students to challenge the validity of what they read or what the instructor says, it is harder to deny what they have seen with their own eyes. Students can be given hands-on assignments outside of class to facilitate this process.

For example, after reading *Portraits of White Racism* (Wellman, 1977), some students expressed the belief that the attitudes expressed by the White interviewees in the book were no longer commonly held attitudes. Students were then asked to use the same interview protocol used in the book (with some revision) to interview a White adult of their choice. When students reported on these interviews in class, their own observation of the similarity between those they had interviewed and those they had read about was more convincing than anything I might have said.

After doing her interview, Patty, a usually quiet White student, wrote:

---

[6] Class size has a direct bearing on my ability to create safety in the classroom. Dividing the class into pairs or small groups of five or six students to discuss initial reactions to a particular article or film helps to increase participation, both in the small groups and later in the large group discussions.

I think I learned a lot from it and that I'm finally getting a better grip on the idea of racism. I think that was why I participated so much in class. I really felt like I knew what I was talking about.

Other examples of creating opportunities for self-generated knowledge include assigning students the task of visiting grocery stores in neighborhoods of differing racial composition to compare the cost and quality of goods and services available at the two locations, and to observe the interactions between the shoppers and the store personnel. For White students, one of the most powerful assignments of this type has been to go apartment hunting with an African American student and to experience housing discrimination firsthand. While one concern with such an assignment is the effect it will have on the student(s) of color involved, I have found that those Black students who choose this assignment rather than another are typically eager to have their White classmates experience the reality of racism, and thus participate quite willingly in the process.

Naming the Problem

The emotional responses that students have to talking and learning about racism are quite predictable and related to their own racial identity development. Unfortunately, students typically do not know this; thus they consider their own guilt, shame, embarrassment, or anger an uncomfortable experience that they alone are having. Informing students at the beginning of the semester that these feelings may be part of the learning process is ethically necessary (in the sense of informed consent), and helps to normalize the students' experience. Knowing in advance that a desire to withdraw from classroom discussion or not to complete assignments is a common response helps students to remain engaged when they reach that point. As Alice, a White woman, wrote at the end of the semester:

> You were so right in saying in the beginning how we would grow tired of racism (I did in October) but then it would get so good! I have *loved* the class once I passed that point.

In addition, sharing the model of racial identity development with students gives them a useful framework for understanding each other's processes as well as their own. This cognitive framework does not necessarily prevent the collision of developmental processes previously described, but it does allow students to be less frightened by it when it occurs. If, for example, White students understand the stages of racial identity development of students of color, they are less likely to personalize or feel threatened by an African American student's anger.

Connie, a White student who initially expressed a lot of resentment at the way students of color tended to congregate in the college cafeteria, was much more understanding of this behavior after she learned about racial identity development theory. She wrote:

I learned a lot from reading the article about the stages of development in the model of oppressed people. As a White person going through my stages of identity development, I do not take time to think about the struggle people of color go through to reach a stage of complete understanding. I am glad that I know about the stages because now I can understand people of color's behavior in certain situations. For example, when people of color stay to themselves and appear to be in a clique, it is not because they are being rude as I originally thought. Rather they are engaged perhaps in the Immersion stage.

Mary, another White student, wrote:

I found the entire Cross model of racial identity development very enlightening. I knew that there were stages of racial identity development before I entered this class. I did not know what they were, or what they really entailed. After reading through this article I found myself saying, "Oh. That explains why she reacted this way to this incident instead of how she would have a year ago." Clearly this person has entered a different stage and is working through different problems from a new viewpoint. Thankfully, the model provides a degree of hope that people will not always be angry, and will not always be separatists, etc. Although I'm not really sure about that.

Conversely, when students of color understand the stages of White racial identity development, they can be more tolerant or appreciative of a White student's struggle with guilt, for example. After reading about the stages of White identity development, Sonia, a Latina previously quoted, wrote:

This article was the one that made me feel that my own prejudices were showing. I never knew that Whites went through an identity development of their own.

She later told me outside of class that she found it much easier to listen to some of the things White students said because she could understand their potentially offensive comments as part of a developmental stage.

Sharon, an African American woman, also found that an understanding of the respective stages of racial identity development helped her to understand some of the interactions she had had with White students since coming to college. She wrote:

There is a lot of clash that occurs between Black and White people at college which is best explained by their respective stages of development. Unfortunately schools have not helped to alleviate these problems earlier in life.

In a course on the psychology of racism, it is easy to build in the provision of this information as part of the course content. For instructors teaching courses with race-related content in other fields, it may seem less natural to do so. However, the inclusion of articles on racial identity development and/or class discussion of these issues in conjunction with the other strategies that have been suggested can improve student receptivity to the course content in important ways, making it a very useful investment of class time. Because the stages describe kinds of behavior that many people have commonly observed in themselves, as well as in their own intraracial and interracial interactions, my experience has been that most students grasp the basic conceptual framework fairly easily, even if they do not have a background in psychology.

Empowering Students as Change Agents

Heightening students' awareness of racism without also developing an awareness of the possibility of change is a prescription for despair. I consider it unethical to do one without the other. Exploring strategies to empower students as change agents is thus a necessary part of the process of talking about race and learning about racism. As was previously mentioned, students find it very helpful to read about and hear from individuals who have been effective change agents. Newspaper and magazine articles, as well as biographical or autobiographical essays or book excerpts, are often important sources for this information.

I also ask students to work in small groups to develop an action plan of their own for interrupting racism. While I do not consider it appropriate to require students to engage in antiracist activity (since I believe this should be a personal choice the student makes for him/herself), students are required to think about the possibility. Guidelines are provided (see Katz, 1978), and the plans that they develop over several weeks are presented at the end of the semester. Students are generally impressed with each other's good ideas; and, in fact, they often do go on to implement their projects.

Joanne, a White student who initially struggled with feelings of guilt, wrote:

> I thought that hearing others' ideas for action plans was interesting and informative. It really helps me realize (reminds me) the many choices and avenues there are once I decided to be an ally. Not only did I develop my own concrete way to be an ally, I have found many other ways that I, as a college student, can be an active anti-racist. It was really empowering.

Another way all students can be empowered is by offering them the opportunity to consciously observe their own development. The taped exercise to which some of the previously quoted students have referred is an example of one way to provide this opportunity. At the beginning of the semester, students are given an interview guide with many open-ended questions concerning racial attitudes and opinions. They are asked to interview themselves on tape as a way of recording their own ideas for future reference. Though the tapes are collected, students are assured that no one (including me) will listen to them. The tapes are returned near the end of the semester, and students are asked to listen to their own tapes and use their understanding of racial identity development to discuss it in essay form.

The resulting essays are often remarkable and underscore the psychological importance of giving students the chance to examine racial issues in the classroom. The following was written by Elaine, a White woman:

> Another common theme that was apparent in the tape was that, for the most part, I was aware of my own ignorance and was embarrassed because of it. I wanted to know more about the oppression of people in the country so that I could do something about it. Since I have been here, I have begun to be actively resistant to racism. I have been able to confront my grandparents and some old friends from high school when they make racist comments. Taking this psychology of racism class is another step toward active resistance to racism. I am trying to educate myself so that I have a knowledge base to work from.
>
> When the tape was made, I was just beginning to be active and just beginning to be educated. I think I am now starting to move into the redefinition stage. I am starting to feel ok about being White. Some of my guilt is dissipating, and I do not feel as ignorant as I used to be. I think I have an understanding of racism; how it effects [*sic*] myself, and how it effects this country. Because of this I think I can be more active in doing something about it.

In the words of Louise, a Black female student:

> One of the greatest things I learned from this semester in general is that the world is not only Black and White, nor is the United States. I learned a lot about my own erasure of many American ethnic groups. . . . I am in the (immersion) stage of my identity development. I think I am also dangling a little in the (encounter) stage. I say this because a lot of my energies are still directed toward White people. I began writing a poem two days ago and it was directed to White racism. However, I have also become more Black-identified. I am reaching to the strength in Afro-American heritage. I am learning more about the heritage and history of Afro-American culture. Knowledge = strength and strength = power.

While some students are clearly more self-reflective and articulate about their own process than others, most students experience the opportunity to talk and learn about these issues as a transforming process. In my experience, even those students who are frustrated by aspects of the course find themselves changed by it. One such student wrote in her final journal entry:

> What I felt to be a major hindrance to me was the amount of people. Despite the philosophy, I really never felt at ease enough to speak openly about the feelings I have and kind of watched the class pull farther and farther apart as the semester went on. . . . I think that it was your attitude that kept me intrigued by the topics we were studying despite my frustra-

tions with the class time. I really feel as though I made some significant moves in my understanding of other people's positions in our world as well as of my feelings of racism, and I feel very good about them. I feel like this class has moved me in the right direction. I'm on a roll I think, because I've been introduced to so much.

Facilitating student development in this way is a challenging and complex task, but the results are clearly worth the effort.

Implications for the Institution

What are the institutional implications for an understanding of racial identity development theory beyond the classroom? How can this framework be used to address the pressing issues of increasing diversity and decreasing racial tensions on college campuses? How can providing opportunities in the curriculum to talk about race and learn about racism affect the recruitment and retention of students of color specifically, especially when the majority of the students enrolled are White?

The fact is, educating White students about race and racism changes attitudes in ways that go beyond the classroom boundaries. As White students move through their own stages of identity development, they take their friends with them by engaging them in dialogue. They share the articles they have read with roommates, and involve them in their projects. An example of this involvement can be seen in the following journal entry, written by Larry, a White man:

> Here it is our fifth week of class and more and more I am becoming aware of the racism around me. Our second project made things clearer, because while watching T.V. I picked up many kinds of discrimination and stereotyping. Since the project was over, I still find myself watching these shows and picking up bits and pieces every show I watch. Even my friends will be watching a show and they will say, "Hey, Larry, put that in your paper." Since they know I am taking this class, they are looking out for these things. They are also watching what they say around me for fear that I will use them as an example. For example, one of my friends has this fascination with making fun of Jewish people. Before I would listen to his comments and take them in stride, but now I confront him about his comments.

The heightened awareness of the White students enrolled in the class has a ripple effect in their peer group, which helps to create a climate in which students of color and other targeted groups (Jewish students, for example) might feel more comfortable. It is likely that White students who have had the opportunity to learn about racism in a supportive atmosphere will be better able to be allies to students of color in extracurricular settings, like student government meetings and other organizational settings, where students of color often feel isolated and unheard.

At the same time, students of color who have had the opportunity to examine the ways in which racism may have affected their own lives are able to give voice to their own experience, and to validate it rather than be demoralized by it. An understanding of internalized oppression can help students of color recognize the ways in which they may have unknowingly participated in their own victimization, or the victimization of others. They may be able to move beyond victimization to empowerment, and share their learning with others, as Sharon, a previously quoted Black woman, planned to do.

Campus communities with an understanding of racial identity development could become more supportive of special-interest groups, such as the Black Student Union or the Asian Student Alliance, because they would recognize them not as "separatist" but as important outlets for students of color who may be at the Encounter or Immersion stage of racial identity development. Not only could speakers of color be sought out to add diversity to campus programming, but Whites who had made a commitment to unlearning their own racism could be offered as models to those White students looking for new ways to understand their own Whiteness, and to students of color looking for allies.

It has become painfully clear on many college campuses across the United States that we cannot have successfully multiracial campuses without talking about race and learning about racism. Providing a forum where this discussion can take place safely over a semester, a time period that allows personal and group development to unfold in ways that day-long or weekend programs do not, may be among the most proactive learning opportunities an institution can provide.

References

Barnard, H. F. (Ed.). (1987). *Outside the magic circle: The autobiography of Virginia Foster Durr.* New York: Simon & Schuster. (Original work published 1985)

Bowser, B. P., & Hunt, R. G. (1981). *Impacts of racism on Whites.* Beverly Hills: Sage.

Braden, P. A., & Quina, K. (Eds.). (1988). *Teaching a psychology of people: Resources for gender and sociocultural awareness.* Washington, DC: American Psychological Association.

Cross, W. E., Jr. (1971). The Negro to Black conversion experience: Toward a psychology of black liberation. *Black World, 20*(9), 13–27.

Cross, W. E., Jr. (1978). The Cross and Thomas models of psychological nigrescence. *Journal of Black Psychology, 5*(1), 13–19.

Cross, W. E., Jr. (1991). *Shades of Black: Diversity in African-American identity.* Philadelphia: Temple University Press.

Cross, W. E., Jr., Parham, T. A., & Helms, J. E. (1991). The stages of black identity development: Nigrescence models. In R. Jones (Ed.), *Black psychology* (3rd ed., pp. 319–338). San Francisco: Cobb and Henry.

Derman-Sparks, L., Higa, C. T., & Sparks, B. (1980). Children, race and racism: How race awareness develops. *Interracial Books for Children Bulletin, 11*(3/4), 3–15.

Helms, J. E. (Ed.). (1990). *Black and White racial identity: Theory, research and practice.* Westport, CT: Greenwood Press.

Highlen, P. S., Reynolds, A. L., Adams, E. M., Hanley, T. C., Myers, L. J., Cox, C., and Speight, S. (1988, August 13). *Self-identity development model of oppressed people: Inclusive model for all?* Paper presented at the American Psychological Association Convention, Atlanta, GA.

Hull, G. T., Scott, P. B., & Smith, B. (Eds.). (1982). *All the women are White, all the Blacks are men, but some of us are brave: Black women's studies.* Old Westbury, NY: Feminist Press.

Katz, J. H. (1978). *White awareness: Handbook for anti-racism training.* Norman: University of Oklahoma Press.

Lester, J. (1987). *What happens to the mythmakers when the myths are found to be untrue?* Unpublished paper, Equity Institute, Emeryville, CA.

McIntosh, P. (1988). *White privilege and male privilege: A personal a account of coming to see correspondences through work in women's studies.* Working paper, Wellesley College Center for Research on Women, Wellesley, MA.

McIntosh, P. (1989, July/August). White privilege: Unpacking the invisible knapsack. *Peace and Freedom,* pp. 10–12.

Parham, T. A. (1989). Cycles of psychological nigrescence. *Counseling Psychologist, 17*(2), 187–226.

Phinney, J. (1989). Stages of ethnic identity in minority group adolescents. *Journal of Early Adolescence, 9,* 34–39.

Phinney, J. (1990). Ethnic identity in adolescents and adults: Review of research. *Psychological Bulletin, 108*(3), 499–514.

Phinney, J. S., & Rotheram, M. J. (Eds.). (1987). *Children's ethnic socialization: Pluralism and development.* Newbury Park, CA: Sage.

Schuster, M. R., & Van Dyne, S. R. (Eds.). (1985). *Women's place in the academy: Transforming the liberal arts curriculum.* Totowa, NJ: Towman & Allanheld.

Wellman, D. (1977). *Portraits of White racism.* New York: Cambridge University Press.

Empowering Minority Students:
A Framework for Intervention

—■ ■ ■—

JIM CUMMINS

During the past twenty years, educators in the United States have implemented a series of costly reforms aimed at reversing the pattern of school failure among minority students. These have included compensatory programs at the preschool level, myriad forms of bilingual education programs, the hiring of additional aides and remedial personnel, and the institution of safeguards against discriminatory assessment procedures. Yet the dropout rate among Mexican American and mainland Puerto Rican students remains between 40 and 50 percent compared to 14 percent for Whites and 25 percent for Blacks (Jusenius & Duarte, 1982). Similarly, almost a decade after the passage of the nondiscriminatory assessment provision of PL94-142,[1] we find Hispanic students in Texas overrepresented by a factor of 300 percent in the "learning disabilities" category (Ortiz & Yates, 1983).

I have suggested that a major reason previous attempts at educational reform have been unsuccessful is that the relationships between teachers and students and between schools and communities have remained essentially unchanged. The required changes involve *personal redefinitions* of the way classroom teachers interact with the children and communities they serve. In other words, legislative and policy reforms may be necessary conditions for effective change, but they are not sufficient. Implementation of change is dependent upon the extent to which educators, both collectively and individually, redefine their roles with respect to minority students and communities.

---

[1] The Education of All Handicapped Children Act of 1975 (Public Law 94-142) guarantees to all handicapped children in the United States the right to a free public education, to an individualized education program (IEP), to due process, to education in the least segregated environment, and to assessment procedures that are multidimensional and nonculturally discriminatory.

Harvard Educational Review Vol. 56 No. 1 February 1986, 18–36

The purpose of this paper is to propose a theoretical framework for examining the types of personal and institutional redefinitions that are required to reverse the pattern of minority student failure. The framework is based on a series of hypotheses regarding the nature of minority students' educational difficulties. These hypotheses, in turn, lead to predictions regarding the probable effectiveness, or ineffectiveness, of various interventions directed at reversing minority students' school failure.

The framework assigns a central role to three inclusive sets of interactions or power relations: (1) the classroom interactions between teachers and students, (2) relationships between schools and minority communities, and (3) the intergroup power relations within the society as a whole. It assumes that the social organization and bureaucratic constraints within the school reflect not only broader policy and societal factors but also the extent to which *individual educators* accept or challenge the social organization of the school in relation to minority students and communities. Thus, this analysis sketches directions for change for policymakers at all levels of the educational hierarchy and, in particular, for those working directly with minority students and communities.

The Policy Context

Research data from the United States, Canada, and Europe vary on the extent to which minority students experience academic failure (for reviews, see Cummins, 1984; Ogbu, 1978). For example, in the United States, Hispanic (with the exception of some groups of Cuban students), Native American, and Black students do poorly in school compared to most groups of Asian American (and White) students. In Canada, Franco-Ontarian students in English language programs have tended to perform considerably less well academically than immigrant minority groups (Cummins, 1984), while the same pattern characterizes Finnish students in Sweden (Skutnabb-Kangas, 1984).

The major task of theory and policy is to explain the pattern of school success and failure among minority students. This task applies both to students whose home language and culture differ from those of the school and wider society (language minority students) and to students whose home language is a version of English but whose cultural background is significantly different from that of the school and wider society, such as many Black and Hispanic students from English language backgrounds. With respect to language-minority students, recent policy changes in the United States have been based on the assumption that a major cause of students' educational difficulty is the switch between the language of the home and the language of the school. Thus, the apparently plausible assumption that students cannot learn in a language they do not understand gave rise in the late sixties and early seventies to bilingual education programs in which students' home language was used in addition to English as an initial medium of school instruction (Schneider, 1976).

Bilingual programs, however, have met with both strong support and vehement opposition. The debate regarding policy has revolved around two intuitively appealing assumptions. Those who favor bilingual education argue that children cannot learn in a language they do not understand, and, therefore, L1 (first language) instruction is necessary to counteract the negative effects of a home/school linguistic mismatch. The opposition contends that bilingual education is illogical in its implication that less English instruction will lead to more English achievement. It makes more sense, the opponents argue, to provide language-minority students with maximum exposure to English.

Despite the apparent plausibility of each assumption, these two conventional wisdoms (the "linguistic mismatch" and "insufficient exposure" hypotheses) are each patently inadequate. The argument that language minority students fail primarily as a result of a home/school language switch is refuted by the success of many minority students whose instruction has been totally through a second language. Similarly, research in Canada has documented the effectiveness of "French immersion programs" in which English background (majority language) students are instructed largely through French in the early grades as a means of developing fluent bilingualism. In spite of the home/school language switch, students' first language (English) skills develop as well as those of students whose instruction has been totally through English. The fact that the first language has high status and is strongly reinforced in the wider society is usually seen as an important factor in the success of these immersion programs.[2]

The opposing "insufficient exposure" hypothesis, however, fares no better with respect to the research evidence. In fact, the results of virtually every bilingual program that has been evaluated during the past fifty years show either no relationship or a negative relationship between amount of school exposure to the majority language and academic achievement in that language (Baker & de Kanter, 1981; Cummins, 1983a, 1984; Skutnabb-Kangas, 1984). Evaluations of immersion programs for majority students show that students perform as well in English academic skills as comparison groups despite considerably less exposure to English in school. Exactly the same result is obtained for minority students. Promotion of the minority language entails no loss in the development of English academic skills. In other words, language minority students instructed through the minority language (for example, Spanish) for all or part of the school day perform as well in English academic skills as comparable students instructed totally through English.

---

[2] For a discussion of the implications of Canadian French immersion programs for the education of minority students, see California State Department of Education (1984).

351

These results have been interpreted in terms of "interdependence hypothesis," which proposes that to the extent that instruction through a minority language is effective in developing academic proficiency in the minority language, transfer of this proficiency to the majority language will occur, given adequate exposure and motivation to learn the majority language (Cummins, 1979, 1983a, 1984). The interdependence hypothesis is supported by a large body of research from bilingual program evaluations, studies of language use in the home, immigrant student language learning, correlational studies of L1-L2 (second language) relationships, and experimental studies of bilingual information processing (for reviews, see Cummins, 1984; McLaughlin, 1985).

It is not surprising that the two conventional wisdoms inadequately account for the research data, since each involves only a one-dimensional linguistic explanation. The variability of minority students' academic performance under different social and educational conditions indicates that many complex, interrelated factors are at work (Ogbu, 1978; Wong-Fillmore, 1983). In particular, sociological and anthropological research suggests that status and power relations between groups are an important part of any comprehensive account of minority students' school failure (Fishman, 1976; Ogbu, 1978; Paulston, 1980). In addition, a variety of factors related to educational quality and cultural mismatch also appear to be important in mediating minority students' academic progress (Wong-Fillmore, 1983). These factors have been integrated into the design of a theoretical framework that suggests the changes required to reverse minority student failure.

A Theoretical Framework

The central tenet of the framework is that students from "dominated" societal groups are "empowered" or "disabled" as a direct result of their interactions with educators in the schools. These interactions are mediated by the implicit or explicit role definitions that educators assume in relation to four institutional characteristics of schools. These characteristics reflect the extent to which 1) minority students' language and culture are incorporated into the school program; 2) minority community participation is encouraged as an integral component of children's education; 3) the pedagogy promotes intrinsic motivation on the part of students to use language actively in order to generate their own knowledge; and 4) professionals involved in assessment become advocates for minority students rather than legitimizing the location of the "problem" in the students. For each of these dimensions of school organization the role definitions of educators can be described in terms of a continuum, with one end promoting the empowerment of students and the other contributing to the disabling of students.

The three sets of relationships analyzed in the present framework — majority/minority societal group relations, school/minority community relations, educator/minority student relations — are chosen on the basis of hypotheses regarding the relative ineffectiveness of previous educational re- forms and the directions required to reverse minority group school failure. Each of these relationships will be discussed in detail.

Intergroup Power Relations

When the patterns of minority student school failure are examined from an international perspective, it becomes evident that power and status relations between minority and majority groups exert a major influence on school performance. An example frequently given is the academic failure of Finnish students in Sweden, where they are a low-status group, compared to their success in Australia, where they are regarded as a high-status group (Troike, 1978). Similarly, Ogbu (1978) reports that the outcast Burakumin perform poorly in Japan but as well as other Japanese students in the United States.

Theorists have explained these findings using several constructs. Cummins (1984), for example, discusses the "bicultural ambivalence" (or lack of cultural identification) of students in relation to both the home and school cultures. Ogbu (1978) discusses the "caste" status of minorities that fail aca- demically and ascribes their failure to economic and social discrimination combined with the internalization of the inferior status attributed to them by the dominant group. Feuerstein (1979) attributes academic failure to the disruption of intergenerational transmission processes caused by the aliena- tion of a group from its own culture. In all three conceptions, widespread school failure does not occur in minority groups that are positively oriented towards both their own and the dominant culture, that do not perceive them- selves as inferior to the dominant group, and that are not alienated from their own cultural values.

Within the present framework, the *dominant* group controls the institu- tions and reward systems within society; the *dominated* group (Mullard, 1985) is regarded as inherently inferior by the dominant group and denied access to high-status positions within the institutional structure of the society. As described by Ogbu (1978), the dominated status of a minority group exposes them to conditions that predispose children to school failure even before they come to school. These conditions include limited parental access to economic and educational resources, ambivalence toward cultural transmis- sion and primary language use in the home, and interactional styles that may not prepare students for typical teacher/student interaction patterns in school (Heath, 1983; Wong-Fillmore, 1983). Bicultural ambivalence and less effective cultural transmission among dominated groups are frequently as- sociated with a historical pattern of colonization and subordination by the dominant group. This pattern, for example, characterizes Franco-Ontarian students in Canada, Finns in Sweden, and Hispanic, Native, and Black groups in the United States.

Different patterns among other societal groups can clearly be distin- guished (Ogbu & Matute-Bianchi, in press). Detailed analysis of patterns of intergroup relations go beyond the scope of this paper. However, it is important to note that the minority groups characterized by widespread school failure tend overwhelmingly to be in a dominated relationship to the majority group.[3]

Empowerment of Students

Students who are empowered by their school experiences develop the ability, confidence, and motivation to succeed academically. They participate competently in instruction as a result of having developed a confident cultural identity as well as appropriate school-based knowledge and interactional structures (Cummins, 1983b; Tikunoff, 1983). Students who are disempowered or "disabled" by their school experiences do not develop this type of cognitive/academic and social/emotional foundation. Thus, student empowerment is regarded both as a mediating construct influencing academic performance and as an outcome variable itself.[4]

Although conceptually the cognitive/academic and social/emotional (identity-related) factors are distinct, the data suggest that they are extremely difficult to separate in the case of minority students who are "at risk" academically. For example, data from both Sweden and the United States suggest that minority students who immigrate relatively late (about ten years of age) often appear to have better academic prospects than students of similar socioeconomic status born in the host country (Cummins, 1984; Skutnabb-Kangas, 1984). Is this because their L1 cognitive/academic skills on arrival provide a better foundation for L2 cognitive/academic skills acquisition, or alternatively, because they have not experienced devaluation of their identity in the societal institutions, namely schools of the host country, as has been the case of students born in that setting?

[3] Ogbu (1978), for example, has distinguished between "caste," "immigrant," and "autonomous" minority groups. Caste groups are similar to what has been termed "dominated" groups in the present framework and are the only category of minority groups that tends to fail academically. Immigrant groups have usually come voluntarily to the host society for economic reasons and, unlike caste minorities, have not internalized negative attributions of the dominant group. Ogbu gives Chinese and Japanese groups as examples of "immigrant" minorities. The cultural resources that permit some minority groups to resist discrimination and internalization of negative attributions are still a matter of debate and speculation (for a recent treatment, see Ogbu & Matute-Bianchi, in press). The final category distinguished by Ogbu is that of "autonomous" groups who hold a distinct cultural identity but who are not subordinated economically or politically to the dominant group (for example, Jews and Mormons in the United States).

Failure to take account of these differences among minority groups both in patterns of academic performance and sociohistorical relationships to the dominant group has contributed to the confused state of policymaking with respect to language minority students. The bilingual education policy, for example, has been based on the implicit assumption that the linguistic mismatch hypothesis was valid for all language minority students, and, consequently, the same types of intervention were necessary and appropriate for all students. Clearly, this assumption is open to question.

[4] There is no contradiction in postulating student empowerment as both a mediating and an outcome variable. For example, cognitive abilities clearly have the same status in that they contribute to students' school success and can also be regarded as an outcome of schooling.

Similarly, the most successful bilingual programs appear to be those that emphasize and use the students' L1 (for reviews, see Cummins 1983a, 1984). Is this success due to better promotion of L1 cognitive/academic skills or to the reinforcement of cultural identity provided by an intensive L1 program? By the same token, is the failure of many minority students in English-only immersion programs a function of cognitive/academic difficulties or of students' ambivalence about the value of their cultural identity (Cohen & Swain, 1976)?

These questions are clearly difficult to answer; the point to be made, however, is that for minority students who have traditionally experienced school failure, there is sufficient overlap in the impact of cognitive/academic and identity factors to justify incorporating these two dimensions within the notion of "student empowerment," while recognizing that under some conditions each dimension may be affected in different ways.

Schools and Power

Minority students are disabled or disempowered by schools in very much the same way that their communities are disempowered by interactions with societal institutions. Since equality of opportunity is believed to be a given, it is assumed that individuals are responsible for their own failure and are, therefore, made to feel that they have failed because of their own inferiority, despite the best efforts of dominant-group institutions and individuals to help them (Skutnabb-Kangas, 1984). This analysis implies that minority students will succeed educationally to the extent that the patterns of interaction in school reverse those that prevail in the society at large.

Four structural elements in the organization of schooling contribute to the extent to which minority students are empowered or disabled. As outlined in Figure 1, these elements include the incorporation of minority students' culture and language, inclusion of minority communities in the education of their children, pedagogical assumptions and practices operating in the classroom, and the assessment of minority students.

Cultural/linguistic incorporation. Considerable research data suggest that, for dominated minorities, the extent to which students' language and culture are incorporated into the school program constitutes a significant predictor of academic success (Campos & Keatinge, 1984; Cummins, 1983a; Rosier & Holm, 1980). As outlined earlier, students' school success appears to reflect both the more solid cognitive/academic foundation developed through intensive L1 instruction and the reinforcement of their cultural identity.

Included under incorporation of minority group cultural features is the adjustment of instructional patterns to take account of culturally conditioned learning styles. The Kamehameha Early Education Program in Hawaii provides strong evidence of the importance of this type of cultural incorporation. When reading instruction was changed to permit students to collaborate in discussing and interpreting texts, dramatic improvements were found in both reading and verbal intellectual abilities (Au & Jordan, 1981).

An important issue to consider at this point is why superficially plausible but patently inadequate assumptions, such as the "insufficient exposure" hypothesis, continue to dominate the policy debate when virtually all the evidence suggests that incorporation of minority students' language and culture into the school program will at least not impede academic progress. In other words, what social function do such arguments serve? Within the context of the present framework, it is suggested that a major reason for the vehement resistance to bilingual programs is that the incorporation of minority languages and cultures into the school program confers status and

Figure 1. Empowerment of Minority Students: A Theoretical Framework

SOCIETAL CONTEXT

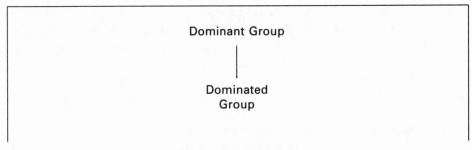

SCHOOL CONTEXT

Educator Role Definitions

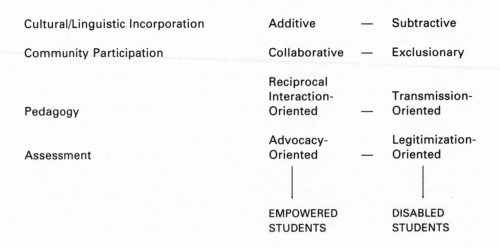

Cultural/Linguistic Incorporation	Additive —	Subtractive
Community Participation	Collaborative —	Exclusionary
Pedagogy	Reciprocal Interaction-Oriented —	Transmission-Oriented
Assessment	Advocacy-Oriented —	Legitimization-Oriented
	EMPOWERED STUDENTS	DISABLED STUDENTS

power (jobs, for example) on the minority group. Consequently, such programs contravene the established pattern of dominant/dominated group relations. Within democratic societies, however, contradictions between the rhetoric of equality and the reality of domination must be obscured. Thus, conventional wisdoms such as the insufficient exposure hypothesis become immune to critical scrutiny, and incompatible evidence is either ignored or dismissed.

Educators' role definitions in relation to the incorporation of minority students' language and culture can be characterized along an "additive-subtractive" dimension.[5] Educators who see their role as adding a second language and cultural affiliation to their students' repertoire are likely to empower students more than those who see their role as replacing or subtracting students' primary language and culture. In addition to the personal and future employment advantages of proficiency in two languages, there is considerable, though not conclusive, evidence that subtle educational advantages result from continued development of both languages among bilingual students. Enhanced metalinguistic development, for example, is frequently found in association with additive bilingualism (Hakuta & Diaz, 1985; McLaughlin, 1984).

It should be noted that an additive orientation does not require the actual teaching of the minority language. In many cases a minority language class may not be possible, for reasons such as low concentration of particular groups of minority students. Educators, however, communicate to students and parents in a variety of ways the extent to which the minority language and culture are valued within the context of the school. Even within a monolingual school context, powerful messages can be communicated to students regarding the validity and advantages of language development.

Community participation. Students from dominated communities will be empowered in the school context to the extent that the communities themselves are empowered through their interactions with the school. When educators involve minority parents as partners in their children's education, parents appear to develop a sense of efficacy that communicates itself to children, with positive academic consequences.

Although lip service is paid to community involvement through Parent Advisory Committees (PAC)[6] in many education programs, these committees are frequently manipulated through misinformation and intimidation (Cur-

---

[5] The terms "additive" and "subtractive" bilingualism were coined by Lambert (1975) to refer to the proficient bilingualism associated with positive cognitive outcomes on the one hand, and the limited bilingualism often associated with negative outcomes on the other.

[6] PACs were established in some states to provide an institutional structure for minority parent involvement in educational decisionmaking with respect to bilingual programs. In California, for example, a majority of PAC members for any state-funded program was required to be from the program target group. The school plan for use of program funds required signed PAC approval.

tis, 1984). The result is that parents from dominated groups retain their powerless status, and their internalized inferiority is reinforced. Children's school failure can then be attributed to the combined effects of parental illiteracy and lack of interest in their children's education. In reality, most parents of minority students have high aspirations for their children and want to be involved in promoting their academic progress (Wong-Fillmore, 1983). However, they often do not know how to help their children academically, and they are excluded from participation by the school. In fact, even their interaction through L1 with their children in the home is frequently regarded by educators as contributing to academic difficulties (Cummins, 1984).

Dramatic changes in children's academic progress can be realized when educators take the initiative to change this exclusionary pattern to one of collaboration. The Haringey project in Britain illustrates just how powerful the effects of simple interventions can be (Tizard, Schofield, & Hewison, 1982). In order to assess the effects of parental involvement in the teaching of reading, the researchers established a project in the London borough of Haringey whereby all children in two primary level experimental classes in two different schools read to their parents at home on a regular basis. The reading progress of these children was compared with that of children in two classes in two different schools who were given extra reading instruction in small groups by an experienced and qualified teacher who worked four half-days at each school every week for the two years of the intervention. Both groups were also compared with a control group that received no treatment.

All the schools were in multiethnic areas, and there were many parents who did not read English or use it at home. It was found, nevertheless, to be both feasible and practicable to involve nearly all the parents in educational activities such as listening to their children read, even when the parents were nonliterate and largely non-English-speaking. It was also found that, almost without exception, parents welcomed the project, agreed to hear their children read, and completed a record card showing what had been read.

The researchers report that parental involvement had a pronounced effect on the students' success in school. Children who read to their parents made significantly greater progress in reading than those who did not engage in this type of literacy sharing. Small-group instruction in reading, given by a highly competent specialist, did not produce improvements comparable to those obtained from the collaboration with parents. In contrast to the home collaboration program, the benefits of extra reading instruction were least apparent for initially low-achieving children.

In addition, the collaboration between teachers and parents was effective for children of all initial levels of performance, including those who, at the beginning of the study, were failing in learning to read. Teachers reported that the children showed an increased interest in school learning and were better behaved. Those teachers involved in the home collaboration found the work with parents worthwhile, and they continued to involve parents with subsequent classes after the experiment was concluded. It is interesting to note that teachers of the control classes also adopted the home collaboration program after the two-year experimental period.

The Haringey project is one example of school/community relations; there are others. The essential point, however, is that the teacher's role in such relations can be characterized along a *collaborative-exclusionary* dimension. Teachers operating at the collaborative end of the continuum actively encourage minority parents to participate in promoting their children's academic progress both in the home and through involvement in classroom activities. A collaborative orientation may require a willingness on the part of the teacher to work closely with mother-tongue teachers or aides in order to communicate effectively, in a noncondescending way, with minority parents. Teachers with an exclusionary orientation, on the other hand, tend to regard teaching as *their* job and are likely to view collaboration with minority parents as either irrelevant or detrimental to children's progress.

Pedagogy. Several investigators have suggested that many "learning disabilities" are pedagogically induced in that children designated "at risk" frequently receive intensive instruction which confines them to a passive role and induces a form of "learned helplessness" (Beers & Beers, 1980; Coles, 1978; Cummins, 1984). This process is illustrated in a microethnographic study of fourteen reading lessons given to West Indian Creole-speakers of English in Toronto, Canada (Ramphal, 1983). It was found that teachers' constant correction of students' miscues prevented students from focusing on the meaning of what they were reading. Moreover, the constant corrections fostered dependent behavior because students knew that whenever they paused at a word the teacher would automatically pronounce it for them. One student was interrupted so often in one of the lessons that he was able to read only one sentence, consisting of three words, uninterrupted. In contrast to a pattern of classroom interaction which promotes instructional dependence, teaching that empowers will aim to liberate students from instruction by encouraging them to become active generators of their knowledge. As Graves (1983) has demonstrated, this type of active knowledge generation can occur when, for example, children create and publish their own books within the classroom.

Two major pedagogical orientations can be distinguished. These differ in the extent to which the teacher retains exclusive control over classroom interaction as opposed to sharing some of this control with students. The dominant instructional model in North American schools has been termed a transmission model (Barnes, 1976; Wells, 1982). This model incorporates essentially the same assumptions about teaching and learning that Freire (1970, 1973) has termed a "banking" model of education. This transmission model will be contrasted with a "reciprocal interaction" model of pedagogy.

The basic premise of the transmission model is that the teacher's task is to impart knowledge or skills that she or he possesses to students who do not yet have these skills. This implies that the teacher initiates and controls the interaction, constantly orienting it towards the achievement of instructional objectives. For example, in first- and second-language programs that stress pattern repetition, the teacher presents the materials, models the language patterns, asks questions, and provides feedback to students about the correctness of their response. The curriculum in these types of programs focuses on the internal structure of the language or subject matter. Consequently, it frequently focuses predominantly on surface features of language or literacy such as handwriting, spelling, and decoding, and emphasizes correct recall of content taught by means of highly structured drills and workbook exercises. It has been argued that a transmission model of teaching contravenes central principles of language and literacy acquisition and that a model allowing for reciprocal interaction among students and teachers represents a more appropriate alternative (Cummins, 1984; Wells, 1982).[7]

A central tenet of the reciprocal interaction model is that "talking and writing are means to learning" (Bullock Report, 1975, p. 50). The use of this model in teaching requires a genuine dialogue between student and teacher in both oral and written modalities, guidance and facilitation rather than control of student learning by the teacher, and the encouragement of student/student talk in a collaborative learning context. This model emphasizes the development of higher level cognitive skills rather than just factual recall, and meaningful language use by students rather than the correction of surface forms. Language use and development are consciously integrated with all curricular content rather than taught as isolated subjects, and tasks are presented to students in ways that generate intrinsic rather than extrinsic motivation. In short, pedagogical approaches that empower students encourage them to assume greater control over setting their own learning goals and to collaborate actively with each other in achieving these goals.

The development of a sense of efficacy and inner direction in the classroom is especially important for students from dominated groups whose experiences so often orient them in the opposite direction. Wong-Fillmore (1983) has reported that Hispanic students learned considerably more English in classrooms that provided opportunities for reciprocal interaction with teachers and peers. Ample opportunities for expressive writing appear to be

---

[7] This "reciprocal interaction" model incorporates proposals about the relation between language and learning made by a variety of investigators, most notably in the Bullock Report (1975), and by Barnes (1976), Lindfors (1980), and Wells (1982). Its application with respect to the promotion of literacy conforms closely to psycholinguistic approaches to reading (Goodman & Goodman, 1977; Holdaway, 1979; Smith, 1978) and to the recent emphasis on encouraging expressive writing from the earliest grades (Chomsky, 1981; Giacobbe, 1982; Graves, 1983; Temple, Nathan, & Burris, 1982). Students' microcomputing networks such as the *Computer Chronicles Newswire* (Mehan, Miller-Souviney, & Riel, 1984) represent a particularly promising application of reciprocal interaction model of pedagogy.

particularly significant in promoting a sense of academic efficacy among minority students (Cummins, Aguilar, Bascunan, Fiorucci, Sanaoui, & Basman, in press). As expressed by Daiute (1985):

> Children who learn early that writing is not simply an exercise gain a sense of power that gives them confidence to write — and write a lot. . . . Beginning writers who are confident that they have something to say or that they can find out what they need to know can even overcome some limits of training or development. Writers who don't feel that what they say matters have an additional burden that no skills training can help them overcome. (pp. 5–6)

The implications for students from dominated groups are obvious. Too often the instruction they receive convinces them that what they have to say is irrelevant or wrong. The failure of this method of instruction is then taken as an indication that the minority student is of low ability, a verdict frequently confirmed by subsequent assessment procedures.

Assessment. Historically, assessment has played the role of legitimizing the disabling of minority students. In some cases assessment itself may play the primary role, but more often it has been used to locate the "problem" within the minority student, thereby screening from critical scrutiny the subtractive nature of the school program, the exclusionary orientation of teachers towards minority communities, and transmission models of teaching that inhibit students from active participation in learning.

This process is virtually inevitable when the conceptual base for assessment is purely psychoeducational. If the psychologist's task is to discover the causes of a minority student's academic difficulties and the only tools at his or her disposal are psychological tests (in either L1 or L2), then it is hardly surprising that the child's difficulties will be attributed to psychological dysfunctions. The myth of bilingual handicaps that still influences educational policy was generated in exactly this way during the 1920s and 1930s.

Recent studies suggest that despite the appearance of change brought about by PL 94-142, the underlying structure of assessment processes has remained essentially intact. Mehan, Hertweck, and Meihls (in press), for example, report that psychologists continued to test children until they "found" the disability that could be invoked to "explain" the student's apparent academic difficulties. Diagnosis and placement were influenced frequently by factors related to bureaucratic procedures and funding requirements rather than to students' academic performance in the classroom. Fueda and Mercer (1985) have also shown that designation of minority students as "learning disabled" as compared to "language impaired" was strongly influenced by whether a psychologist or a speech pathologist was on the placement committee. In other words, with respect to students' actual behavior, the label was essentially arbitrary. An analysis of more than four hundred psychological assessments of minority students revealed that although no diagnostic conclusions were logically possible in the majority of assessments, psychologists were most reluctant to admit this fact to teachers and parents (Cummins, 1984). In short, the data suggest that the structure within which psychological assessment takes place orients the psychologist to locate the cause of the academic problem within the minority student.

An alternative role definition for psychologists or special educators can be termed an "advocacy" or "delegitimization" role.[8] In this case, their task must be to delegitimize the traditional function of psychological assessment in the educational disabling of minority students by becoming advocates for the child in scrutinizing critically the societal and educational context within which the child has developed (Cazden, 1985). This involves locating the pathology within the societal power relations between dominant and dominated groups, in the reflection of these power relations between school and communities, and in the mental and cultural disabling of minority students that takes place in classrooms. These conditions are a more probable cause of the 300 percent overrepresentation of Texas Hispanic students in the learning disabled category than any intrinsic processing deficit unique to Hispanic children. The training of psychologists and special educators does not prepare them for this advocacy or delegitimization role. From the present perspective, however, it must be emphasized that discriminatory assessment is carried out by well-intentioned individuals who, rather than challenging a socioeducational system that tends to disable minority students, have accepted a role definition and an educational structure that makes discriminatory assessment virtually inevitable.[9]

Empowering Minority Students: The Carpinteria Example

The Spanish-only preschool program of the Carpinteria School District, near Santa Barbara, California, is one of the few programs in the United States that explicitly incorporates the major elements hypothesized in previous sections to empower minority students. Spanish is the exclusive language of instruction, there is a strong community involvement component, and the program is characterized by a coherent philosophy of promoting conceptual development through meaningful linguistic interaction.

The proposal to implement an intensive Spanish-only preschool program in this region was derived from district findings showing that a large majority of the Spanish-speaking students entering kindergarten each year lacked

[8] See Mullard (1985) for a detailed discussion of delegitimization strategies in anti-racist education.

[9] Clearly, the presence of processing difficulties that are rooted in neurological causes is not being denied for either monolingual or bilingual children. However, in the case of children from dominated minorities, the proportion of disabilities that are neurological in origin is likely to represent only a small fraction of those that derive from educational and social conditions.

adequate skills to succeed in the kindergarten program. On the School Readiness Inventory, a districtwide screening measure administered to all incoming kindergarten students, Spanish-speaking students tended to average about eight points lower than English-speaking students (approximately 14.5 compared to 23.0, averaged over four years from 1979 to 1982) despite the fact that the test was administered in students' dominant language. A score of 20 or better was viewed by the district as predicting a successful kindergarten year for the child. Prior to the implementation of the experimental program, the Spanish-background children attended a bilingual preschool program — operated either by Head Start or the Community Day Care Center — in which both English and Spanish were used concurrently but with strong emphasis on the development of English skills. According to the district kindergarten teachers, children who had attended these programs often mixed English and Spanish into a "Spanglish."

The major goal of the experimental Spanish-only preschool program was to bring Spanish-dominant children entering kindergarten up to a level of readiness for school similar to that attained by English-speaking children in the community. The project also sought to make parents of the program participants aware of their role as the child's first teacher and to encourage them to provide specific types of experiences for their children in the home.

The preschool program itself involved the integration of language with a large variety of concrete and literacy-related experiences. As summarized in the evaluation report: "The development of language skills in Spanish was foremost in the planning and attention given to every facet of the pre-school day. Language was used constantly for conversing, learning new ideas, concepts and vocabulary, thinking creatively, and problem-solving to give the children the opportunity to develop their language skills in Spanish to as high a degree as possible within the structure of the pre-school day" (Campos & Keatinge, 1984, p. 17).

Participation in the program was on a voluntary basis and students were screened only for age and Spanish-language dominance. Family characteristics of students in the experimental program were typical of other Spanish-speaking families in the community; more than 90 percent were of low socioeconomic status, and the majority worked in agriculture and had an average educational level of about the sixth grade.

The program proved to be highly successful in developing students' readiness skills, as evidenced by the average score of 21.6 obtained by the 1982–1983 incoming kindergarten students who had been in the program, compared to the score of 23.2 obtained by English-speaking students. A score of 14.6 was obtained by Spanish-speaking students who experienced the regular bilingual preschool program. In 1983–1984 the scores of these three groups were 23.3, 23.4, and 16.0, respectively. In other words, the gap between English-background and Spanish-background children in the Spanish-only preschool had disappeared; however, a considerable gap remained for Spanish-background students for whom English was the focus of pre-school instruction.

Of special interest is the performance of the experimental program students on the English and Spanish versions of the Bilingual Syntax Measure (BSM), a test of oral syntactic development (Hernandez-Chavez, Burt, & Dulay, 1976). Despite the fact that they experienced an exclusively Spanish preschool program, these students performed better than the other Spanish-speaking students in English (and Spanish) on entry to kindergarten in 1982 and at a similar level in 1983. On entrance to grade one in 1983, the gap had widened considerably, with almost five times as many of the experimental-program students performing at level 5 (fluent English) compared to the other Spanish-background students (47 percent v. 10 percent) (Campos & Keatinge, 1984).

The evaluation report suggests that

> although project participants were exposed to less *total* English, they, because of their enhanced first language skill and concept knowledge, were better able to comprehend the English they were exposed to. This seems to be borne out by comments made by kindergarten teachers in the District about project participants. They are making comments like, "Project participants appear more aware of what is happening around them in the classroom," "They are able to focus on the task at hand better" and "They demonstrate greater self-confidence in learning situations." All of these traits would tend to enhance the language acquisition process. (Campos & Keatinge, 1984, p. 41)

Campos and Keatinge (1984) also emphasize the consequences of the preschool program for parental participation in their children's education. They note that, according to the school officials, "the parents of project participants are much more aware of and involved with their child's school experience than non-participant parents of Spanish speakers. This is seen as having a positive impact on the future success of the project participants — the greater the involvement of parents, the greater the chances of success of the child" (p. 41).

The major relevance of these findings for educators and policymakers derives from their demonstration that educational programs *can* succeed in preventing the academic failure experienced by many minority students. The corollary is that failure to provide this type of program constitutes the disabling of minority students by the school system. For example, among the students who did not experience the experimental preschool program, the typical pattern of low levels of academic readiness and limited proficiency in both languages was observed. These are the students who are likely to be referred for psychological assessment early in their school careers. This assessment will typically legitimize the inadequate educational provision by attributing students' difficulties to some vacuous category, such as learning disability. By contrast, students who experienced a preschool program in which (a) their cultural identity was reinforced, (b) there was active collaboration with parents, and (c) meaningful use of language was integrated into every aspect of daily activities were developing high levels of conceptual and linguistic skills in *both* languages.

Conclusion

In this article I have proposed a theoretical framework for examining minority students' academic failure and for predicting the effects of educational interventions. Within this framework the educational failure of minority students is analyzed as a function of the extent to which schools reflect or counteract the power relations that exist within the broader society. Specifically, language-minority students' educational progress is strongly influenced by the extent to which individual educators become advocates for the promotion of students' linguistic talents, actively encourage community participation in developing students' academic and cultural resources, and implement pedagogical approaches that succeed in liberating students from instructional dependence.

The educator/student interactions characteristic of the disabling end of the proposed continua reflect the typical patterns of interaction that dominated societal groups have experienced in relation to dominant groups. The intrinsic value of the group is usually denied, and "objective" evidence is accumulated to demonstrate the group's "inferiority." This inferior status is then used as a justification for excluding the group from activities and occupations that entail societal rewards.

In a similar way, the disabling of students is frequently rationalized on the basis of students' "needs." For example, minority students need maximum exposure to English in both the school and the home; thus, parents must be told not to interact with children in their mother tongue. Similarly, minority children need a highly structured drill-oriented program· in order to maximize time spent on tasks to compensate for their deficient preschool experiences. Minority students also need a comprehensive diagnostic/prescriptive assessment in order to identify the nature of their "problem" and possible remedial interventions.

This analysis suggests a major reason for the relative lack of success of the various educational bandwagons that have characterized the North American crusade against underachievement during the past twenty years. The individual role definitions of educators and the institutional role definitions of schools have remained largely unchanged despite "new and improved" programs and policies. These programs and policies, despite their cost, have simply added a new veneer to the outward facade of the structure that disables minority students. The lip service paid to initial L1 instruction, community involvement, and nondiscriminatory assessment, together with the emphasis on improved teaching techniques, has succeeded primarily in deflecting attention from the attitudes and orientation of educators who interact on a daily basis with minority students. It is in these interactions that students are disabled. In the absence of individual and collective educator role redefinitions, schools will continue to reproduce, in these interactions, the power relations that characterize the wider society and make minority students' academic failure inevitable.

To educators genuinely concerned about alleviating the educational difficulties of minority students and responding to their needs, this conclusion may appear overly bleak. I believe, however, that it is realistic and optimistic, as directions for change are clearly indicated rather than obscured by the overlay of costly reforms that leave the underlying disabling structure essentially intact. Given the societal commitment to maintaining the dominant/dominated power relationships, we can predict that educational changes threatening this structure will be fiercely resisted. This is in fact the case for each of the four structural dimensions discussed earlier.[10]

In order to reverse the pattern of widespread minority group educational failure, educators and policymakers are faced with both a personal and a political challenge. Personally, they must redefine their roles within the classroom, the community, and the broader society so that these role definitions result in interactions that empower rather than disable students. Politically, they must attempt to persuade colleagues and decisionmakers — such as school boards and the public that elects them — of the importance of redefining institutional goals so that the schools transform society by empowering minority students rather than reflect society by disabling them.

References

Au, K. H., & Jordan, C. (1981). Teaching reading to Hawaiian children: Finding a culturally appropriate solution. In H. Trueba, G. P. Guthrie, & K. H. Au (Eds.), *Culture and the bilingual classroom: Studies in classroom ethnography* (pp. 139–152). Rowley, MA: Newbury House.

Baker, K. A., & de Kanter, A. A. (1981). *Effectiveness of bilingual education: A review of the literature.* Washington, DC: U.S. Department of Education, Office of Planning and Budget.

Barnes, D. (1976). *From communication to curriculum.* New York: Penguin.

Beers, C. S., & Beers, J. W. (1980). Early identification of learning disabilities: Facts and fallacies. *Elementary School Journal, 81,* 67–76.

Bethell, T. (1979, February). Against bilingual education. *Harper's,* pp. 30–33.

Bullock Report. (1975). *A language for life* (Report of the Committee of Inquiry appointed by the Secretary of State for Education and Science under the Chairmanship of Sir Alan Bullock). London: HMSO.

California State Department of Education. (1984). *Studies on immersion education: A collection for United States educators.* Sacramento: Author.

Campos, J., & Keatinge, B. (1984). *The Carpinteria preschool program: Title VII second year evaluation report.* Washington, DC: Department of Education.

[10] Although for pedagogy the resistance to sharing control with students goes beyond majority/minority group relations, the same elements are present. If the curriculum is not predetermined and presequenced, and the students are generating their own knowledge in a critical and creative way, then the reproduction of the societal structure cannot be guaranteed — hence the reluctance to liberate students from instructional dependence.

Cazden, C. B. (1985, April). *The ESL teacher as advocate.* Plenary presentation to the TESOL Conference, New York.

Chomsky, C. (1981). Write now, read later. In C. Cazden (Ed.), *Language in early childhood education* (2nd ed., pp. 141–149). Washington, DC: National Association for the Education of Young Children.

Cohen, A. D., & Swain, M. (1976). Bilingual education: The immersion model in the North American context. In J. E. Alatis & K. Twaddell (Eds.), *English as a second language in bilingual education* (pp. 55–64). Washington, DC: TESOL.

Coles, G. S. (1978). The learning disabilities test battery: Empirical and social issues. *Harvard Educational Review, 48,* 313–340.

Cummins, J. (1979). Linguistic interdependence and the educational development of bilingual children. *Review of Educational Research 49,* 222–251.

Cummins, J. (1983a) *Heritage language education: A literature review.* Toronto: Ministry of Education.

Cummins, J. (1983b). Functional language proficiency in context: Classroom participation as an interactive process. In W. J. Tikunoff (Ed.), *Compatibility of the SBIS features with other research on instruction for LEP students* (pp. 109–131). San Francisco: Far West Laboratory.

Cummins, J., Aguilar, M., Bascunan, L., Fiorucci, S., Sanaoui, R., & Basman, S. (in press). *Literacy development in heritage language program.* Toronto: National Heritage Language Resource Unit.

Curtis, J. (1984). *Bilingual education in Calistoga: Not a happy ending.* Report submitted to the Instituto de Lengua y Cultura, Elmira, NY.

Daiute, C. (1985). *Writing and computers.* Reading, MA: Addison-Wesley.

Feuerstein, R. (1979). *The dynamic assessment of retarded performers: The learning potential assessment device, theory, instruments, and techniques.* Baltimore: University Park Press.

Fishman, J. (1976). *Bilingual education: An international sociological perspective.* Rowley, MA: Newbury House.

Freire, P. (1970). *Pedagogy of the oppressed.* New York: Seabury.

Freire, P. (1973). *Education for critical consciousness.* New York: Seabury.

Giacobbe, M. E. (1982). Who says children can't write the first week? In R. D. Walshe (Ed.), *Donald Graves in Australia: "Children want to write"* (pp. 99–103). Exeter, NH: Heinemann Educational Books.

Goodman, K. S., & Goodman, Y. M. (1977). Learning about psycholinguistic processes by analyzing oral reading. *Harvard Educational Review, 47,* 317–333.

Graves, D. H. (1983). *Writing: Teachers and children at work.* Exeter, NH: Heinemann Educational Books.

Hakuta, K., & Diaz, R. M. (1985). The relationship between degree of bilingualism and cognitive ability: A critical discussion and some new longitudinal data. In K. E. Nelson (Ed.), *Children's language* (Vol. 5, pp. 319–345). Hillsdale, NJ: Erlbaum.

Heath, S. B. (1983). *Ways with words.* Cambridge, Eng.: Cambridge University Press.

Hernandez-Chavez, E., Burt, M., & Dulay, H. (1976). *The bilingual syntax measure.* New York: The Psychological Corporation.

Holdaway, D. (1979). *The foundations of literacy.* Sydney, Australia: Ashton Scholastic.

Jusenius, C., & Duarte, V. L. (1982). *Hispanics and jobs: Barriers to progress.* Washington, DC: National Commission for Employment Policy.

Lambert, W. E. (1975). Culture and language as factors in learning and education. In A. Wolfgang (Ed.), *Education of immigrant students* (pp. 55–83). Toronto: O.I.S.E.

Lindfors, J. W. (1980). *Children's language and learning.* Englewood Cliffs, NJ: Prentice-Hall.

McLaughlin, B. (1984). Early bilingualism: Methodological and theoretical issues. In M. Paradis & Y. Lebrun (Eds.), *Early bilingualism and child development* (pp. 19–46). Lisse: Swets & Zeitlinger.

McLaughlin, B. (1985). *Second language acquisition in childhood: Vol. 2. School-age children.* Hillsdale, NJ: Erlbaum.

Mehan, H., Hertweck, A., & Meihls, J. L. (1986). *Handicapping the handicapped: Decision making in students' educational careers.* Palo Alto: Stanford University.

Mehan, H., Miller-Souviney, B., & Riel, M. M. (1984). Research currents: Knowledge of text editing and control of literacy skills. *Language Arts, 65,* 154–159.

Mullard, C. (1985, January). *The social dynamic of migrant groups: From progressive to transformative policy in education.* Paper presented at the OECD Conference on Educational Policies and the Minority Social Groups, Paris.

Ogbu, J. U. (1978). *Minority education and caste.* New York: Academic Press.

Ogbu, J. U., & Matute-Bianchi, M. E. (in press). Understanding sociocultural factors: Knowledge, identity and school adjustment. In California State Department of Education (Ed.), *Sociocultural factors and minority student achievement.* Sacramento: Author.

Ortiz, A. A., & Yates, J. R. (1983). Incidence of exceptionality among Hispanics: Implications for manpower planning. *NABE Journal, 7,* 41–54.

Paulston, C. B. (1980). *Bilingual education: Theories and issues.* Rowley, MA: Newbury House.

Ramphal, D. K. *An analysis of reading instruction of West Indian Creole-speaking students.* Unpublished doctoral dissertation, Ontario Institute for Studies in Education, 1983.

Rosier, P., & Holm, W. (1980). *The Rock Point experience: A longitudinal study of a Navajo school.* Washington, DC: Center for Applied Linguistics.

Rueda, R., & Mercer, J. R. (1985, June). *Predictive analysis of decision making with language-minority handicapped children.* Paper presented at the BUENO Center 3rd Annual Symposium on Bilingual Education, Denver.

Schneider, S. G. (1976). *Revolution, reaction or reform: The 1974 Bilingual Education Act.* New York: Las Americas.

Skutnabb-Kangas, T. (1984). *Bilingualism or not: The Education of minorities.* Clevedon, Eng.: Multilingual Matters.

Smith, F. (1978). *Understanding reading* (2nd ed.). New York: Holt, Rinehart & Winston.

Temple, C. A., Nathan, R. G., & Burris, N. A. (1982). *The beginning of writing.* Boston: Allyn & Bacon.

Tikunoff, W. J. (1983). Five significant bilingual instructional features. In W. J. Tikunoff (Ed.), *Compatibility of the SBIS features with other research on instruction for LEP students* (pp. 5–18). San Francisco: Far West Laboratory.

Tizard, J., Schofield, W. N., & Hewison, J. (1982). Collaboration between teachers and parents in assisting children's reading. *British Journal of Educational Psychology, 52,* 1–15.

Troike, R. (1978). Research evidence for the effectiveness of bilingual education. *NABE Journal, 3,* 13–24.

Wells, G. (1982). Language, learning and the curriculum. In G. Wells, (Ed.), *Language, learning and education* (pp. 205–226). Bristol, Eng.: Centre for the Study of Language and Communication, University of Bristol.

Wong-Fillmore, L. (1983). The language learner as an individual: Implications of research on individual differences for the ESL teacher. In M. A. Clarke & J. Handscombe (Eds.), *On TESOL '82: Pacific perspectives on language learning and teaching* (pp. 157–171). Washington, DC: TESOL.

Discussions at the Symposium on "Minority Languages in Academic Research and Educational Policy" held in Sandbjerg Slot, Denmark, April 1985, contributed to the ideas in the article. I would like to express my appreciation to the participants at the Symposium and the Safder Alladina, Jan Curtis, David Dolson, Norm Gold, Monica Heller, Dennis Parker, Verity Saifullah Khan, and Tove Skutnabb-Kangas for comments on earlier drafts. I would also like to acknowledge the financial support of the Social Sciences and Humanities Research Council (Grant No. 431-79-0003), which made possible participation in the Sandbjerg Slot Symposium.

Uncertain Allies:
Understanding the Boundaries
of Race and Teaching

—■ ■ ■—

MARILYN COCHRAN-SMITH

Two trends in the United States have converged during the 1990s to make revision of the pre-service teacher education curriculum not just necessary, but urgent. First, the population of schoolchildren increasingly includes an array of racial, ethnic, and cultural groups, particularly in large urban areas, where the majority is now from minority groups (Banks, 1991). In border states such as New Mexico, Texas, and California, many schools include at least three minority groups, and few include only White European American students (Quality Education for Minorities Project, 1990). In states such as Alaska, Arizona, and South Dakota, large proportions of the school population are Native Americans. Concurrently, the racial composition of those entering the teaching force is overwhelmingly White European American; African Americans, Asian Americans, Latinos, and Native Americans together represent less than 10 percent of prospective teachers, and this percentage is steadily declining (American Association of Colleges of Teacher Education, 1987).

At the same time the demographics of the school population have been changing, so have our understandings about the difficulties inherent in the educational system at every level in the United States. There is increasing evidence, for example, that teachers are most able to understand, set appropriate expectations, and provide strategic support for students who are like themselves in culture, race, and ethnicity (Hilliard, 1974; McDiarmid, 1990), and that it is difficult for teachers to avoid misunderstandings and effectively teach "other people's children" (Delpit, 1988; Kozol, 1991). This intensifies the educational import of the disparity between the nation's teaching force

Harvard Educational Review Vol. 56 No. 1 Winter 1995, 541–570

and its schoolchildren and has enormous implications for the pre-service teacher education curriculum.

Faced with this disparity and acknowledging the limitations of people's knowledge about values and experiences different from their own, teacher educators across the nation have been attempting to open a discourse about race, racism, and teaching in the pre-service curriculum (e.g., Hilliard, 1974; Rosenberg, in press–a; Tatum, 1992, 1994). Many prospective teachers and teacher educators find this discourse powerful but unsettling, in part because it is often difficult to reconcile new understandings with their own prior experiences and assumptions about the meritocracy of the U.S. educational system, and in part because they realize that no obvious solutions exist. Indeed, when we "unleash unpopular things" (Britzman, 1991) by making race and racism explicit parts of the curriculum, responses are often strongly emotional (Rosenberg, in press–b), and resistance, misunderstanding, frustration, anger, and feelings of inefficacy may be the outcomes (Britzman, 1991; Tatum, 1992, 1994).

As teacher educators attempt to open the unsettling discourse of race in the pre-service curriculum, they need to examine how this discourse and its implications for particular schools, communities, and classrooms are constructed and interpreted. In this article, I attempt to do so by juxtaposing the written and oral inquiries of two student cohorts from one teacher education program with analysis of some of my own efforts as the program's director and as architect/instructor of its core courses in language and learning. First, I suggest that these student teachers' construction of the issues of race, racism, and teaching was a process characterized by both rewriting autobiography and constructing uncertainty — terms I define below. I draw on the words of student teachers, both written and oral, to provide a sense of the depth of their thoughtful intellectual work as they wrestled with the tenacious complexity of these issues. Next I attempt, as a teacher educator, to interrogate my own construction of the issues by exposing the images embedded in our pre-service teacher education program — images of passion, power, and truth, and the image of the center of the curriculum. Reflexivity about my own efforts suggests that teacher educators and their pre-service programs may convey contradictory messages about the responsibilities of teachers who work with students who are both like them and not like them in race, culture, and ethnicity.

Race, Racism, and Teaching:
Opening an Unsettling Discourse in the Pre-Service Curriculum

Designed during the teacher education reform period in the latter part of the 1980s (Clift, Veal, Johnson, & Holland, 1990; Cochran-Smith, 1991a; Feiman-Nemser, 1990; Holmes Group, 1990), Project START is a fifth-year pre-service program designed to support student teachers' efforts to engage in inquiry as an integral part of the activity of teaching and to "teach against the grain" (Cochran-Smith, 1991b) of many standard school practices.[1] The program was intended to build the social, organizational, and intellectual contexts necessary to support pre-service education as both inquiry and reform.

Pre-Service Education as Reform and Inquiry

When experienced Philadelphia-area teachers and University of Pennsylvania teacher educators collaboratively designed Project START, we agreed on several major premises. First, we assumed that teaching is a political activity (as opposed to a neutral one) in which every teacher participates by engaging in practices that either perpetuate or challenge the educational system and the inequities embedded within it (Aronowitz & Giroux, 1985; Zeichner, 1986). Second, we took the perspective that teaching is an intellectual activity as opposed to a technical one (Zumwalt, 1982). In the technical view, it is assumed that the teacher applies generalized principles, implements curriculum and instructional plans generated by others, and translates theory into practice. Instead, we regarded the teacher as decisionmaker and generator of knowledge, perspectives, and theories, and, like her students, as an active agent in her own learning, using the classroom as a site for inquiry and continuously interrogating her own and others' assumptions (Cochran-Smith & Lytle, 1993). This view of teaching is linked to our third assumption about knowledge as something that is fluid and socially constructed, and hence as something that changes and is able to be changed over time. Along these lines, we understood that teachers and students together construct classroom life and the learning opportunities that are available there (Bloome & Green, 1984; Erickson, 1986), essentially negotiating curriculum, as well as what counts as knowledge, instruction, and critique.

From the beginning, then, the goal of Project START was not reproduction of "current best practice" or implementation of "the knowledge base," but educational reform with the intention that pre-service teachers would develop an intellectual and socially responsible stance toward teaching and design their own roles as agents for school and social change. This viewpoint is related to our final premise about learning to teach. As we designed the program, we assumed that students could not learn to be reforming, researching, and reflecting teachers only at the university from individuals whose work was *about* schools but did not take place *in* schools. In other words, we believed that student teachers could not learn to be reformers at the university and then go "do reform" in the schools. We acknowledged that outsiders' perspectives (often university generated) are important in pre-service teacher education, but also and at least as importantly, we asserted

[1] Project START is currently supported by the Graduate School of Education at the University of Pennsylvania and by grants from the Milken Family Foundation; research about the relationships of student teachers' inquiry, knowledge, and practice is supported by a major grant from the Spencer Foundation.

that student teachers need to learn in the company of school-based mentors who have developed critical perspectives based on their work inside schools — on their own struggles to work both with and against the grain of prevailing practices and perspectives by staying inside the system (Cochran-Smith, 1991b).[2]

Teacher Educator as Researcher

Penn is a large research university in urban Philadelphia. The student population is primarily White European American, although the university's next-door neighbors in West Philadelphia are African American and Asian communities and schools, and, in parts of North and Northeast Philadelphia, Latino communities. Seventy-nine percent of the students in Project START, who range in age from early twenties to early forties, are White European American, while 21 percent are African American, Asian American, or Latino/a.[3] Twenty-six percent and 23 percent of cooperating teachers and supervisors, respectively, are African American or Latino, with the remainder White European American. Our student teachers work in public schools and a few independent schools in the Philadelphia area where, desegregation efforts notwithstanding, many school populations are homogeneous in terms of race as well as socioeconomic class. In schools that appear on the surface to be more integrated, the racial tension is sometimes intense, with individual groups insulated from or even hostile toward one another.

---

[2] Several social and organizational structures were designed to support pre-service education as inquiry and reform. Student teachers progress in two cohorts of 20-25 each, participating together in study groups, seminars, courses, and teacher research groups over a twelve-month period. Each student teacher simultaneously completes university coursework and a full year of student teaching in the same classroom with the same teacher (four months of student teaching two days per week, four months of student teaching five days per week). Methods courses emphasize critical issues in theory and practice, and require teacher research projects that are implemented in student teaching classrooms and evaluated by both university and school mentors and by course instructors. Groups of three to four student teachers are placed at specially selected elementary school sites with cooperating teachers who, in a variety of ways, are involved in school, curricular, and community reform efforts (e.g., curriculum redesign projects, teacher research and publication, alternative schools and programs, grassroots parent-teacher community groups, teacher networks and collaboratives, and other teaching and school reform efforts). Each small group of student teachers, their cooperating teachers, and a university supervisor meet weekly as a school-site teacher researcher group to read, write, think, and talk about serious issues in teaching, learning, and schooling.

In addition, all groups meet monthly for a university-site seminar on teaching, learning, and learning to teach. University supervisors and program faculty meet regularly in a teacher-educator-as-researcher group to inquire about their own theories and practices of teacher education. Supervisors, faculty, and cooperating teachers meet twice yearly to assess and revise the program. All participants in the program are regarded as teachers, learners, and researchers. They have opportunities to participate in a variety of teacher research activities through course assignments, school- and university-site activities, in-house and regional publications and professional forums, and the larger professional community.

[3] These are the figures for the 1993–1994 academic year (START class of 1994); the figures for the START class of 1995 are slightly different, with 75 percent of students White European American and 25 percent African American, Asian American, and Latino/a. The START class of 1996 includes 78 percent White European American and 22 percent African American, Asian American, and Latino/a students.

In our pre-service program, members of the START community — faculty, supervisors, and cooperating teachers — have been trying to revise the curriculum to meet the needs of students and teachers in the local Philadelphia context, as well as in the changing scene nationwide. For years, a central thread of the curriculum has been the examination of race, class, and culture and the ways these structure both the U.S. educational system and the experiences of individuals in that system. For years our students have read Ogbu, Comer, Delpit, Bell, and Heath, as well as Giroux, Taylor and Dorsey-Gaines, Ladson-Billings, Rodríguez, Rose, Sleeter and Grant, and Steele, and recently they have been exposed to Asante, Fordham, Foster, Tatum, Seale, Dorris, and McIntosh.[4] They have also read the published and unpublished writings of other student teachers, experienced teachers, and teacher educators from the local teacher research community, and those of teacher research groups across the nation. They have participated in class discussions, teacher research group school-site meetings, oral inquiry processes, cultural diversity workshops, and cross-school visitations and seminars intended to explore the relationships of race and teaching. In addition, they have written hundreds and hundreds of pages of reflective journal entries, essays about course readings, personal narratives, and small-scale studies, attempting to link their own educational experiences to their student teaching classrooms and to the empirical and conceptual writings of others.

As director of the program, my general commitment to opening and sustaining a discourse about race and teaching is unflagging. Over the last few years, however, I have become increasingly uncertain about what this unsettling discourse means for the students and teachers in our program and in teacher education programs more generally, and about how this discourse informs beginning teachers as they set out to teach in urban, suburban, small town, and rural schools. Part of my uncertainty stems from the rapid growth of national attention to issues of multicultural education. While I believe that many goals of the movement are essential, I also find parts of it cause for concern. I wonder if slickly packaged multicultural materials, preplanned diversity activities, and school assemblies featuring the "the culture of the month" sometimes take on a life of their own in K-12 teaching, as well as in teacher education programs, and thus obscure a more direct confrontation of race and racism.

The more gnawing part of my uncertainty, however, lies closer to home. It is about my own program, my own institution, and my own teaching. Despite more than twenty years as a teacher and teacher educator, with most of them in urban areas, I realize how little I really know about how to do this work. I know little, for example, about how student teachers really make sense of their year in our pre-service program. I worry about who and what we are reading — the race and ethnicity of the authors, their perspectives

---

[4] Bibliographic information for each reading is provided in the references section at the end of this article.

about language and curriculum, the balance of the personal and more distanced accounts of school experiences that are included in the syllabus. I worry about the implicit — and powerful — messages we convey, considering that our school has so few faculty of color. I wonder what racial perspective is perceived as "regular" or "normal" in our curriculum and what that means for White students and for students of color. I worry about divisions student teachers perceive between "progressive" and "traditional" curricula, suburban and urban schools, Black and White teachers, poor and privileged children, their own and others' families — divisions that may be subtly reinforced rather than challenged by students' field experiences across school sites and by the critical and more or less progressive perspectives that our pre-service program espouses.

I worry about how we can have more open discussions about race and teaching among our own staff, many of whom have worked pleasantly together for many years, let alone among our student teachers and their cooperating teachers who know each other much less well. How can we open up the unsettling discourse of race without making people afraid to speak for fear of being naive, offensive, or using the wrong language? Without making people of color do all the work, feeling called upon to expose themselves for the edification of others? Without eliminating conflict to the point of flatness, thus reducing the conversation to platitudes or superficial rhetoric? In short, over the past several years, I have become certain only of uncertainty about how and what to say, whom and what to have student teachers read and write, about who can teach whom, who can speak for or to whom, and who has the right to speak at all about the possibilities and pitfalls of promoting a discourse about race and teaching in pre-service education.

With these questions in mind, I set out to examine how student teachers construct the issues of race and teaching during their pre-service program. My analysis was part of a larger program-wide effort to interrogate our attempts as teacher educators to help student teachers understand the real and imagined, visible and invisible boundaries of race, racism, and teaching. My part, as director of the program and instructor of courses on language, learning, and literacy, was to examine class discussions that explicitly dealt with race and teaching, as well as the critical essays and personal narratives that student teachers completed for my course.[5] Toward this end, I reviewed 126 essays, forty-two personal narratives, and more than three hundred pages

---

[5] "Language, Learning and Looking in Elementary Classrooms," one of the courses that I teach, is a two-semester course that explores the relationships among language, learning, and culture, and their implications for the teaching of reading, writing, and oral language in elementary classrooms. The course draws on the writing of university-based and school-based teachers, writers, and researchers. Closely connected to classroom fieldwork and seminars, the course is designed to help students think through the relationships of theory and practice, learn how to learn from children, and construct perspectives about teaching and learning language and literacy. Over the two semesters, students explore and study modes of teacher inquiry as well as reading/writing pedagogy and assessment. Three threads run throughout the course: critical perspectives on the relationships of literacies and race, class, gender, and ethnicity; a view of

of transcriptions of small and large group discussions that occurred over the period of about a month in my class. I found that my students' questions served as powerful lenses for seeing my own questions and prompted me to interrogate some of my own assumptions and constructions about race and teaching.

Student Teachers' Constructions of the Issues of Race and Teaching

In my language and learning class, we talked extensively about hegemony and privilege in the context of many of the works referred to earlier: about the fact that U.S. society writ large is not a meritocracy but is embedded in social, political, economic, and educational systems that are deeply and fundamentally racist; and about the ways and the extent to which each of our individual lives is structured by the privileges or disadvantages conferred upon us by virtue of race, gender, ethnicity, and language orientation. We used Sleeter and Grant's (1987) conceptual framework for definitions of "multicultural education," ranging from crafts and ethnic food days all the way to pedagogies that are intended to be both multicultural and politically and socially reconstructionist. These discussions served as the backdrop for the segment of the class explicitly devoted to issues of race and teaching.

Analysis of the topics and themes that run throughout the data revealed that during this segment of the class, students were doing two kinds of intellectual work that I came to think of as *rewriting autobiography* and *constructing uncertainty*.[6] By intellectual work, I mean the particular interpretive tasks that were taken on by individuals and groups of student teachers: the problems posed about children and families, the dilemmas considered unanswerable, the knowledge made problematic, the evidence sought in order to document and explore issues, the bodies of knowledge brought to bear on classroom situations, the ways experiences were connected, and the themes that were made central in the struggle to understand the issues of race and teaching (Cochran-Smith, 1991b).

---

teaching as an intellectual activity and knowledge for teaching as socially constructed; and a theory- and research-based approach to the construction and critique of instructional and assessment practices.

Following an initial segment on "Learning from Children: Observation, Reflection, and Teacher Research," the course introduces "Critical Perspectives on Teaching, Learning, and Schooling." For this segment, the 1994 students read selections by Sleeter and Grant, Giroux, Comer, Asante, Brown, Joe, Heath, Rose, McIntosh, Carrier, Tatum, Seale, Delpit, Garcia et al., Sola and Bennett, and Muldanado.

[6] My analysis of my students' construction of the issues represents my perspective as a teacher educator on their work and their words. I make no pretense that I speak for them or interpret their discourse in ways that are identical to theirs. In an effort to provide a richer sense of people's varying perspectives, however, I sent the students multiple drafts of this article and invited them to respond, especially to tell me where their perspectives diverged from mine. I have tried to indicate, primarily through footnotes, points about which students disagreed or offered alternative interpretive perspectives.

Rewriting Autobiography

Many students responded to readings and class discussions by doing what I came to think of as "rewriting their autobiographies," or reinterpreting some of their own life stories and/or previous experiences. McIntosh's (1989) discussion of White privilege and her distinction between prejudice, on the one hand, as individual acts of kindness or meanness, and racism, on the other, as the invisible system of unearned privileges and disadvantages embedded in our entire system, was extremely powerful. Many White students and students of color were prompted to revise some parts of their life stories, based on the realization that no matter how much or how little they had already acknowledged the role race played in their lives and the lives of others, there had still been too little acknowledgment of it and too much silence about it.

For some White students, the process was literally a re-seeing of their lives, not as morally neutral and average, but as filled with the privileges conferred by race. This was a powerful and sometimes painful process. As the following excerpt from a small group discussion reflects, students often opened their comments with qualifiers such as, "I feel really naive and stupid when I say this, but I've never considered White privilege before. It's embarrassing," or, "It's very humbling to realize these things."[7]

> *Kristin Gusick:* When I was reading McIntosh, I just thought that this related so much to what I . . . what I was learning in my high school in that I never even like realized all these different things that show that we White people have privilege. I just never even thought of them. I just took them for granted and you know, I thought everyone was like this. And I thought all of my friends were normal and that I was normal, that I wasn't oppressing anybody because I never did anything wrong. But, um, I realized that there were a lot of like unconscious things going on that I just never took time to look at and realize that they were there. . . . It is so embedded within me it's frightening.

The next example is excerpted from a readings essay written by a START student just prior to the one highlighted above; I use it here because it connects so directly to Gusick's comments and provides some sense of the consistency of students' concerns with these issues across the years. In her essay, Peggy Kaplan, a student teacher who entered teaching after several years as a homemaker and mother, confronted the realization that the current arrangements of schools and society not only provided unearned privi-

---

[7] Examples included here are excerpted from three kinds of course inquiries: small group or whole class discussions that took place as part of regular class sessions; written essays wherein students responded to the ideas presented in selected readings and explored the issues and questions they found most important; and personal narratives wherein students wrote about experiences that had influenced their individual perspectives on race or class. Each example is used with permission.

leges for members of the majority, including herself and her own children, but also handicapped the children she was teaching in her student-teaching classroom, children who were not part of that majority in either language or race (Cochran-Smith, 1995):

> *Peggy Kaplan:* Hegemony is a large and complex concept. It is also a lofty way to say prejudice. Except this concept is covert, insidious, and often-times unconscious, which makes it much more difficult to battle. Many times it is even hard to recognize. However, it is a useful concept that has helped to clarify so much of what I am witnessing in my [student teaching] school and in my life.
>
> McIntosh's article spoke about me when it said, "I think Whites are carefully taught not to recognize White privilege." I know I was. I was taught everyone was equal. It never occurred to me that I got what I did because I could fit into the system. . . . McIntosh must have shared my experiences because again she captured my sentiments when she wrote, "My schooling gave me no training in seeing myself as an oppressor, as an unfairly advantaged person, or as a participant in a damaged culture. Because I succeeded through the system am I more likely to perpetuate it, even if it is unwillingly or unknowingly?"
>
> I recognize I am a classic by-product of this system. How, as a teacher, can I impart another set of values? Hunter [an urban public school with a large Hispanic population in a poor area with serious drug and crime problems] is a perfect example of hegemony, but more importantly so is Merion [a public school in an affluent White suburb where nearly all children go to college]. I student teach at Hunter; I am the proud parent of a second grader at Merion. Neither school is trying to change the system and therefore Merion will always succeed in reproducing the "future executives" and Hunter will always be struggling to have its children merely come to class daily. Merion will be able to win all the awards because standardized tests seem to be stacked in its favor while Hunter [won't] measure up.
>
> Case in point: Hunter had been told to test all kindergartners . . . in memorization, word, and letter skills. Over half the children in my [kindergarten] class speak Spanish at home and know only minimal English. The test will be given in English. . . . I see these young and eager children possibly being placed on the path of low expectation and failure.
>
> I feel the unfairness is the consequence of hegemony. I am wrestling with its implications. But how do I fight against a system that gives my own children the life I want them to have? I moved from the city to give them the same advantages I had. My husband and I chose Lower Merion Township because it offered the lifestyle and schools we wanted. I will have a tough time bucking a system that works for myself and my children. Does that mean I am part of the problem and not the solution?

While many White students struggled to rewrite their autobiographies by shifting the story from one that was morally neutral to one structured by unearned privilege that also disadvantaged others, some students of color wrote about how they had consciously tried not to think about race in their lives, attempting to assimilate into mainstream culture by "acting White" and shunning people and events of their own race or by attempting to be "race-less" (Fordham, 1988). The following is an excerpt from a personal narrative:

Julie Wang: "Chink!" "Flat face!" Listening to my fourth grade classmate hurl these insults at me brought tears to my eyes. I knew that she was jealous of my test score, but why did she have to hurt me in this way? At that moment, all I could feel was embarrassment and shame. Why did I have to look different from the other girls? Why couldn't I be "normal" so that I would not be made fun of? What turned out to be a desire to be "normal" eventually became a long struggle to separate myself from anything re-motely Asian. . . . The unspoken pressure between siblings and friends to be "American" and not "too Asian" pervaded my life. At times, I was told that my hair was too black and too straight. . . . I had to be careful that my pant legs were not too short; otherwise I would be "FOB" also known as "fresh off the boat." My sisters, friends and I discouraged each other from being interested in Asian boys. . . .

I did not participate in any cultural organization's activities [at college] because I did not want to be exclusionary. How ironic it was when I chose to be part of a [sorority] system that was associated with exclusion and elitism. . . . My years at Penn went smoothly. I was involved with my studies and my sorority, hardly questioning the issue of race and culture as it pertained to me. . . .

[But later] as president I represented Penn's chapter at a biannual con-vention in Orlando. In a crowd of hundreds of collegiate women repre-senting their sorority chapters, I was only one of two Asian Americans pre-sent. This was the nineties! Why were they still all White? Why were there no other minorities represented? I knew the answer [then]. I felt like a stranger who did not belong.

Particularly in response to Tatum's (1992) discussion of the development of racial identity, both White students and students of color also examined their own prejudice even though they also all qualified their comments with openers such as, "I don't like to think of myself as a prejudiced person." One of the students quoted in Tatum's article was a White woman who was angry with herself after taping her responses to a questionnaire on racial attitudes. She commented that she was surprised and upset when she discovered that she responded differently to the same questions about different races. First, quoting from Tatum's students' comments in her small discussion group, an African American woman in my class stated that she also was angry when she acknowledged some of her own stereotyped notions about African American men:

Dawn Lazarus Goode: I, as a Black female, share [some of the stereotypes about Black men] in spite of my "openness to people of all races." [I realize] I have been socialized to believe that [a] cautionary reaction is common sense in an urban community, rather than racist. The important thing is not being innocent or guilty. Steele suggests [that] often by presuming our innocence we are, in fact, declaring our guilt. What is important to me is that all of us, Blacks and Whites, recognize and identify with prejudices so that we may move forward.

Each of these examples offers a glimpse of ways student teachers began to reconsider and reconnect their personal experiences to new understandings and insights about race and racism, and the ways these both shape and are embedded in the institutions in which we live, especially our educational institutions. Part of what was important in this sort of inquiry was that students struggled to identify and locate themselves within those institutions. The point was not for student teachers to accept blame or guilt because they had been part of a system based on hegemony rather than meritocracy. It was, rather, to interrogate the ways they as educators from that point on would understand and act on the successes and failures of individual students and groups of students, the actions and apparent inaction of parents and community members, and the educational categories and labels often assigned by educational experts and diagnosticians.

Asante's (1991) provocative and controversial argument for an Afrocentric curriculum and his critique of the standard "neutral" U.S. curriculum as Eurocentric and biased prompted more students to rewrite their autobiographies, particularly regarding their own educational experiences. For example, many students were astounded by the realization that although they thought they had had solid liberal and supposedly "liberating" educations at some very fine undergraduate institutions, the breadth of their studies was actually very narrow. The following excerpt from a small group discussion gives some sense of this:

David Smith: It's stunning to me that no one talks about this stuff! In college, I didn't have a single advisor who encouraged me to take a Black History course. Not one! And that blows me away! Because I wasn't going to do it on my own. I did not have the background that would say, "Go take a Black History course." But if an advisor had sat down and said, "I think you'd really benefit from this and I think you'd learn a lot." . . . These articles are just blowing me away! I wonder where they've been all my life, you know?

Liz Duffey: Yeah.

Alexandra don Konics: You want to give these articles to everyone else so that they're thinking about this too!

David Smith: You do, you really do!

Liz Duffey: And you were supposed to have this liberal arts education that was supposed to cover so many different facets . . .

David Smith: You know what blows me away? I had two majors [at Oberlin College] . . . one of them was philosophy, and I suddenly thought back [and realized that] every single philosopher I had studied was a White European male. That's what we studied! And it's like, well, *what about the other people?* And I never thought of that until a week or two ago when it suddenly dawned on me, "My God, I read *nothing but* White European male philosophers!"

Liz Duffey: I didn't take any Black History classes [at Duke] either and I really . . . am I ever going to get the opportunity to do that again?

David Smith: That's how I feel. That's what you're supposed to do in college — be exposed to this kind of thinking. . .

Monica Goldberg: [While a Penn undergraduate], I took "History of the South," but it was [listed] under "History" and I think "Anthropology," and it wasn't [listed] under African American Studies so there were very few Black women and men. And I know my roommate now is taking an African American Studies course and it's all Black people in it, and there's three White people, you know? They don't come to the White classes and we don't go to those classes. It's just stupid.

Liz Duffey: Although I understand more [having read Asante and Tatum] why people of color would be more reluctant to go to "White History" classes [in college] because for the first time at the collegiate level they [can choose] to put themselves in the center of their own education. And that's got to be a phenomenal experience. . . .

David Smith: Most people have *already had* twelve years of "White History" anyway . . . only the teachers just called it history.

Much discussion occurred in response to reading Asante about whether all students should have an *Afro*-centric curriculum. Students raised thoughtful questions: Shouldn't Latino students have a Latino-centered curriculum? What do you do in classes where there are various racial and cultural groups represented? They asked these questions in class, they wrote about them in their essays and inquiry projects, and, when Asante came to speak to our group later in the year, they asked him to elaborate on and clarify his position. Interestingly, however, there was little overt resistance to his fundamental premise that all students should have the opportunity to learn within the context of their own cultural references (Asante, 1991).

At a certain level, I think students displayed little resistance because they realized that locating all students within the context of their own cultural references was an obviously important thing to do, once they connected the fact of cultural and racial hegemony to their personal realizations about privilege and prejudice. Although unsettled, they were receptive to Asante's and others' claims that European history is not the only history nor its starting point, that the European "discovery" of the American continent was not discovery at all but encounter, enslavement, and even genocide, and that European perspectives are not universal standards of the evolution of higher order thought, but culturally and socially constructed habits of mind developed in a particular context to serve particular purposes.[8]

I do not want to suggest, however, that students naively or blithely accepted the idea of decentering and then radically reconstructing the curriculum, or that all student teachers immediately went out and altered the curriculum in their student-teaching schools. I also do not want to suggest that all students were responsive to dealing intensely with issues of race or that they consistently understood or acknowledged its implications for every aspect of teaching, learning, and schooling. Over the years that our program and my courses have emphasized issues of race and teaching, some groups of students have asserted that the focus was much too heavy. Occasionally, a few have threatened to refuse to attend future seminars or classes if we continued to talk about it. At the same time, some students have complained bitterly that we did not do enough to help them deal with the issues of race and teaching, and still others have offered that what we were doing was just right, an entirely appropriate balance.

For the two cohorts analyzed here, however, these positions did not surface (at least not in the public discourse contexts of course discussions and papers). I found that the student teachers in these groups participated quite thoughtfully in constructing a complex set of questions about what the issues of race and teaching might mean for their own lives and for their work lives as teachers. For the most part, the issues they constructed were about uncertainty.

Constructing Uncertainty

I use the term "construct" as I describe the student teachers' knowledge of race and teaching in order to suggest that the process was not simply a matter of grasping or understanding ideas — full-blown and clear — that already existed. It was instead a labor-intensive and in some cases protracted process

---

[8] Deirdre Flint, a student, pointed out that some START students came into the program fully aware of the narrow perspectives they had been taught in school and indeed perhaps chose the program because of the congruence with their own political commitments. She wrote in response to a draft of this article:

> I can tell you from the endless discussions we had about START outside of classrooms, that at least a handful of us were certainly not unsettled. Although I had far from what I considered to be an Afrocentric curriculum when I taught a ninety-eight percent African American fifth grade class for two years . . . I spent a great deal of time researching and trying to present American History (which I was required to teach) in the context of the African American experience. . . . Many of my friends in the START program had not had the opportunity to teach, but certainly had reflected upon the shortcomings, fallacies and narrowness of the dominant historical perspectives they had been taught. Thus, Asante's ideas particularly concerning European history were not a shock or revelation but rather served to affirm and expand their own reflections and beliefs.

of students' invention of the issues in ways that made sense for them, given their own prior experiences with families, schools, and communities, their own status as raced and gendered persons in the world, and their own field-work situations as student teachers. This construction of knowledge, however, was not like the process of constructing a house, wherein one stands outside the basic structure and places each brick or board so that it rests on the ones beneath and in turn supports the ones yet to be mortared or hammered in and from which, when the roof nicely overarches everything, and the house is finished, the constructor can walk away or move inside.

The process of constructing knowledge about race and teaching was more akin to building a new boat while sitting in the old one, surrounded by rising waters. In this kind of construction process, it is not clear how or if the old pieces can be used in the new "boat," and there is no blueprint for what the new one is supposed to look like. It is also not clear whether the new boat will float, hold the weight of its builder, or hold back the water. And, of course, as one is trying to build the new boat, one is stuck inside the old one, struggling to negotiate tricky waters, not to mention rapids, hidden rocks, and unpredictable currents.

If this metaphor works at all, it should be clear that the students' construction of the issues was punctuated with uncertainty — with an unending string of such comments as, "Yes, but then what about this or that?" or, "I've been thinking about this all week, and I still don't understand how these things fit together" or, "I see things now that I hadn't seen before, but I don't see my place in all this" or, "This whole thing makes me so angry I really don't know what to do" or, "I'm sick of talking about this all the time." Constructing uncertain knowledge about race and teaching meant feeling doubtful, confused, angry, and surprised (or "blown away" as some students liked to say) by new realizations. These are psychic conditions that are difficult and very different from the conditions successful students are used to feeling in school where the point, as we know, is often to get the right answer, summarize the major points, or, in some college classrooms, restate the teacher's point of view.

In pre-service education, when both teacher and students own uncertainty, it causes stress and unrest and challenges some of the foundations of what "going to school" and "being a student" have meant in the educational history of student teachers. It is not surprising that this process sometimes explodes in unpredicted, off-putting, and even harsh directions.

Delpit's (1988) writing about the "culture of power" in schools and classrooms was important to these students struggling with uncertainty. Delpit argues that, although it may well not be the way we would like it to be, there is a culture of power in the schools that operates according to certain codes — codes that children from dominant racial and cultural groups often come to school understanding better than children not from those groups. As the small group discussion below reveals, student teachers wrestled with what this meant in their urban classrooms and in their suburban classrooms —

with what implications this had for preparing children who were from both minority and majority cultural or racial groups to live in a society that revolved around the majority groups and their gatekeepers:

Susan Tiedemann: I'm really committed to change and activism . . . but at the same time, it's really hard not to do certain things that I know go against what I believe in, but I know will help the children with the way society is today.

Elizabeth Zack: For example?

Susan Tiedemann: For example, I am a strong proponent of journal writing, but I also know that children have to have expository writing because if you can't write clearly and logically in the way society works today, and if you don't know grammar rules, [which goes against what I believe in about language learning,] you're not going to be able to write college essays, and you're not going to be able to get jobs. . . . I want my kids to be able to . . . Although I don't like the ways things are today, I want my children to be able to survive with the ways thing are today.

Laura Kripp: It's like in the one article where the children were studying . . . African literature. . . . The reason the teacher brought that up was because she really wanted them to become involved in literature, and wanted to spark their interest and [wanted them] to associate with what was going on in the literature. But the parents were upset because it wouldn't serve the aims of . . . integrat[ing their children] better into society.

Susan Tiedemann: [offers the example of reading Zora Neale Hurston instead of Shakespeare] It's really hard, because there is only so much time in the day. There are only so many things you can cover.

Elizabeth Zack: A goal of mine . . . is you want to get kids involved in what they're doing, and once they are excited about literature, then maybe you can say, "Oh, and by the way, here's Shakespeare, and let's read it and talk about it." You can talk about the values of it, and the history and everything else, but do that as well as Langston Hughes and Hurston, and Maya Angelou and Amy Tan.

Susan Tiedemann: I know, but it's just hard because there is so much to accomplish.

Discussions like these focused on the tension between student teachers' wanting to build on the linguistic and cultural resources children brought to school with them, but also to prepare all children to be able to participate in the dominant culture and to negotiate the existing power structures, even if ultimately to help dismantle them. Student teachers acknowledged that this dual agenda required some kind of balance — children need to know something about the "canon" of history and literature and how and when to utilize the conventions of standard English, but they also need to see their own experiences reflected in novels and history books, and they need to draw on and develop their considerable linguistic resources. How to do both was a year-long theme for many students and is, I would venture, a life-long theme for many teachers and teacher educators.

A related tension was how to teach about the culture of power and prepare children to participate in it, but at the same time not appear to endorse the inequities of that culture or to promote assimilation into it. After a fairly lengthy discussion trying to link Delpit, Asante, and McIntosh, one student questioned:

> *Lynn Parsons:* Does that mean we call for Afrocentrism but teach . . . culture of power too?

> *Traci Reisner:* We need to do both . . . and you need to be wary when you're teaching about power . . . that [you don't imply] that you agree with it, that that's how it should be, and the kids should know that, that just because you are learning the tools to be in power . . . [you don't agree with the power structure].

> *Lynn Bouck:* I think that's what's so important, because you have to explain to them why, I mean that a dialect, for example, is good, you know, and that there's nothing bad about it. But [you also need to] say that to get along in this society, just because it's the nature of the way it is right now, it's almost like we have to speak this way sometimes.

> *Traci Reisner:* In other words, like . . . teaching is more [about] acknowledging that you don't necessarily agree that the power should lie in formal English, [for example] . . .

> *Lynn Parsons:* But right now it is?

> *Traci Reisner:* Right. But be honest with your kids that you don't necessarily agree with that . . .

The students also constructed uncertainty about the differences between generalizations regarding various groups that promoted insights about communities, families, and individuals, versus stereotypes about groups that simply bolstered unexamined assumptions and were in and of themselves racist perspectives:

> *Laura Kripp:* I think [one of the central questions is] should we see a child as an individual? When does race confine them? And when does it help to define them?

> *Susan Tiedemann:* That is good . . . confining versus defining. And is defining confining in and of itself?

Elizabeth Zack: It's the difficulty of seeing people as individuals, people as a group, who defines who you are, who defines what group you're from, how are you defined. As a teacher, what centricity do you teach from? It's all related.

Julie Friedman: It relates a lot to my [point] when [people] say "[all] Asians are good at math" or . . . "all Natives are good craftsmen" . . . [instead of] "you're talented." [They mean] you were born with that talent, it's inherent in you [not that you did anything yourself]. So how do you make students feel that their individual talents are individual and unique without placing them in the culture and the race and the gender that they came from?

Some conversations further stretched the tension between stereotypes and understandings of groups other than one's own, and raised legitimate questions about the value or harm of "expert" anthropological information on groups of "others":

Gay Auerbach: Does ethnographic information constitute another form of stereotyping? . . . The kind of thing that I guess Erickson or Heath did . . . analyzing the culture of the community and then using that as information in the classroom. But in some settings I think it's much harder to get a sense of the culture of a community. . . . This is a progressive view of children, that you have to deal with what you have. And your job as a teacher is to find out how to meet their educational needs given who they are. Forget if they got it from their culture . . . where they got it. That's irrelevant. Because in a way, making those assumptions is stereotyping a whole culture.

Another group followed along the same lines in their discussion:

Elizabeth Zack: But, what's interesting though is [what happens] if we don't make generalizations. We keep talking about classifying people and we keep talking about different races and having a centric view, but if we don't make generalizations because we're saying that they're stereotypes, how can we then define how we are different [from one another]?

Laura Kripp: That's my argument. Teaching to individuals as opposed to teaching to groups of people. Because then you can't really go wrong, because you realize that every person is different, and although they bring things . . .

Elizabeth Zack: But, from what perspective are you teaching? Are you going to teach about lots of different cultures or . . . ?

Students were certain that they wanted to include information about many different groups in the curriculum, but they were uncertain about how to avoid add-ons (the "racial or cultural group of the week" syndrome); calling unwelcome attention to a particular child or children who were different from the majority in a given classroom (the "would you now like to share with us the African American or Chicano perspective" syndrome); or implying that the *real* cultural norm in the classroom was White and mainstream (the "I have several 'culturally diverse' children in my classroom" syndrome).

One student began to get at this issue by describing a problem with the "multicultural bookshelf" in her student teaching classroom:

> *Renee Wallach:* We're dealing with this right now in our classroom and actually my cooperating teacher is going to talk about this later on today. . . . We have a section in our classroom with books on a shelf and they're all [multicultural]. . . . There are Native American books and books about Chinese [people] and books about all different groups. But there is not one book on that shelf that's about White people, and the assistant teacher in the other class said, "Well, does that mean that by not having them on that shelf where the other ethnic groups are, . . . does that mean that we're excluding Whites [as a diverse group]?" [So I wonder, does that mean] that we're saying that the White people are the norms . . . they are the normal ones, and these are the exceptions — and how do you incorporate everyone into multiculturalism, not just those who are the minority?

Student teachers carried the discussion of stereotypes directly into their conversations about constructing new curricula with children, finding alternative materials and resources, and thinking about standard materials with new eyes. Responding to Native American educator Doris Seale's (1992) powerful argument for removal and withholding of books with damaging stereotypes, student teachers worried about censorship, selection and rejection of curriculum materials, and what revisionist views implied about the "the canon" of children's classics:

> *Marisol Sosa:* [Seale talks about] how images are perpetuated in children's literature that is really *revered* like *Little House on the Prairie* and how those negative images can impact those children in the classroom. But also, this passage/article was specifically about Indians. I think it was important to see how all images in all literature — how it's important to look at them critically and see, to keep in mind, "What is the negative impact that *this image* would have on *this child?*" It's important to be sensitive to that.

> *Liz Duffey:* I loved the Laura Ingalls Wilder books when I was little and I started to go back and reread sections of [them], and I was blown away because I had never had that perspective before and then I started to think it was like *The Education of Little Tree.* Does that mean there's no place for Laura Ingalls Wilder anymore in education?

> *Deirdre Flint:* [We talked last summer about censorship] and I'm still not sure whether or not I would censor things. I really was impressed by Doris Seale's view that in a way she *would* censor things, and sometimes I feel like I would with some of the really insulting books out there and the racist

books. It's interesting to find somebody that says, "I would rather not give any book to a child than one that's filled with misrepresentations and outright lies."

Finally, many student teachers admitted their personal uncertainties about how to talk about issues of race, especially in racially mixed groups. Some small group discussions touched gingerly on the question, but other students chose to write about it instead. The following excerpt is from one student's readings essay:

Dawn Lazarus Goode: Generally speaking, I do not believe that non-White people, particularly African Americans, share the same resistances to talking and learning about race and racism. Instead, African Americans tend to talk about racism in oppressor/oppressee terms where the roles of guilt and innocence are clearly defined. Thus the discussions of race between a group of Black students take on a very different nature than discussion in a predominantly White classroom involving Black students. It is both an example of what DuBois refers to as the "dual souls of Black folks" and a representation of the hopelessness that many feel about their situation and other people's understanding of it. I sometimes refrain from commenting on issues in class because I think "Why bother, they just don't understand" (thus the expression, it's a Black thing, you wouldn't understand it). Therefore, African Americans do not allow for many opportunities for White people to discuss and hear Blacks' points of view.

A mixed-race group of student teachers constructed this uncertainty in a small group discussion, wrestling with their own lack of experience talking candidly with others about race and feeling comfortable in groups with racial or cultural "others." This was especially evident in their recycling of phrases, their repeatedly beginning again, correcting themselves, groping for words:

Julie Wang: I think maybe . . . I'm trying to figure out my words here. . . . Maybe before this program or before this class, whatever, regardless of whatever stereotypes or feeling that we had about culture and race. . . . Now, it's like a common, kind of a determination for all of us to . . . kind of, be politically active in our approach towards race and culture because we are going to be future educators. It seems like before . . . you didn't really [have to] deal with the issue and I didn't really deal with the issues. . . . But now, I mean, we're all going to be teachers and that's our common ground here. And we're all going to be tackling this issue, hopefully, in the right way.

Art Kaiser: Then [the central question is] how we can, as teachers, encourage our students to get out of their . . . to be able to identify their own culture . . . [and] be able to learn from other cultures.

Dawn Lazarus Goode: Yeah . . . we don't have any control about who our kids are, unless you want to take yourself out of the school, out of the situation. Given what we're given, how do we bridge the gap between these cultures? How do we realize we have these stereotypes of people? [Let's say] we realize that. Okay, now that we can identify them, how do we deal with these children? How do they deal with us? How do we introduce them to other cultures as well as themselves without having this tension, this uneasy feeling of being out of control?

Eventually the student teachers in this group pieced together their central uncertainty: How do we help children develop their own racial and cultural identities and establish meaningful relationships with children of other races and cultures when we ourselves are uncomfortable with that? When, in fact, we have failed for most of our adult lives to talk directly and constructively with others about issues of race and culture?

What can be said about how these students understood the issues of race and teaching? From my perspective as their teacher, the students' discourse was always interesting and articulate, often poignant and insightful, and sometimes powerful, even painful. It was also in some ways refreshingly naive, lacking the broader, more experienced and realistic (perhaps cynical is the more accurate term) interpretive perspectives of their mentor teachers who had spent years in urban and suburban classrooms, struggling inside the confines of school bureaucracies, and working with communities and families in complex social, historical, and cultural contexts. The students' perspectives tended to be more hopeful. Although clearly uncertain about how to do what they wanted to do and sometimes very discouraged, they were for the most part positive and committed to making a difference in children's lives. I was heartened by their optimism, but I also worried about its longevity. I wondered, for example, whether the students' commitment to teaching children the skills they need to survive in (and work to alter) the dominant power structure would eventually become — depending on the pressures exerted by parents, schools, and local and national interest groups — an intellectual rationale for teaching only the standard curriculum. I wondered whether efforts to teach from a multi-centered perspective would result in an add-on curriculum where the center was still mainstream, White, and Eurocentric. And I worried about some students' insistence that "the answer" to the complex questions about culture, race, and language diversity was teaching all children as individuals. I wonder whether this was really a sophisticated way of resorting to color blindness (Cochran-Smith, 1995) and resisting confrontation of race and culture issues in the classroom.[9]

[9] One student, David Smith, strongly disagreed with my framing the concern this way. He wrote in response to an early draft of this article:

I must disagree with your comment that teaching students as individuals allows one to "resort to color blindness." I hold a very firm conviction that each student must be viewed, approached, and treated as an individual. For example, because of this belief, I would never . . . ask a person of color to speak for his or her race during a discussion on race.

It also needs to be said, of course, that my students' writings and conversations were partial representations of adults' values, beliefs, and attitudes, which were unlikely to change in a short period of time and were perhaps not related to their actions and decisions as teachers anyway. Although I would like to believe that my courses have a lasting impact on students and that all of their discourse is genuine, I am resigned to the reality that part of what it represents is the effort of a very smart and successful group of students who have figured out how to talk the talk and play the game in a graduate course taught by the director of a program with an explicit political stance on teaching.

A Teacher Educator's Construction of the Issues of Race and Teaching in Pre-Service Education

Research during the last decade has demonstrated that the formal aspects of pre-service teacher preparation do little to alter students' outlooks and practices, while the less formal, experiential aspects of student teaching — fieldwork experiences and especially exposure to the cultures of schools and teaching — are potentially significant influences (Feiman-Nemser, 1983; Zeichner, Tabachnick, & Densmore, 1987). My experience tells me that this is largely true, but I have come to think that the images that are implicit in pre-service pedagogy itself may also be among the most potent informal influences on how prospective teachers construct the issues of race and teaching. By implicit images, I mean the ways we teacher educators talk about "others" in our teaching, include or ignore multiple perspectives in discussions, express public uncertainty, interrogate our own assumptions, and make visible successful and failed efforts to alter our own teaching. What I want to argue here is that embedded in our pedagogy is a powerful subtext about the boundaries of race and teaching in schools and larger educational systems, not simply what we say to students about the kinds of teachers they should become, but in what we show them about the norms in our own classrooms. In the sections that follow, I attempt to expose two important images that existed beneath the surface of the discourse both in my classes and in the program more generally — *images of passion, power and truth* and *the image of the center of the curriculum.*

It's insulting to that person's individuality. But, in focusing on the individual, one must keep in mind that a part of that individual will likely have been formed or affected by the tripartite interaction between that person's race, culture, social class, gender, etc., and the society (i.e., the dominant group's society) of which he or she is a part, and the individual person. Race [and other factors] aren't ignored; on the contrary, they are very much taken into account in exploring who that person is; however, that is a far cry from simply assuming that a particular person is a particular person because of their specific race, class, culture, etc.

Images of Passion, Power, and Truth

As a teacher, I make no pretense that my courses present an unbiased array of perspectives about language, learning, and culture from which students are invited to mix and match their favorites. My courses have an explicit and (I hope) coherent point of view, and I do not apologize for the critical and generally progressive perspectives I assert about pedagogy, schooling, and society. But my courses also espouse a constructivist perspective — that is, that all viewpoints are historically, culturally, and socially located, that students and teachers together socially constitute meanings rather than transmit/receive ideas full-blown, and that students of all ages learn most felicitously by wrestling with difficult questions, considering conflicting interpretations, and interrogating their own assumptions. These principles and perspectives would seem to suggest a democratic and learner-centered pedagogy, wherein the teacher is facilitator and fellow traveler rather than shrewd influencer or even artful manager of students' responses to competing claims.

Transcriptions of whole class discussions about race and teaching, however, provided evidence to the contrary. They showed that as a teacher, I was neither democratic nor unbiased, that I frequently exhorted the class with passion and the ring of "truth" about the responsibilities of teachers. I clearly took a revisionist view of history and a critical view of the institutional arrangements that differentially distribute power and resources among groups who differ in race, class, gender, and culture. I urged student teachers to reconstruct the curriculum so that all children could find themselves in it and so that, despite the groups that might or might not be represented in a particular classroom, a Eurocentric White perspective not be portrayed as the universal or "normal" one. I tried to push students beyond the idea that we need simply to enlarge the curriculum by adding materials about "other" cultures and toward the idea that we need fundamentally to rethink what our notions of "other," "diverse," "normal," "progress," and "American" imply.

In the excerpt that follows, for example, I responded to several student teachers' questions about how, on a practical and fairly concrete level, they could actually do what we were reading about — this thing called "multicultural teaching" or constructing a "differently centered" curriculum or creating "socially reconstructionist" pedagogy:

Marilyn Cochran-Smith: You could ask me [how to do this exactly in a classroom] and I would say, "I don't know either." I think that one thing that Asante's saying that seems to be generally important is that every child needs to be able to find himself or herself in the curriculum. Now, that's a general kind of thing. What does that mean? Certainly, every child needs to find him or herself in the books that are used . . . but it's more than just having books, and I think we all know that . . . it's much more than that. It's [realizing that] there *is* a historical center to all this — [it's a center of] European history — and American history has been essentially European history — and it begins and ends with European discoveries of other parts of the world. . . . I think you need something else . . .

Do you know those posters that they [photographed] from space, that they made after the astronauts went into space? There was this . . . huge sort of from-space [cosmic] view of the world, and [then] there was this tiny little speck and there was an arrow [pointing to the speck] saying, "You are here." I think there's something about trying to help the kids have a different "you are here" perspective if they are in the dominant group, where everything about the media and the history books, etc., is telling them *not* "you are here — this tiny little speck," but "YOU ARE HERE!" Then [if that's the case], you need to help them get a smaller perspective.

[But] if they're in a group that isn't the dominant group and everything around them is telling them that they can't even find themselves, then maybe you need to be helping them find a "YOU ARE HERE" perspective that's bigger. And [even] with all this other stuff that's going on, "Here's *your* history and *your* ancestors and *your* literature" . . . I mean, it seems more that there are lots of different answers and all of it isn't spelled out in this article [or any other] and it's confusing and it raises enormous questions: Are we helping? . . . And what's this going to lead to? Is it going to make things worse than they already are? And yet in some ways, how can it be worse than it already is? . . . I don't know how to do it. And I think part of [the] argument [in these readings] is that *every* curriculum *is* centered whether you like it or not. It's not a choice, it has to have a center.

My motivation during this discussion was to make it clear that there was no particular lesson or unit a teacher could include that would make him or her a "multicultural" or "reconstructionist" teacher, just as I would suggest later in the course that there was no particular practice that necessarily qualified one as a "whole language" teacher (Edelsky, Altwerger, & Flores, 1991). Rather, I wanted to argue that critical pedagogy and whole language teaching were not matters of method, but were instead matters of the intellectual frameworks and political commitments that guided teachers' decisions, interpretations, and questions about both the immediacy of classroom life and the larger issues of curriculum, instruction, and social justice. I also wanted to emphasize that curricula are unavoidably value laden and historically situated, whether or not teachers realize that they are or intend them to be. My consistent theme was that, given the inevitability of teaching as political and value based, teachers were responsible for constructing pedagogy and curriculum with the explicit intention of reconstructing the system for social justice.

My comments above may or may not have made those points. But, examined in a different way, they expose one of the central tensions inherent in promoting a discourse about race in pre-service teaching — the tension between inviting students to formulate new and perhaps disconcerting insights, on the one hand, and, on the other hand, using the power of one's position as a professor to impose those perspectives. Paine's (1989) discussion of relativism, radical pedagogy, and paralysis in college English classrooms is useful here. He points out that despite extreme differences in ideology, an ironic similarity sometimes obtains between conservatives' and liberal humanists' fears of relativism and their apparent espousal of universal values. Paine argues that if critical theorists and radical pedagogues purport that all structures of knowledge and critique are relative, they must acknowledge that their own emancipatory visions and values are also relative, rather than the inevitable result of enlightened critical thinking:

> Teachers need to keep well in mind that equality and democracy are not transcendent goods that inevitably emerge when one learns to seek the truth through critical thinking. Rather, if those are the desired values, the teacher must recognize that he or she must influence (perhaps manipulate is the more accurate word) students' values through charisma or power; otherwise, one must depend on the assumption that those values are latent in students, and the teacher's job is merely to help the student bring them to the surface. It must be recognized, then, that emancipation is not a transcendental vision, but is a value, which, like all values, is contingent, and that if the teacher wishes to instill such a vision in students, he or she must accept the role as manipulator. (p. 563)

Paine's analysis rightly points out that we cannot both claim that all viewpoints are value laden and socially constituted, on the one hand, and argue for the ultimate right and truth of teaching for social justice on the other.

The tension between imposition and invitation in the pre-service discourse about race and teaching is uncomfortable and rather unappealing to me personally, but recognizing it is important. Part of what I found as I read and reread transcriptions of discussions in my classes was that when student teachers asked for answers about classroom teaching, I always said, "It depends," trying to convey that there are no universals in teaching, no recipes that work in every classroom, no algorithms for figuring out the tough questions. But through my lack of public uncertainty about the critical perspectives I espouse about race and schooling, I have come to realize that I gave them contradictory messages about the nature of knowledge and the role of power in teaching. Examining some of the formal and informal discourse in my courses helped me realize the importance of acknowledging my own uncertainties about the boundaries of race and teaching, and of revealing how my students' questions continuously magnify and intensify my own.

As teachers of and through critical pedagogy, whether our students are children or adults, the best we can do is openly admit our convictions and own our agendas. Then we must acknowledge the fact that if we influence students' views about race and teaching, it is not because we open their eyes to *the truth*, but to a great extent because we use professional status and personal charisma to persuade them of the perspectives we believe will support their efforts for social justice through the orchestration of readings, written assignments, discussion topics, and school experiences.

The Image of the Center

My students and I drew especially on the work of Delpit, McIntosh, and Asante to interrogate the White and often Eurocentric bias of much of the curriculum in U.S. schools. Asante (1991) explains the notion of "centricity" in education as follows:

> In education centricity refers to a perspective that involves locating students within the context of their own cultural references so that they can relate socially and psychologically to other cultural perspectives. . . . The centrist paradigm is supported by research showing that the most productive method of teaching any student is to place his or her group within the center of the context of knowledge. . . . For White students in America this is easy because almost all the experiences discussed in American classrooms are approached from the standpoint of White perspectives and history. . . . Consequently non-White students are also made to see themselves and their groups as the "acted upon." . . . [However,] a person educated in a truly centric fashion comes to view all groups' contributions as significant and useful. Even a White person educated in such a system does not assume superiority based upon racist notions. Thus, a truly centric education is different from a Eurocentric racist . . . education. (p. 171)

Asante's argument here and in later work (1994) is that teachers have to know their students, draw on their cultural and racial references, and build a center that does not privilege the dominant racial group over all others. As the first section of this article has demonstrated, student teachers struggled with what it would mean in schools and classrooms to "decenter" and/or "recenter" the curriculum of elementary schooling. At my urging, they raised questions about traditional teaching units such as Columbus's discovery of America or the Pilgrims' first Thanksgiving, classic children's texts such as *Little House on the Prairie* and Grimm's fairy tales, and standard European perspectives in science and history on civilization, progress, and forms of knowledge.

Despite my convictions about the kind of curriculum my student teachers should struggle to construct in their classrooms and despite the fact that student teachers of color represent some 20 percent of our program participants, I have come to see that the center of our curriculum and of my own teaching is indeed White in terms of racial perspective. I am not talking here about my personal perspective and experience; of course, as a White European American woman, my perspective and my position in the world are White and can never be anything else. What I mean is that I have come to see through close analysis of the program and of my students' discourse that the center of the program is helping White prospective teachers prepare to teach children who may not be like them in race and/or culture, rather than helping all student teachers, with full regard for race, interrogate their experiences and be prepared to teach in an increasingly multiracial and multicultural society. I believe that this image of the center, revealed in the informal discourse of the program and underlying the formal discourse, may be more powerful than my exhortations to the contrary and more powerful than the images specified in the formal discourse.

I have been worried about this for some time, worried that I am most effective at getting White students to explore issues of race and teaching because I am more able to locate them within the context of their own references, and because I come at these issues from perspectives and experiences that are more similar to theirs than to those of students of color. Several critical moments that occurred over the course of the program year have contributed to this growing realization.

In October, during the time that my class was having the discussions excerpted in the first part of this article, HBO aired the documentary, "I Am A Promise," which was filmed at the Stanton Elementary School in urban Philadelphia and was later to win an Academy Award. In a meeting of supervisors and staff, we watched the film when it was first aired, and then, partly in response to students' requests, showed it later that same day to them. The discussion in our supervisory group was deeply felt — some adamantly progressive teachers complained that the film did not show enough teaching, that we did not get a chance to see what was going on inside classrooms. Other supervisors countered that the film was not about classroom instruction but about the fact that society as a whole cares very little about what is happening to young urban African American children.

Some supervisors and staff were concerned about the stereotypes the film conveyed and about the strong images of Whites and Blacks it offered — a strong White principal committed to making a difference in children's lives, a Black disciplinarian with a bull horn yelling at the children on the playground, a White teacher who appeared unaware that one of the children in her class could not read, a Black older man who had more or less adopted a young girl when her family simply abandoned her, a Black male teacher who was teaching an experimental (and highly successful) class of Black five- and six-year-old boys, and many Black parents who were portrayed as inaccessible, violent, abusive, or involved in drugs and crime. One supervisor spoke bitterly about what she called a "conspiracy" in the Philadelphia schools where central administrators showed no interest in helping children, fostering a system that was tacitly designed to keep Black children in their place. She also pointed out that other schools — with White populations but just as difficult and hopeless as the one portrayed in the documentary — could have been filmed in urban Philadelphia to convey quite a different message. And all of us talked about the fact that film-makers unavoidably convey a very particular, very selective portrait when they construct so-called true-to-life documentaries, despite the fact that skillful films also create the illusion of an uncrafted natural view.

When student teachers viewed the film, the response was again heartfelt and intense. Many were visibly shaken and struggled to deal with what they saw as absolute hopelessness, wondering how they could make even the most remote difference in children's lives. Some expressed guilt, realizing that their own families, their own children, would never experience the kind of school and the kind of life revealed in the film. A few days later one student, Luke Sullivan, wrote about the film as part of an essay for my class. Technically, he had not followed instructions for the assignment, which explicitly required that students respond to course readings, but I began to realize that he was telling me something important with his essay, and I began to think about his critique of the film as an important comment about the image of the center embedded in our program:

"I Am A Promise" is a story told by White film-makers about a White principal working in a poor Black community. The principal is obviously a sincere and well intentioned person. It would be fair, from what we were shown in the film, to characterize her methods as traditional. It would also be fair to characterize her results, as portrayed in the film, as failing. Academic failure was depicted in the scene with the faculty at the end of the year as they went over the rankings of the students' scores relative to the rest of the city. Social failure was portrayed in the film's focus on the principal's constant efforts to get the children to behave, implying that she spent all her time during the school day on this issue. The scene of the White school guard in uniform dragging the nine year old boy across the school yard was particularly disturbing. Without any imagination it would be possible to see this as a scene from one of the TV law enforcement shows popular today. The ultimate failure was represented in the principal leaving the school system, for reasons unknown, at the end of the school year.

The film was shown on HBO, and is a mainstream depiction of a non-mainstream community. It is a story that the mainstream tells many times and serves to perpetuate the stereotypes of African Americans as a failed community. This portrayal is not balanced in the mainstream media with healthy and successful realistic images of non-mainstream African American communities. Just as the first grade boy stated that the only White men he saw were drug dealers with guns, many mainstream people have seen only unhealthy images of African Americans. This can also be said about some of the students in the START program. Race is a very difficult issue at Penn. I cannot think of an African American who is a member of the GSE faculty. The number of students who are "of color" is very small. Dr. Mitchell led the discussion on the film, the only time she has done so this year. Is she an expert on race because she is Black? . . .

After viewing the tape, I peeked at the paper of a female African American student sitting next to me and in regards to the film, she had written, "same ol' same ol'." Interestingly, she folded the paper up when she realized I was peeking, and I don't remember her saying anything in the discussion. . . . A male African American friend later said he believed the most damaging thing about the kind of portrayal found in "I Am A Promise" is that it misleads Black people into thinking that White people are their friends. His argument was that African Americans need less of the altruistic intentions and failed methods that have been tried in the past and more empowerment of African Americans to run their own affairs. He would argue that the all-male first grade classroom supported this view.

Two other incidents helped expose the image of the center underlying the curriculum. During the portion of my course devoted to critical perspectives, Susie Suk Yee Hung wrote me a note and later, at the urging of her supervisor, came to my office. She was upset that my course readings about race and culture did not include any articles or personal narratives about Asian American groups. She wondered how she was to find herself in the curriculum if the majority of readings described the experiences of African Americans, a few centered on Latinos and Native Americans, and none highlighted Asian Americans. Did I not consider Asians and Asian Americans minority groups in U.S. education? Had we not had Asian Americans in the student body previously? Or, was it possible that by omission, my course implied that Asians did not have problems or issues in the educational system based on their experiences of racism and their status as minority groups? Her questions left me with few ready answers. Initially, I felt somewhat defensive — after all, how could I possibly represent every group on my syllabus (and anyway, I was sure that I already paid more attention to questions of race and teaching than did many other teacher educators). But deep inside, I knew she was right. I was telling her — with passion, power, and the ring of "truth" — that all children needed to be able to find themselves in the curriculum, but I was not giving her that opportunity in my courses or in the program. It was clear which message she perceived as the more powerful one.[10]

Finally, during what was for many their last course in the program, a number of students took a course about minority experiences in educational settings taught by Paul Ongtooguk, an Alaska Native (Inupiat or "Northern Eskimo"), who was on our campus as a visiting instructor from the University of Alaska-Fairbanks. Many students — both White and students of color —

[10] Lynn Bouck, a student, confirmed Susie Suk Yee Hung's concerns in a response she wrote to a draft of this article. Bouck, a White European American woman who student taught at a school with a mixed Asian, White, African American, and Latino population, commented:

I do hope this results in some change. . . . Working at Lowell School opened my eyes to the same concerns that [Susie] felt albeit in a much less personal way. But I had such an overwhelming sense that through START, I was not being encouraged to look at the world through the eyes of students/people from all cultures, but instead mostly through the African American culture. It did unfortunately offend those working at such a diverse school as Lowell, I think.

commented directly to me and other staff members or wrote on their course evaluations about the tremendous impact this course had on their thinking about issues of teaching, race, and culture. They emphasized how different it was to discuss issues of race and teaching when the teacher spoke from both an outside and an inside perspective — a perspective that was outside the racial and cultural mainstream of the university and of schooling generally, and at the same time was inside the experience of a minority group that had suffered the disastrous social and economic consequences of racist educational policy and practice for many years. David Smith, a student, commented in a letter to me:

> Paul Ongtooguk's legacy to me is a presumption of the collected intelligence and wisdom of every culture. It's always there; if you don't see it at first, then you have to look harder. . . . As a teacher, you fight to get your students to understand that. Boldly put, you take every kid out to the desert, to the mountains, to the arctic tundra and say, "Deal with this." And sometime (hopefully before they die) you let them hear or read how people who have lived in those conditions for millennia have learned to deal with it. And the intelligence and wisdom of those people shine through.

With almost no exceptions, this course was the only one students in our program had that was taught by a person of color.

What concerns me most about these incidents are the powerful and probably not so hidden lessons they teach my student teachers about teaching and race. As I struggled to make sense of my student teachers' uncertainties, they helped me realize how important it was for me and my colleagues in teacher education to examine closely the assumptions and structures of our own program — to consider whose perspectives are accounted for and whose are not, who finds herself or himself in the curriculum and who does not, to examine how White students and students of color, men and women, younger and more mature students, students from middle-class professional backgrounds and those from working-class backgrounds, experience the program.

I have begun to wonder whether those for whom my course content (and perhaps the curriculum more generally) fits most comfortably — even when they are dealing with admittedly difficult issues — are White women students who can identify most easily with me and my perspectives, since we are alike in many ways and they are at the center. And, I have come to think that teacher educators who are committed to preparing teachers who are able to build on and enrich the linguistic and cultural resources of all children, whether like them or not like them in race, culture, class, and gender, have an essential and difficult task. We must look unflinchingly at our own teaching and our own programs — at what we say about a multicentered, multicultural curriculum on the one hand, and what we demonstrate about it on the other.

Uncertain Allies

People who lead cultural and racial diversity courses and workshops often talk about the importance of becoming allies to others — that is, becoming sensitive to issues of race from perspectives other than our own and working actively with others to promote not simply *non*-racist, but *anti*-racist educational views and practices. The notion of *teacher as ally* or activist is akin to Aronowitz and Giroux's (1985) more general concept of the teacher as transformative intellectual who develops critical pedagogy, to Sleeter and Grant's (1987) promotion of teaching that is multicultural as well as socially reconstructionist, and to my arguments (Cochran-Smith, 1991a) for teachers who challenge the inequities in the system by learning to teach against the grain. Each of these assumes that the teacher ought to be accountable for the construction of pedagogy and curriculum that, at the appropriate developmental and intellectual levels, help students of all ages understand and then prepare to take action against the social and institutional inequities that are embedded in our society.

In her recent article about teaching White students about racism, Tatum (1994) discusses the model of the "White ally" specifically, contrasting it with other models of Whiteness she asserts are commonly available in the culture — the "actively racist White supremacist" model wherein Whites fully embrace the notion that people of color are inferior; the "what Whiteness?" model wherein Whites do not acknowledge race as a personally significant category in their own and others' lives; and the "guilty White" model wherein Whites with a heightened awareness of racism in society experience shame and guilt (p. 471). Tatum argues that another alternative to the "White ally" model is located within the history of White protest against racism. She also notes, however, that although most White students can name nationally known White people whom they would consider racist, they are not readily familiar with the notion of Whites as allies to people of color, and usually cannot come up with the name of a nationally known White person whom they would consider an anti-racist activist. Tatum argues that both White students and students of color need to learn about and explore this alternative model. They need to know that White people can be allies to people of color by moving beyond guilt, resisting racist socialization, and working directly for social change.

I have deliberately used the phrase "uncertain allies" as the title of this article. It is intended both to refer to the notion of "ally" as discussed above and to convey the uncertainty of student teachers and teacher educators who are struggling to understand issues of race and teaching. It is also intended to underline the complexity of trying to open and sustain a discourse about race in pre-service education and the difficulty involved when prospective teachers and teacher educators want to become allies to other teachers, as well as to children and parents, who are not of the same racial or cultural groups.

But "uncertain" has several meanings in addition to those that refer to not knowing, doubtful, or not clearly defined. Webster's dictionary reminds us that "uncertain" also suggests *not* reliable, *un*trustworthy, *not* constant. My final concern is that teacher educators unintentionally may be unreliable, not constant allies of all students, teachers, and parents, and particularly that White teacher educators may be unreliable allies of students of color. Unless we unflinchingly interrogate the explicit and implicit images in our pre-service pedagogy and then work to alter our own teaching and programs, it is unlikely that we can help student teachers do the same.

References

American Association of Colleges for Teacher Education (AACTE). (1987). *Teaching teachers: Facts and figures.* Washington, DC: Author.

Aronowitz, S., & Giroux, H. (1985). *Education under siege.* New York: New World Foundation.

Asante, M. K. (1991). The Afro-centric idea in education. *Journal of Negro Education, 62,* 170–180.

Asante, M. K. (1994). *The Afro-centric curriculum* (Presentation for Project START Monthly Seminar on Teaching and Learning). Philadelphia: University of Pennsylvania.

Banks, J. (1991). Teaching multicultural literacy to teachers. *Teaching Education, 4*(1), 135-144.

Bell, D. (1992). *Faces at the bottom of the well: The permanence of racism.* New York: Basic Books.

Bloome, D., & Green, J. (1984). Directions in the sociolinguistic study of reading. In P. D. Pearson (Ed.), *Handbook of reading research* (pp. 395–421). New York: Longman.

Britzman, D. P. (1991). *Practice makes practice: A critical study of learning to teach.* New York: State University of New York Press.

Brown, S. P. (1993). Lighting fires. In M. Cochran-Smith & S. Lytle (Eds.), *Inside/outside: Teacher research and knowledge* (pp. 241–249). New York: Teachers College Press.

Carrier, B. (1992). *Rethinking White privilege.* Unpublished manuscript.

Clift, R., Veal, M. L., Johnson, M., & Holland, P. (1990). Restructuring teacher education through collaborative action research. *Journal of Teacher Education, 41*(2), 52–62.

Cochran-Smith, M. (1991a). Reinventing student teaching. *Journal of Teacher Education, 42,* 104–118.

Cochran-Smith, M. (1991b). Learning to teach against the grain. *Harvard Educational Review, 61,* 279–310.

Cochran-Smith, M. (1995). Color blindness and basket making are not the answers: Confronting the dilemmas of race, culture, and language diversity in teacher education. *American Educational Research Journal, 32*(3), 493–522.

Cochran-Smith, M., & Lytle, S. L. (Eds.). (1993). *Inside/outside: Teacher research and knowledge.* New York: Teachers College Press.

Comer, J. P. (1989). Racism and the education of young children. *Teachers College Record, 90,* 352–361.

Delpit, L. (1988). The silenced dialogue: Power and pedagogy in educating other people's children. *Harvard Educational Review, 58,* 280–298.

Dorris, M. (1992). I is not for Indian. In B. Slapin & D. Seale (Eds.), *Through Indian eyes: The native experience in books for children* (3rd ed., pp. 27–28). Philadelphia: New Society.

Edelsky, C., Altwerger, B., & Flores, B. (1991). *Whole language: What's the difference?* Portsmouth, NH: Heinemann.

Erickson, F. (1986). Qualitative methods in research on teaching. In M. Wittrock (Ed.), *Handbook of research on teaching* (pp. 119–161). New York: Macmillan.

Feiman-Nemser, S. (1983). Learning to teach. In L. S. Shulman & G. Sykes (Eds.), *Handbook of teaching and policy* (pp. 150–170). New York: Longman.

Feiman-Nemser, S. (1990). Teacher preparation: Structural and conceptual alternatives. In W. R. Houston (Ed.), *Handbook of research on teacher education* (pp. 212–233). New York: Macmillan.

Fordham, S. (1988). Racelessness as a factor in Black students' school success: Programmatic strategy or pyrrhic victory? *Harvard Educational Review, 58,* 54–84.

Foster, M. (1990). The politics of race through African-American teachers' eyes. *Journal of Education, 172*(3), 123–141.

Garcia, A., Kaufman, D., Muldanado, C., Parham, K., Smith, J., & Whitney, K. (1992, February). *Teaching ain't no crystal stair.* Paper presented at the Ethnography in Education Forum, Philadelphia.

Giroux, H. (1984). Rethinking the language of schooling. *Language Arts, 61,* 33–40.

Heath, S. B. (1982). What no bedtime story means: Narrative skills at home and school. *Language in Society, 11,* 49–76.

Hilliard, A. (1974). Restructuring teacher education for multicultural imperatives. In W. A. Hunter (Ed.), *Multicultural education through competency-based teacher education* (pp. 40–55). Washington, DC: American Association of Colleges for Teacher Education.

Holmes Group. (1990). *Tomorrow's schools.* East Lansing, MI: Author.

Joe, S. (1993). Rethinking power. In M. Cochran-Smith & S. Lytle (Eds.), *Inside/outside: Teacher research and knowledge* (pp. 290–298). New York: Teachers College Press.

Kozol, J. (1991). *Savage inequalities.* New York: Harper.

Ladson-Billings, G. (1990). Culturally relevant teaching. *College Board Review, 155,* 20–25.

McDiarmid, G. W. (1990). *What to do about differences? A study of multicultural education for teacher trainees in the Los Angeles Unified School District* (Research Report No. 90-11). East Lansing: Michigan State University, National Center for Research on Teacher Education.

McIntosh, P. (1989). White privilege: Unpacking the invisible knapsack. *Peace and Freedom, 49*(4), 10–12.

Ogbu, J. (1978). *Minority education and caste.* New York: Academic.

Paine, C. (1989). Relativism, radical pedagogy, and the ideology of paralysis. *College English, 51,* 557–570.

Quality Education for Minorities Project. (1990). *Education that works: An action plan for the education of minorities.* Cambridge, MA: Author.

Rodríguez, R. (1982). *Hunger of memory: The education of Richard Rodríguez.* New York: Bantam.

Rose, M. (1989). *Lives on the boundary.* New York: Penguin Books.

Rosenberg, P. (in press–a). The presence of an absence: Issues of race in teacher education in a predominantly White college. In M. Dilworth (Ed.), *Consideration of culture in teacher education: An anthology.* Washington, DC: American Association of Colleges of Teacher Education.

Rosenberg, P. (in press–b). *Underground discourses: Exploring whiteness in teacher education.* In M. Fine, L. Powell, & L. Weiss (Eds.), *Off White: Readings on society, race, and culture.* New York: Routledge.

Seale, D. (1992). Let us put our minds together and see what life we will make for our children. In B. Slapin & D. Seale (Eds.), *Through Indian eyes: The native experience in books for children* (3rd ed., pp. 11–17) Philadelphia: New Society.

Sleeter, C. E., & Grant, C. A. (1987). An analysis of multicultural education in the United States. *Harvard Educational Review, 57,* 421–444.

Sola, M., & Bennett, A. (1985). The struggle for voice: Narratives, literacy, and consciousness in an East Harlem School. *Journal of Education, 167*(1), 88–110.

Steele, S. (1991). *The content of our character: A new vision of race in America.* New York: Harper Perennial.

Tatum, B. D. (1992). Taking about race, learning about racism: The application of racial identity development theory in the classroom. *Harvard Educational Review, 62,* 1–24.

Tatum, B. D. (1994). Teaching White students about racism: The search for White allies and the restoration of hope. *Teachers College Record, 95,* 462–476.

Taylor, D., & Dorsey-Gaines, C. (1988). *Growing up literate. Learning from inner city families.* Portsmouth, NH: Heinemann.

Zeichner, K. (1986). Preparing reflective teachers: An overview of instructional strategies which have been employed in pre-service teacher education. *International Journal of Educational Research, 7,* 565–575.

Zeichner, K., Tabachnick, B., & Densmore, K. (1987). Individual, institutional, and cultural influences on the development of teachers' craft knowledge. In J. Calderhead (Ed.), *Exploring teachers' thinking* (pp. 21–59). London: Cassell.

Zumwalt, K. K. (1982). Research on teaching: Policy implications for teacher education. In A. Lieberman & M. McLaughlin (Eds.), *Policy making in education: 81st yearbook of the National Society for the Study of Education* (pp. 215–248). Chicago, IL: University of Chicago Press.

Marjorie Perloff, both teaching assistant for the course described here and research assistant for this and larger projects in student teachers' learning, spent many hours sorting, reading, and categorizing students' writing and transcriptions of class discussions. Her organizational, analytical, and teaching skills were invaluable in the preparation of this article, and I wish to acknowledge her tremendous contribution.

ABOUT THE CONTRIBUTORS

—■—■—■—

David Wallace Adams is an Associate Professor at the Cleveland State University College of Education. His major field of research is the history of American education, with emphasis on minorities in the Far West. His most recent publications include "From Bullets to Boarding Schools: The Educational Assault on the American Indian Identity" in *The American Indian Experience: A Profile* (edited by P. Weeks, 1988) and *Education for Extinction: American Indians and the Boarding School Experience, 1875–1928* (1995).

Cynthia Ballenger is a Senior Research Associate at TERC, Cambridge, Massachusetts. Her professional interests concern the teaching and learning of science in bilingual classrooms, issues of literacy for bilingual children, and the field of teacher research. Her publications include *Language and Literacy in a Haitian Preschool: A Perspective from Teacher Research* (1994).

Marilyn Cochran-Smith is Associate Professor of Education and Director of Project START at the University of Pennsylvania Graduate School of Education. Her professional interests center around teacher education, teacher research, and language and literacy. Her published works include *Learning to Write Differently: Young Children and Word Processing* (with C. Paris and J. Kahn, 1991) and *Inside/Outside: Teacher Research and Knowledge* (with S. L. Lytle, 1993).

Jim Cummins is a Professor at the Ontario Institute for Studies in Education, Toronto. His major research interest is cultural diversity. He is author of *Bilingualism in Education: Aspects of Theory, Research and Policy* (with M. Swain, 1986), *Empowering Minority Students* (1989), and coauthor of *Brave New Schools: Challenging Cultural Illiteracy through Global Learning Networks* (with D. Sayers, 1995).

Lisa D. Delpit, Benjamin E. Mays Professor of Urban Educational Leadership at Georgia State University in Atlanta, is interested in urban education. Her recent publications include *Other People's Children: Power and Pedagogy in Multicultural Classrooms* (1995) and "The Village Tok Ples School Scheme of Papua New Guinea" in *Cross-Cultural Perspectives on Literacy in the Black Community* (edited by I. McPhail and M. R. Hoover, in press). She was awarded a MacArthur Fellowship in 1990.

Donna Deyhle is Associate Professor in the Department of Educational Studies and Ethnic Studies at the University of Utah in Salt Lake City. She is interested in anthropology and education, American Indian education, and cultural conflict and change. Her most recent publications include "Culture and Child Development: Navajo Youth and the Middle School" in *Theory Into Practice* (1994), which received an award from the Educational Press Association of America, and "Navajo Mothers and Daughters: Schools, Jobs, and the Family" in *Anthropology and Education Quarterly* (with F. Margonis, 1995).

Signithia Fordham, Assistant Professor at the University of Maryland in Baltimore, is interested in diasporic populations and success. Her numerous publications include "Black Students' School Success: Coping with the Burdens of 'Acting White'" in *Urban Review* (with J. Ogbu, 1986), and *Blacked Out: Dilemmas of Race, Identity and Success at Capital High* (in press).

John J. Halcón is currently serving as Special Assistant to the Provost of California State University, Monterey Bay, in Seaside. He is on leave from the University of Northern Colorado where he is an Associate Professor of Education. His research centers on the organization of schools and the development of public policy as it affects historically under-represented and under-achieving students. His publications include "Bilingual Education Research, Policy, and the 'Trickledown' Reform Agenda" in *Critical Perspectives in Bilingual Education Research* (edited by R. Padilla and A. Benavides, 1992).

Carol Locust is a Clinical Professor at the University of Arizona College of Medicine, Native American Research and Training Center. Her major professional interest is Native American Studies. Her published works include "American Indian 101: Basic Course for Cultural Sensitivity" in *Cultural Sensitivity Issues in Minority Health* (1994) and "The Impact of Differing Belief Systems Between Native Americans and Their Rehabilitation Service Providers" in *Rehabilitation Education* (1995).

Beverly McElroy-Johnson (Folásadé Oládélé) is an English teacher at Havenscourt Junior High School in Oakland, California. She is also a Performance Assessor for Teach For America. Her major research interests are international and multicultural curriculum development. She is a recipient of the Marcus A. Foster Institute's award for Most Outstanding Educator.

Jacquelyn Mitchell is a Visiting Scholar at the Laboratory of Human Cognition, University of California, San Diego. Her professional interests include culture and pedagogy in the college classroom, and teaching research methods and theories to minority students. She is author of "Pedagogical Strategies to Teach Social Theories and Methods in African-American Studies" in *African American Studies: Working Together to Create a Future* (edited by L. Reed, 1995) and "Roles, Ritual, and Routines in a Black Home-School: A Community View of Schooling" in *Anthropology and Education Quarterly* (forthcoming).

María de la Luz Reyes is Professor of Education at California State University, Monterey Bay. Her areas of expertise include English language arts, literacy for linguistically diverse students, and ethnic minority faculty in higher education. She is author of "Emerging Biliteracy and Cross-Cultural Sensitivity in Language Arts Classrooms" in *Language Arts* (with E. A. Laliberty and J. A. Orbanosky, 1993) and *A Tapestry of Language and Culture: Weaving the Literacy Web* (with J. D. Comas and P. Mason, forthcoming).

David Spener is Research Director of the Program in Border and Migration Studies at the Population Research Center, University of Texas at Austin. His research interests include comparative international development, economic sociology, international migration, and race and ethnicity. He is editor of *Adult Biliteracy in the United States* (1994), and author of "Small Firms, Social Capital, and Global Commodity Chains: Some Lessons from the Tex-Mex Border in the Era of Free Trade" in *Latin America in the World Economy* (edited by R. P. Korzeniewicz and W. C. Smith, in press.)

Beverly Daniel Tatum is Associate Professor in the Department of Psychology and Education at Mount Holyoke College, South Hadley, Massachusetts. Her research interests include racial identity development theory, identity development of African American adolescents raised in predominantly White communities, and pedagogical issues involved in teaching about oppression. She is author of *Assimilation Blues: Black Families in a White Community* (1987).

Emilie V. Siddle Walker is Assistant Professor in the Division of Educational Studies at Emory University, Atlanta. Her professional interests focus on learning environments and the social context of education, as well as the history of education. She is coeditor of the original edition of *Facing Racism in Education* (with N. Hidalgo and C. McDowell, 1990), and author of *Their Highest Potential: A Case of African American Schooling in the Segregated South* (forthcoming).

Janie V. Ward, Associate Professor of Education and Human Services at Simmons College, Boston, is interested in the psychological development of African American adolescents and Black family studies. She is coeditor of *Mapping the Moral Domain: A Contribution of Women's Thinking to Psychological Theory and Education* (with C. Gilligan and J. Taylor, 1989).

Arlette Ingram Willis is an Assistant Professor at the University of Illinois at Urbana-Champaign. Her professional interests include secondary reading methods, multicultural literature, and trends and issues in reading research. Her publications include "Ideological Representation in the Multicultural Discourse on Curriculum Reform" in *Beyond the Comfort Zones: Multiculturalism and Teacher Education*, edited by S. Jackson and J. Solís (with C. McCarthy, 1994).

ABOUT THE EDITORS

—■—■—■—

D. Smith Augustine is a doctoral candidate in Human Development and Psychology at the Harvard Graduate School of Education. Her concentration is the psychosocial development of children, especially those placed at academic risk as a result of unequal educational and economic opportunity. The focus of her research is the healthy development and resilience of low-income children labeled at risk, with a special interest in low-income African American girls.

Tamara Beauboeuf-Lafontant is a doctoral candidate in Human Development and Psychology at the Harvard Graduate School of Education. In previous graduate work in literature, she explored the psychological and cultural experiences of schooling among women of the African diaspora. She is currently writing a dissertation on the psychological development of political resistance among African American women teachers.